FINANCIAL
ACCOUNTING

FINANCIAL ACCOUNTING

Ronald M. Copeland
UNIVERSITY OF SOUTH CAROLINA

Paul E. Dascher
DREXEL UNIVERSITY

Dale L. Davison
ARIZONA STATE UNIVERSITY

JOHN WILEY & SONS
NEW YORK
CHICHESTER
BRISBANE
TORONTO

Material from the Certificate in Management
Accounting Examinations, copyright © 1976, 1977,
1978, and 1979 by the National Association of
Accountants, is adapted with permission.

Material from the Uniform CPA Examinations and
Unofficial Answers, copyright © 1977, 1978 by the
American Institute of Certified Public Accountants,
Inc., is adapted with permission.

Library of Congress Cataloging in Publication Data:

Copeland, Ronald M
    Financial accounting,
    Includes index.
    1. Accounting. I. Dascher, Paul E., joint author.
    II. Davison, Dale L., joint author. III. Title.
HF5635.C7614   657   79-18276
ISBN 0-471-17173-5

Printed in the United States of America

10 9 8 7 6 5 4 3 2 1

ABOUT THE AUTHORS

Ronald M. Copeland is the Business Partnership Foundation Fellow and Professor of Accounting at the University of South Carolina. He received a B.B.A. degree from the University of Massachusetts, an M.S. degree from The Pennsylvania State University, and a Ph.D. from Michigan State University. He has been a member of the faculties of Elizabethtown College, The Pennsylvania State University, and Michigan State University. Professor Copeland has coauthored several books including *Financial Statements*, and *Advanced Accounting*, and has contributed a chapter to the *Accountants' Handbook*. In addition, he has written many articles for leading academic and professional journals, and is an active member of several academic and professional organizations. His current research interest is in the development of new techniques for applying managerial accounting to nonprofit organizations.

Paul E. Dascher received B.S., M.S., and Ph.D. degrees from The Pennsylvania State University. Currently he is Dean of the College of Business and Administration of Drexel University. He has taught on the accounting faculties of Virginia Polytechnic Institute, The Pennsylvania State University and Drexel University. He has written many articles that have appeared in leading academic and professional journals. Professor Dascher has served as President of the Philadelphia Chapter of the National Association of Accountants, Vice President of Administrators of Accounting Programs Group, American Accounting Association, and Vice President of Community Accountants, in addition to other professional duties. He has served on the editorial board of *The Accounting Review* and was the founder and original director of the Intercollegiate Clearing House for Computer Programs. Drs. Dascher and Copeland have coauthored a book, *Managerial Accounting,* which is designed to be a companion to the current book.

Dale L. Davison is Associate Professor of Accounting at Arizona State University. Before joining Arizona State, Dr. Davison taught at the University of South Carolina, Clemson University, and the University of Georgia. He has assumed an active role as member of several committees of the American Accounting Association, and as faculty advisor to Beta Alpha Psi. In addition, Dr. Davison has written several articles that have appeared in accounting journals. Dr. Davison earned a B.S. Degree in Accounting from Northeast Lousiana University, and both the M.B.A. and Ph.D. degrees from the University of Georgia.

PREFACE

Financial Accounting is an introductory level textbook, appropriate for a one-semester or a two-quarter elementary accounting course. No previous exposure to the material is assumed and the book is intended to be used alone or enriched with appropriate supplemental materials at the option of the instructor.

This book does not make a radical departure from the traditional approach to financial accounting. Instead, it focuses on the underlying theory of the discipline and enhances the presentation with an organization and approach that match the developing thrust of current practice. Consistent with this organization is the goal of presenting concepts and exploring underlying theory through discussion and generalized examples. The text is divided into five major sections.

Section one presents an introduction to accounting and is intended to orient the student. It begins by emphasizing the importance and usefulness of financial statements and develops a basic set—including balance sheet, income statement, and funds flow statement—from a realistic example. In essence, this establishes parameters for the book and provides a context for the remaining chapters.

Section two leads into the fundamentals of the accounting process. The debit/credit, mechanism, the journal, and the ledger are introduced and explained. This section uses procedural illustrations to view accounting as a processing system, developed and functioning in a manner parallel to other information systems.

Section three views the accounting process in the context of the income statement. At this point, the text begins to emphasize income determination.

Section four deals with particular issues involved in recording and reporting asset, liability, and equity items. These chapters, while developed with a recognition of the importance of reporting earnings, provide specific treatments on subjects that affect particular transaction-based accounts.

Section five presents topics that can enhance the student's grasp of accounting. The capstone of this section is a chapter dealing with the total financial report, including footnotes, auditor's opinion, SEC disclosures, and the conceptual framework project. Written at an understandable level, this section serves as a bridge to allow the student to enter the total context of the development, environment, and future of the accounting profession.

Although the chapters are organized on the basis of subject content, attention has been given to the amount of material included. Several chapters are subdivided into two or more *parts* to provide flexibility of coverage. This division into parts also enables the instructor to continue the pace of assignments at a constant rate.

The order of chapter sequence has been developed to reflect the structure of the instructional goal. Other arrangements and sequences may be developed by instructors without altering the flow of the material. For example, some users have suggested that Chapter 8 could be taught immediately after Chapter 6. Individuals can structure chapter assignments to meet goals of particular courses or to accommodate professorial individuality. This book has been prepared to complement the instructor, not to restrict or inhibit teaching style in any way.

Each chapter is accompanied by a *supplementary discussion.* They provide an expanded set of tools that may be used at the instructor's option without affecting the continuity of coverage. The material is presented in a narrative form and is intended to enrich the student's understanding of accounting and its business environment. Supplementary discussions range from accounting history, through inventory control systems, to nonprofit organizations and international accounting.

Supplementary discussions are positioned in the text on the basis of one of two criteria. They may support or logically build on the material presented in the chapter. Alternatively, they may present material at a place in the text where a student's exposure to accounting is sufficient to benefit from the discussion.

Assignment materials are important elements of introductory textbooks. The assignment materials here are divided in *questions, exercises,* and *problems* and are provided in sufficient numbers to ensure adequate selection. Questions are designed to focus on concepts, definitions, and descriptions. Exercises generally require data-manipulating steps that relate to chapter illustrations in a straightforward manner. Problems are based on the textual material but present reasonably complex analytical or discussion situations. All of the assignment materials have been class tested to ensure their reliability and relevance. Care has been taken to guarantee that each point covered in the chapter is reinforced by at least three assignment items. While appropriate for the level of the text, the assignment items draw on realistic situations and develop problems from pertinent data. Several questions appearing in the Uniform CPA Examination and the Certificate in Management Accounting Examination have been included in the assignments. In all these cases, the problems have been specifically adapted to this book but with review and modification of some requirements in terms of the chapter coverage.

Several learning materials are available to aid instructors and students using *Financial Accounting.* A *Student Study Guide to Accompany Finan-*

cial Accounting has been prepared by Professor Fred Jacobs of the University of Tennessee. A *Practice Set* has been developed by Professor Stanley Kratchman of Texas A&M University. *Working Papers* and *Check Figures* are also available. The *Instructor's Manual* contains extensive teaching notes for each chapter and a set of simple demonstration problems for class use. *Transparencies* for all Problem Solutions and Achievement Tests, are also available to users.

Throughout this book, an attempt has been made to explicitly recognize that accounting is practiced by both men and women and that business and commercial ventures attract competent and capable individuals without regard to sex. In some discussions, the impersonal pronouns *he, him,* and *his* have been used for reasons of style and accepted English usage. In all these cases, the terms *she, her,* and *hers* obviously could be substituted.

We are indebted to many people for their ideas and assistance in preparing this book. The following professors made very constructive and helpful comments on earlier drafts of the manuscript:

Andrew Barnett (Arizona State University)
Michael Barrett (University of Missouri at Kansas City)
James Benjamin (Texas A&M University)
Wayne Bremser (Villanova University)
Vincent Brenner (Louisiana State University)
Dale Buckmaster (University of Delaware)
Charles Calhoun III (University of Miami)
John Cerepak (Fairleigh Dickinson University)
Jesse Dillard (Ohio State University)
Christopher Flynn, Jr. (Boston College)
Joseph Ford (Drexel University)
William Grasty (Murray State University)
Robert Ingram (University of South Carolina)
Stanley Kratchman (Texas A&M University)
Robert E. Malcom (Pennsylvania State University)
Philip Reckers (University of Maryland)
Janis Reeder (Pennsylvania State University)
Howard Sanders (University of South Carolina)
Ralph Skelly (University of Missouri)
Robert Strawser (University of Houston)

Graduate students Anthony Rollo of Drexel University and Julia Magann of the University of South Carolina were invaluable in preparing the manuscript. Our colleagues at Drexel, South Carolina, and Arizona State were helpful with suggestions, comments, and encouragement. We would also like to recognize the support of Jim Kane, Herb Raynes, and Russ Petersen who provided an administrative climate conducive to creating this book.

A special measure of thanks is due the staff of John Wiley & Sons for their interest in and commitment to this project. To Don Ford who dreamed with us and to Serje Seminoff who made those dreams a reality, go our deepest appreciation.

Many students read the manuscript and worked the problems to ensure that they were readable and as free as possible from error. Our students also contributed ideas and materials that helped in revising manuscript chapters and preparing problems. Appreciation goes to the American Institute of Certified Public Accountants and the National Association of Accountants for their permission to quote from their copyrighted publications. Material from the Uniform CPA Examination, copyright © by the American Institute of Certified Public Accountants, Inc., is adapted with permission. Material from the CMA Examination, copyright © by the Institute of Management Accounting, is adapted with permission. Although we have not cited authors whose original contributions are so widely felt that they are now an integral part of accounting practice, needless to say, we owe them our thanks. Finally, we welcome comments from the users of this book.

Ronald M. Copeland
Paul E. Dascher
Dale L. Davison

CONTENTS

14 FINANCIAL STATEMENT ANALYSIS

□ 1
THE ACCOUNTING INFORMATION SYSTEM

INFORMATION AND ACCOUNTING

ACCOUNTING DEFINED

ELEMENTS OF THE ACCOUNTING MODEL

A BUSINESS VENTURE

ACCOUNTING ENTITY

TRANSACTIONS

ACCOUNTS

USERS OF ACCOUNTING INFORMATION

ECONOMIC DESCRIPTIONS

ASSETS

EQUITIES

CHANGES IN ASSETS AND EQUITIES

ACCOUNTING REPORTS

THE BALANCE SHEET

THE INCOME STATEMENT

THE CASH FLOW STATEMENT

CRITERIA FOR EVALUATING ACCOUNTING INFORMATION

SUMMARY

A SUPPLEMENTARY DISCUSSION: THE PROFESSION OF ACCOUNTING

FINANCIAL ACCOUNTING

AUDITING

TAXATION

COST AND MANAGERIAL ACCOUNTING

NOT-FOR-PROFIT ACCOUNTING

OTHER ACCOUNTING EFFORTS

□ OBJECTIVES

AFTER STUDYING THIS CHAPTER, YOU SHOULD BE ABLE TO DO THE FOLLOWING:

1. DEFINE ACCOUNTING AND DESCRIBE ITS GENERAL FUNCTION OR PURPOSES.

2. IDENTIFY THE VARIOUS ELEMENTS OF THE ACCOUNTING MODEL AND DISCUSS THEIR INTERRELATIONSHIPS.

3. DEFINE THE TERMS ASSETS, LIABILITIES, OWNER'S EQUITY, REVENUE, AND EXPENSE.

4. CONSTRUCT SIMPLIFIED VERSIONS OF THE BALANCE SHEET, THE INCOME STATEMENT, AND THE CASH FLOW STATEMENT.

5. LIST SOME QUESTIONS THAT COULD BE ANSWERED WITH DATA CONTAINED IN THE TYPICAL ACCOUNTING REPORTS.

Everyone regularly uses the services of different information specialists. News and weather reporters study data and provide news and weather forecasts to the general public. Medical doctors review diagnostic information and report to patients about their health problems. Lawyers advise clients about the legal ramifications of certain actions after reviewing the relevant laws and court decisions. Accountants also are information specialists. They collect, process, and report economic information about specific financial events for business or noncommercial activities. Some reports issued by accountants become part of the public domain and are available for use by anyone who is interested in financial statements.

Actually, accounting originated several thousand years ago when human beings first developed a need to accumulate information about economic resources such as land, livestock, and other personal property.[1] Throughout history, the accounting profession has continued to grow in response to the financial information needs of individuals and societies. Today, in the United States, several hundred thousand individuals are engaged in professional accounting activities; millions of others throughout the country depend on accountants for information that affects their personal and professional lives.

Information and Accounting

We can collect many types of data about an object or activity. For example, when considering a building, we can note its age, height, volume, location, cost, or structural composition. For any given purpose, some data are extremely useful, while other data are irrelevant. When buying a new car, the price of the vehicle and the purchaser's available cash are important pieces of data, but the expiration date of the purchaser's driver's license is not. However, if the purchaser plans to operate the new car, the license expiration date is extremely important. Thus, data can be useful or not, depending on the situation or on the decision to be made. Useful data are termed *information*, and information represents the goal, or desired end product, of an information system.

All human activity depends on information. For example, we, as individuals, collect, process, and use information to decide when to get up, how to dress, and what to do throughout the day. Ordinarily, more information is used to make important decisions than is used to make trivial ones. Business decisions often require economic information that is provided by the accounting system.

Accounting Defined. The accounting information system includes all of the procedures, techniques, methods, and resources needed to collect and

[1] Accounting records dating from 5000 B.C. have been discovered in the ruins of the ancient Babylonian and Egyptian civilizations.

THE ACCOUNTING INFORMATION SYSTEM

disseminate relevant economic information to interested users. A recent definition offers the following description of the accounting process:

"[Accounting is] the process of identifying, measuring, and communicating economic information to permit informed judgements and decisions by users of the information."[2]

Although the fundamentals of accounting have remained unchanged for centuries, specific procedures have been altered to reflect today's business activity.

All accounting procedures, methods, and techniques are oriented toward ultimately providing information to users. Accounting information is communicated to users in the form of accounting reports that are the culmination, or desired end result, of the accounting process.

The traditional accounting model, or the basis for the accounting process, relies on three major assumptions about business and commerce. The first is that business activity is conducted by distinct *entities* or identifiable business units. Second, it is assumed that business activity is conducted through economic *transactions* that may be observed and measured. Finally, the assumption is made that a transaction can be described meaningfully in terms of standard units of information, or *accounts*. A better understanding of these assumptions may be gained by considering a specific business venture.

Elements of the Accounting Model

A Business Venture.   Two longtime friends, Harry Hawke and William Wizzard, decide to start a business upon graduation from college. Each has a limited amount of cash to invest, but they have received assurances of a sizable loan from a local bank. After a brief period of negotiation, they receive authorization to act as a local distributor for a manufacturer of electronic calculators. The terms of the distributorship agreement call for Wizzard and Hawke to form a company that will buy calculators at a wholesale price from the manufacturer and, then, resell them to college students at a higher price. The agreement specifies that they can add 75 percent to the wholesale price to arrive at a retail selling price.

During the month of June, the business was organized. The owners of the business, Hawke and Wizzard, each invested $5,000 in the venture and named their company Basic Calculators. Recognizing that the business needed a supply of calculators for *inventory,* the owners, acting through Basic Calculators, borrowed $10,000 from the local bank. The terms of the

[2] American Accounting Association Committee to Prepare a Statement of Basic Accounting Theory, *Statement of Basic Accounting Theory* (Evanston: American Accounting Association, 1966), p. 1.

loan called for the business to pay 12 percent annual interest, or $100 each month that the loan was outstanding ($10,000 × 0.12 × 1/12).

During the month of August, Basic Calculators opened for business, and several things happened quickly. First, the company rented a store for $500 a month and promptly paid the first month's rent. Store furnishings of $5,000 and calculators worth $7,000 (the wholesale price) were purchased for cash. A salesman was hired at a salary of $700 per month. At the end of the month, the first $100 interest payment was made to the bank and the salesman was paid. During the month, the salesman sold $3,000 worth of the calculators for a retail price of $5,250 ($3,000 cost plus 75 percent of $3,000), which was promptly collected from the customers.

Accounting Entity. An accountant seeking to compile information about this particular business would first clearly *identify* the business organization for which to account. The specific organization under consideration is referred to as the **accounting entity.** Therefore, Harry Hawke, as an individual, may be an accounting entity; financial data pertaining to Harry may be collected, measured, and reported. Similarly, Basic Calculators, the company owned by Hawke and Wizzard, may be an entity. Basic Calculators is the entity of interest in this example.

All accounting entities are treated independently of one another. Thus, data relating to the entity Harry Hawke (the individual) are not confused with, or included in, data concerning Basic Calculators (the company). This assumption—which restricts the accountant's attention to a specific individual or organization—is known as the **separate entity assumption.** Under the separate entity assumption, a business is treated as being separate and distinct from its owners. The accounting records of Basic Calculators should reflect economic events relating solely to that entity.

Transactions. After an entity has been identified, the accounting model measures the economic effect of *transactions* on the business. A **transaction** is a simultaneous exchange between the accounting entity and other parties such as customers, suppliers, employees, or owners. The exchange is characterized by each party giving and receiving something of value. Thus, an exchange of economic value must take place for a transaction to occur.

Examples of transactions would include the following:

☐ Sale of goods for cash—an exchange of property for cash took place.

☐ Purchase of store furnishings for cash—the firm received store furnishings and exchanged (gave) cash for it.

☐ Paying a salesperson's salary—the business received the salesperson's services and gave cash in return.

The transactions concept relies on the assumption of a rational, economic individual; people and organizations are always assumed to exchange things of equal value. For example, if a college student buys a best-selling novel for $15, it is assumed that the book was worth exactly $15 to the student, or she wouldn't have exchanged her money for it. The same logic prevails with respect to the seller of the book and with all business transactions inlcuded in the accounting system.

Such an assumption of economic rationality aids in valuing accounting transactions; once one element of a transaction is valued, the value of the other element is also known. Thus, if $3,000 is paid for store furnishings, the furnishings will be valued at $3,000 by their new owner. The transaction concept also adds to the definition of an entity. An accounting entity must be an economic unit capable of entering into transactions.

A list of transactions for Basic Calculators during its first month of operations is given below. Observe that the dollar impact of objectives given and received is the same. Each transaction between a business and another party can be characterized in a similar fashion.

Objects or Services Received	Objects or Services Given	Dollar Impact
Money	Promise to repay bank (Note)	$10,000
Use of store (Rent)	Money	500
Furnishings	Money	5,000
Salesman's labor	Money	700
Use of bank's money (Interest)	Money	100
Money	Calculators	5,250

Furthermore, most business transactions are evidenced by *source documents* that describe the event. For example, a promissory note is a legal instrument that provides evidence of borrowing money. A purchase order, sales slip, shipping invoice, and canceled check all evidence the acquisition of furnishings. Business forms, documents, and memos reflect each transaction. Creating source documents coincident to a business transaction lies at the heart of most accounting systems, since these documents usually activate the accounting process.

Accounts. Accounting systems classify transactions into broad groups such as sales transactions, purchase transactions, and borrowing transactions. Data relating to each type of transaction is accounted for, or recorded and processed, in the same manner as all other transactions of the same class. They are recorded consistently. For example, identical accounting procedures are applied to all sales for cash even though one sale is of calculators and another of typewriters; similarly, it makes no difference that Mrs. Jones is the first customer and that Mr. Johnson is the second. Preprinted source documents or business forms ensure that corresponding data are collected for similar transactions.

Information in the accounting system is recorded in accounts that reflect the characteristics of various types of transactions. Accounts are used to accumulate information about both elements of each transaction —that is, what an entity receives and what it gives in a transaction. An *account* identifies the name under which information about a specific element of data is recorded. Accounts represent the names of objects or activities that are accepted as part of the recording vocabulary. Similar transaction components are recorded in the same account. Thus, all information relating to cash will be reflected in the *Cash* account. (Following standard practice, names of specific accounts are capitalized.) The ability to record, classify, and summarize information in accounts is fundamental to the operation of all accounting systems.

Users of Accounting Information

Although accounting information can be collected for any organization, we will concentrate on accounting for business organizations. A wide cross section of our society uses accounting information. Most of these users, however, fall within the following general classes:

- ☐ Managers or decision makers within the business organization.
- ☐ Stockholders or owners who do not play an active managerial role and consequently are considered to be outside of the organization.
- ☐ Governmental regulating agencies.
- ☐ Labor unions and individual employees of the organization.
- ☐ Creditors.
- ☐ Private regulatory bodies, such as a stock exchange.
- ☐ Potential investors in a business.

This list could be expanded greatly, since many individuals have some interest in the present and potential future performance of business enterprises.

Economic Descriptions

Reporting information to interested users requires that the accounting system describe various aspects of a firm's economic condition as well as the activities that a firm initiates. Part of this description includes indentifying and measuring the value of resources owned by the business. These resources are termed *assets* by the accountant.

Assets. Basically, assets are resources, or things of value, owned and controlled by the business. Assets have future service potential or economic value to the firm. Thus, a building, future occupancy rights, or a debt owed by a customer (future economic value to be collected) are assets. Normally, the accountant will establish specific accounts to summarize data on each type of asset, such as Cash, Land, or Buildings.

THE ACCOUNTING INFORMATION SYSTEM

An accountant initially measures assets at their dollar cost to the firm. This is consistent with the description of a transaction. For example, if $10,000 cash is given for a plot of land, the land is measured at $10,000. In the previous example, when Basic Calculators started operations, it had one asset: cash that was valued at $20,000.

Equities.   Our free enterprise system recognizes the private ownership of property; and our courts determine property rights whenever questions of ownership arise. Businesses are "owned" in varying degrees by those who supply the assets and those who therefore have legal claims against them. If Basic Calculators were to cease operations at the beginning of the month, the following legal claims would be honored against its $20,000 of assets: the local bank, $10,000; Harry Hawke, $5,000; and William Wizzard, $5,000.

As this example shows, there are two parts, or distinct sides, to an accounting description of this or any business. On one side, there are the assets, or resources, with which the firm may operate. These resources are owned or controlled by the firm. On the other side, there are the claims against the assets of the firm. Claims correspond to sources of the assets of a business, in that suppliers of assets have corresponding claims. Accountants refer to these claims as equities.

Legally, these claims are divided into two distinct types or classifications—*liabilities* and *owners' equity*. Liabilities are claims by creditors of a business and commit the firm to convey assets or perform services at some future time. Liabilities are usually definite in amount and rank high in priority. In constrast, owners' equity represents all of the claims of owners that are recognized under our system of private enterprise. Among other rights, there is the right of owners to designate who will manage the business, as well as the rights to profits earned by their firm. In the case of Basic Calculators, Hawke and Wizzard are owners, and their claims are classified as owners' equity; whereas the local bank is a creditor, and its claim is classified as a liability. Normally, the claims of creditors take priority over the claims of owners.

Economic information associated with two transactions of Basic Calculators is shown below:

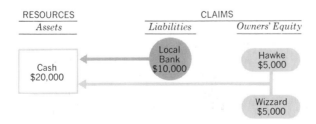

The $20,000 of assets are matched in amount by corresponding claims of creditors and owners.

Changes in Assets and Equities. During the first month of its operations, Basic Calculators engaged in several transactions that changed the asset and equity descriptions of the business. At the end of the month, the asset Cash has been reduced to $11,950. This resulted from payments made by the company for Rent ($500), Store Furnishings ($5,000), Calculators ($7,000), Salary ($700), and Interest ($100), and from collections by the company from its customers ($5,250).[3]

While cash decreased, two additional assets were recognized. The company acquired $5,000 worth of store furnishings and has $4,000 of calculators remaining at the end of the month ($7,000 were purchased and $3,000 were sold). The effect of these changes in the assets of the firm could be portrayed as shown in this figure:

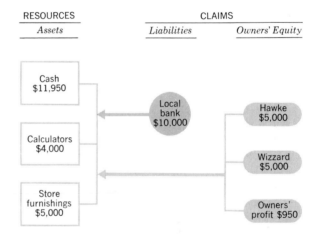

The total dollar value of assets has increased from $20,000 to $20,950. The increase in assets resulting from successful business operations is called *profit,* or *net income,* and belongs to the owners. Therefore, it is reflected as a corresponding increase in the owners' accounts.

Generally, all increases and decreases in assets resulting from business operations are reflected by corresponding changes in the claims of owners. This characteristic of owners' equity differentiates it from liabilities; owners' claims change in reaction to business success or failure, while creditors' claims remain *constant* until they are paid.

Individual ownership rights and liabilities are related to all of the assets

---

[3]Following tradition, the first letter of account names (titles) are capitalized throughout this text. Thus, the word *Cash* refers to the Cash account, while the word *cash* refers to money.

in general. The Cash balance is not sufficient to satisfy all of the claims. Thus, all of the assets must be used to satisfy all of the claims against these assets. Since the size of owners' claims change with business success, the total amount of claims will always equal the total amount of the assets.

Accounting Reports

Although schematic presentations can reveal information about a business venture, they are limited. A thorough understanding of most business organizations and their activities demands other means of reporting. Accounting reports attempt to present relevant information about a specific entity. These reports culminate several activities, including:

☐ *Measurement*—Economic information about business transactions is measured and quantified.

☐ *Collection*—Pertinent economic information is collected and entered into the accounting system.

☐ *Summarization*—Data in the accounting system are summarized to facilitate reporting.

☐ *Classification*—Summarized data are classified and combined to prepare accounting reports.

Three kinds of accounting reports are prepared regularly to address different aspects of a business.

The Balance Sheet. On August 31, the owners of Basic Calculators, Harry Hawke and William Wizzard, wanted to know the status of their investment in the venture. Accordingly, their accountant prepared a *balance sheet* or *statement of financial position* (shown in Exhibit 1-1).

EXHIBIT 1-1
BALANCE SHEET

BASIC CALCULATORS
Balance Sheet
August 31, 19X6

Assets		*Claims (Equities)*	
Cash	$11,950	Liabilities	
Calculators	4,000	Bank Loan	$10,000
Store Furnishings	5,000	Owners' Equity	
		Hawke Investment	5,000
		Wizzard Investment	5,000
		Owners' Profit	950
Total Assets	$20,950	Total Claims	$20,950

The balance sheet shows the specific assets, or resources, of the venture and the specific claims against these assets at one particular point in time. The report is called a balance sheet because it discloses the "balances," or summaries, of the various assets and claims. Also, the statement is "in balance," since conventional accounting procedures automatically equate assets and claims.

The balance sheet identifies the balances of specific asset liability and equity accounts as of a specific date. Since account balances change in response to additional transactions, balance sheets at different dates present different balances. Therefore, the balance sheet usually is prepared on a regular schedule, such as annually, quarterly, or monthly, and it reflects the final position as of one period in time.

Consider the example of Hawke and Wizzard. The August 31 balance sheet reflects the items of economic value controlled by Basic Calculators: three assets, cash, calculators, and store furnishings. Also, the balance sheet discloses the nature and extent of claims against these assets: a bank claim of $10,000 and the owners' claims of $10,950. Although this information is important, it does not relate directly to questions about the efficiency of the business venture. For example, the cash balance decreased from an initial balance of $20,000 to its current level of $11,950. Although the balance sheet reports a $950 profit, the owners could question how this profit was determined. An *income statement* relates information about a venture's profitability.

The Income Statement. As its name implies, the income statement presents information about the profitability, or income, earned by a business venture. An income statement for Basic Calculators is presented in Exhibit 1-2. This statement shows the results for the first month of operations—August. Basically, it is a summary of sales activity (distributing goods and services to customers) and expense activity (utilizing goods and services to generate sales).

The income statement first identifies the sales made during the period, which is measured by the total amount of cash that was or that will be received from customers. This portion of the statement shows the amount customers paid or promised to pay the business for the product or service that they received. In accounting terminology, this is called *revenue*, or *sales revenue,* or *sales.*

The next section of the income statement focuses on the cost of providing the product or service to customers of the business. These costs are referred to as *expenses.* The expenses of Basic Calculators included the cost to the company of the calculators sold during the month, the rental fee for the store, the salesman's salary, and the interest on the bank loan. These expenses represent the cost of doing business for the month of August.

THE ACCOUNTING
INFORMATION
SYSTEM

EXHIBIT 1-2
INCOME STATEMENT

BASIC CALCULATORS
Income Statement
For the Month of August 19X6

Sales to Customers (as measured by cash paid or promised to be paid)—Revenue		$5,250
Cost of Operation (as measured by cash paid out or promised to be paid out to make sales to customers) —Expenses:		
Cost of calculators sold	$3,000	
Rental of store	500	
Salesman's salary	700	
Interest paid on loan	100	
Total Cost of Operation		4,300
Profit on Month's Operations		$ 950

The last section of the income statement shows the difference between revenues and expenses, or the *profit*. Common synonyms for profit are *earnings* and *income*. In this case the specific profit figure indicates that Basic Calculators earned $950 more than the expenses incurred to distribute the product to its customers. Profit can be considered as the return to owners for initiating the business. The $950 profit of Basic Calculators compensates the owners for investing $10,000 in the business, lending their managerial skills and time to the venture, and performing an entrepreneurial function—that is, starting a business and assuming any risks that may be involved.

The income statement provides management with an insight into strategies for price policy. It gives answers to questions such as: "Are prices high enough to recover costs?" The income statement also provides the user with the information needed to review expenses and evaluate their magnitude and relationships. The summarization and classification included in the statement makes this task feasible.

Owners of a business may also want to know how resources were used during a particular period of time. For example, Hawke and Wizzard might be concerned about the decrease in the cash balance from $20,000 to $11,950 during the month of August. The *funds flow statement,* or *cash flow statement,* describes the changes that affect specific resources, such as cash, during a time period.

The Cash Flow Statement. A cash flow statement for Basic Calculators is shown in Exhibit 1-3. This statement isolates activities that affected the

EXHIBIT 1-3
CASH FLOW STATEMENT

BASIC CALCULATORS
Cash-Flow Statement
For the Month of August 19X6

Cash Balance, August 1, 19X6		$20,000
Sources of Cash During the Month:		
Received from customers		5,250
Total Cash Available to Be Used during the Month		$25,250
Uses of Cash During the Month:		
Purchased calculators	$7,000	
Store furnishings	5,000	
Store rental	500	
Saleman's salary	700	
Interest payment	100	
Total Uses of Cash During the Month		13,300
Cash Balance, August 31, 19X6		$11,950

asset Cash during the month of August. Sources and uses of cash are identified, and the change from the beginning balance to the ending balance is
explained.

After establishing the beginning balance, all sources and uses of cash
are presented in the statement. The difference between the sources and
uses represents the change in the Cash balance (cash decreased by
$8,050, from $20,000 to $11,950). The cash flow statement for Basic
Calculators for the month of August was very similar to its income statement, but this merely reflects (a) the low number of transactions initiated
during August, (b) that most of these transactions dealt with revenue or expense activities, and (c) that none of the transactions involved the use of
credit. In a more typical example, the cash-flow statement reflects activites
different from those shown on the Income Statement.[1]

**Criteria for
Evaluating
Accounting
Information**

The three accounting reports for Basic Calculators illustrate a complete set
of the financial accounting information that is normally prepared by all
business enterprises. Although the complexity and the size of the reports
will increase as the size of the business increases, the basic structures will
remain the same. The information in these accounting reports are usually
evaluated according to these criteria:

[1]Many businesses prepare a funds flow statement rather than a cash flow statement. We will
discuss funds flow in more detail in Chapter 13.

Relevance—Accounting reports give financial data about a specific entity to a broad cross section of individuals involved in decision situations. Relevant accounting reports provide information that answers questions asked by the decision maker.

Verifiability—If accounting procedures, techniques, and methods were standardized, two accountants independently working with the same data would produce the same report. Since modern accounting practice is not standardized, verifiability requires that professional judgments be supported by objective evidence.

Timeliness—In all cases, reports should be prepared and delivered promptly and received when they are needed. This may require that some reports be prepared on a prearranged schedule, while other reports must be prepared when needed.

Clarity—All reports should be clear and understandable. Clarity is a function of both form and content. A good report is neat and legible. Like items are grouped together, and unlike terms are segregated.

Conciseness—No unnecessary information should be included in a report: good reports contain only necessary information. Also, the report must be complete and include all vital information.

Freedom from Bias—Accounting information should be neutral, in the sense of not assigning benefits to one group at the expense of another group.

Comparability—All similar reports should be either directly comparable or capable of being recast into a comparable form. This criterion aids in comparing accounting data between companies or within a company between time periods.

Summary

This chapter considered the importance of information to individual decision makers. Information, defined as useful data, must possess certain general characteristics to be of value to a user. These characteristics include relevance, verifiability, timeliness, clarity, conciseness, freedom from bias, and comparability.

Accounting information specifically relates to economic data about organizations. This information is used by individuals in a wide cross section of society. The accounting information system encompasses all of the procedures, techniques, methods, and resources necessary to produce and distribute relevant financial information to interested users.

The means of transmitting this information is through accounting reports. Three basic accounting reports—the balance sheet, the income statement, and the cash-flow statement—were discussed in this chapter. The balance sheet reports, as of a particular moment in time, the resources (assets) of a business organization and the claims (liabilities and owner's equity) against these resources. The income statement, often considered to be the most important financial statement, summarizes output and input activity as the revenues and expenses that relate to business operations during a particular time period and discloses the profit or loss. Finally, the cash-flow statement details the changes in a firm's cash resources that occurred during the period under consideration.

These three statements are important to virtually all decision makers associated with a business. Although these reports can become more complex as the size of a business increases, their basic forms and purposes remain the same. A major part of the total accounting effort is devoted to processing the underlying transaction data to produce these reports.

A Supplementary Discussion: The Profession of Accounting

The potential users of accounting information include all individuals involved in any form of economic decision making. This ranges from personal decisions to situations involving large, multinational corporations such as General Motors, General Electric, or International Telegraph and Telephone. The broadness of this user base and the diversity of the resulting information needs has fostered specialization within the accounting profession.

FINANCIAL ACCOUNTING

Financial accounting is concerned with collecting, recording, classifying, and reporting business information about economic events that have involved a specific accounting entity. Financial accounting is based on a set of *generally accepted accounting principles,* which provide a framework for the accountant's activities. The output of the process is a financial history of an organization, primarily reported to users through three main financial statements—the balance sheet, the income statement, and the funds flow statement. Each year, copies of these reports are distributed to corporate stockholders. Our government, acting through the Securities and Exchange Commission, has imposed public reporting requirements on large, publicly owned businesses. The Federal Trade Commission demands and receives financial accounting reports from selected entities that are in a position to initiate monopolistic or anticompetitive practices. All stock exchanges and most banks require client businesses to submit timely financial statements. Most metropolitan newspapers devote daily space to data obtained from annual reports of selected companies. In other words, widespread attention is focused on financial accounting data.

The public accounting profession, acting especially from associations with three formal institutions, has had a tremendous impact on establishing accounting standards. The American Institute of Certified Public Accountants (AICPA), a professional association of over 90,000 CPAs, historically has dominated the control of accounting thought in the United States. More recently, a seven-member Financial Accounting Standards Board (FASB) has assumed quasi-regulatory authority for the development and promulgation of generally accepted accounting theory. However, the ultimate control over American accounting practice rests with the Securities and Exchange Commission, an agency of the U.S. Government that has legal authority to specify accounting principles and to demand that any business falling under its jurisdiction must follow them. For the most part, the three dominant accounting organizations work in concert in the development of contemporary accounting standards for financial reporting.

AUDITING

The auditor provides an independent, thrid-party evaluation of financial accounting reports and testifies to their fairness, consistency, and conformity to predetermined standards through the issuance of an opinion. Thus, auditing extends the financial accounting function and lends credibility to the results.

Independent audits are conducted by *Certified Public Accountants* (CPAs) retained by a company to express an opinion on its financial statements. These opinions accompany the firm's financial statements that are presented to stockholders and, in many instances, to the public. CPAs are licensed by the individual states; they are professionals who have passed a comprehensive examination (the *Uniform CPA Examination*) and have met certain education and experience requirements.

CPAs rely on generally accepted accounting principles, acceptable auditing standards, and the official pronouncements of the Financial Accounting Standards Board, the Securities and Exchange Commission, and other authorative sources as an indication of proper reporting by a company. The CPA bears personal legal liability for his work and may be sued by stockholders and other interested parties if he performs in an unprofessional or negligent manner.

TAXATION

Personal and corporate income tax payments are based on calculations using certain accounting information. The purpose of tax accounting is to determine the proper amount of a tax payment and to aid in future tax planning so that tax benefits (in the form of a reduced liability) may be acquired, if deserved. Tax accounting, then, combines the techniques of accounting with the requirements of various federal, state, and local laws. Normally, tax accountants report to the management of an organization and will interact with the taxing body on the behalf of the organization.

COST AND MANAGERIAL ACCOUNTING

Another distinct phase of accounting relates to reporting information useful to managment decision makers within the firm. Managers charged with planning and control of an enterprise have different information needs than do investors or the general public. Forecasts, budgets, cost reports, performance reports, and special analyses characterize these needs.

This type of information is normally supplied by a cost, or managerial, accountant working within the firm. The managerial accountant relies on economic decision models, quantitative techniques, and an appreciation of the specific needs of users to arrive at an acceptable report for each request. The companion volume to this textbook, *Managerial Accounting,* specifically deals with this subject.

NOT-FOR-PROFIT ACCOUNTING

Governmental units and other not-for-profit organizations pursue different goals than the typical business organization. Basically, they are not profit-oriented; instead, they seek to deliver a particular product or service to satisfy social needs. Most of the accountants engaged in not-for-profit accounting refer to specific laws for guidance in their work.

OTHER ACCOUNTING EFFORTS

Like other professions, accounting is performed in many environments under a variety of situations. There are accounting historians and accountants engaged in law enforcement (special agents of the Federal Bureau of Investigation, for example). Accountants contribute services to the National Aeronautics and Space Administration and they are also involved in environmental monitoring. Accounting firms engage in feasibility studies, systems design or installation, and personnel recruitment activities. While the accounting discipline has far-reaching interests and innumerable opportunities for service, financial accounting—the subject of this book—focuses on the narrower range of activities described in this chapter.

Key Terms	Information
	Accounting
	Accounting entity
	Separate entity assumption
	Transaction
	Account
	Assets
	Liabilities
	Owners' equity
	Profit
	Net income
	Balance sheet
	Income statement
	Revenue
	Expenses
	Funds flow statement
	Cash flow statement
	Generally accepted accounting principles

1. Define the word *accounting.*

2. Define the word *information.* Do accounting reports provide information?

3. List three elements of the accounting model.

4. What is the purpose of a source document?

5. Describe the components of an accounting information system.

6. Specify three assumptions about business that are implied in the accounting model.

7. What does the separate entity assumption entail?

8. Define *transaction* and explain the exchange concept embodied in the definition.

9. Give some examples of users of different types of accounting information.

10. Define assets, liabilities, and owner's equity.

11. What is net income?

12. List the four activities that culminate in accounting reports.

13. Compare the content of the balance sheet and the income statement. How does the bottom line of the income statement relate to the balance sheet?

14. What does the cash flow statement disclose?

15. List and discuss the criteria for evaluating information contained in accounting reports.

16. Which organization has ultimate control over American accounting practice?

17. What does an auditor contribute to financial accounting reporting?

18. Define *revenue.* On which financial statement is revenue reflected?

19. List some areas of specialization in accounting.

1. Indicate whether each of the following situations constitutes an accounting transaction.
(a) Company A bought a machine from a supplier for $100.
(b) Company A agreed to supply Company B with widgets for the next 10 years.
(c) Land reflected on the books of Company A at $1,000 has been recently appraised at a fair market value of $5,000.
(d) Company A paid rent of $500 for office space to Company B.
(e) Company A bought $200 of supplies from Company B and agreed to pay within 30 days.

2. Determine which of the following accounts are listed on the balance sheet and which are on the income statement. The company manufactures and sells boats.
(a) Cash on hand.
(b) Sales for the year.
(c) Equipment used for manufacturing boats.
(d) Boats in stock.

(e) Salary paid to salesman.

(f) Rent paid for office space.

(g) The owner's investment in the business.

3. List the following transactions under the three headings: *Objects/Services Received, Objects/Services Given,* and *Dollar Impact.*

(a) Owner invested $5,000 in business.

(b) Company paid $200 for office supplies.

(c) Company promised to pay $300 in 30 days for merchandise that was obtained for resale.

(d) Company borrowed $1,000 from bank.

(e) Company pays rent of $200 for use of office space.

4. Some financial statements report the financial activities of a firm over some period of time, while others report the condition of a firm at one point in time. Classify the income statement, balance sheet, and cash-flow statement as to whether they report activities over a period of time, such as a year, or whether they report the condition of a firm at one point in time.

5. During 19X4, Ace Company had an increase in assets from $100,000 to $125,000. What sources could have attributed to this growth?

6. Assuming that no loans were made and no investment equity was issued in Exercise 5, what caused the increase?

7. During the month of June, The Art Shop Company had the following transactions: borrowed $10,000 from bank, rented a shop and made an obligation to pay rent of $1,000 for the first year, purchased paintings costing $15,000, sold some of the paintings for $22,000. List each transaction, and determine what was received and given and the dollar impact.

8. Assuming that the Jay Company had the following account balances, arrange the information into a balance sheet. Cash, $8,200; Inventory, $3,200; Other Assets, $500; Jay's Investment, $10,000; Liabilities, $200; Profit,?

9. Determine whether each of the following accounts would be classified as asset, liability, or owner's equity accounts on the balance sheet of a firm:

(a) Cash.

(b) Wages Payable.

(c) Land.

(d) Property, Plant, and Equipment.

(e) Jane Webber, Equity (Jane owns the business).

(f) Interest Payable.

(g) Note Payable.

(h) Office Furniture and Fixtures.

10. A cash flow statement for AAA Company reflects a beginning balance of $20,000, sources of cash of $8,000, and uses of cash of $6,000. What amount is the ending cash balance?

11. Gordon's Barber Shop has the following transactions during the month of June: revenues from hair cuts, $1,205; wages paid, $350; rental expenses for shop, $250;

supplies used, $30; utilities, $105; interest expense on bank loan paid, $20; union dues paid by business, $20. Prepare an income statement for Gordon's Barber Shop for the month of June, using the format shown in Exhibit 1-2.

12. Complete the blanks in the following table:

Case	Assets	Liabilities	Owner's Equity
1	$ 3,000	$ 1,900	_____
2	15,600	_____	6,800
3	_____	47,000	3,800
4	12,000	_____	9,600
5	62,000	47,000	_____

13. Haried Company received $6,000 in cash from customers during the month of July and paid $500 in rent, $1,000 in salaries, and $3,500 for an automobile during the month of July. Prepare a cash flow statement for the company assuming its beginning cash balance on July 1, 19X5, was $2,700. Use the format shown in Exhibit 1-3.

Problems

1. John Smart operates his own business. He sells tires. Last year John had revenue from sales of $14,000. Repairs last year for the delivery truck cost him $150. He uses the truck to transport his tires from the manufacturer to his place of business, which is 250 miles round trip. He makes this trip four times a year and buys 200 tires each trip at $20 for each tire, selling them at $28 each. John pays $0.50 per gallon of gas, and his truck gets 25 miles to the gallon. He sold 500 tires during the year.

REQUIRED:
Prepare an income statement, as shown in Exhibit 1-2.

2. Rita Wright owns and operates her own business. She writes and sells a CPA exam guide. Her cash account on 1/1/X8 had a balance of $5,000. The following business events occurred during January 19X8:
(a) Sold 50 guides for $2,000 in cash.
(b) Borrowed $10,000 cash from the bank.
(c) Sold 40 guides for $1,500 on credit.
(d) Bought a new printing press for $30,000, half of which was paid for in cash.
(e) Rita invested $4,000 additional cash in the business.
(f) Promised to sell guides to students next month for $4,000 in cash.
(g) Paid rent of $500 in cash.

REQUIRED:
Prepare a simple cash flow statement for the month of January, as shown in Exhibit 1-3.

3. Ben and Mary Higgins operate a shoe shop. Their balance sheet accounts at year end, December 31, 19X6, had the following balances:

Cash	$ 2,600
Supplies	600
Land	10,000
Buildings	21,000
Store Furnishings	3,900
Bank Loan	25,000
Higgins' Equity	6,000
Owners' Profit	7,100

REQUIRED:

Prepare a balance sheet for the Higgins Shoe Shop as of December 31, 19X6, as shown in Exhibit 1-1.

4. Redman Brothers Pharmacy is interested in acquiring additional funds to expand the business. Susan Olsen is considering investing in the business and is interested in getting answers to these questions:
(a) What is the current financial condition of the business?
(b) How profitable is the business?
(c) How much are employees paid in salary?
(d) How much does the firm pay in rent?
(e) Is the cash flow of the business positive (inflows exceed outflows)?
(f) How much is owed to creditors?
(g) How much cash is currently available for expansion of the business?

REQUIRED:

Indicate which financial statements will provide answers to these questions.

5. Wayne Plumbing Company's account balances as of December 31, 19X4, are as follows:

Cash	$ 1,210
Supplies	1,800
Tools	2,240
Office Furnishings	1,300
Bank Loan	500
Wayne Equity	1,000
Revenues	13,680
Salary Expense	5,800
Supplies Expense	2,780
Interest Expense	50

REQUIRED:

Prepare an income statement and a balance sheet for the year ended December 31, 19X4, for Wayne Plumbing Company.

6. The Hemphill Company's cash account details the following transactions for the first month the business is in operation:

Owner's investment in business	$ 3,000
Purchased equipment	1,200
Rented office space	700
Received from customers	1,500
Paid wages	1,100
Purchased store furnishings	1,400
Paid interest	40

REQUIRED:

Prepare a cash flow statement for Hemphill Company for this month.

7. Henderson Dry Cleaners is owned by George Henderson. George rents all his equipment and store space and uses a calendar year for the business. The account balances for Henderson Dry Cleaners are shown below as of December 31, 19X4:

Accounts Payable	$ 1,200
Accounts Receivable	6,900
Advertising Expense	2,000
Cash	18,200
Insurance Expense	600
Miscellaneous Expense	210
Rent Expense	18,000
Sales	41,400
Salaries Payable	300
Salary Expense	14,300
Supplies	8,100
Supplies Expense	3,900
Taxes Expense	3,050
Utilities Expense	4,250
Henderson, Equity	36,610

REQUIRED:

(a) Prepare an income statement for Henderson Dry Cleaners for 19X4, using the format shown in the chapter.

(b) Having calculated owner's profit, prepare a balance sheet for Henderson Dry Cleaners as of December 31, 19X4.

8. Below are the account balances for Midland Service Company as of June 30, 19X7, its fiscal year end:

Accounts Payable	$12,000
Accounts Receivable	20,000
Advertising Expense	21,000
Cash	15,000
General Operating Expenses	13,000
Interest Expense	2,000
Land, Buildings and Equipment	10,000
Salary and Wage Expense	75,000
Sales	250,000
Rental Expense	60,000
Selling Expenses	57,000
Owners' Equity	11,000

REQUIRED:

(a) Prepare an income statement for Midland Service Company for the year ended June 30, 19X7.

(b) Prepare a balance sheet for Midland Service Company as of June 30, 19X7.

9. A summary of important events and transactions for the Victor Company for the month of June 19X8 is shown below:

(a) Purchased a car for company use, paying $1,000 and signing a note for $6,000.

(b) Paid wages, $3,700 in cash.

(c) Purchased supplies, $650 in cash.

(d) A small fire destroyed supplies costing $100 that had been acquired in a prior month.

(e) Sales to customers totaled $16,000; half was received in cash, the remainder was recorded as accounts receivable.

(f) Collected accounts receivable, totaling $3,800 during the month.

(g) Signed a new rental agreement, requiring $600 per month in rents. Paid the June rental.

(h) Owners invested $1,000 in the business.

REQUIRED:

Prepare a cash flow statement for the Victor Company for June 19X8, assuming its opening cash balance was $3,500.

☐ 2
ACCOUNTING PRINCIPLES AND INFORMATION PROCESSING

THE ENVIRONMENT OF ACCOUNTING

COMPLEXITY

OWNERSHIP AND CONTROL

PUBLIC INFORMATION

EFFICIENCY

PROCESSING ACCOUNTING DATA

AN EXAMPLE

INFORMATION REPORTING

OTHER ACCOUNTING PRINCIPLES

TRANSACTIONS AND FINANCIAL STATEMENTS

THE ACCOUNTING EQUATION

EXPANDING THE EQUATION

CLASSIFYING INFORMATION

AN ILLUSTRATION

RECORDING THE EVENTS

REVENUES AND EXPENSES

STATEMENT PREPARATION

SUMMARY

A SUPPLEMENTARY DISCUSSION: THE DEVELOPMENT OF THE ACCOUNTING PROFESSION AND ACCOUNTING PRINCIPLES

ANCIENT TIMES

MODERN ACCOUNTING

ACCOUNTING INSTITUTIONS

THE SECURITIES AND EXCHANGE COMMISSION

THE AMERICAN INSTITUTE OF CERTIFIED PUBLIC ACCOUNTANTS

THE FINANCIAL ACCOUNTING STANDARDS BOARD

□ OBJECTIVES

AFTER STUDYING THIS CHAPTER, YOU SHOULD BE ABLE TO DO THE FOLLOWING:

1. DESCRIBE THE BUSINESS ENVIRONMENT THAT AFFECTS ACCOUNTING.

2. EXPLAIN SELECTED, GENERALLY ACCEPTED ACCOUNTING PRINCIPLES.

3. RELATE SPECIFIC ACCOUNTING PRINCIPLES TO THE DATA COLLECTION, DATA PROCESSING, AND INFORMATION REPORTING PROCESSES.

4. STATE THE ACCOUNTING EQUATION AND EXPLAIN ITS UNDERLYING RELATIONSHIP.

5. EXTEND THE ACCOUNTING EQUATION (BY ADDING REVENUE, EXPENSE, OWNERS' INVESTMENT, AND WITHDRAWAL VARIABLES TO THE PREVIOUS ELEMENTS), AND USE THE EQUATION TO RECORD TRANSACTIONS.

6. CONSTRUCT FINANCIAL STATEMENTS FROM ACCOUNT BALANCES.

When writing a book, a term paper, a business letter, or a note to a friend, certain rules and procedures must be followed. Communication is possible only with a common understanding of the meaning of words and a system to interrelate such words. English grammar and syntax combine with definitions to provide meaning to communicated expressions. Form is also an important part of the communication process. In English, we write from left to right and from top to bottom. These accepted procedures enable the reader to follow the flow of thought intended by the author.

The accounting process also is based on predetermined rules, procedures, and form. These concepts and standards which underlie financial accounting are referred to as *Generally Accepted Accounting Principles,* or *GAAP.* GAAP have evolved over a period of several centuries.[1] Specific principles developed in response to changes in available data, information processing technology, and the information needs of users. Financial accounting practices in the United States are fairly well specified in the pronouncements of the Securities and Exchange Commission (*SEC*), the American Institute of Certified Public Accountants (*AICPA*), and the Financial Accounting Standards Board (*FASB*). Characteristics of these organizations and historical perspectives on the development of accounting are presented in the Supplementary Discussion at the end of this chapter.

The Environment of Accounting

Accounting principles result from needs and reflect the environment of the profession. Several factors characterize the environment of accounting: the *complexity* of modern business organizations, the separation of business *ownership* and *control,* the public's *"right to know,"* and a concern for *efficiency* fostered by the profit motive of free enterprise.

Complexity. Most business enterprises operate as individual proprietorships or partnership ventures. These forms of organization generally limit the size and scope of activities that can be undertaken. However, the greatest bulk of business volume is conducted by entities that adopt the corporate form of organization. The corporation provides a means for many individuals to pool their financial resources for large-scale commercial ventures. For example, the growth of the steel, railroad, and automobile industries in this country is directly related to the ability of individual investors to collectively invest.

By combining vast amounts of resources in a single organization, corporations can become huge. Size and complexity create a need for significant quantities of accounting information. Many modern corporations

---

[1] The history of modern accounting dates from the development of formalized Italian bookkeeping practices during the fifteenth century.

operate in multinational markets, adding additional dimensions to accounting information needs.

Ownership and Control.   As business operations expand, those who supply economic resources to the organization become farther removed from directly controlling the resources. For example, when a neighborhood laundry adds a truck for pickups and deliveries, the owner of the laundry (the supplier of the resources) relinquishes direct control of that delivery truck (a resource) to a driver. In large corporations directed by professional managers, the owners (stockholders) effectively relinquish all direct control to the managers. Managers of large organizations require information about the business operations, while the owners require information about the resource stewardship of management.

Public Information.   In organized societies, governments exercise control over many aspects of life for the betterment of those who are governed. Such control requires information. The significant impact of business on modern society has heightened the need for government to be informed of business activities and to monitor compliance with laws and regulations. The administrative complexities of societal controls have magnified requirements for accounting information.

Efficiency.   Businessmen have always been concerned about the efficient use of economic resources of immediate concern to their own business, such as materials, labor, plant, and equipment. Efficient use of these resources is directly reflected in accounting-derived profit measurements—a widely recognized performance index in both socialistic and capitalistic economies. Historically, less concern was directed at measuring the consequences of employee safety, pollution, and other ecological factors. Today, however, a growing social awareness has broadened the focus and concerns of the accounting field.

Financial accounting is primarily concerned with historical events. Data relating to *completed transactions* represent the focus of accounting attention. Measurements are primarily based on *historical costs*, or values recorded at the time a transaction was completed, instead of current or future values. Under the historical cost concept, land that was acquired by an entity in 1950 for $120,000 would be reflected in the accounts at $120,000 today, despite known changes in real estate values. The use of historical cost provides an objective measurement for processing accounting data—the value of the land is $120,000 because it was purchased for this amount in 1950. While striving for objectivity, accountants will sometimes record estimates and other judgments if the presentation enhances the usefulness of resulting reports.

Processing Accounting Data

There are various ways to record descriptions of transactions. *Qualitative descriptions* rely heavily on judgment and interpretation. For example, if a friend says, "I paid a lot of money for my new car," he has described a transaction in qualitative terms. However, the phrase "a lot of money" can be interpreted quite differently by different individuals; contrast the reactions of an eight-year-old and someone earning a salary in excess of $100,000 per year.

Quantitative descriptions leave no room for judgmental errors or misinterpretations. "The car cost $7,000" conveys the same meaning to everyone. Therefore, accountants focus on the available quantitative information about transactions. The *monetary-unit-of-measure-concept* identifies money as a common denominator and the basis for quantifying transactions.

The usefulness of historical costs is related to the *going concern assumption.* This assumption directs the accountant to treat each entity as though it were to continue in existence indefinitely. But since information users require periodic reports to make informed decisions, the concept of *periodicity* supports the preparation of periodic accounting reports about a business. While periodic reports could be prepared for periods spanning any interval, almost all entities prepare an annual report. The business year is called a *fiscal year* and it may or may not coincide with a calendar year. A fiscal year could run from July 1 through June 30 or any other contiguous 12-month period. The reporting period for some businesses ignores the common convention of months and subdivides the business year into 13 periods, each containing four weeks.

Periodic reporting requires that income for the business entity under consideration be calculated. Two classes of accounts are important in making such an income determination:

Revenue—results from the sale of a product or service. Revenue is measured by the corresponding increase in assets (or resources) received as payment for the item sold.

Expense—is associated with the goods or services consumed by the revenue generation process. They are measured as a decrease in the assets (or resources) that result from making a sale of a product or service, that is, the historical cost of the assets given up in the sale or consumed to make the sale.

In preparing a periodic income statement, expenses are related to revenues for the particular period in question. The *matching concept* relates expenses with corresponding revenues during a period and reports the difference between them as net income (or loss). Expenses are recognized and reported when revenue is generated.

The foregoing concepts are used in accounting practice to determine how data are collected and processed in the accounting system. The following example illustrates how these concepts are employed by the accountant.

On June 1, 19X6, Nancy Byrne and Jane Rice opened the Campus Book Store and hired an accountant. In this case, the *accounting entity* is the Campus Book Store and its *fiscal year* will run from June 1, 19X6, through May 31, 19X7. The accountant is interested in recording *transactions* data relative to this business.

Throughout the year, the following business events occurred:

1. A store was purchased for $20,000.
2. Books costing $15,000 were purchased from publishers.
3. One-half of the books were sold for $12,000.
4. The remaining 980 books were unsold at the end of the year—one wholesale book company offered to buy them for $3,000 and another offered $5,000, but Jane felt that they were worth about $9,000.
5. A salesman was paid $4,000 in salary for the year.

In reviewing this information throughout the year, the accountant did several things. Using *historical costs* and *monetary units of measure,* he recorded the store at $20,000, the books at $15,000, and the salesman's services at $4,000. He assumed that the business would keep going in the future (*going concern* concept); thus, he ignored the offers of the wholesale book companies. The only information that he recorded concerned *completed transactions.*

To provide the owners with information, he employed the concept of *periodicity* and produced reports at the end of the fiscal year. One report, the income statement, *matched* revenues and expenses. *Revenue,* valued at $12,000, related to sales made during the year. The *expenses* matched to this revenue were books of $7,500 (one-half of the total cost of all the books) and salaries of $4,000. When these were *matched,* they resulted in net income of $500.

We can see from this example that most accounting principles are not applied in any predetermined sequence. Instead, they are introduced as needed. The accountant regularly exercises professional judgment in applying principles.

Once transaction data have been collected, other accounting conventions are introduced to the reporting process. First, the principle of *conservatism* should be observed; conservatism is translated to mean that accounting reports should anticipate (or disclose) all likely losses, but gains should not be reported until they actually occur. Thus, accounting reports reflect a pessimistic view when dealing with uncertain events. For example, conservatism would call for a financial statement that discloses a possible loss that could result from suits against the firm—even though legal counsel believes that the case is not well-founded. However, if the company had instituted a lawsuit, no accounting entry would be made until the suit was finally settled, even if chances of winning were excellent.

Financial statements provide a basis for comparative analysis, where data for two companies are compared or where the changes over time (between reports) of one company are isolated. *Consistency* is a necessary characteristic that promotes comparative analyses. Consistency requires the entity to use similar accounting procedures over time. Therefore, if a company acquires two similar assets in two consecutive years, it must classify the asset in similar fashion. To do otherwise is inconsistent and would hinder comparability.

While the accountant supplies useful information, expedients are taken so that time and money are not wasted on trivial problems. The concept of *materiality* calls for precise classification of all significant information and implies that insignificant data may be classified in an expedient fashion. For example, a large business organization might classify a newly acquired screwdriver as an expense rather than as an asset. Materiality is measured relative to the entity under consideration. Thus, the misclassification of $100 of assets may be significant, or material, to a small business. However, General Motors, with over $18 billion of assets, would consider a $100 misclassification as immaterial.

Other Accounting Principles. A compilation of generally accepted accounting principles would include many more than those we have discussed so far. However, this set provides a basis for an initial discussion. In appropriate places throughout the book, other principles will be introduced as they become applicable.

Transactions and Financial Statements

In Chapter 1, the three basic financial statements were introduced—the balance sheet, the income statement, and the cash flow statement. The balance sheet, or statement of financial position, discloses the nature and value of the investment in assets, or resources, of the entity and the claims against these assets, referred to as liabilities and owners' equity. In a condensed fashion, this statement appears as follows:

BALANCE SHEET

Assets	Liabilities + Owners' Equity
Total Assets	Total Liabilities and Owners' Equity

The form of the statement approximates the letter "T," with assets on the left-hand side and liabilities and owners' equity on the right-hand side. The dollar value of the assets is exactly equal to the dollar value of the claims against those assets—liabilities and owners' equity. This fundamental interrelationship of assets, liabilities, and owner's equity is referred to as the *accounting equation.*

The Accounting Equation.   In algebraic form the accounting equation is expressed as:

$$Assets = Liabilities + Owners' Equity$$

Relying on this relationship, we can see that if any two parts of the balance sheet are known, the third may be found by substitution. For example, if assets are $100 and liabilities are $80, then owners' equity must equal $20 for the basic equation to hold. Knowing that liabilities are $200 and that owners' equity is $400, we can imply that assets must equal $600.

The accounting equation is related to the transaction concept. Transactions are characterized by giving and receiving consideration of equal economic value. Therefore, if the economic effects of transaction items given and received are recorded in the balance sheet, the equality of the accounting equation will hold.

For example, if a business buys a used truck for $1,000, the asset Truck will increase in value by $1,000 and the asset Cash will decrease by $1,000. Total assets are unchanged by this transaction and the equality of the accounting equation stays the same. If the business initially had $10,000 of cash, an $8,000 bank loan, and $2,000 of owners' investment, its balance sheet, expressed in equation form, looked like this before acquiring the truck:

$$Assets = Liabilities + Owners' Equity$$

				Owners'	
Cash	$10,000	Loan	$8,000	Investment	$2,000
Total	$10,000	=	$8,000	+	$2,000

After acquiring the truck, the equation underlying the balance sheet still holds, as shown below:

$$Assets = Liabilities + Owners' Equity$$

				Owners'	
Cash	$ 9,000	Loan	$8,000	Investment	$2,000
Truck	1,000				
Total	$10,000	=	$8,000	+	$2,000

The same equality will hold as long as the accountant consistently records all parts of a transaction. Assume that the company also buys a building for $20,000, paying $5,000 in cash and securing a $15,000 mortgage. Properly recorded, this information still maintains the equation:

Assets = Liabilities + Owners' Equity

				Owners'	
Cash	$ 4,000	Loan	$ 8,000	Investment	$2,000
Truck	1,000				
Building	20,000	Mortgage	15,000		
Total	$25,000	=	$23,000	+	$2,000

In this case, assets were increased by $20,000 due to the acquisition of the building. They were simultaneously decreased by $5,000 because of the outflow of cash. Liabilities were increased by the $15,000 mortgage. The overall effect of this transaction was to increase assets by $15,000 (from $10,000 to $25,000) and to increase liabilities by $15,000 (from $8,000 to $23,000).

Exhibit 2-1 presents a summary of possible effects on the balance sheet from various types of transactions. Recognize that in each case the equality of the underlying accounting equation has been preserved.

Expanding the Equation. The accounting equation provides a basis for all accounting activity. The general form parallels the format of the balance sheet. The income statement explains, or elaborates on, part of the change that may occur between two balance sheets—specifically, the effect of normal operations on a firm's financial position.

Owners' equity, or the owners' claim against the business, results from the net effect of the owners' investments in, and withdrawals from, the business plus any income (less any losses) from operations. In tabular form, these effects are summarized below:

Action or Event	Effect on Owners' Equity
Investment by owner	INCREASE in owners' equity
Withdrawal by owner	DECREASE in owners' equity
Income from operations	INCREASE in owners' equity
Loss from operations	DECREASE in owners' equity

Income is measured by matching *revenue* and *expenses*. To the extent that revenue exceeds expenses, income has been earned. If expenses exceed revenue, a loss has been incurred. The basic accounting equation can be expanded to reflect this detail as follows:

Assets = liabilities + owners' equity

Assets = liabilities + (investment − withdrawal) + (revenue − expenses)

EXHIBIT 2-1
TRANSACTION EFFECTS ON THE BALANCE SHEET

Possible Change			
Increase	*Decrease*	*Possible Explanation*	*Effect on Balance Sheet*
Assets		A truck (asset) is purchased for cash (asset).	No effect on totals.
	Assets		
Liabilities		A bank loan (liability) is made to pay a supplier's bill (liability).	No effect on totals.
	Liabilities		
Owners' equity		One owner (owners' equity) sells his interest to another (owners' equity).	No effect on totals.
	Owners' equity		
Assets		Supplies (assets) are purchased on credit (liability).	Assets increase. Liabilities increase.
Liabilities			
	Assets	Cash (asset) is used to pay off a bank loan (liability).	Assets decrease. Liabilities decrease.
	Liabilities		
Assets		Cash (asset) is invested in a business by an owner (owners' equity).	Assets increase. Owners' equity increases.
Owners' equity			
	Assets	An owner withdraws cash (asset) from a business for personal use (owners' equity).	Assets decrease. Owners' equity decreases.
	Owners' equity		
Liabilities		An owner satisfied part of his claim (owners' equity) by taking a note from the business (liability).	Liabilities increase Owners' equity decreases.
	Owners' equity		
Owners' equity		A creditor satisfied his claim (liability) by becoming an owner (owners' equity).	Liabilities decrease. Owners' equity increases.
	Liabilities		

The expanded equation includes the impact of the ***net owners' investment*** (Investment − Withdrawals) and the ***net income*** (Revenue − Expenses). In accounting terminology, the word "net" indicates that a subtraction has occurred.

Classifying Information

Fundamentally, the recording process is based on the accounting equation; each transaction involving the entity may be analyzed in terms of its impact on the equation. Parts of the equation may be subclassified into various types of assets, liabilities, and owners' equity items, while preserving the equality. Classifying the data in this manner facilitates the preparation of the financial statements. For example, changes in the asset "Cash" may be separated from changes affecting the asset "Building."

Exhibit 2-2 provides a comprehensive illustration of this classification approach, based on the following example.

An Illustration. On September 1, 19X6, Mr. Phil Weiss decided to open a boat dealership named the Weiss Boat Company. During the month of September, the following economic events (transactions) occurred relative to this business:

Event	Description
1	Mr. Weiss invested $20,000 in the business.
2	A bank loan of $50,000 was obtained.
3	A store was rented for $2,000 per month, paid in cash.
4	$10,000 of equipment for use in the store was purchased for cash.
5	Boats costing $40,000 were purchased. Mr. Weiss paid the supplier $20,000 in cash and agreed to pay the balance in 60 days.
6	$500 was spent on advertising in local papers.
7	Six boats which cost $30,000 were sold for $75,000.
8	Salaries of $2,000 were paid.
9	A boat which cost $3,000 was sold for $1,000 in cash, with the purchaser's promise to pay $6,000 in 30 days.
10	$15,000 of the amount owed to the boat supplier was paid.

These transactions are analyzed in Exhibit 2-2. The accounting equation has been expanded to provide subclassifications of the various asset, liability, and equity items affecting the firm. In this case, specific column names were selected and inserted as events were recorded. The columns are used to represent *accounts,* or classes of information, that will be captured by the accounting system. Thus, the column Cash is an account that contains information about the movement of cash into or out of the business. Separate rows were used for each transaction to provide a chronological listing. Since transactions are characterized by inflows and outflows, each transaction row should have at least two entries in account columns. Because the accounting equation underlies the entire process, the equation should remain in balance after each row is complete.

Recording the Events. The accounting analysis for each of the 10 transactions involving the Weiss Boat Company is explained in the following list. You may relate the description to the record in Exhibit 2-2.

ACCOUNTING PRINCIPLES AND INFORMATION PROCESSING

EXHIBIT 2.2

ANALYZING AND CLASSIFYING TRANSACTIONS

| | Assets | | | | = | Liabilities | | + Revenue − | | Owner's Equity Expenses | | | | + Owner's Investment |
| | Cash + | Accounts Receivable + | Boats (Inventory) + | Equipment = | Bank Loan + | Accounts Payable + | Sales Revenue − | Rent Expense − | Advertising Expense − | Salary Expense − | Cost of Goods Sold + | Investment |
Event Number												
1	$20,000											$20,000
2	50,000				$50,000							
3	(2,000)							$2,000				
4	(10,000)			$10,000								
5	(20,000)		$40,000			$20,000						
6	(500)								$500			
7a	75,000						$75,000					
7b			(30,000)								$30,000	
8	(2,000)									$2,000		
9a	1,000	$6,000					7,000					
9b			(3,000)								3,000	
10	(15,000)					(15,000)						
Totals	$96,500	$6,000	$ 7,000	$10,000	$50,000	$ 5,000	$82,000	$2,000	$500	$2,000	$33,000	$20,000

Note: Parentheses denote negative numbers and decreases.

Event 1—The business (which is the accounting entity) received $20,000 in cash and gave Mr. Weiss a corresponding $20,000 ownership claim. Thus, the asset Cash is increased by $20,000 and the Owner's Investment account is also increased by $20,000.

Event 2—The business received $50,000 in cash, reflected by an increase in this amount in the Cash account. The corresponding claim is not held by an owner, but by a creditor. Therefore, the liability Bank Loan is increased by $50,000.

Event 3—The $2,000 store rent represented an outflow of cash; the Cash account was decreased by this amount. A corresponding increase was made to the Rent Expense account, since the "right to use the store" was acquired. Recognize that the increase in the Expense account represents a decrease in owner's equity; thus, the accounting equation maintains its equality.

Event 4—Equipment, valued at $10,000, was received by the entity and recorded as an increase in the Equipment account. Another asset, Cash, is reduced by $10,000, reflecting its outflow from the business.

Event 5—The acquisition of boats increases the Inventory account by the amount of their cost, $40,000. Two distinct outflows relate to this event: a $20,000 reduction of Cash, and a $20,000 promise to pay the supplier. This type of promise to pay is commonly called an Accounts Payable. Because the supplier is a creditor, the $20,000 increase in Accounts Payable is placed as a liability.

Event 6—Advertising is a business expense. Thus, the $500 payment is reflected by an increase in the Advertising Expense account and a decrease in the asset Cash.

Event 7—The entry to record this sale is shown in two parts, 7a and 7b respectively, although it could have been combined on a single line. The business received $75,000 in cash, which is shown as an increase in the Cash account. The $75,000 represents a receipt from a customer for a product or service; so it is shown as an increase in the Sales Revenue account. The cost of goods sold is shown in row 7b. The account Boats is reduced by $30,000; this reflects the historical cost of the boats that were sold. Since these resources (boats) are of no future benefit to the firm (i.e., no longer belong to the firm), they are included as an increase of $30,000 in the Cost of Goods Sold (expense) account.

Event 8—The receipt of labor services from employees is an expense to the firm. Thus, the account Salary Expense is increased by $2,000. Since the salaries were paid in cash, the Cash account is reduced by a corresponding amount.

Event 9—Like event 7, the entry for event 9 is separated into two parts, 9a and 9b. The total revenue to be recognized is $7,000, including a $1,000 increase in the Cash account and a receipt of the purchaser's promise to pay $6,000. Such promises are termed Accounts Receivable, and this account is increased by $6,000. The $7,000 revenue is recorded by an increase to the Sales Revenue account. The value of the boat that was sold, $3,000, is shown as a decrease in the Inventory account and an increase in the Cost of Goods Sold (expense) account.

Event 10—Making a payment to the supplier reduced the cash. Thus, the Cash account is decreased by $15,000. Also, the outstanding promise to pay, Accounts Payable, has been reduced by $15,000.

Revenues and Expenses. One further point should be mentioned concerning the disclosure of revenues and expenses. Examine event 7: the entry could have increased the Cash by $75,000, decreased Boats by $30,000, and increased Owner's Equity by $45,000—the gain or profit on the sale. However, this approach obscures the revenue and expense information needed to prepare an income statement. By separating the entry into two parts, and separately identifying revenues and expenses, income reporting is facilitated. Recognize that both methods have the same effect on the balance sheet. Once revenue of $75,000 is matched with expenses of $30,000, the resulting net income of $45,000 belongs to the owner and eventually becomes part of the owner's equity.

After all of the transactions for the fiscal period have been recorded, financial statements can be prepared. As a first step, all accounts are totaled to determine their balances. Check that the sum of the asset account balances equals the sum of the liability account balances plus the owner's equity account balances. The transactions information has been *recorded* (in a form paralleling the accounting equation), *classified* (chronologically by transaction and by class and type of account), *summarized* (totaled by account) and is also available for reporting.

Statement Preparation

The income statement discloses revenues, expenses, and net income. Revenue and expense account balances for the Weiss Boat Company were used to prepare an income statement, as shown in Exhibit 2-3. Recognize that the form of this statement differs from previous examples. Cost of goods sold has been separated from the cost of operating the business (operating expenses), as is commonly done. *Gross margin* represents the difference between the amounts a company pays for its goods and the price it charges its customers.

The balance sheet presents the balances of those accounts not included in the income statement. Instead of reporting details of revenues and expenses, the balance sheet carries forward net income or net loss as part of

EXHIBIT 2-3
INCOME STATEMENT

WEISS BOAT COMPANY
Income Statement
For the Month Ended September 30, 19X6

Sales Revenue		$82,000
Cost of Goods Sold		33,000
Gross Margin on Sales		$49,000
Operating Expenses		
Rent Expense	$2,000	
Advertising Expense	500	
Salary Expense	2,000	4,500
Net Income		$44,500

owner's equity. A balance sheet for the Weiss Boat Company is presented in Exhibit 2-4. Note that the term, investment, is used to represent the owner's financial contribution to the business. Other terms are commonly used as synonyms, the most frequent of which is *capital*. Capital, owner's equity, and other terms introduced later in the text will be used interchangeably, as is widespread in business practice.

EXHIBIT 2-4
BALANCE SHEET

WEISS BOAT COMPANY
Balance Sheet
As of September 30, 19×6

Assets		*Liabilities*		
Cash	$96,500	Accounts Payable	$ 5,000	
Accounts Receivable	6,000	Bank Loan	50,000	
Boats (Inventory)	7,000	Total Liabilities		$ 55,000
Equipment	10,000	*Owner's Equity*		
		Owner's Investment	$20,000	
		Net Income*	44,500	
		Total Owner's Equity		64,500
		Total Liabilities and		
Total Assets	$119,500	Owner's Equity		$119,500

Source: Income Statement, Exhibit 2-3

Summary

Financial accounting practices and techniques are based on generally accepted accounting principles. Transactions for specific accounting entities are the focus of attention. The principles of historical cost, going concern, monetary unit of measure, and periodicity all relate to processing accounting data. Periodic income determination requires that revenues and expenses are clearly identified and matched to yield net income. Conservatism, consistency, and materiality are guides for the reporting process.

All accounting activities are based on the accounting equation:

$$\text{Assets} = \text{liabilities} + \text{owners' equity}$$

This equation can be modified to reflect additional classifications of owners' equity:

$$\text{Assets} = \text{liabilities} + (\text{investment} - \text{withdrawals}) + (\text{revenue} - \text{expenses})$$

Properly recorded transaction information maintains the equality of the accounting equation. Account balances provide a basis for preparing the income statement and the balance sheet of the entity.

A Supplementary Discussion: The Development of the Accounting Profession and Accounting Principles

Accounting emerged in response to the need for information about economic resources of distinct entities.

ANCIENT TIMES

The organized use of the accounting function has been traced back to 4,000 B.C. Taxes were levied in the Babylonian Empire on the basis of accounting records maintained on clay tablets. Similarly, about 3,000 B.C., the Incan civilization in Peru advanced to a stage where accounting information was needed. A knotted string, known as a *quipu,* was used as an accounting device—even *before a written language had emerged* among these people.

The Roman and Greek civilizations advanced the practice of accounting in response to the commercial needs of the times. For example, interest, at the rate of 20 percent, was recorded on outstanding debts in 542 B.C. Partnerships and commercial companies also flourished in Greece about 400 B.C., and in 300 B.C. the Greeks created the governmental position of treasurer. During the year 5 A.D., the Roman Emperor Augustus prepared the first budget.

As these and other civilizations emerged, numbering systems and symbolic languages developed to facilitate recording and reporting economic information—that is, accounting was born. The emergence of modern accounting systems has been traced directly to the Italian city-states of the fifteenth century.

MODERN ACCOUNTING

With the development of major trade routes linking diverse civilizations, business ventures and ownership interest became more complex. The need for a system able

A SUPPLEMENTARY
DISCUSSION: THE
DEVELOPMENT OF THE
ACCOUNTING
PROFESSION
AND ACCOUNTING
PRINCIPLES

to account for multiple ownership interests led to the introduction of double-entry bookkeeping in much the same form as we know it today. The practices constituting this system was first described in a mathematics book written by an Italian priest, Luca Pacioli, in 1494.[2] The continuity and acceptance of such a system is based on its logical structure, efficiency, effectiveness, and flexibility. As specific information needs changed in response to the business environment, the general nature of the basic accounting system was able to accommodate the change.

Following Pacioli's effort, other events occurred in diverse parts of the world that shaped the profession. Some, of the more interesting and important of these include the following[3]:

1581—The first accounting association was formed in Italy.

1645—The first public accountant began to practice accounting in Scotland.

1789—The Congress of the United States passed a law providing for an auditor and a comptroller within the Treasury Department.

1805—Napoleon of France decreed that an examination and an apprenticeship were necessary before anyone could practice accounting.

1881—John Wharton established the first collegiate school of business in America. It was to become a part of the University of Pennsylvania.

1896—The New York legislature enacted legislation that regulated public accounting and created the title of Certified Public Accountant (CPA).

1899—The first woman CPA in the United States was recognized.

1904—The First International Congress of Accountants was held in St. Louis.

The half million professional accountants of today are involved with a variety of organizations. However, all practice a profession that is centuries old and has developed as a mandate of civilization.

ACCOUNTING INSTITUTIONS

Accounting information is used by many people to make a variety of economic decisions. The growth of large and diverse corporations during the early 1900s emphasized some inadequacies in existing accounting practices. Following the stock market crash of 1929, general dissatisfaction with then current accounting practice stimulated the accounting profession, the government, and the major stock exchanges to take a more active interest in regulating and controlling accounting practice.

The accounting profession practices self-regulation through various professional organizations, the most notable being the *American Institute of Certified Public Accountants (AICPA)*. As an extension of private, professional control, the *Financial*

---

[2]This book describes a double-entry accounting system, the one which is used in modern accounting practice.

[3]Based on George Abs et al, "Historical Dates in Accounting," *The Accounting Review* (July 1954), pp. 486–93.

Accounting Standards Board (FASB) was authorized to establish generally accepted accounting principles. Governmental control of financial accounting is exercised primarily through the **Securities and Exchange Commission (SEC).**

The Securities and Exchange Commission.   The Securities and Exchange Commission, a Federal regulatory body, was created in the 1930s to oversee all activities related to public securities markets, including the financial reporting practices of companies that are traded on the various stock exchanges. SEC initiates its regulatory power by requiring that subject companies submit periodic reports. This reported information then becomes publicly available. In addition, SEC also requires that each business under its jurisdiction issue periodic reports to its stockholders. These reports must be examined by a certified public accountant who certifies that the reports were prepared in conformity with generally accepted accounting principles. By this action, SEC delegated power to the CPAs to control the financial reporting practices of publicly owned companies.

The Securities and Exchange Commission has the legal power and practical ability to formulate accounting principles. However, over the years, the Commission has used this power sparingly, relying on the accounting profession itself to play a leadership role in developing and promulgating accounting principles.

The American Institute of Certified Public Accountants.   The AICPA is the national professional association of Certified Public Accountants in the United States. Since the early 1900s, the Institute has sought to codify and promote generally accepted accounting principles. Through a variety of special and continuing committees, the AICPA has addressed itself to the areas of accounting principles and auditing standards.

In 1959, the AICPA created the **Accounting Principles Board** (APB) to advance the development of accounting principles and to reduce the existing inconsistencies which characterized common practice. Over its 14-year existence, the APB issued a series of 31 opinions. These opinions constituted official pronouncements by the Board about specific areas of controversy. All members of the American Institute of Certified Public Accountants in the United States were bound to adhere to these principles and procedures in preparing financial statements. Responsibility for establishing accounting standards shifted in 1973 from the APB to the Financial Accounting Standards Board, an independent body. However, the AICPA has retained its control over the establishment of *auditing* standards and continues to support a variety of research and professional educational endeavors that are aimed at continually enhancing the profession and its members.

The Financial Accounting Standards Board.   The Accounting Principles Board was composed of members of the AICPA. Over the years, it received substantial criticism concerning its lack of independence and its inability to respond quickly to emerging problems. Following the recommendations of a study group, the AICPA supported the establishment of an independent organization to promulgate accounting principles. FASB was established to meet this need.

The Financial Accounting Standards Board consists of seven full-time members drawn from public accounting, industry, education, and government. The Board is supported by an extensive staff and has the ability to research, evaluate, and react

A SUPPLEMENTARY
DISCUSSION: THE
DEVELOPMENT OF THE
ACCOUNTING
PROFESSION
AND ACCOUNTING
PRINCIPLES

to new situations in a reasonable time. The Board's activities are structured to provide the broadest base of input into their deliberations concerning accounting principles.

Like its predecessor, the Accounting Principles Board, the Financial Accounting Standards Board promulgates reporting and disclosure principles for use by the profession. The Board has received the cooperation and support of the Securities and Exchange Commission, which has legislative authority to force compliance.

Other organizations, boards and commissions also have an influence on accounting practice. Because of the breadth of the profession, the focus of some of these activities is not restricted to financial accounting. The impact on the financial records of an entity may be indirect in nature. Advanced study in accounting will expose students to information about many of these organizations, their activities, authority and accomplishments.

Key Terms

Generally accepted accounting principles
Historical costs
Monetary unit of measure concept
Going concern assumption
Periodicity
Revenue
Expense
Matching concept
Conservatism
Consistency
Materiality
Accounting equation
Gross margin
Capital
Investment

Questions

1. Name three organizations that specify rules for financial accounting practices.

2. Which factors characterize the environment of accounting?

3. Distinguish between qualitative and quantitative descriptions. Which is most applicable to accounting?

4. What assumptions underlie the use of historical costs for financial statements?

5. Define the terms, *revenue* and *expense.*

6. How does the principle of conservatism affect the reporting of gains or losses?

7. Why is the principle of consistency necessary for the evaluation of comparative financial statements related to consecutive periods?

8. How is insignificant data treated under the concept of materiality? Give an example.

9. Describe the format of a conventional balance sheet.

10. Distinguish between the "accounting equation" and the "expanded accounting equation."

11. List four events that can affect owner's equity.

12. What steps are taken in the preparation of financial statements to assure that correct information is reported?

13. Define the term *gross margin,* and explain what information can be derived from it.

14. Discuss the powers and duties of the three organizations that regulate the accounting profession.

15. Explain the matching concept.

16. Identify the concept that is associated with the preparation of *annual* financial statements.

17. Name the accounting concept that instructs that all measures listed in financial reports prepared for distribution in the United States be stated in terms of dollars.

18. From which sources do CPAs obtain information required in their work? Are CPAs legally liable to clients for the quality of their work?

19. List five technical areas of accounting used in many businesses.

20. Describe the objectives of three accounting reports listed in this chapter.

21. Accounting reports are used in making various business decisions. List three examples of decisions that are commonly based on accounting information.

1. Just prior to going out of business, the Smith Corporation prepared a balance sheet as follows:

Exercises

Assets (no cash)	$50,000
Liabilities	30,000
Owners' equity	20,000

Assets were subsequently sold for $40,000 in cash.

REQUIRED:
(a) Prepare a balance sheet immediately after the sale of assets.
(b) Explain how the cash should be distributed.

2. On January 1, 19X6, the Inventory account of the Harper Company showed a balance of $100,000. During the year, the company purchased $50,000 worth of inventory, and delivered $55,000 of goods to customers. What is the balance of the Inventory account on December 31, 19X6?

3. The Jones partnership was established on July 1, 19X6. It adopted a June 30 year-end. Each of three partners contributed $1,000 on July 1, 19X6. On June 30, 19X7, the following amounts were determined: (1) $2,050 was in the checking account; (2) amounts due from customers for services rendered, $1,000; (3) office supplies on hand $2,000; (4) $1,500 in notes payable, owed to a local bank; and (5) amounts due to suppliers of $500.

REQUIRED:

(a) Using the accounting equation, what is the balance of the partners' capital accounts (in aggregate) at June 30, 19X7?

(b) Prepare a balance sheet for the Jones partnership at June 30, 19X7.

4. Barbara James and Heather Holmes opened Dallas Used Cars, Inc. They hired an accountant at the end of their first year of operations who determined that the following transactions took place during the year:

(a) A bank account was opened with a deposit of $70,000.

(b) Used cars were purchased for $60,000.

(c) Cars that cost $20,000 were sold for $30,000.

(d) The remaining cars had fair market value of $80,000.

(e) Barbara's brother-in-law was paid $6,000 salary as a salesman.

REQUIRED:

Perform an analysis similar to the one shown in Exhibit 2-2.

5. Below are independent events. Indicate the effect (increase, decrease, no effect) and the amount on assets, liabilities, and owner's equity:

(a) In starting a new business, owners contribute $100,000 cash, a building worth $50,000, and land worth $40,000.

(b) Office furniture and calculators were purchased for $5,000.

(c) A mortgage of $30,000 was taken out on the building.

(d) Salesmen's commissions are paid by cash—$200.

(e) Inventory was purchased on account—$500.

6. Westward Photographers, Inc., has a fiscal year closing of June 30. For fiscal year 19X7 you have determined the following account balances:

Sales	$100,000
Cost of goods sold	60,000
Advertising Expense	5,000
Rent Expense	7,200
Salary Expense	10,000

REQUIRED:

Prepare an income statement for Westward Photographers, Inc.

7. Determine the dollar amount that would be recorded by an accountant for the following events.

(a) Land purchased 10 years ago for $10,000 has a fair market value today of $200,000. What is the land valued at on the books?

(b) A salesperson was paid $8,000 in commissions for the past year. He is expected to sell enough products this year to receive $10,000 in commissions.

(c) The author of a book was offered $1,000 by a publishing company for his book.

(d) A company received $10,000 for the sale of mineral rights on its land. The rights had a fair market value of $12,000, but the company needed the money right away.

8. The Vivian Company balance sheet on December 31, 19X1, contains the following totals:

Assets	Liabilities	Owner's Equity
$10,000	1,000	9,000

Keep a cumulative running total showing the effect each of the following transactions has on the totals of the balance sheet, as in Exhibit 2-2.
(a) Bought truck for $5,000 cash.
(b) Owner invested $10,000 of additional cash in business.
(c) Business borrowed $10,000 on a note to the bank.
(d) Sold merchandise for cash—$3,000.
(e) Paid off a note to the bank—$1,000.

9. Show the effects (increase +. decrease −, or no change 0) in the proper columns of the balance sheet—Assets (A), Liabilities (L), Owner's Equity (OE)—for the following transactions.
(a) Owner withdraws cash.
(b) Equipment sold for cash.
(c) Bought truck on credit.
(d) Truck purchased for cash.
(e) One owner sells his interest to another owner.
(f) A bank loan is obtained to pay an overdue bill.

10. (a) The assets of a company total $2 million and the owner's equity totals $1.4 million. What is the amount of total liabilities?
(b) The total liabilities of a company are worth $100,000. This figure is 50 percent of the total assets. What is the amount of Owner's Equity.

11. Determine whether each of the following events constitutes a recordable transaction.
(a) Owners invested $10,000 cash into the business.
(b) Purchased truck for $8,000, payment to be made next year.
(c) Employed salesman at $1,000 per week. He will start work tomorrow.
(d) Paid $400 for telephone bill for previous month.
(e) Paid for truck in (b).

12. Indicate whether the effect on each of the following transactions is to increase, decrease, or have no effect on the total assets of the business as shown on its balance sheet.

Transaction	Asset Increase	Asset Decrease	No Effect
(a) Owners invest cash in business	_____	_____	_____
(b) Customers pay for services	_____	_____	_____
(c) Business purchases supplies for cash	_____	_____	_____
(d) Business purchases equipment for cash	_____	_____	_____
(e) Supplies are purchased for credit	_____	_____	_____
(f) A liability is paid in cash	_____	_____	_____
(g) Owners withdraw cash	_____	_____	_____
(h) An asset is destroyed by fire	_____	_____	_____

13. Show the effect of each of the following transactions on Owner's Equity by completing the following table.

	Effect on Owner's Equity		
Transaction	Increase	Decrease	No Effect
(a) Owner invested cash	_____	_____	_____
(b) Business purchases land	_____	_____	_____
(c) Business pays rental expenses	_____	_____	_____
(d) Customers pay for services	_____	_____	_____
(e) Owners withdraw cash	_____	_____	_____
(f) A liability is paid	_____	_____	_____
(g) A creditor satisfies his claim by becoming an owner	_____	_____	_____

14. Compute the unknown amounts on each of the four unrelated business balance sheets.

	A	B	C	D
Accounts Receivable	_____	$ 400	$1,000	$ 3,000
Accounts Payable	$ 9,000	800	1,000	8,000
Cash	12,000	_____	1,300	7,000
Equipment	32,000	9,000	6,000	13,000
Land	6,000	8,000	2,000	5,000
Salaries Payable	8,000	600	_____	2,500
Supplies	500	1,000	1,000	1,500
Owner's Equity	46,000	20,000	8,000	_____

Problems

1. Below are transactions for the Rogers Company for the month of April 19X9:
   (a) Clay Rogers invested $50,000 in the business.
   (b) $5,000 of equipment was purchased for the business for cash.
   (c) $50,000 of merchandise was purchased for resale *on account.*
   (d) Clay Rogers invested $50,000 of additional cash in the business.
   (e) Advertising of $500 was paid with cash.
   (f) Merchandise costing $10,000 was sold for $40,000 cash.
   (g) Rent of $10,000 for the company's office building was paid for in cash.
   (h) Merchandise costing $20,000 was sold for $50,000, $10,000 of which was paid in cash, and the rest was owed on account.
   (i) Salaries of $25,000 were paid in cash.
   (j) Clay Rogers withdrew $10,000 cash from the business.
   (k) $10,000 of the amounts owed the company were paid in cash.
   (l) Merchandise costing $3,000 was sold for $6,000 cash.

REQUIRED:
   (a) Set up an expanded accounting equation in the same form shown in Exhibit 2-2. Record the transactions for the Rogers Company.

(b) After all transactions have been recorded, prepare a simple income statement and balance sheet.

2. The balance sheet for the Blackburn Company on January 1, 19X9, is as follows:

Blackburn Company
Balance Sheet
January 1, 19X9

Assets		Liabilities	
Cash	$10,000	Accounts Payable	$2,000
Accounts Receivable	15,000	Notes Payable	4,000
Inventory	4,000		6,000
Equipment	17,000	*Owner's Equity*	
		Net Investment	40,000
	$46,000		$46,000

The following transactions took place during 19X9:
(a) Sold merchandise costing $1,000 for $5,000 cash.
(b) Bert Blackburn, owner, invested additional cash of $20,000 in the business.
(c) Received $10,000 in cash as payment of accounts from customers.
(d) Bought merchandise for $10,000 on account.
(e) Advertising of $500 for the year was paid in cash.
(f) Equipment was purchased for $1,000 cash.
(g) Sold merchandise costing $5,000 for $15,000, $10,000 of which was paid in cash.
(h) Paid off $3,000 of note payable with cash.
(i) Paid salaries of $10,000 with cash.

REQUIRED:
Prepare income statement and balance sheet for Blackburn Company.

3. Prepare a balance sheet for the McCummen Company for December 31, 19X9, using the following information.

Accounts Payable	$14,000
Accounts Receivable	8,275
Buildings	64,000
Land	30,000
Cash	?
Equipment	2,100
Notes Payable	30,000
Truck	3,420
Jim McCummen, Capital	80,000

4. The financial data for the Howard Company (an electronics servicing firm) for the month of April are summarized in equation form below. Each line shows the effect of each transaction on the equation.

	Cash	+ Accts Rec	+ Supplies	+ Equip	= Accts Pay	+ Capital	+ Revenue	− Expense
Balance	$11,000	$4,000	$450	$ 6,000	$4,450	$17,000		
1	2,000						$2,000	
2	−100				−100			
3			−200					+$200
4	−400		+400					
5	+1,000					+1,000		
6	−200							+200
7	−1,500					−1,500		
8					+4,000	+4,000		
9		+300					+300	
10	+2,000	−2,000						
	$13,800 +	$2,300 +	$650 +	$10,000 =	$8,350 +	$16,500 +	$2,300 −	$400

REQUIRED:
(a) Describe the probable nature of each transaction.
(b) What is the net change in cash and owner's equity for the month?
(c) What is the net income for the month?

5. Below are transactions for the Howard Company for the month of May:

5/1   Ann Howard, owner, invested $40,000 cash.
5/3   The company borrowed $8,000 cash from bank on a note payable.
5/4   The company buys $20,000 worth of equipment, pays $10,000 and promises to pay the other $10,000 within 30 days.
5/12 Cash received for services is $12,000.
5/14 Services performed for customers who agree to pay within 30 days is $4,000.
5/16 Salaries are paid in cash, totaling $4,500.
5/19 The company pays $2,000 of the note payable owed to the bank.
5/22 The company pays $50 of interest on note with cash.
5/24 Customers pay $1,000 of amount owed to company.
5/27 An order is received from a customer for services to be rendered next week, which will be billed at $1,000.
5/31 Utilities bill of $560 is paid in cash.

REQUIRED:
(a) Using the following form of the expanded accounting equation, enter each transaction.

Date	Cash	Accounts Receivable	Equipment	Accounts Payable	Notes Payable	Owners Equity	Revenue	Expenses

(b) Calculate net income for the month of May.

6. Given below are the statements of financial position and the income statement of the Logan Company.

LOGAN COMPANY
Statement of Financial Position

	April 30, 19X8	May 31, 19X8
Assets		
Cash	$ 8,000	$12,000
Accounts Receivable	12,000	10,000
Prepaid Rent	3,000	2,000
Total Assets	$23,000	$24,000
Liabilities and Owner's Equity		
Liabilities	$ 6,000	$ 3,000
Total Owner's Equity	17,000	21,000
	$23,000	$24,000

LOGAN COMPANY
Income Statement
For The Month Ended 5/31/X8

Revenue		$15,000
Expenses		
Utilities	$10,000	
Rent	1,000	11,000
Net Earnings		$ 4,000

REQUIRED:

Assume that all revenues earned were received in cash. State the probable cause of the changes in each of the statements of financial position accounts during May.

7. Below are the transactions of Lightfoot Service Company for the month of March 19X4:
   (a) Received $800 for services performed for customers, not previously billed.
   (b) Paid $300 accounts payable.
   (c) Paid rent of $300 for March.
   (d) Received $1,000 on account from customers.
   (e) Purchased $200 of supplies, paying cash.
   (f) Purchased $2000 of equipment on account.
   (g) Withdrew $200 for owner's personal use.
   (h) Paid wages in cash, $1,300.
   (i) Paid utilities in cash, $100.
   (j) Used $100 in supplies.

REQUIRED:
(a) Complete the following expanded accounting equation for each of these transactions:

Cash + Accts Rec + Supplies + Equip = Accts Pay + Capital +
Bal: $12,000 + 3,000 +   500 + 6,000 = 2,000 + 19,500 +

    Revenue − Expenses

Bal: _____ _____

(b) Prepare a balance sheet as of March 31, 19X4.

8. Savannah TV Repair Company's records show the information listed below for 19X3 and 19X4:

	Dec. 31, 19X3	Dec. 31, 19X4
Accounts Receivable	$9,000	$6,000
Accounts Payable	4,000	1,500
Cash	6,000	7,200
Equipment	8,800	7,700
Supplies	1,500	900
Notes Payable	3,000	2,000
Owner's Investment	?	?

REQUIRED:
(a) Prepare a balance sheet for Savannah TV Repair Company for each year.
(b) Assuming that the owner withdrew $1,000 during 19X4 for personal needs, calculate net income for 19X4.

9. The transactions for the Mint Company for the month of October 19X2 are shown below:
(a) Purchased auto for business use on credit.
(b) Billed customer for services provided.
(c) Paid rent for the month.
(d) Collected cash from customer for rendering services.
(e) Received amount due from customer.
(f) Paid wages.
(g) Purchased supplies for cash.
(h) Withdrew cash for owner's personal use.
(i) Paid utility bills when received.

REQUIRED:
Using Exhibit 2-1 as a guide, show the effect of each of these transactions on the balance sheet totals of Assets, Liabilities, and Owner's Equity.

□ 3
THE ACCOUNTING CYCLE

THE GENERAL LEDGER

MAINTAINING ACCOUNTS

FORMAT OF THE LEDGER

DEBITS AND CREDITS

NORMAL ACCOUNT BALANCES

DOUBLE ENTRY RECORDING

ANALYZING TRANSACTIONS

REVENUE AND EXPENSE TRANSACTIONS

EXPENSES

REVENUES

RECORDING REVENUES AND EXPENSES

THE GENERAL JOURNAL

FORMAT OF THE JOURNAL

THE COMPLETE RECORDING PROCESS

THE TRIAL BALANCE

THE CLOSING PROCESS

SUMMARY

A SUPPLEMENTARY DISCUSSION: FORMS OF BUSINESS ORGANIZATION

PROPRIETORSHIPS

PARTNERSHIPS

CORPORATIONS

FINANCIAL STATEMENTS AND FORMS OF ORGANIZATION

□ OBJECTIVES

AFTER STUDYING THIS CHAPTER, YOU SHOULD BE ABLE TO DO THE FOLLOWING:

1. DESCRIBE THE FORMAT AND PURPOSE OF THE GENERAL LEDGER.
2. RECORD TRANSACTIONS IN THE LEDGER, GIVING PROPER CONSIDERATION TO DEBITS AND CREDITS.
3. PREPARE GENERAL JOURNAL ENTRIES.
4. PREPARE A TRIAL BALANCE.
5. COMPLETE THE ACCOUNTING CYCLE BY JOURNALIZING AND POSTING CLOSING ENTRIES.

All complex, purposeful activities require organization if they are to achieve their intended goal. A baseball game or a college class would deteriorate into chaos if they were not organized. Organization implies a predetermined system or set of related procedures that govern the activity. In a baseball game, the rules specify who is at bat, who is in the field, and what specific actions may be taken at a given time. Rules organize the game.

The organization of many related parts is referred to as a system. A system regulates activities and functions in such a way that an overall goal may be attained. The accounting system directs all accounting activities toward a goal of reporting useful and usable information. The sequence of activities followed in an accounting system is referred to as the *accounting cycle,* and it includes procedures to collect, record, and process financial data into a report of meaningful economic information. The process is continuous and ongoing, leading to the use of the term "cycle."

The General Ledger

An account is a unit of information about a particular economic object or event: in a physical sense, it is a form on which data are summarized. Thus, a Cash account would maintain information about increases or decreases in cash. A personal checkbook could serve as an account; increases and decreases in available cash are *recorded* on the checkstub. The checkstub also *summarizes* (produces a balance) of all transactions involving items *classified* as cash, that is, all checks and deposits relate to one type of asset—cash. Like a checkstub, an account facilitates recording, summarizing, and classifying information about any one element of a transaction.

Maintaining Accounts. To properly record all of the transactions of an entity, many accounts are needed. Specifically, a separate account is kept for each item on a firm's balance sheet and income statement. Thus, there can be many asset, liability, and owner's equity accounts, plus revenue and expense accounts.

Accounts are kept and maintained in a *ledger.* In manual accounting systems, the ledger is a large book with a separate page for each account. In computerized systems, the ledger is a set of reserved storage locations with sublocations reserved for each account. In either case, the ledger provides a summarization of the transaction effects on the various parts of the financial statements.

Format of the Ledger. Each ledger account should provide the following information:

1. *Account Name.* Each account is identified by a name consistent with that used in the financial statements. Without becoming too restrictive, the number of accounts is normally limited to provide a reasonable amount of summarization.

2. *Account Number.* In most accounting systems, ledger accounts are numbered. Numbering aids in indexing and locating accounts, as the numbering system may be structured to identify groups of related items. For example, all assets could be identified with three digit numbers where the first digit is always a "1." By sorting on this digit, assets could quickly be identified. Liability account numbers might start with the numeral "2," owner's equity with a "3," and so on.

3. *Date Column.* The date of record is noted for every entry in the account. Dating each entry allows balances to be determined as of a specific date, knowledge that is absolutely necessary for preparing financial statements.

4. *Explanation Column.* The explanation column in the ledger provides room to describe the underlying transaction that affected the account. In many cases, explanations will be unnecessary as the reference column entry will provide an adequate description of the event.

5. *Reference Column.* The reference column indicates the source and location of the data that was recorded in the ledger. This is a control procedure to facilitate cross checking the original recording with the summarization.

6. *Amount Columns.* Each ledger has two amount columns: one for increases in the account, the other for decreases from the account. The double-column format reduces possibilities for error associated with using plus and minus signs in a single column.

7. *Balance Columns (optional).* Ledger accounts may include specific columns for maintaining a running total of the account balance. The balance is the difference between the debits and credits. When a balance column is not used, the account is periodically totaled, or *footed,* to facilitate reporting.

8. *Number of Accounts in the Ledger.* The number of accounts contained in the ledger is determined by the amount and type of information demanded by the organization. Additional accounts are added when more information is required. Organizational form also influences the number of accounts contained in the ledger, as described in the Supplementary Discussion at the end of this chapter. For example, information about the equity of a sole proprietorship is contained in one account called Owner's Equity, while equity accounts for a corporation are titled Common Stock and Retained Earnings.

A standard, four-column ledger account will appear in the following form:

Account Title					Account Number		
						Balance	
Date	Explanation	Post Ref.	Debit Amount	Credit Amount		Debit	Credit

Specific forms of ledger accounts can vary, depending on the particular business environment in which they are used. However, each will have the general characteristics identified above. A ledger account can be represented by the letter "T:"

ACCOUNT TITLE

Debit Amount | Credit Amount

While form is important and should not be ignored, the "T" account representation is an excellent way to illustrate the effect of transactions on the accounts. As is traditional in accounting textbooks, we shall employ the "T" account format.

Debits and Credits Amount columns of general ledger accounts have been identified as *debit* and *credit,* respectively. Literally, these terms refer to the side of an account where an entry is to be placed. **Debits** relate to entries on the *left-hand side* of an account, and **credits** relate to entries on the *right-hand side.* Such entries will either increase or decrease an account, depending on its *normal balance.*

Normal Account Balances. The normal balance of an account depends on its traditional classification and placement on the balance sheet. By treating the balance sheet as a large "T" account, with left- and right-side balances, and by superimposing specific accounts on it, the normal account balances become obvious, as illustrated in Exhibit 3-1.

EXHIBIT 3-1

Debit Side	Credit Side
Assets	*Liabilities*

Asset 1

Debit +	Credit −

Asset 2

Debit +	Credit −

Asset 3

Debit +	Credit −

Liability 1

Debit −	Credit +

Liability 2

Debit −	Credit +

Owner's Equity

Debit −	Credit +

Total Assets = <u>Debit Balance</u>

Total Liabilities & Owner's Equity
= <u>Credit Balance</u>

Assets that appear on the left side, or debit side, of the balance sheet are increased by debits and have a normal debit balance. Conversely, the normal balances of liability and owner's equity accounts are credits and credit entries will increase them. In a summary fashion, the relationships between the accounts and debits and credits can be expressed as follows:

☐ Asset Accounts
    Normal balance is on the left side—*debit.*
    Increases are recorded by *debit* entries.
    Decreases are recorded by *credit* entries.

☐ Liability Accounts
    Normal balance is on the right side—*credit.*
    Increases are recorded by *credit* entries.
    Decreases are recorded by *debit* entries.

☐ Owner's Equity Accounts
   Normal balance is on the right side—*credit.*
   Increases are recorded by *credit* entries.
   Decreases are recorded by *debit* entries.

Double-Entry Recording. A transaction was defined as an exchange in which the entity gives and receives consideration of equal economic value. Therefore, any transaction must be recorded by entries to, at least, two accounts—one showing what was given in the transaction and the other what was received. Furthermore, the debits recorded for a transaction must equal the recorded credits, since accountants equate values for both parts of the transaction.

The duality of this process—debits equal credits—is the basis of double-entry accounting, where each transaction results in, at least, two entries—a debit and a credit of equal value. Verification of the equality of debits and credits in each transaction provides the accountant with some assurance that the complete effect of transaction was recorded.

Analyzing Transactions

The accountant must analyze transactions to (1) determine which accounts are affected, and to (2) determine the proper debit and credit amounts needed to record the transaction. An advantage of the general ledger is its flexibility; accounts may be added as needed. The following transactions illustrate how information is recorded in the general ledger. Each transaction assumes that the accounts do have sufficient amounts of their normal balance to facilitate the exchange. Account names include the parenthetical notation of A, L, or OE, representing asset, liability, or owner's equity, respectively. Also, the debit and credit captions include a notation of either + or − to indicate the effect on the normal balance of this type of account.

1. *Type:* Exchange of an asset for an asset.
   Example: A new truck is purchased for $6,000 cash.

Truck (A)		Cash (A)	
Debit (+)	Credit (−)	Debit (+)	Credit (−)
$6,000			$6,000

2. *Type:* Exchange of an asset for a liability.
   Example: Land, costing $28,000, is purchased through a mortgage.

Land (A)		Mortgage Payable (L)	
Debit (+)	Credit (−)	Debit (−)	Credit (+)
$28,000			$28,000

3. *Type:* Exchange of an asset for owner's equity.
   Example: An owner invests $20,000 cash in the business.

Cash (A)			Owners' Equity (OE)	
Debit (+)	Credit (−)		Debit (−)	Credit (+)
$20,000				$20,000

4. *Type:* Reduction of a liability in exchange for an asset.
   Example: Cash of $10,000 is paid to reduce an outstanding mortgage. (Reduction of a liability can be conceived of as the return or receipt of your prior promise to pay.)

Cash (A)			Mortgage Payable (L)	
Debit (+)	Credit (−)		Debit (−)	Credit (+)
	$10,000		$10,000	

5. *Type:* Reduction of owner's equity in exchange for an asset.
   Example: An owner withdraws $4,000 of her investment from a business.

Cash (A)			Owner's Equity (OE)	
Debit (+)	Credit (−)		Debit (−)	Credit (+)
	$4,000		$4,000	

6. *Type:* Reduction of a liability in exchange for owner's equity.
   Example: A creditor, to whom the company owes $8,000, is permitted to invest that amount in the business in exchange for canceling the liability.

Accounts Payable (L)			Owner's Equity (OE)	
Debit (−)	Credit (+)		Debit (−)	Credit (+)
$8,000				$8,000

In each of the foregoing transactions, the complete entry required the debits to equal the credits, thus maintaining the equality of the accounting equation.

Revenue and expense transactions have not been analyzed to this point. Data obtained from recording these activities become the central elements of an income statement.

Revenue and Expense Transactions

Expenses. When a business acquires an asset, it is valued at its *cost* to the firm and reported on the balance sheet. *Costs* are *incurred,* or recognized, whenever the acquisition of an asset is recorded. In a functioning business, assets are sold or consumed as a part of normal operations. When an asset is sold, its future service potential is given up by the selling entity; it is no longer owned or controlled by that entity. The value of what has been given up or consumed is termed an *expense* and reported on the income statement. At the time of sale or consumption, the cost of the resource should be reclassified from an asset to an expense so that it is reflected in the income statement rather than on the balance sheet.

Exhibit 3-2 illustrates the relationship between costs and expenses for two entities that are exchanging assets.

The service potential of some resources expires when they are sold. Inventory, for example, will generally become an expense after a sale has been made. Other items are used up immediately in the course of business. Electricity is consumed as soon as it is acquired. Thus, it could be classified as an expense at the time it is acquired. Similarly, labor generally has no *future* service potential to a business; its value is consumed immediately as the time and effort are expended. Therefore, labor too could be an immediate expense entry.

Revenue. When resources are acquired, they are valued at their cost to the firm. When resources are sold by the firm, they are valued again in the market. The selling value is termed *revenue,* and it is measured as the amount received by the firm in exchange for the resource given up. Revenue results from business activities where a product or a service is sold. Examples of revenue-producing transactions include renting property, lend-

EXHIBIT 3-2

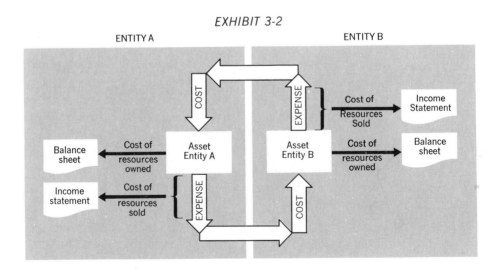

EXHIBIT 3-3

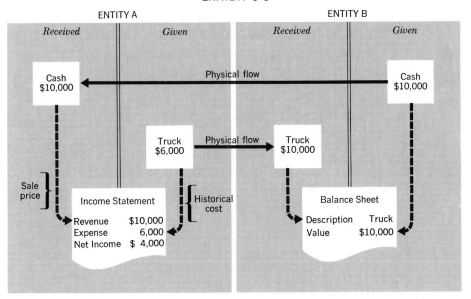

ing money, selling goods, or providing a professional service. Exhibit 3-3 illustrates some relationships between and measurements of expenses and revenues.

In the illustration, Entity A, an automotive distributor, sold Entity B a truck for $10,000. The truck originally cost Entity A $6,000. When the truck was sold, Entity A treated the $6,000 historical cost of the truck as an expense. The $10,000 cash that was received is an asset. Also, this inflow established the value of Entity A's revenue from the sale. The $4,000 difference between the $10,000 revenue and the $6,000 expense is *income,* and it will be reported on the income statement.

From the view of Entity B, the truck is an asset valued at its historical cost to B, $10,000. This asset will be reported on B's balance sheet.

Recording Revenues and Expenses. Revenue and expense accounts are used to calculate net income as reported on the income statement. The effects of debits and credits on these accounts are as follows:

☐ Revenue Accounts
  Normal balance is on the right side—*credit.*
  Increases are recorded by *credit* entries.
  Decreases are recorded by *debit* entries.

☐ Expense Accounts
    Normal balance is on the left side—*debit.*
    Increases are recorded by *debit* entries.
    Decreases are recorded by *credit* entries.

Using this structure, the entries to record the sale of the truck described in the previous example would be as shown below. The parenthetically noted R and E refer to revenue and expense accounts, respectively, and the debit and credit captions include a notation showing the effect on the normal balance of the accounts.

1. Reclassifying costs from assets to expenses—assets must be reduced by $6,000 and expenses must be increased by $6,000.

Truck (A)		Cost of Goods Sold (E)	
Debit (+)	Credit (−) $6,000	Debit (+) $6,000	Credit (−)

2. Recognizing the revenue from the sale—assets must be increased by $10,000 and revenue of $10,000 must be recognized.

Cash (A)		Sales Revenue (R)	
Debit (+) $10,000	Credit (−)	Debit (+)	Credit (−) $10,000

Revenues and expense jointly determine income, and income belongs to the owners of the entity. Thus, the revenue and expense accounts are used primarily to determine income and then enable accountants to value the owner's equity section of the balance sheet.

The General Journal

In the previous examples, transactions were recorded directly into the general ledger accounts. While this method facilitates the preparation of financial statements, it is not conducive to recording transaction activity in an orderly fashion. Before the first 100 transactions are recorded in the ledger, the details of any particular transaction would be obscured, since the general ledger classifies activity by type of account rather than by type of transaction.

In contrast, the *journal* contains a chronological listing of each transaction. Hence, the journal is a place of *original entry.* Transactions are initially recorded in the journal. However, the journal does not sort activity by accounts but is organized by sequence of occurrence. Therefore, transactions are *posted,* or transcribed in appropriate ledger accounts.

Format of the Journal. The general journal normally is structured to provide the following information:

1. *Date Column.* The date when each transaction occurred is recorded in the date column.
2. *Accounts.* The names of the ledger accounts to be debited and credited are recorded in this section.
3. *Reference.* The reference column identifies the ledger account number of each account to be posted. Normally, these numbers are inserted when posting occurs, thereby providing a control over the posting process.
4. *Amount Columns.* Separate columns are maintained for recording the debit and credit accounts corresponding with each account.

A standard journal will appear in the following form:

Date	Accounts	Reference	Debit	Credit
19X6 July 15	Land Cash To record the purchase of building lot number A-176	10 1	$4,200	$4,200

Recognize two additional characteristics of the journal entry. First, the debit account in the Accounts column is slightly left adjusted and the credit account is slightly right adjusted. This placement represents a generally used form for recording journal entries. Second, the entry itself is followed by a brief description of the transaction. These descriptions are used sparingly, when necessary, to provide details about a transaction or to disclose important information about the transaction not evident from the journal entry.

To place the entire recording process in context, consider the following transactions of the Tell-A-Phone Answering Service:

The Complete Recording Process

1. June 1, 19X6—Mr. William Tell invested $5,000 in the Tell-A-Phone Answering Service.
2. June 2, 19X6—The business bought a store for $20,000, paying $4,000 in cash and getting a mortgage for the balance.
3. June 2, 19X6—The business leased telephone equipment for $1,000 a month and paid the first month's charge.
4. June 7, 19X6—The business negotiated a $7,000 bank loan and received the cash.
5. June 8, 19X6—Two employees were paid salaries that totaled $300.
6. June 10, 19X6—Collections from customers for answering services amounted to $1,000.

7. June 11, 19X6—Customers were billed $3,000 for answering services.
8. June 15, 19X6—Employees were paid salaries of $300.
9. June 16, 19X6—Customers billed on June 11 paid $1,000, one-third of the balance due.

These transactions are recorded in the general journal of the business, or *journalized,* as shown in Exhibit 3-4. The reference column would not be completed as entries are journalized. At a subsequent date, each entry in the journal would be individually transcribed or posted in the general ledger, with the reference information being completed at this time. Reference notations confirm that the data were posted and will help locate the data if cross checking is desired. The results of this posting process are illustrated in Exhibit 3-5.

EXHIBIT 3-4
GENERAL JOURNAL

Date	Accounts	Ref.	Debit	Credit
19X6				
6/1	Cash	1	$ 5,000	
	Owner's Equity	6		$ 5,000
	Investment in business by Mr. Tell			
6/2	Store	3	20,000	
	Cash	1		4,000
	MortgagePayable	5		16,000
	Purchase of a new store			
6/2	Equipment Expense	9	1,000	
	Cash	1		1,000
	Rental charge for new telephone equipment			
6/7	Cash	1	7,000	
	Bank Loan Payable	4		7,000
	Loan of $7,000 from the Smith Bank			
6/8	Salary Expense	8	300	
	Cash	1		300
	Weekly salaries are paid			
6/10	Cash	1	1,000	
	Service Revenue	7		1,000
	Cash collections from customers			
6/11	Accounts Receivable	2	3,000	
	Service Revenue	7		3,000
	Owed by customers for service performed			
6/15	Salary Expense	8	300	
	Cash	1		300
	Weekly salaries are paid			
6/16	Cash	1	1,000	
	Accounts Receivable	2		1,000
	Collections of account from customers			

EXHIBIT 3-5

Cash (A)	No. 1	Accounts Receivable (A)	No. 2

Debit (+)		Credit (−)		Debit (+)		Credit (−)	
6/1	$5,000	$4,000	6/2	6/11	$3,000	$1,000	6/16
6/7	7,000	1,000	6/2				
6/10	1,000	300	6/3		2,000		
6/16	1,000	300	6/15				
	8,400						

Store (A)	No. 3	Bank Laon Payable (L)	No. 4

Debit (+)		Credit (−)	Debit (−)	Credit (+)	
6/2	$20,000			$7,000	6/7

Mortgage Payable (L)	No. 5	Owner's Equity	(OE) No. 6

Debit (−)	Credit (+)		Debit (−)	Credit (+)	
	$16,000	6/2		$5,000	6/1

Service Revenue (R)	No. 7	Salary Expense (E)	
			No. 8

Debit (−)	Credit (+)		Debit (+)		Credit (−)
	$1,000	6/10	6/8	$300	
	3,000	6/11	6/15	300	
	4,000			600	

Equipment Expense (E)	No. 9

Debit (+)		Credit (−)
6/2	$1,000	

The Trial Balance. After transactions have been posted in the ledger, ledger accounts are periodically *footed,* or totaled. A single line through the account indicates that a balance appears on the following line. Balances are set out by a double underline. Recognize that some accounts have a debit, or left side, balance, while others have a credit, or right side, balance.

Partial verification of journalizing and posting accuracy is obtained from a *trial balance*. The trial balance is a listing of all of the account balances as of a particular date. The total dollar amount of accounts with debit balances should equal the total of accounts with credit balances. If they are not equal, a journalizing or posting error has been made. The accountant should locate and correct the error.

Equality of trial balance debits and credits does not insure that the recording process has been correctly performed. Instead, it indicates that *certain* errors have not been made. Among the errors which a trial balance will *not* detect are:

A transaction posted to the wrong account.

An incorrect dollar value used consistently in both the debit and the credit of a transaction.

Recording a transaction more than once.

Correctly posting a transaction that was incorrectly journalized.

Failure to record a transaction.

A trial balance as of June 30, 19X6 for the Tell-A-Phone Answering Service is shown in Exhibit 3-6.

The Closing Process. Revenue and expense account balances are not

EXHIBIT 3-6
TRIAL BALANCE

Tell-A-Phone Answering Service Trial Balance June 30, 19X6		
Account	Debit	Credit
Cash	$ 8,400	
Accounts Receivable	2,000	
Store	20,000	
Bank Loan		$ 7,000
Mortgage Payable		16,000
Owner's Equity		5,000
Service Revenue		4,000
Salary Expense	600	
Equipment Expense	1,000	
	$32,000	$32,000

cumulative. These accounts are maintained on an annual basis (i.e., start with a zero balance and accumulate data for a whole year) to facilitate the preparation of an income statement. At the end of the period, revenue and expense accounts are "closed out," or turned back to zero, so that they can start off with a fresh start for the next period. The closing process also helps confirm the net income calculation. Net income becomes part of the owner's equity in the business. The closing process can be used to transfer the net income to the owner's equity accounts. The process of determining net income and clearing the revenue and expense accounts is referred to as the _closing process;_ the revenues and expense accounts are closed for the year.

The closing process introduces a special, temporary account called "Income Summary" as a vehicle for computing net income and transferring it to the owner's equity account. In a sequential fashion, the steps of the closing process are as follows:

Closing revenue accounts by _debiting_ them for their balance and _crediting_ income summary.

Close expense accounts by _crediting_ them for their balance and _debiting_ income summary.

Determine the balance of the Income Summary account. A debit balance indicates a loss. A credit balance indicates income.

Close the Income Summary account with a _debit_ balance by _crediting_ Income Summary and _debiting_ Owner's Equity. Close the Income Summary account with a _credit_ balance by _debiting_ Income Summary and _crediting_ Owner's Equity.

When the closing process is complete, all revenue and expense accounts should have a zero balance and the net income or loss should be included in the owner's equity account. Three closing entries would be necessary for the Tell-A-Phone Answering Service:

Date	Accounts	Debit	Credit
June 30	Service Revenue	$4,000	
	Income Summary		$4,000
	To close the revenue account		
June 30	Income Summary	1,600	
	Salary Expense		600
	Equipment Expense		1,000
	To close the expense accounts		
June 30	Income Summary	2,400	
	Owner's Equity		2,400
	To close the income summary account		

Exhibit 3-7 shows the general ledger after the closing entries have been posted and final balances taken. The closing entries are identified by a parenthetical "c."

After the closing process is complete, any account with a nonzero balance is reported on the balance sheet. The revenue and expense accounts, as well as the income summary account, all have zero balances. These accounts supply data used in preparing the income statement.

Summary

The accounting cycle consists of a periodic process that encompasses all accounting events from the recording of original transactions to the ultimate preparation of financial statements. Each transaction is analyzed in terms of its effect on two or more accounts. Both (all) effects are chronologically listed in the general journal, a formal book of original entry that identifies account names, as well as debit and credit dollar amounts. Every entry in the journal specifies whether an account is to be increased or decreased, an effect related to the traditional (but arbitrary) "normal" balance of an account. Normally asset and expense accounts maintain debit balances, while liability, owner's equity, and revenue accounts have credit balances.

Subsequent to the original entry, data from the journal is transcribed or posted in the ledger. The ledger is a collection of accounts, each of which has a title (name) and account number, and columns for debit, credit, and balance entries. Posting from the journal to the ledger sorts all transaction effects by account name, so that each account balance represents the accumulated summary up to a particular point in time. A trial balance summarizes debit and credit account balances and provides a limited validity check on the recording process.

Revenue and expense accounts are periodically closed, or transferred, to a special account called income summary. Income summary is used to compute the net income or loss resulting from a series of transactions and to clear the balances of the revenue and expense accounts for future accumulations of transaction activity. The Income Summary account is closed by transferring its balance to the owner's investment account. After the closing process is complete, accounts with remaining balances are reported on a balance sheet. The revenue, expense, and income summary accounts are used to prepare the income statement.

A Supplementary Discussion: Forms of Business Organization

Virtually all of the 13 million businesses in the United States are organized and operated as proprietorships, partnerships, or corporations. While proprietorships represent the largest number of businesses, recent Internal Revenue Service statistics indicate that the 1.5 million domestic corporations generated over 80 percent

EXHIBIT 3-7
FINAL GENERAL LEDGER BALANCE

Cash (A)	No. 1
$5,000	$4,000
7,000	1,000
1,000	300
1,000	300
8,400	

Accounts Receivable (A)	No. 2
Debit (+)	Credit (−)
$3,000	$1,000
2,000	

Store (A)	No. 3
Debit (+)	Credit (−)
20,000	

Bank Loan Payable	No. 4
Debit (−)	Credit (+)
	7,000

Mortgage Payable (L)	No. 5
Debit (−)	Credit (+)
	16,000

Owner's Equity (OE)	No. 6
Debit (−)	Credit (+)
	5,000
	2,400 (c)
	7,400

Service Revenue	No. 7
Debit (−)	Credit (+)
(c) 4,000	1,000
	3,000
	0

Salary Expense (E)	No. 8
Debit (+)	Credit (−)
300	600 (c)
300	
0	

Equipment Expense (E)	No. 9
Debit (+)	Credit (−)
1,000	1,000 (c)
0	

Income Summary	No. 10
Debit	Credit
(c) 1,600	4,000 (c)
(c) 2,400	
	0

of the total business receipts in the United States. Features of the organizational forms can explain these results. Although the basic accounting framework applies to all organizational forms, each form does require some few unique accounting procedures.

PROPRIETORSHIPS

Proprietorships are organized around a single owner of the business venture. In the legal sense, a proprietorship is not considered to be separate and distinct from its owner; thus, it is treated as an extension of the individual. Nevertheless, a proprietorship is treated as a distinct accounting entity.

Proprietory ventures may be started without prior legal authorization and may, therefore, be initiated or terminated quickly. Taxes are levied against the owner at individual tax rates, and business and personal income are combined. Most proprietorship ventures are fairly small, because they operate on the capital, or investment, of a single owner.

There are two major disadvantages to the proprietorship form of business organization, including the following:

Legal liability.   The business venture is not considered independent of its owner. Therefore, creditors may satisfy debts and other claims against the business by seizing or attaching the owner's personal property, such as home or car.

Limited life.   Proprietorships lack continuity, because they are associated with a particular individual. When the individual leaves the business, either through sale or death, the proprietorship ceases to exist.

In spite of these limitations, over 10 million business ventures are organized as proprietorships—probably because of the ease of formation.

PARTNERSHIPS

The partnership is a form of business organization where ownership is shared among two or more co-owners (called partners). Although some minimal legal controls over a partnership are imposed, it, like a proprietorship, is considered to be an extension of its owners.

Taxes are levied against partners as individuals, and partnership income is combined with personal income in determining the annual tax liability. In contrast to proprietorships, partnerships can be quite large, because many individuals may combine their individual resources under this form of organization. Many certified public accounting firms and law firms are organized as partnerships, some of which have hundreds of partners.

Although partnership form permits the investment of several individuals, it still has the same disadvantages as does the proprietorship:

Legal liability.   Each partner is individually and personally liable for all of the debts of the partnership.

Limited life.   Each partnership represents a combination of specific individuals. When a partner dies, retires, or sells an interest in the business, the old partnership is terminated; continuity requires the formation of a new partnership.

Approximately one million businesses are organized as partnerships in the United States.

CORPORATIONS

A corporation is legally defined as being separate and distinct from its owners; it is considered to be an artificial legal entity. Any number of individuals may simultaneously invest in a corporation by buying *shares* of its *capital stock*. These shares represent a proportionate ownership interest in the business. An individual investor's liability for debts of a corporation is legally limited to the amount he originally invested in the shares of stock.

Shares of stock, or ownership interests, are freely traded on stock exchanges throughout the country; transferability of ownership is easily facilitated by the corporate form of organization. Also, the death of any stockholder does not terminate the business, since the stock can be sold or given to someone else; thus, continuity of ownership is promoted.

For these reasons, corporations have been able to attract significant amounts of investment over the years. Several large corporations have assets (resources) measured in the billions of dollars.

There are disadvantages to the corporation including the following:

Organizational costs. Corporations must be chartered or approved by either a state government or by the Federal government. Significant amounts of legal work, involving time and money, are generally required to secure this approval.

Taxation. Corporations are taxed on their earnings at rates that are normally less than those applying to individuals. However, this tax applies to earnings before they are distributed to the owners (investors). When earnings are distributed, they are taxed again to the individual recipients as personal income. Thus, corporate earnings are, in effect, taxed twice.

Corporations clearly dominate other forms of organization in terms of volume of business activity. Many investors feel that the advantages outweigh the disadvantages.

FINANCIAL STATEMENTS AND FORMS OF ORGANIZATION

The income statement and cash (funds) flow statement of a business would not, in themselves, provide an indication of the form of organization used by the business. The reported information in these two statements is not dependent on organizational form.

However, one section of the balance sheet will vary with the form of organization. While resources (assets) and creditor claims (liabilities) are independent of the organizational form, the owners' equity is not. The owners' equity section of the balance sheet reflects the particular type of owners' claims that are outstanding; these claims are related to the form of business organization.

Exhibit 3-8 presents three different forms of a hypothetical owners' equity section for proprietorships, partnerships, and corporations. In practice, only one form would be used to reflect the prevailing organization structure.

A SUPPLEMENTARY
DISCUSSION:
FORMS OF BUSINESS
ORGANIZATION

EXHIBIT 3-8
Illustrative Balance Sheet

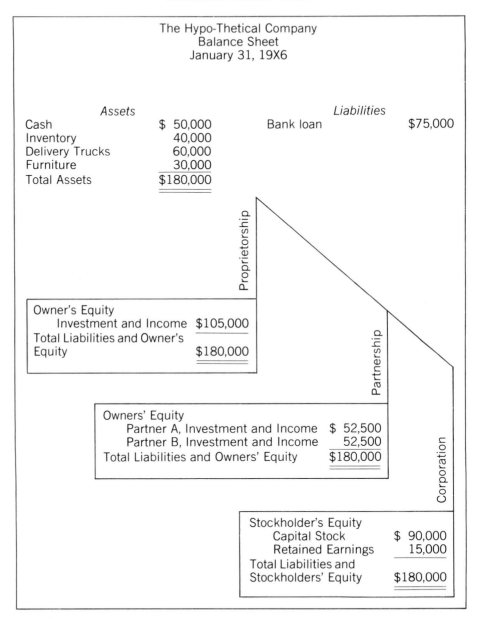

The Hypo-Thetical Company
Balance Sheet
January 31, 19X6

Assets		*Liabilities*	
Cash	$ 50,000	Bank loan	$75,000
Inventory	40,000		
Delivery Trucks	60,000		
Furniture	30,000		
Total Assets	$180,000		

Owner's Equity
    Investment and Income $105,000
Total Liabilities and Owner's
Equity $180,000

Owners' Equity
    Partner A, Investment and Income $ 52,500
    Partner B, Investment and Income   52,500
Total Liabilities and Owners' Equity $180,000

Stockholder's Equity
    Capital Stock $ 90,000
    Retained Earnings   15,000
Total Liabilities and
Stockholders' Equity $180,000

Proprietorship

Partnership

Corporation

The impact of organizational forms on accounting is discussed in later chapters of the text.

Accounting cycle
Ledger
Debits
Credits
Journal
Posted
Journalized
Footed
Trial balance
Closing process
Retained Earnings
Common Stock

Questions

1. Describe the format and purpose of the general ledger.

2. Are debit or credit balances normally found in asset accounts? In liability accounts? In owners' equity accounts?

3. In posting to the ledger, will a debit or a credit perform the following functions?
(a) Increase a liability.
(b) Increase an owners' equity.
(c) Decrease an asset.
(d) Decrease a liability.
(e) Increase an asset.
(f) Decrease an owners' equity.

4. Define the word transaction.

5. What must an accountant determine when analyzing a transaction before journalizing it?

6. In the following transactions, indicate whether assets (A), liabilities (L), or owners' equity (OE) increase (+), decrease (−), or remain constant (0). The business:
(a) Receives an asset for a liability (e.g., borrows money from a bank).
(b) Exchanges an asset for an asset (e.g., buys inventory for cash).
(c) Satisfies a liability for an asset (e.g., pays off a debt).
(d) Distributes money to an owner.
(e) Receives money from an owner.

7. Explain the difference between a cost and an expense. Give an example of each.

8. On which side (debit, credit) of the T account are the following situations entered?
Normal Balance—Expense Accounts
Increase—Expense Account
Increase—Revenue Account
Decrease—Expense Account
Normal Balance—Revenue Account

9. Does the general ledger summarize account activity before or after entries are made in the general journal?

10. Describe the format and purpose of the general journal.

11. Specify the purpose of the reference column in the general journal.

12. List some of the errors a trial balance *will not* detect.

13. What is the purpose of the closing process in the accounting cycle?

14. List the steps in the closing process.

15. Why are revenue and expense accounts "closed out" at the end of the accounting cycle?

16. Why are asset and liability accounts not "closed out" at the end of the accounting cycle?

17. Which of the following accounting principles are most closely related to the accounting cycle: materiality, consistency, or matching?

Exercises

1. Draw, in good form, the standard form column ledger account using the rules for format of the ledger described in the book.

2. Set up separate T accounts as needed and record the following transactions. Assume accounts have sufficient beginning balances to facilitate the exchanges.
(a) Equipment purchased for $4,000 cash.
(b) Purchased merchandise worth $2,000 on account
(c) The owner withdraws $10,000 cash from the business.
(d) Paid $8,000 cash to a creditor on account.
(e) Owner invests $4,000 cash in business.

3. The Cash account for ABC Company had a $5,000.00 balance on July 1. During July, cash sales amounted to $4,000.00, but the bookkeeper mistakenly recorded this amount in the Cash account with a credit rather than with a debit. By how much will the Cash account be misstated as a result of this error?

4. Set up the T accounts as needed and record the following transactions in them.
(a) Received $900 cash for services rendered.
(b) Sold truck costing $8,000 for $8,000 cash.
(c) Sold merchandise costing $200 *on account* for $400.

5. The preliminary trial balance of Mouton Equipment Co. presented below does *not* balance. A review of the records shows that the (a) debits and credits in the cash account total $14,000 and $11,000 respectively. (b) The balance of the equipment account is $2,200. (c) Four hundred dollars of accounts receivable was not posted to the ledger accounts receivable account. (d) Each account should reflect a *normal balance.*

MOUTON COMPANY
Trial Balance
June 30, 19X0

Cash	$ 4,200	
Account Receivable	3,000	
Prepaid Insurance		$ 400
Equipment	2,000	
Land		4,000
Account Payable		6,000
Notes Payable	1,000	
K. Mouton—Capital		6,000
Sales		400
Ad Expense		200
Selling Expense	200	
	$10,400	$17,000

REQUIRED:
Prepare a corrected trial balance.

6. Give journal entries for the following transactions:
(a) Paid $6,000 cash for a new truck.
(b) Paid vendor $2,000 for outstanding accounts payable.
(c) Bought inventory on account for $3,000.
(d) Sold inventory that originally cost $5,000 for $20,000 cash.
(e) Paid $2,000 for current rent.
(f) Cash payment on mortgage was $10,000 consisting of principal $9,000 and interest $1,000.

7. Give journal entries for the following transactions, for a new business, the National Bookbinders Company:
(a) Deposited $50,000 in checking account in the formation of the business.
(b) Borrowed $50,000 from the bank.
(c) Purchased equipment on account for $40,000.
(d) Paid $600 rent for the current month.
(e) Paid $1,200 for wages.
(f) Cash sales for the month amounted to $8,000.
(g) Issued check for $20,000 in part payment of equipment purchased [see item (c)].
(h) Bought merchandise on account for $5,000.
8. Specify the normal balance for the following accounts.
(a) Cash.
(b) Owner's Equity.
(c) Accounts Payable.
(d) Truck.
(e) Insurance Expense.
(f) Prepaid Insurance.
(g) Sales.

(h) Salary Expense.
(i) Income Tax Expense.
(j) Income Tax Payable.
(k) Land.
(l) Notes Payable.

9. Prepare closing entries for the following accounts.

	Debit	Credit
Cash	$ 2,300	
Supplies	300	
Tools	3,500	
Bank Loan Payable		$ 500
Owner's Equity		1,600
Sales		16,000
Wages Expense	8,000	
Materials Expense	1,600	
Rent Expense	2,400	
	$18,100	$18,100

10. Below are transactions for Susan's Beauty Shop for one month.
(a) Sales totaled $1,440 in cash.
(b) Purchased supplies for $200 cash.
(c) Paid wages to employee, $400 in cash.
(d) Purchased new equipment for $600 in cash.
(e) Borrowed $1,000 from bank.
(f) Paid $200 rent.
Prepare general journal entries for these transactions and post these to T accounts.

11. Prepare a trial balance for the following accounts, assuming all accounts have a normal balance. Then prepare a balance sheet and an income statement.

Cash	$ 6,100
Accounts Receivable	850
Supplies	450
Land	18,000
Buildings & Equipment	32,000
Bank Note Payable	5,000
Wages Payable	3,200
Owners' Equity	40,200
Sales	36,000
Wages Expense	20,000
Materials Expense	6,000
License Fee Expense	500
Interest Expense	500

12. From the following financial data, prepare a trial balance, and closing general journal entries:

Cash	$ 630
Accounts Receivable	200
Materials	1,000
Equipment	1,800
Bank Loan Payable	300
Owners' Equity	2,730
Sales	5,000
Wage Expense	2,000
Materials Expense	2,000
Rent Expense	400

13. Construct a balance sheet with T accounts as shown in Exhibit 3-1, with these accounts and normal balances: Cash, $3,000; Accounts Receivable, $2,000; Equipment, $8,000; Accounts Payable, $1,000; Bank Note Payable, $1,000; Owner's Equity, $11,000. Post each of the following transactions in the appropriate accounts and check to see that the balance sheet still balances:
(a) Owner invests $3,000 cash.
(b) Firm purchases supplies on account, $200.
(c) Firm purchases equipment for $500 cash.
(d) Customers pay $600 on account.
(e) Firm pays $500 on bank loan.
(f) Firm pays $700 on accounts payable.
14. Which of the following accounts are *not* closed in making closing entries?
(a) Cash.
(b) Owner's Equity.
(c) Accounts Payable.
(d) Truck.
(e) Insurance Expense.
(f) Prepaid Insurance.
(g) Sales.
(h) Salary Expense.
(i) Income Tax Expense.
(j) Income Tax Payable.
(k) Land.
(l) Notes Payable.

15. Prepare the necessary closing entries in general journal format for the following financial data for Goddard Company. How much is its net income?

	Debit	Credit
Cash	$13,000	
Accounts Receivable	13,000	
Accounts Payable		$ 5,000
Supplies	1,500	
Sales		80,000
Salary Expense	21,000	
Supplies Expense	15,000	
Insurance Expense	1,000	
Rent Expense	12,000	
Notes Payable		12,000
Utilities Expense	2,000	
Owner's Equity		6,500
Equipment	25,000	

Problems

1. The Johns Company repairs air conditioners. Transactions for the month of December 19X9 were:

12/1	Received cash for services—$2,400
12/3	Customers billed for services—$2,800
12/5	Collected on customer account—$2,000
12/7	Bought supplies for cash—$400
12/9	Paid miscellaneous expenses—$200
12/12	Bought supplies on account—$400
12/15	Received cash for services—$8,000
12/18	Bought equipment for cash—$2,000
12/27	Paid wages to employees for December—$500
12/29	Paid miscellaneous expense for December with cash—$400
12/30	Supplies used during month—$400
12/31	Rent for December is paid in cash—$400

REQUIRED:
(a) Prepare general journal entries to record these transactions.
(b) Prepare a general ledger and post the journal entries to the accounts. (Assume that beginning balances are large enough to accommodate the new transactions.)
(c) Prepare a trial balance *in good form.*
(d) Prepare journal entries to close the revenue and expense accounts.

2. The following transactions for the Darling Company, a computer dating service, were incurred in the month on April 19X9.

4/1 Received cash for services—$8,000
4/4 Purchased supplies for $1,000 and equipment for $3,000 on account
4/5 Billed customers $10,000 for services rendered.
4/8 Paid for Advertising—$1,000
4/12 Paid cash to creditors on Account—$2,000
4/14 Returned equipment that was faulty to seller for full credit—$500
4/16 Paid Miscellaneous Expenses—$100
4/18 Bought truck on Account—$3,000
4/22 Received cash for services—$12,000
4/26 Paid cash to creditors on account—$4,000
4/30 Paid Rent for April—$300
4/30 Paid Wages to Employees—$500

REQUIRED:
(a) Determine the account affected and the amounts debited and credited. Enter these amounts into properly labeled T accounts. (Assume beginning balances exist in the accounts in amounts sufficient to accommodate the new transactions.)
(b) Prepare Trial Balance from T accounts as of April 30, 19X9.

3. Wheeler Company has the following trial balance on December 31, 19X4:

Account	Debit	Credit
Cash	$28,000	
Accounts Receivable	18,000	
Supplies	4,000	
Equipment	30,000	
Prepaid Rent	2,000	
Truck	8,000	
Accounts Payable		$ 8,500
Notes Payable		500
Owner's Equity		55,000
Revenue		33,000
Rent Expense	1,000	
Operating Expense	500	
Insurance Expense	2,500	
Administrative Expense	3,000	

REQUIRED:
(a) Indicate which accounts are balance sheet accounts and which accounts are income statements accounts.
(b) Prepare journal entries to close out all appropriate accounts to the Income Summary.
(c) Prepare journal entry to close Income Summary into Owner's Equity.

4. Collins, Inc. was organized January 1 and carried out several transactions prior to opening for business on February 1.

1/1   Ed Collins, owner, invested $90,000 in business.
1/4   Purchased land worth $9,400 for $4,000 cash and issued note payable for balance.
1/14 Purchased office building for $36,000.
1/17 Purchased cash register for $1,600 from Bar and Co. on account.
1/30 Paid $700 of account payable to Bar and Co.

REQUIRED:
    (a) Prepare a general journal and ledger. Record and post the transactions.
    (b) Prepare a trial balance.
    (c) Prepare a balance sheet as of February 1.

5. Jim Rich is in the business of selling football equipment. The following list shows the account balances at June 30, 19X0.

Accounts Payable	$ 7,410	Notes Receivable	$ 1,200
Accounts Receivable	2,850	Office Building	33,000
Trucks	6,800	Office Supplies	400
Owner's Equity	50,000	Net Profit for Month	6,270
Cash	?	Bonds Payable	10,000
Equipment	58,950		
Furniture & Fixtures	5,400		
Warehouse	4,970		
Land	16,740		
Notes Payable	79,800		

REQUIRED:
    (a) Prepare a trial balance. (Compute balance for cash.)
    (b) Prepare a balance sheet as of June 30, 19X0.

6. Arens Company has the following transactions for the month of July that affect cash:
    (a) Paid rent, $600 (July 3).
    (b) Purchased supplies for cash, $350 (July 5).
    (c) Received $1,250 from customers on account (July 8).
    (d) Received $5,700 from customers for cash sales (July 16).
    (e) Paid wages, $3,000 (July 23).
    (f) Paid utilities, $170 (July 29).

REQUIRED:
    (a) Prepare general journal entries to record these transactions.
    (b) Prepare a four-column general ledger account for Cash, and post these transactions to the Cash account. Assume a beginning cash balance of $3,200.

7. Wayne Plumbing Company has the following account balances as of December 31, 19X5:

Cash	$ 1,210
Accounts Receivable	2,200
Supplies	1,800
Tools	2,240
Furniture and Fixtures	1,300
Note Payable	500
Owner's Equity	3,000
Sales	14,500
Rental Expense	3,400
Salary Expense	3,600
Supplies Used	2,000
Interest Expense	250

REQUIRED:

(a) Prepare a trial balance for these accounts.

(b) Prepare closing entries in general journal format.

(c) Prepare a balance sheet and income statement.

8. Harper Shoe Service had the following transactions for May 19X7:

(a) Purchased supplies on account, $1,000.

(b) Paid May rent, $400.

(c) Paid utilities, $60.

(d) Received $4,000 cash for services performed.

(e) Billed customers $200 for services performed.

(f) Paid wages, $1,200.

(g) Purchased equipment on account, $3,000.

(h) Paid $1,000 note.

(i) Paid $50 interest on note in (h) above.

(j) Used $1,000 in supplies.

Harper had the following trial balance *after* closing entries on April 30, 19X7:

Cash	$3,000	
Accounts Receivable	100	
Equipment	3,000	
Supplies	1,500	
Accounts Payable		$ 100
Notes Payable		1,000
Owner's Equity		6,500

REQUIRED:

(a) Record the transactions for May in general journal format.

(b) Post the journal entries to four-column general ledger accounts.

(c) Prepare a trial balance for May 31, 19X7.

(d) Prepare closing entries as of May 31, 19X7.

(e) Prepare a balance sheet and income statement for the period ended May 31, 19X7.

□ 4
FINANCIAL STATEMENT RELATIONSHIPS AND ADJUSTMENTS

☐ OBJECTIVES

AFTER STUDYING THIS CHAPTER, YOU SHOULD BE ABLE TO DO THE FOLLOWING:

1. EXPLAIN THE RELATIONSHIP BETWEEN COSTS AND ASSETS, EXPENSES AND LOSSES.

2. DESCRIBE THE INTERRELATIONSHIPS BETWEEN ACCOUNTS ON THE BALANCE SHEET AND THOSE ON THE INCOME STATEMENT.

3. RELATE ACCRUAL/DEFERRAL INFORMATION TO SPECIFIC ACCOUNTS.

4. PREPARE ADJUSTING ENTRIES. IDENTIFY EFFECTS OF ADJUSTMENTS ON FINANCIAL STATEMENTS.

5. CONSTRUCT AND COMPLETE AN ADJUSTMENT WORKSHEET.

6. PREPARE ADJUSTING AND CLOSING JOURNAL ENTRIES.

7. PREPARE FINANCIAL STATEMENTS.

Well over 100,000 publicly owned companies publish and distribute annual financial reports. Most of these firms also distribute interim and special reports throughout the year. These reports are supplemented by other financial information filed by these companies with the Securities and Exchange Commission and the major stock exchanges. Millions of partnerships and proprietorships also prepare financial reports for use by owners, creditors, and other interested parties. Financial statements and accounting reports are the most widely distributed, regularly published source of financial information in the United States, aside from newspapers and news magazines.

Anyone attempting to use published financial information effectively must have a thorough knowledge of the accounting process. This chapter will describe the adjusting process and its effects on the financial statements.

Costs—Assets, Expenses, and Losses

The term "cost" is used by accountants to imply several different meanings. Most often, the word cost is used to refer to the valuation of goods or services acquired by the accounting entity. When cost is used in this sense, the good or service being acquired will be classified as an asset or an expense. Some writers, however, use the term "cost" as a synonym for the object being valued. In this sense, an asset is an *unexpired cost.* Both expenses and losses are called *expired costs.* If the firm has experienced a benefit from a good or service that has expired, the expired cost is classified as an expense: if no benefit is derived from an expired cost, the classification as a loss is appropriate.

Exhibit 4-1 illustrates the relationships between costs and assets, expenses and losses. The acquisition value of all goods and services received by an entity are recognized as costs. When these costs are journalized, a choice must be made to classify the productive input as either an asset or an expense. Ordinarily, acquired *goods* are classified as assets, and acquired *services* are classified as expenses. Services usually yield an immediate benefit. Thus, they would flow from an asset classification to an expense classification with such speed that recording them as expense is justified. Similarly, goods that flow quickly through an organization, such as fuel for a delivery truck, may be classified immediately as an expense. These primary relationships are denoted by arrows 1 and 2, respectively. At some date after the acquisition of a good has been recognized, additional journal entries may reclassify assets as expenses or losses whenever the asset loses its future service potential to the firm. These subsequent reclassifications are illustrated as arrows 3 and 4 in Exhibit 4-1.

Chapter 3 contains several examples of primary cost classifications. For example, the acquisition of merchandise inventory by a firm was classified as an asset, and the acquisition of labor services from salesmen was clas-

EXHIBIT 4-1

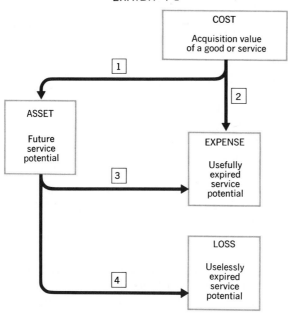

sified as an expense. Arrow 3, reclassification of an asset as an expense, describes the actions taken by the accountant when goods out of inventory are delivered to customers. The relationship shown as arrow 4 is discussed in a later chapter.

Another example of a reclassification, arrow 3, follows.

If a building was rented on June 1 for $500 a month, the prepaid rent would be considered an asset on June 1. Future service potential in the form of the right to use the building for the next month has been acquired. The journal entry to record this transaction would be:

    June 1   Prepaid Rent (Asset) $500
                    Cash (Asset) $500
              To recognize acquisition of property use right for June

At the end of 30 days, the right to use the building for June has expired. It is appropriate, therefore, to reclassify the cost (Prepaid Rent) from an asset to the corresponding expense (Rent Expense). The following journal entry will accomplish this:

        June 30   Rent Expense (Expense) $500
                        Prepaid Rent (Asset) $500
                   To recognize the expiration of a property right

**Revenues—
Unearned Income**

A revenue transaction involves an exchange between the firm and its customers. The firm receives cash or promises for future cash payments (accounts receivable), and it delivers goods and/or services to the customer. The accounting for revenue transactions usually occurs whenever the accountant receives one of two types of source documents. The receipt of cash, a check, or a note of the customer can initiate the accounting for a revenue transaction. Also, the recording of a revenue transaction may be triggered by the receipt of an invoice signed by the customer. This signed invoice indicates that the customer has received the goods and/or services delivered by the firm.

Three types of revenue transactions are commonly encountered in business. First, the cash receipt may occur simultaneous to the delivery of goods or services. This case presents no new accounting problem. Second, the cash receipt may occur after the delivery of the goods and services. For this type of transaction, the generally accepted accounting principle usually calls for the recognition of revenue at the point of delivering goods and services. The accountant recognizes an account receivable from the customer at the point of sale; a subsequent transaction recognizes the exchange of cash from the customer for the account receivable. Since this subsequent transaction involves an exchange of one asset for another asset, revenue is not affected. A third type of revenue transaction involves the receipt of cash by the firm and a delayed delivery of goods or services. That is, the accounting entity merely promises future delivery of goods or services. The accounting term for the promise of future delivery is *unearned income.* Unearned income is a liability that will be satisfied by future delivery of goods or services. A subsequent transaction is necessary to reclassify unearned income to revenue whenever goods and services are ultimately delivered.

**Financial
Statement
Interrelationships**

Revenue transactions ordinarily affect both revenue and asset accounts. Expense transactions ordinarily affect expense and asset (or liability) accounts. Thus, "income activity" is inherently related to financial position. Transactions that affect an income statement also affect the balance sheet. Exhibit 4-2 illustrates the relationships between accounts on both the income statement and the balance sheet.

Assets, Expenses, and Equities. Revenues affect both financial statements. Revenues increase reported net income, which, in turn, increase owner's equity on the balance sheet. Also, the corresponding inflows associated with recognizing revenue, cash or receivables, lead to an increase in assets reported on the balance sheet. As assets are used, they are reclassified as expenses. This process reduces the assets reported on the balance sheet and increases the expenses included in the income statement.

EXHIBIT 4-2

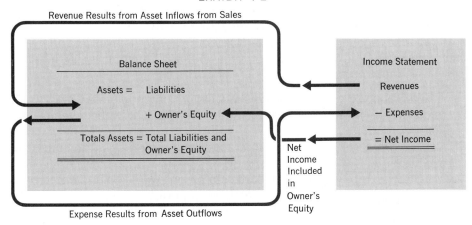

Revenue Results from Asset Inflows from Sales

Balance Sheet

Assets = Liabilities

+ Owner's Equity

Totals Assets = Total Liabilities and Owner's Equity

Income Statement

Revenues

− Expenses

= Net Income

Net Income Included in Owner's Equity

Expense Results from Asset Outflows

The increase in expenses will reduce net income, and consequently, will lead to a reduction in owner's equity. These interrelationships are consistent with the equality of the accounting equation.

(1)	Assets	=	Liabilities + Owners' Equity

(2)	Assets + Cash or Receivables − Inventory or Other Assets	=	Liabilities + Owners' Equity + Revenue − Expense

The Effects of Errors. A single error in recording a transaction can produce multiple effects, given the relationships that exist between the financial statements. For example, if an asset valued at $1,200 were consumed during the course of a business year but was not listed as an expense, the following errors in the financial statements would result:

1. *Assets,* reported on the balance sheet, are overstated by $1,200, because the consumed resource is still (improperly) shown as an asset.
2. *Expenses,* reported on the income statement, are understated by $1,200, because the consumed resource was (improperly) not expensed.
3. *Net income,* reported on the income statement is overstated by $1,200, because a legitimate expense was not deducted from revenue.
4. *Owner's equity,* reported on the balance sheet, is overstated by $1,200, because net income, overstated by $1,200, was added to the beginning owner's equity balance.

In spite of these errors, the balance sheet will still balance, because both assets and owner's equity are overstated by $1,200.

Other errors can also have serious multiple effects on the financial statements. By tracing the facts through an analysis such as shown in Exhibit 4-2, the full impact of these errors may be isolated.

If revenue, relating to a particular $2,000 sale, was not recognized in the accounts of an entity, a series of errors would again be introduced into the financial statements:

1. *Assets,* reported on the balance sheet, would be understated by $2,000, because the corresponding asset inflow associated with the revenue was not recorded.
2. *Revenue,* reported on the income statement, would be understated by $2,000.
3. *Net income,* reported on the income statement, would be understated by $2,000, because less revenue has been reported.
4. *Owner's equity,* reported on the balance sheet, would be understated by $2,000, because net income, understated by $2,000, was added to the beginning owner's equity balance.

The accounting system must be designed, implemented, and controlled to ensure that errors are not committed. Some errors can be minimized if the source documents that initiate accounting activity are automatically generated by transactions. However, errors will still occur if the accounts are not updated periodically to reflect all changes which have taken place, even if source documents are automatically generated.

Desired Statement Information

When information is reported in the balance sheet or income statement, certain assumptions generally are made about the reported data. Some of these include the following:

☐ Assets: The asset accounts should contain the historical cost valuations of those resources that have a future service potential to the entity.
☐ Liabilities: The value and description of creditor claims against the entity should be disclosed. This includes all debts owed by the entity as of the balance sheet date.
☐ Owner's Equity: The value of the owner's claim against the entity should be shown, including the effect of income or loss for the period ended on the balance sheet date.
☐ Revenue: The income statement should include all revenues that were earned during the current period, whether or not payment has been received.
☐ Expense: The historical cost of all resources consumed during the current period should be related to current revenue and included as expenses on the income statement, whether or not paid.

At times, this diverse information has not been recorded, because documents supporting formal transactions have not been received. At other times, accounts that should have been reclassified have not been. In these cases, *adjusting entries* can make the accounts conform with reporting expectations.

Four common combinations of accounts are generally affected by adjusting entries. These include:

1. Expenses and Assets.
2. Expenses and Liabilities.
3. Revenues and Assets.
4. Revenues and Liabilities.

Three general steps are necessary to complete the adjusting process at the end of an accounting period:

1. Decide what *should be* the proper balance of an account.
2. Identify what is the *actual* balance of the account.
3. Make a journal entry to bring the *actual balance* to the *proper balance.*

The most common expense and asset adjustments relate to prepayments for future services and utilization of resources that are owned. Failure to adjust the accounts for expiration of prepayments lead to misstatements of expenses and assets and multiple statement errors as discussed in the previous section.

Expense and Asset Adjustments

Prepayments. When advance payments are made, the common entry is to increase an asset account (debit) and to decrease the cash account (credit). At the end of the accounting period, that portion of the asset which has been consumed should be removed from the asset account and reclassified in the appropriate expense account.

Rent is often paid in advance, and no source document is received to indicate the expiration associated with use over time. Assume that the Ample Company rented a warehouse on June 1, 19X8, for $18,000 a year and paid the first year's rent in advance. The following journal entry would be made on June 1 to record this transaction:

> Prepaid Rent $18,000
>   Cash $18,000
> To recognize prepayment of one year's rent

The asset, Prepaid Rent, was debited to record the inflow to the company. Ample Company received the right to use the warehouse for the next 12 months—a resource having future service potential.

By the end of December 19X8, seven-twelfths of the resource, Prepaid Rent, has been consumed by virtue of occupying the warehouse for seven months. Although no transaction has occurred, an adjusting reclassification is necessary. Since the $18,000 annual rental is equivalent to $1,500 per month ($18,000 ÷ 12), the five remaining months (after December 31) have an asset value of $7,500 ($1,500 × 5). Accordingly, the $10,500 difference between $7,500 and the $18,000 original balance of the account represents the amount of the rent expense (that portion of the asset that was consumed). The adjusting entry that reflects this information is:

Rent Expense $10,500
     Prepaid Rent $10,500
To reclassify expired Prepaid Rent

Recognize that the balance of the Prepaid Rent account is $7,500 after the adjusting entry has been posted. The Rent Expense account has a balance of $10,500.

Insurance premiums are ordinarily paid in advance and represent another example of an asset (prepaid expense). *Prepaid expenses* are future expense items that have been acquired, paid for, and recorded prior to their use. Assume that Ample Company had purchased a three-year insurance policy for $3,600 on August 15, 19X6. The appropriate journal entry to record this transaction on August 15 would be as follows:

Prepaid Insurance $3,600
     Cash $3,600
To recognize the acquisition of a three-year insurance policy

The debit to the asset account, Prepaid Insurance, reflects the receipt of a resource—insurance protection for a three-year period.

If financial statements were prepared on December 31, the Prepaid Insurance account is overstated, because part of the coverage period has expired; therefore, an adjusting entry is necessary. The adjustment should reduce the asset account balance to the $31\frac{1}{2}$ months remaining on the policy ($36-4\frac{1}{2}$) and also recognize insurance expense for $4\frac{1}{2}$ months. The following adjusting entry would be appropriate:

Insurance Expense $450
     Prepaid Insurance $450
To reclassify expired prepaid insurance

The amount of the adjustment was calculated by multiplying the monthly cost of insurance coverage—$100 ($3,600 ÷ 36)—by the $4\frac{1}{2}$ months that elapsed between August 15 and December 31. The Rent Expense account is adjusted to $450 and the balance in Prepaid Insurance is reduced to $3,150 as a result of the adjusting entry.

Utilization. Many assets used by a business in its operations, such as plant and equipment, lose value with the passage of time or with an amount of usage. A factory building may have a service life of 40 to 50 years, after which it must be replaced. As time passes, the building loses its future service potential, and the financial statements should reflect this change in asset and expense accounts. Similarly, equipment may have a service life related to the number of units produced. A delivery truck, for example, may be able to accumulate 180,000 miles before it must be replaced. As more miles are actually driven, future service potential is lost, and an adjustment should be made to the asset and expense accounts.

The process to adjust the accounts for asset usage is termed *depreciation.* Depreciation expense is the amount of an asset's cost that is deemed to have expired during the course of an accounting period. Instead of directly reducing a related asset account when recording depreciation expense, accounting practice supports the preservation of historical cost information through the use of a contra account commonly titled, *Accumulated Depreciation.* This **contra account** is directly related to the particular portion of the asset that is being reclassified as an expense, and it is used to reflect the cumulative amount of reductions in the asset. Contra accounts may be used to reduce the balance of asset, liability, or equity accounts. They permit the preservation of the initial balance in their related account. The asset and the contra asset accounts are always disclosed together in the financial statements, and the net difference between the two is reported as the net book value of the asset. Two accounts are used to reflect two different types of information: the historical cost reflected in the asset account is supported by *facts* (original acquisition price), but the balance reflected in the accumulated depreciation account is only an estimate.

The balance sheet disclosure of a particular depreciated asset, using equipment as an example, is shown below:

Balance Sheet Segment	12/31/19X6	12/31/19X7
Assets		
Equipment (original acquisition cost)	$100,000	$100,000
Less Accumulated Depreciation (sum of annual depreciation charges)	1,800	3,600
Net Book Value of Equipment	$ 98,200	$ 96,400

The historical cost of the asset, equipment, will not change over the life of the equipment. The annual charge to Depreciation Expense is accompanied by a credit to the contra account, Accumulated Depreciation, rather than directly reducing the asset account. While Depreciation Expense will be cleared annually in the closing process, Accumulated Depreciation (being an asset classification) will not be closed: its balance increases over the life of the asset. This cumulative balance is deducted from the historical cost to produce the **net book value** or carrying value of the asset.

To illustrate this process, assume that a company purchased a new building on January 1, 19X6, for $100,000. The building is expected to have a useful life of 50 years, at which time it is expected to have a *residual value* of $10,000; that is, after 50 years, the building may be salvaged or sold for $10,000.

On January 1, 19X6, the acquisition of the building would be recorded with the following entry:

```
Buildings    $100,000
    Cash                     $100,000
To record acquisition of building
```

Recognize that acquisitions are recorded at the historical cost regardless of expectations about residual values.

On December 31, 19X6, the amount of depreciation expense for this building must be determined, and an adjustment must be made. One method of calculating depreciation is called the *straight-line method,* which generates an even flow of expense over the life of the asset. Straight-line depreciation is computed as follows:

$$\text{Annual depreciation} = \frac{\text{Cost} - \text{Residual value}}{\text{Useful Life in years}}$$

In terms of the example, the amount of depreciation expense would be:

$$\text{Annual depreciation} = \frac{\$100,000 - \$10,000}{50}$$
$$= \$1,800 \; per \; year$$

Thus, the proper adjusting entry for 19X6 would be as follows:

```
Depreciation Expense                          $1,800
    Accumulated Depreciation—Buildings                $1,800
To record depreciation for one year
```

The balance sheet would contain the following information in the Asset section:

```
Assets
    Buildings                                     $100,000
    Less Accumulated Depreciation—Buildings          1,800   $98,200
```

If this method is followed consistently, net book value will equal the residual value of the asset at the end of 50 years. The balance sheet will appear as follows at that time:

```
Assets
    Buildings                                     $100,000
    Less Accumulated Depreciation—Buildings         90,000   $10,000
```

Adjustments for depreciation are essential if the income statement is expected to match against revenues the costs of all inputs that helped generate the revenue. The depreciation calculations rely on estimations of residual value and useful life; thus, depreciation expense is an estimate. However, an informed estimate of expired cost is better than completely ignoring the expiration of future service potential. Other acceptable methods of calculating depreciation will be discussed in a later chapter.

Most expense and liability adjustments relate to transactions where goods or services are acquired by the entity *before* receipt of the documents that normally initiate the recording process. Two examples are utilities and salaries. If adjusting entries are not made at the end of an accounting period, the related expense accounts will be understated.

Expense and Liability Adjustments

Utilities Expense. If utility payments for power or water are made when bills are received, the normal accounting treatment is to record the transaction at that time. Therefore, if a $10,000 electricity bill is received and paid on the 10th of the month, the entry to recognize an expense is:

```
Utility Expense        $12,000
    Cash                            $12,000
To record payment of utility bill
```

However, if the accounting period extended to the end of the month, the account balances at the month end would not be correct, since utility expense for the period from the 10th through the 30th would not have been recorded.

An adjusting entry can correct the accounts for the proper amount of expense. Accordingly, the adjusting entry at the end of the month would estimate expense for two-thirds of the month:

```
Utility Expense                 $8,000
    Accrued Utility Payable              $8,000
To accrue unbilled utility liability
```

The term "accrued" indicates that a transaction occurred and has been recognized, but that it has not been billed or paid. The next utility payment made on the 10th of the following month will recognize expense for the first 10 days of that period, and will also satisfy the accrued liability for the last 20 days of last month.

```
Utility Expense              $4,000
Accrued Utility Payable       8,000
    Cash                                 $12,000
To record payment for first utility bill of the new period
```

Thus, the adjusting process insures that utility expenses charged to both accounting periods are correct.

Salary Expense. In most businesses, employee salaries are paid on a regular basis—weekly, bimonthly, or monthly. The normal entry to record the payment of salaries is to debit salary expense and to credit the asset Cash; thus, the costs of securing employee services are recognized. However, when an accounting period ends before a regular payday, an adjusting entry is needed to recognize the full salary expense attributable to the period.

Assume that a company has a regular weekly payroll of $12,000, which is normally paid on Fridays, and that the last day in an accounting period is Wednesday. Two days will elapse after the period before salaries will be paid; however, salary expense for the first part of the week should be recognized as attributable to the period just ended. The following adjusting entry records salary expense incurred for the first three days in the week, which are attributable to the period just ended:

Salary Expense	$7,200	
Accrued Salaries Payable		$7,200
To record unpaid salary liability		

Accrued Salaries Payable indicates a liability arising from the acquisition of labor services which have not been paid. When salaries are actually paid on Friday, the entry will recognize that this liability has been satisfied:

Salary Expense	$4,800	
Accrued Salaries Payable	7,200	
Cash		$12,000
To record payment for the first payroll of the new period		

Revenue and Asset Adjustments

Adjustments to revenue and asset accounts are required when some revenue items are earned, even though no source document is received by the end of the accounting period. These revenues are generally collected on a regular basis, and the collection date falls in the next accounting period. Income determination requires that the full amount of revenue earned in the current period must be recognized.

Interest Revenue. Interest revenue increases gradually with the passage of time and therefore must be adjusted if the collection date does not coincide with the last day of the accounting period. Throughout the period, revenue would be recognized whenever an interest payment is collected. For example, consider the collection of a semi annual interest payment on a $100,000, 8 percent loan: receipt of the $4,000 interest would be recorded as follows:

Cash	$4,000	
Interest Revenue		$4,000
Collection of semiannual interest ($100,000 $\times$ .08 $\times$ $\frac{1}{2}$)		

If the fiscal year ended on September 30, but the semiannual interest was due on June 30 and December 31, the interest revenue account will not reflect the actual amount of interest revenue earned by the end of the fiscal year. An adjusting entry can correct revenue to the amount earned for the period. The entry must record three months of interest revenue and a corresponding accrued receivable reflecting that the revenue has been realized (earned) but not collected.

Accrued Interest Receivable	$2,000	
Interest Revenue		$2,000
To accrue three months of interest		

Part of the interest collected on December 31 pertains to the receivable and the remainder is treated as revenue.

Cash	$4,000	
Accrued Interest Receivable		$2,000
Interest Revenue		2,000
Collection of semiannual interest		

Thus, the adjusting entry divided an interest payment into two parts, half as revenue in the new accounting period and half as revenue in the old period.

Whenever payment is received in advance for a product or a service to be supplied over time, revenue and liability accounts should be adjusted at the end of the accounting period. Generally, revenue is recognized in the accounting records when bills are distributed or cash is received. If an accounting period ends before all of the revenue has been earned, an adjustment must be made.

Revenue and Liability Adjustments

For example, on September 1, the New Say Magazine Company received 1,000 annual subscriptions at $12 each for their monthly news journal. The entry to record this collection is as follows:

Cash	$12,000	
Subscription Revenue		$12,000
To record receipts for new subscriptions		

The Company has fulfilled one-third of its publication commitment by December 31. Consequently, revenue is overstated by $8,000 ($\frac{2}{3} \times$ $12,000). An adjusting entry will reduce revenue and establish a liability for future commitments; the company must deliver magazines to its subscribers for the following eight months. The proper adjusting entry would be:

Subscription Revenue	$8,000	
Deferred Subscription Revenue		$8,000
To adjust the revenue account		

The account, Deferred Subscription Revenue, is a liability account. Unlike other liabilities, deferred subscription revenue will be satisfied by providing goods or services, rather than by cash payments. *Deferral* implies the postponement of income recognition. In the example, $8,000 of revenue is deferred until the next accounting period. Deferred revenue or deferred expense accounts are reflected on the current balance sheet but eventually will be recognized in future income statements.

Adjustments in Perspective

Adjustments can be classified as *accruals* or *deferrals.* Accruals build up gradually from continuous activity associated with the passage of time. They are unrecorded prior to adjustment, because no source document has been received to initiate the accounting process. Both revenues and expenses can be accrued. Recognition of accrued revenues results in the creation of a receivable (asset). Recognition of an accrued expense results in the creation of a liability.

Many business transactions relate to continuous activities. Rent is associated with an ongoing right to use property owned by another entity; interest relates to the right to use a sum of money for a period of time. Other activities requiring accruals are associated with the accounts Utilities, Income Taxes, and Labor. In these cases, expenses and revenues build up as a function of time or usage, even though bills are received or payments occur later. Transactions ordinarily are recorded when a source document initiates the accounting process; however, continuous activity frequently occurs well before the receipt of a source document. If an accounting period ends before the source document for a continuous activity is received, an adjusting entry must be made to correctly state the account balances. Adjusting entries insure that income statements reflect earned revenue and expired costs and that unearned revenue or unexpired costs are reflected on the balance sheet.

Deferred costs or revenues are associated with prepayments. Deferred costs are assets that are unexpired at the end of the period; deferred revenues are precollected but unearned. Deferred cost adjustments reclassify expenses to assets. Deferred revenue adjustments reclassify revenues to liabilities.

Alternative adjustments.   The objective of the adjusting process is to bring selected accounts to their proper balances at a particular point in time. Adjustments require a basic review of underlying facts to determine appropriate account balances. The specific adjustment needed in a particular case is dependent on the original journal entry.

Exhibit 4-3 illustrates how one transaction can be recorded in two ways. A prepayment was initially recorded as an asset or, alternatively, as an expense. Either treatment may be acceptable. At the end of the period, how-

EXHIBIT 4-3
ADJUSTMENTS AND RECORDING ALTERNATIVES

January 1, 19X7: A premium of $3,600 is paid on a three year insurance policy.

Record as an Asset		*Record as an Expense*	
Prepaid Insurance $3,600		Insurance Expense $3,600	
Cash $3,600		Cash $3,600	

| Prepaid | Insurance | Prepaid | Insurance |
Insurance	Expense	Insurance	Expense
$3,600			$3,600

December 31, 19X7: Adjustment at the end of the year is necessary

Insurance Expense $1,200		Prepaid Insurance $2,400	
Prepaid Insurance $1,200		Insurance Expense $2,400	

| Prepaid | Insurance | Prepaid | Insurance |
Insurance	Expense	Insurance	Expense
$3,600 1,200	$1,200	$2,400	$3,600 1,200
2,400			$2,400

After adjustment

Results are the same

ever, both the asset and expense accounts must be properly stated. The adjusting entry made in each case will differ, but both sets of adjustments produce identical ending balances in each pair of accounts: the two Prepaid Insurance accounts contain $2,400, while the two Insurance Expense accounts contain $1,200.

Processing Adjustment Data

The accounting system includes various procedures to assist the accountant in manipulating data. These procedures also provide for efficient processing of information. The worksheet helps accountants organize data for the adjusting process. The worksheet is an intermediate processing device employed to develop meaningful information for other accounting uses. Worksheets are prepared solely for use within the accounting function and are rarely shown to report users.

The Worksheet

The *worksheet* is a document prepared by and for accountants as a part of the process of preparing adjusting entries and formulating financial statements. Deferral and accrual entries are first prepared on a worksheet before they are officially recognized by the journalizing and posting process. In effect, the worksheet becomes the source document that authorizes the recognition of deferral and accrual entries.

A tabular format is used to construct the worksheet. Account titles and preadjustment balances are obtained from the ledger. Adjusting entries are formulated from this and other supporting data and entered in the appropriate debit/credit columns. Combining the original account balances with the adjusting amounts will produce an adjusted trial balance. This trial balance provides the data used to develop the balance sheet and income statement, which are also presented in a columnar fashion. Note that the choice of information to be recorded in the worksheet requires accounting expertise and judgments.

An Example. The fiscal year for High Way Air Freight Company ends on December 31. At the end of 19X8, the accountant prepared the worksheet illustrated in Exhibit 4-4. The unadjusted account balances on the worksheet came from the general ledger. The following pertinent information was also available:

1. On September 1, one year's rent of $12,000 was paid in advance for the use of a terminal building.
2. Equipment, which cost $100,000, is to be depreciated on a straight-line basis at the rate of $10,000 per year.
3. Wages and salaries of $2,000 per week are normally paid on Fridays. December 31 is a Tuesday.

EXHIBIT 4-4
HIGH WAY AIR FREIGHT COMPANY
Worksheet
For the Year Ended December 31, 19X8

Account Titles	Trial Balance		Adjustments		Adjusted Trial Balance		Income Statement		Balance Sheet	
	Debit	Credit	Debit	Credit	Debit	Credit	Debit	Credit	Debit	Credit
Cash	$ 35,300				$ 35,300				$ 35,300	
Accounts Receivable	22,400				22,400				22,400	
Prepaid Rent	12,000			(a)$ 4,000	8,000				8,000	
Notes Receivable	12,500				12,500				12,500	
Equipment	100,000				100,000				100,000	
Accumulated Depreciation		$ 30,000		(b) 10,000		$ 40,000				$ 40,000
Accounts Payable		6,600				6,600				6,600
Deferred Service Revenue		1,000	(e)$ 400			600				600
Capital Stock*		80,000				80,000				80,000
Retained Earnings*		45,400				45,400				45,400
Service Revenue		140,700		(e) 400		141,100		$141,100		
Interest Revenue		500		(d) 250		750		750		
Salary Expense	102,000		(c) 800		102,800		$102,800			
Insurance Expense	5,700				5,700		5,700			
Maintenance Expense	11,500				11,500		11,500			
Miscellaneous Expense	2,800				2,800		2,800			
	$304,200	$304,200								
Rent Expense			(a) 4,000		4,000		4,000			
Depreciation Expense			(b) 10,000		10,000		10,000			
Accrued Salaries Payable				(c) 800		800				800
Accrued Interest Receivable			(d) 250		250				250	
			$15,450	$15,450	$315,250	$315,250	$136,800	$141,850	$178,450	$173,400
Net Income							5,050			5,050
							$141,850	$141,850	$178,450	$178,450

*These accounts represent owners' equity in a corporation. They are explained in more detail in the Supplementary Discussion of Chapter 3.

4. The Company had loaned some of its surplus cash to an officer of the firm in exchange for an interest-bearing note. The note provides for interest payments of $500 to be made to the firm twice a year, on March 31 and September 30.
5. One customer paid $1,000 in advance for 10 shipments. At the end of the year, 4 of these shipments had been made.
6. All other expenses were paid as incurred, and all other revenues were collected as realized.

Completing the Worksheet

Completing a worksheet is somewhat mechanical, although accounting judgment is needed to interpret the data. The worksheet is arranged with titles of specific accounts listed vertically in the first column. Columns are provided to record specific monetary amounts for the trial balance, adjusting entries, an adjusted trial balance, the income statement, and the balance sheet.

Trial Balance. Throughout the year, information concerning specific transactions was recorded in the journal and posted to the ledger. At the end of the year, the ledger accounts were *footed,* or summed, and the balances were developed into a trial balance. This trial balance is reproduced in the first two columns of the worksheet. The equality of the debits and the credits ($304,200 and $304,200) tends to support the integrity of the accounting system. The trial balance provides the basis for initiating adjustments.

Adjustments. Using the trial balance information and supplemental data, the accountant formulates specific accrual and deferral adjustments that should be made to the accounts. "Journal entries" reflecting these adjustments are recorded in the two adjustment columns. The debit and credit parts of each adjusting entry are coded together [(a) through (e)] for future reference. If additional accounts are needed in the adjusting process, they are added to the list of account titles. The High Way Air Freight Company required five adjusting entries:

Entry a—Prepaid Rent: The unadjusted trial balance reported prepaid rent as an asset. However, three months have elapsed since the rental payment was made. Therefore, one-third of the prepaid rent should be reclassified as rent expense to indicate that it has been consumed. This may be accomplished by debiting Rent Expense and crediting Prepaid Rent.

Entry b—Depreciation: The annual charge for depreciation is reflected in the adjusting entry which increases Depreciation Expense (debit) and increases the account Accumulated Depreciation (credit). Since the account Depreciation Expense was not included in the trial balance, it was added to the account title column.

Entry c—Accrued Salaries: The end of the accounting period fell between company paydays. Consequently, it is necessary to recognize an expense and a corresponding liability for that amount of salary which has been earned, but not yet paid. The adjustment to salary expense is $800, representing two-fifths (two days out of five days) of the $2,000 weekly payroll. The adjusting entry includes a debit to Salary Expense and a credit to Accrued Salaries Payable.

Entry d—Accrued Revenue: The Company received an interest-bearing note on March 31 of this year. To date, $500 of interest revenue has been recognized, because an interest payment was received on September 30. However, at the year-end, $250 of interest has been earned but not received. To properly include this information in the financial statements, it is necessary to establish an accrued asset, Accrued Interest Receivable (debit) and to increase the Interest Revenue account (credit).

Entry e—Deferred Revenue: Sometime during the year, the Company received an advanced payment from a customer for services to be provided in the future. At that time, the advanced payment was recorded as an unearned, or deferred revenue, and treated as a liability. At the year end, 40 percent of the service has been provided (4 shipments were made out of the 10 that were contracted). Therefore, a corresponding percentage of the revenue (40 percent) should be recognized as earned. This may be accomplished by an adjusting entry which decreases the Deferred Service Revenue account (debit) and increases the Service Revenue account (credit).

After all the adjusting entries have been completed, the two adjustment columns (debit and credit) are summed and checked for equality. While not conclusive, this provides some assurance that all parts of the adjustments were recorded.

Adjusted Trial Balance. The adjusted trial balance is an optional part of the worksheet—it may be omitted without limiting the usefulness of the worksheet. The account balances in these columns represent the extension across or horizontal summation of the trial balance and adjustments columns. Note that the summation of debits and credits to the same account requires a subtraction [e.g., Prepaid Rent (a)]. The summation of two debits or two credits is accomplished by addition [e.g., Salary Expense (c) and Accumulated Depreciation (b)].

For example, the account Cash had a debit balance of $35,300 and was not affected by the adjusting entries. Therefore, a debit balance of $35,300 was extended over to the adjusted trial balance. Prepaid Rent had a trial balance total of $12,000. However, a credit adjustment of $4,000 was made to this account. The combined effect ($12,000 debit and $4,000 credit) results in a debit balance of $8,000, which was extended over to the adjusted trial balance.

The adjusted trial balance provides a summary of account balances prior to the preparation of financial statements. Therefore, all of the accounts listed on the adjusted trial balance will either be reported on the balance sheet or on the income statement.

Income Statement. The income statement provides disclosure for all of the revenue and expense accounts. The revenue and expense account balances reported in the adjusted trial balance are carried over to the income statement columns. Since the adjusted trial balance represents a summation of all previous activity concerning these accounts, the account balances in the income statement columns reflect all available information.

After the revenue and expense balances have been placed in the income statement columns, the columns are footed. If the credit column (revenue) exceeds the debit column (expense), net income has resulted. Conversely, if the debit column exceeds the credit column, a loss has resulted. The amount of the income (or loss) is inserted to offset the difference between the two columns (i.e., to bring both columns into balance). The debit of $5,050 equates both columns at $141,850.

Balance Sheet. The asset, liability and equity accounts are all reported on the balance sheet. As with the income statement, account balances from the adjusted trial balance are extended to the balance sheet columns. No revenues or expenses that appeared in the income statement should also appear in the balance sheet.

After the account balances have been carried over, the debit and credit columns are footed. A difference between the columns equals the amount of the net income or loss should result. For the example, net income of $5,050 exactly balances the remaining two columns. This income will eventually be added to the equity account Retained Earnings. In the context of the worksheet, obtaining a final balance provides some assurance of consistency between the income statement and the balance sheet.

Using the Worksheet

The worksheet provides the accountant with a focal point for analyzing adjusting entries and tracing their effects through to the financial statements. After the worksheet has been prepared, it is used as a guide for the clerical or bookkeeping tasks that remain.

The adjusting entries formulated on the worksheet must be reflected in the actual accounts. Consequently, these entries would be recorded in the journal and then posted to the ledger. The journal entries made for the High Way Air Freight Company are illustrated in Exhibit 4-5.

EXHIBIT 4-5
ADJUSTING ENTRIES: HIGH WAY AIR FREIGHT COMPANY

Date	Accounts	Debit	Credit
12/31	Rent Expense	$ 4,000	
	Prepaid Rent		$ 4,000
12/31	Depreciation Expense	10,000	
	Accumulated Depreciation		10,000
12/31	Salary Expense	800	
	Accrued Salaries Payable		800
12/31	Accrued Interest Receivable	250	
	Interest Revenue		250
12/31	Deferred Service Revenue	400	
	Service Revenue		400

The worksheet also contains information needed to construct the balance sheet and the income statement. The worksheet information should parallel the information found in the accounts after the adjusting entries have been posted. The balance sheet and income statement for the High Way Air Freight Company are illustrated in Exhibits 4-6 and 4-7, respectively.

Closing Entries. After the adjusting entries have been made and the financial statements have been prepared, the worksheet provides direction for journalizing closing entries. The income statement columns provide annual balances for the revenue and expense accounts. These accounts must be closed to the appropriate owner's equity account to complete the accounting cycle.

When the closing process is complete, all of the revenue and expense accounts will have a zero balance. In the case of the High Way Air Freight Company, the resulting net income will eventually be closed to the Retained Earnings account, since the company is a corporation. The closing entries necessary for this example are shown in Exhibit 4-8.

Summary

Resources and services acquired by an entity are valued at their cost and considered to be an asset as long as they have a future service potential. Assets are reported on the balance sheet. When the future service potential of an asset expires, either through use or sale, the asset is reclassified as an expense and transferred from the balance sheet to the income statement.

Expenses are matched with revenues on the income statement. Revenues are valued at the dollar amounts exchanged for goods and services

EXHIBIT 4-6
HIGH WAY AIR FREIGHT COMPANY: BALANCE SHEET

HIGH WAY FREIGHT COMPANY
Balance Sheet
December 31,10X8

Cash		$ 35,300	
Accounts Receivable		22,400	
Prepaid Rent		8,000	
Accrued Interest Receivable		250	
Notes Receivable		12,500	
Equipment	$100,000		
Accumulated Depreciation	40,000	60,000	
Total Assets		$138,450	

Accounts Payable		$ 6,600
Accrued Salaries Payable		800
Deferred Service Revenue		600
Total Liabilities		$ 8,000
Stockholders' Equity		
Capital Stock	$ 80,000	
Retained Earnings*	50,450	
Total Stockholders' Equity		130,450
Total Liabilities and Stockholders' Equity		$138,450

*Beginning Retained Earnings balance ($45,400) plus Net Income ($5,050) will equal the closing Retained Earnings Balance

EXHIBIT 4-7
HIGH WAY AIR FREIGHT COMPANY: INCOME STATEMENT

HIGH WAY AIR FREIGHT COMPANY
Income Statement
For the Year Ended December 31, 19X8

Service Revenue	$141,100	
Interest Revenue	750	
Total Revenue		$141,850
Operating Expenses		
Salary Expense	$102,800	
Insurance Expense	5,700	
Maintenance Expense	11,500	
Miscellaneous Expense	2,800	
Rent Expense	4,000	
Depreciation Expense	10,000	136,800
Net Income		$ 5,050

distributed to customers. Net income, a positive difference between revenues and expenses, leads to an increase in owner's equity. The financial statements are articulated, in the sense that revenue and expense transactions affect both the balance sheet and income statement. Errors in recording these transactions are likely to distort both financial statements.

Account balances may not be properly stated at the end of the period, because formal source documents that initiate the accounting process have not been received for all transactions. These situations require ad-

EXHIBIT 4-8
HIGH WAY AIR FREIGHT COMPANY: CLOSING ENTRIES

Date	Accounts	Debit	Credit
12/31	Service Revenue	$141,100	
	Interest Revenue	750	
	Income Summary		$141,850
12/31	Income Summary	136,800	
	Salary Expense		102,800
	Insurance Expense		5,700
	Maintenance Expense		11,500
	Miscellaneous Expense		2,800
	Rent Expense		4,000
	Depreciation Expense		10,000
12/31	Income Summary	5,050	
	Retained Earnings		5,050

justing entries. Adjusting entries recognize new information and, accordingly, adjust account balances for accruals, deferrals, or reclassifications. For the most part, a need for adjustments results from a difference in timing that severs the two parts of a transaction, for example, the prepayment for goods or services, the early delivery of goods or services, or the gradual use of goods or services. Several common combinations of accounts are affected by the adjustment process. Accrual entries accelerate the recognition of new transaction information by journalizing events before the accompanying source documents arrive. Deferral adjustments postpone (accelerate) income by linking revenue-liability accounts or asset-expense accounts.

The primary objective of the adjusting process is to bring the accounts of an entity to their proper balances at a point in time. To achieve these balances, the accountant must review the available facts and exercise professional judgment.

The accountant may use a worksheet in the adjusting process. The worksheet provides a concise form on which to summarize and manipulate account data, and to prepare draft copies of adjusting entries and financial statements. The worksheet then serves as the source document that authorizes the journalization of adjusting entries.

A Supplementary Discussion: Reversing Entries

The accounting departments of all but the smallest of organizations consist of several people performing a variety of complementary functions. Some of the tasks that are done require relatively low levels of accounting knowledge while other accounting operations require sophisticated insight into accounting theory and practice. For example, the process of journalizing recurring transactions in ongoing systems can be performed by persons with little technical knowledge, and this function is usually done by clerks. The clerk who posts entries from the journal to the ledger accounts can be trained to do this function in less than one day. On the other hand, the person who prepares the end-of-period adjusting entries must make precise accounting judgments.

Clerks can journalize and post recurring entries in ongoing systems whenever standard operating procedures are developed and implemented. For example, the journal clerk can be trained to debit an expense account and credit a payable (liability) account whenever a bill is received, as would happen with the electric bill, the water bill, or employee time cards (i.e., the labor bill). These bills do represent expenses: in the normal course of business, custom specifies that the bill is to be determined only after the service has been delivered. On the other hand, the clerk can be directed to debit an asset account and credit a liability on receipt of an insurance premium notice, a rent bill, or an invoice for materials purchased: in the normal course of business, these bills usually are paid before the service is consumed. Journal clerks are trained to recognize specific accounts, and only those accounts, in response to the receipt of specific source documents: if no document arrives, no entry is made.

ADJUSTING ENTRIES AND
STANDARD OPERATING PROCEDURES

Journal clerks who follow prescribed accounting standard operating procedures record the December electric, water and labor expenses in January, when the bills are received, even though December and January may fall in different fiscal years. At the same time, the clerk typically would not record the expiration of prepaid insurance or rent, since no document will be prepared to initiate such a journal entry. In other words, the implementation of standard operating procedures in the typical accounting system creates end-of-period account balances that must be adjusted, and such adjustment requires the intervention of an accountant with relatively high levels of technical knowledge.

The exact nature of the adjustment made by an accountant depends on the directions given to the clerk who journalizes the original transactions, as described in the main body of this chapter under the heading, *Alternative Adjustments*. One set of adjustments is required if business costs are first recorded as assets, and another set of adjustments is required if the costs are first recorded as expenses.

ADJUSTMENTS AND
ENTRIES IN THE FOLLOWING PERIOD

Unfortunately, adjustments to account balances made at the end of the preceding period may cause misstatements in the current period, unless additional intervention by the accountant is performed. Consider, for example, the first adjustment described in the chapter under the heading *Expense and Liability Adjustments*. Because the last utility bill received during the year considered services provided until December 15, the following adjusting entry was made to estimate for the last half of December:

Utility Expense	$5,000	
Accrued Utility Payable		$5,000
To accrue unbilled utility liability, assuming expense is $10,000 per month		

The Utility Expense account is closed out at the end of the year; that is, the total balance in the account, including the $5,000 estimate made as an adjustment, is included in the income statement for the year just ended, and the Utility Expense account is set back to a zero balance so that the new expenses for the current year may be accumulated. However, the Accrued Utility Payable account will still reflect its $5,000 credit balance in the current year.

When the first utility bill ($10,000) for the current year arrives on January 15, the journal clerk will follow standard operating procedure, and make the following entry:

Utility Expense	$10,000	
Utility Payable		$10,000
To record the utility bill received January 15		

However, half of this $10,000 relates to last year, and the other half to the current year. The journal clerk must follow standard operating procedure, even if the results are misleading.

Ongoing accounting systems are designed to be operated by clerks, without the frequent intervention of accountants. If the accountant did intervene in this case (an unlikely event), an entry might have been prepared as follows:

Utility Expense	$5,000	
Accrued Utility Payable	5,000	
Utility Payable		$10,000
To record the utility bill for the first half of January		

This entry does properly measure Utility Expense, and it does reflect the liability of $10,000. Unfortunately, it also requires the intervention of the accountant.

REVERSING ENTRIES
FOR EXPENSE ACCRUALS

Reversing entries represent a second order adjustment made by the accountant as part of the normal closing process. Reversing entries are designed to correct expected future misstatements resulting from the application of standard operating procedure *before* the misstatements are recorded. For example, consider the following three journal entries:

12/31	Utility Expense	$ 5,000	
	Accrued Utility Payable		$ 5,000
	To accrue utility liability of period 12/15–12/31		
12/31	Income Summary	120,000	
	Utility Expense		120,000
	To reflect expenses on income statement and close expense account		
1/1	Accrued Utility Payable	5,000	
	Utility Expense		5,000
	To reverse December 31 adjusting entry		

This last entry, a reversing entry, is made by the accountant as part of the normal year-end adjustments, in anticipation of the entry to be recorded by the journal clerk upon arrival of the utility bill. When the bill is received on January 15, the clerk will make the following entry:

1/15	Utility Expense	$10,000	
	Utility Payable		$10,000
	To record utility bill of 1/15		

The combination of the reversing entry and the regular entry made in accordance with standard operating procedure will produce the correct account balances, as reflected in the following set of ledger accounts:

Date	Explanation	Utility Expense		Utility Payable	
12/31	Adjusting	$ 5,000			$ 5,000
12/31	Balance	120,000			5,000
12/31	Closing		$120,000		
12/31	Balance	0			5,000
1/1	Reversing		5,000	$5,000	
1/1	Balance		5,000		0
1/15	1/15 bill	10,000			10,000
1/15	Balance	5,000			10,000

Thus, reversing entries are made in conjuction with other end-of-period adjustments in an effort to produce accounts with proper balances.

Reversal entries are applied to some, but not all, of the expense adjustments. In particular, adjustments that reclassify assets as expenses need not be reversed. Included in this category are reclassifications of Inventory as Cost of Goods Sold, the recognition of Depreciation Expense, and the transfer from prepaid expenses (rent, insurance) to expenses.

REVERSING ENTRIES
FOR REVENUE ACCRUAL

Reversing entries are also appropriate for some end-of-year revenue accrual adjustments. Whenever the accountant makes an adjustment to recognize income or revenue that is earned but has not been collected, reversing entries are appropriate. That is, the end-of-year adjustment is made before the receipt of source documents evidencing completion of the earning process: a reversing entry will anticipate and correct for the double counting that occurs when the journal clerk records the revenue item upon receipt of the source documents in the current year. For example, consider the first example described above under the heading, *Revenue and Asset Adjustment.* Here the fiscal year ends on September 30, but the semiannual interest on a $100,000, 8 percent loan is due on June 30 and December 31. At year-end, September 30, the following entry was made to recognize interest earned but not collected:

> Accrued Interest Receivable $2,000
>   Interest Revenue $2,000
>   To accrue interest from July 1 to September 30

The Interest Revenue account would then be closed out to include the $8,000 full year of interest ($100,000 × 8%) in the income statement and to set the Interest

Revenue account back to zero so that it may accumulate fresh information for the new year.

        Interest Revenue $8,000
             Income Summary $8,000
        To reflect revenue in the income statement and close revenue account

A reversing entry is then made by the accountant as part of the year-end adjustments, as follows:

            Interest Revenue $2,000
                 Accrued Interest Receivable $2,000
            To reverse the September 30 adjusting entry

When the December 31 interest check is received, the journal clerk will recognize the whole six-month collection ($100,000 × 8% × ½), $4,000, as income, even though the amount earned during the current year applies to the period October 1 to December 31, that is, $2,000. The clerk makes the following entry, in conformity with accounting standard operating procedure:

            Cash $4,000
                 Interest Revenue $4,000
            To record the December 31 collection of interest.

The ledger accounts will reflect the correct balances, since the reversing entry anticipated the December 31 collection entry.

Date	Explanation	Accrued Interest Receivable		Interest Revenue	
9/30	Adjusting	$2,000			$2,000
9/30	Balance	2,000			8,000
9/30	Closing			$8,000	
9/30	Balance	2,000			0
10/1	Reversing		$2,000	2,000	
10/1	Balance	0		2,000	
12/31	Collection				4,000
12/31	Balance	0			2,000

Thus, the reversing entry, in conjunction with other end-of-period adjusting entries and the application of standard operating procedures for the journal entries, will produce correct account balances.

Reversal entries are applied to some, but not all, of the revenue adjustments. In particular, adjustments that transfer Deferred Revenue (a liability) into Earned Revenue, need not be reversed. For example, a magazine publisher may record prepaid subscriptions by crediting Deferred Subscription Revenue. Year-end adjustments are as follows:

Deferred Subscription Revenue   XXX
     Subscription Revenue   XXX
To recognize portion of subscription earned

This entry does not have to be reversed.

Key Terms

Expired costs
Unearned income
Prepaid expenses
Depreciation
Contra account
Net book value
Accruals
Deferrals
Worksheet

Questions

1. Describe the difference between an expense and a loss.

2. Provide a synonym for the term "unexpired cost."

3. What are adjusting entries? Which combination of accounts generally are affected by adjusting entries?

4. Closing entries serve what purpose? Which accounts typically are closed?

5. Why are worksheets prepared as part of the closing cycle?

6. Will an increase in revenues only affect the income statement?

7. Which accounts are affected by the failure to recognize $100 in accrued but unpaid labor cost (wages)?

8. Which accounts are affected if $100 in earned interest revenue has not been received and, therefore, has not been journalized?

9. For each of the following items, indicate which accounts are debited and credited in recording end-of-period adjusting entries:
(a) Insurance was purchased during the year and debited to prepaid insurance.
(b) Supplies were purchased during the year and debited to supplies.
(c) Rent received in advance from a tenant was credited to deferred revenue.
(d) Advances from a customer were credited to a revenue account.

10. Define the net book value of an asset. Does this amount approximate the market value of the asset?

11. Define the term *"depreciation."*

12. What information does a contra account report to the financial statement user?

13. Do all adjusting entries have an effect on the determination of net income? Explain.

14. What does the term "accrued" mean to an accountant?

15. What is deferred revenue?

16. Assume that the end-of-the-year adjustments ignored (1) depreciation on equipment and (2) accrued but unpaid property taxes. Which accounts will be misstated on the financial statements as a result of each error?

17. Distinguish between a trial balance and a balance sheet.

18. Define the term "unearned income."

19. Explain the probable nature of each of the entries in the account shown below.

INSURANCE EXPENSE

6/30	1,000	(a)	750	(b)	12/31
			250	(c)	12/31

Exercises

1. Certain account balances taken from the ledger of Plum Co. prior to adjustments on December 31 are shown below:

	Debit	Credit
Prepaid Insurance	$ 1,000	
Office Supplies	500	
Unearned Income		$2,000
Salaries Expense	10,000	
Interest Revenue		0

Information required for period-end adjustments is as follows:
(a) The insurance policy was purchased on October 1 of the current year and covers a period of two years.
(b) The inventory of supplies taken on December 31 revealed that $150 of supplies were on hand.
(c) One fourth of the unearned income has been earned as of December 31.
(d) Salaries earned, but not paid, as of December 31 amounted to $200.
(e) The company received a $1,000, 60-day, 6 percent note receivable from a customer on December 1.

REQUIRED:
Prepare the necessary adjusting entries that should be made on December 31.

2. Stabler Co. acquired a new machine on January 1, 19X2, for $11,000. The machine has an estimated life of five years, and its is anticipated that the residual value at the end of that time will be $1,000. The company uses the straight-line method of calculating depreciation.

REQUIRED:
(a) Give the entries necessary to record the purchase of the machine and to record the depreciation expense at the end of 19X2.

(b) Show how the machine would be reported in the balance sheet at December 31, 19X4.

3. The bookkeeper of Griffin Company made a number of errors during 19X8:

(a) The company purchased a machine on January 1, 19X8, for $11,000. The machine had an estimated useful life of 10 years, a $1,000 estimated residual value, and the company planned to use straight-line depreciation. The bookkeeper mistakenly debited the purchase to Supplies Expense.

(b) The company received an advance payment of $1,000 for services to be rendered during 19X9. The bookkeeper credited this amount to Revenue.

(c) The company purchased supplies during the year for $500 and debited the amount to Supplies Inventory. At the end of the year, all of the supplies had been consumed, but the bookkeeper neglected to make the appropriate adjusting entry.

(d) Wages earned during the last week of 19X8 but not payable until January 4, 19X9, amounted to $500. The bookkeeper failed to make the appropriate adjusting entry.

Indicate the effects of these errors by placing a O (overstate), U (understate) or N (no effect) in the chart below.

	Assets	Liabilities	Owner's Equity	Revenues	Expenses
(a)					
(b)					
(c)					
(d)					

4. On April 1, 19X9, a company purchased office supplies for $1200. The count of office supplies on hand on December 31, 19X9, totaled $300. Prepare the necessary adjusting entry at December 31 assuming that the purchase on April 1 was debited to Office Supplies. Prepare a second entry assuming that the April debit was to Office Supplies Expense.

5. Below is a list of accounts that might appear in the adjusted trial balance columns of a worksheet. The income statement columns and the balance sheet columns of a worksheet are shown to the right of the list of accounts. For each account listed, indicate with a check (✔) the normal account balance.

	Income Statement		Balance Sheet	
Account	Debit	Credit	Debit	Credit
1. Revenue				
2. Cash				
3. Accounts Payable				
4. Equipment				
5. Salary Expense				
6. Accumulated Depreciation				
7. Capital Stock				
8. Depreciation Expense				
9. Accrued Salaries Payable				
10. Deferred Revenue				
11. Prepaid Insurance				
12. Retained Earnings				
13. Insurance Expense				

6. Selected account balances for Smith Co. on December 31 prior to adjusting entries are shown below.

Revenue	$47,000
Unearned Revenue	6,000
Prepaid Insurance	4,000
Equipment	100,000
Accumulated Depreciation	20,000
Salary Expense	25,000
Supplies	4,000

Data for adjustments are as follows:

(a) On June 30, a two-year insurance policy was purchased and debited to prepaid insurance.

(b) Supplies on hand as of December 31 amounted to $500.

(c) Accrued salaries on December 31 amounted to $700.

(d) Depreciation expense on equipment for the year is computed to be $10,000.

(e) The company received a $6,000 advance from a customer on September 1 and credited the amount to unearned revenue. As of December 31, one-half of this amount was earned.

REQUIRED:

(a) Prepare the adjusting entries that should be made on December 31.

(b) Prepare an income statement for the year ended December 31.

7. On July 1, 19X8, Jones Co. accepted a $5,000, 1-year, 8 percent note from Ames Co. in settlement of an overdue account receivable. Ames Co. paid the note plus the interest on June 30, 19X9. Prepare the necessary entries relating to the issuance and payment of this note and the adjusting entry on December 31, 19X8, on the books of Jones Co.

8. The following four combinations of accounts are generally affected by adjusting entries:
(a) Expenses and assets.
(b) Expenses and liabilities.
(c) Revenues and assets.
(d) Revenues and liabilities.
Indicate the nature of each of the following adjustments by choosing the appropriate letter from the above list.
(a) Recording depreciation on equipment.
(b) Recording interest accrued on a notes receivable.
(c) Recording salaries earned by employees but not paid as of the end of the year.
(d) Warehouse space was rented to another company on June 30, and the tenant paid one year's rent in advance. The payment was credited to unearned revenue.
(e) Office supplies purchased during the year were debited to an asset account. A year-end inventory revealed that a portion of the supplies was still on hand.

9. Certain account balances of Hine Co. before and after adjustment are listed below. For each account, give the probable adjusting entry that caused the balance to change.

	Balance Before Adjustment	Balance After Adjustment
1. Prepaid Rent	$ 1,200	$ 600
2. Interest Receivable	0	50
3. Office Supplies	0	400
4. Accumulated Depreciation	3,000	4,000
5. Revenue	50,000	53,000
6. Wage Expense	26,000	27,000
7. Interest Expense	750	1,000

10. Listed below are the balances in the adjusted trial balance columns of the worksheet for Carter Co. at the end of 19X6. Complete the worksheet by extending the amounts to the income statement and balance sheet columns.

	Adjusted Trial Balance		Income Statement		Balance Sheet	
Account	Debit	Credit	Debit	Credit	Debit	Credit
Cash	5,000					
Accounts Receivable	10,000					
Prepaid Insurance	1,000					
Equipment	50,000					
Accumulated Depreciation		15,000				
Accounts Payable		6,000				
Notes Payable		9,000				
Deferred Revenue		5,000				
Capital Stock		10,000				
Retained Earnings		7,500				
Revenue		70,000				
Wage Expense	40,000					
Insurance Expense	500					
Rent Expense	12,000					
Depreciation Expense	5,000					
Interest Revenue		500				
Interest Receivable	500					
Wages Payable		1,000				
	124,000	124,000				

11. Copley Company paid $3,000 to acquire a 24-month insurance policy on its business property. The policy covered the period from July 1, 19X3, to June 30, 19X5. Copley uses a calendar year-end. Record the acquisition of the policy and any adjusting entries required on December 31, 19X3, 19X4, and 19X5, first assuming the policy was originally recorded as an expense and, second, assuming it was originally recorded as an asset.

12. Van Horn Company acquired an automobile for use in its business that cost $7,600. The auto was acquired on April 2, 19X3, and is expected to have a useful life of three years, at the end of which it is expected to have a salvage value of $1,000. If the firm uses a March 31 year-end, complete the following depreciation schedule for this automobile, calculating depreciation using the straight-line method:

Date	Depreciation Expense	Accumulated Depreciation	Remaining Book Value
April 2, 19X3	0	0	$7,600
March 31, 19X4	_____	_____	_____
March 31, 19X5	_____	_____	_____
March 31, 19X6	_____	_____	_____

13. Listed below are the balances in the trial balance column of the worksheet for Keck Company at December 31,19X9:

	Trial Balance		Adjustments	
Account	Debit	Credit	Debit	Credit
Cash	2,600			
Accounts Receivable	4,050			
Prepaid Rent	1,200			
Equipment	26,000			
Accumulated Dep.		9,000		
Accounts Payable		6,000		
Notes Payable		2,000		
Owner's Equity		7,900		
Revenue		41,000		
Salary Expense	29,000			
Insurance Expense	950			
Utilities Expense	2,100			
	65,900	65,900		

Using the data given below, prepare the necessary adjustments in the adjustment columns to the worksheet:

(a) Rent was prepaid on November 1, 19X9, for three months.

(b) All of Keck's equipment has a 10-year life and was acquired less than five years ago. None was acquired in the current year. Only $1,000 is expected to be realized as salvage for all the equipment.

(c) The notes payable balance represents a $2,000, 3-year, 6 percent note, dated June 30, 19X9.

(d) Wages totaling $1,000 were earned by employees up to December 31, 19X9, but unpaid at that date.

(e) The insurance policy was a six-month accident policy dated February 1, 19X9. The firm elected not to renew it.

14. Coleman, Incorporated, purchased a machine on January 1, 19X0, for $10,000. Coleman will depreciate the machine on a straight-line basis over a five year life, with no estimated salvage value. The Company's fiscal year ends on June 30th. Prepare a depreciation schedule showing the annual depreciation expense and the net book value of the asset for the years 19X0 through 19X4 inclusive (AICPA adapted).

1. Listed below are selected data concerning the operations of Aggie Co. during 19X9:

(a) The company purchased a two-year insurance policy for $600 on April 1, 19X8, and the premium was debited to prepaid insurance.

Problems

(b) The company purchased supplies during the year for $1,000 cash and debited supplies expense. The supplies on hand on December 31 amounted to $240.

(c) Equipment was purchased on January 1, 19X4, for $20,000. The estimated life was 10 years with zero residual value, and the straight-line method is used to compute depreciation.

(d) Aggie rented a warehouse to another company on June 1 for $100 a month. The tenant paid one year's rent in advance at that time, and the amount was credited to deferred revenue.

(e) The Aggie Co. received a $1,000 advance from a customer for future deliveries. The receipt was credited to a revenue account. As of December 31, $200 of products remained to be delivered to the customer.

(f) The company borrowed $1,000 from the City National Bank on December 1 for 90 days with interest of 9 percent per year.

(g) Income taxes for 19X9 are estimated to be $25,000.

(h) Employee salaries for the week of December 26 were $1,000 to be paid on January 4.

(i) The company rented office space to ABC Co. on September 1, 19X9, at a monthly rental of $200. The rent was to be paid by the last day of the month, but the December rent had not been received as of December 31.

(j) Accrued interest on notes receivable at December 31 amounted to $180.

REQUIRED:

For each item, prepare the adjusting entry necessary at the end of the company's accounting period, December 31, 19X9.

2. Listed below is information concerning the operations of the Watkins Company during 19X9:

(a) Watkins Co. pays all salaries on the 15th of each month. Salary expense for a whole month is $8,000.

(b) On June 30, the company paid $5,000 for license fees to the city and debited Prepaid Licenses, an asset. The licenses expire one year from date of purchase.

(c) A truck was purchased on January 1, 19X5, for $6,000. Its estimated life is 10 years and it has no salvage value. Depreciation is recorded using the straight-line method.

(d) Watkins Co. purchased a 5-year insurance policy on March 1, 19X7, and debited Prepaid Insurance at the time of purchase. The policy cost $10,000.

(e) On January 1, 19X8, the company received an advance payment for services to be rendered over the next two full years. An Unearned Revenue account was credited at the time, and an adjusting entry was made on December 31, 19X8, transferring one-half of the amount to Revenue. The amount of advance payment was $18,000.

(f) Watkins Co. borrowed $20,000 for one year to finance operations on October 1, 19X9. The annual interest rate is 10 percent payable every April and September.

(g) Purchased $500 worth of supplies during the year and debited an expense account. An inventory shows $150 worth of supplies left on December 31, 19X9.

(h) Interest owed, but not paid, as of the end of year on Bonds Payable amounted to $4,000.

(i) Watkins Co. rented office space on June 30 of this year from Mr. Lynn, a good friend of the president. They paid $4,000 for a full year's rent in advance on that date, and debited Rent Expense.

REQUIRED:

Prepare the adjusting entries necessary at the end of the company's accounting period, December 31, 19X9.

3. The ledger account balances after adjustment of Daniel Co. as of December 31, 19X9, are listed below. The balance of the retained earnings account has been intentionally omitted. All accounts reflect their normal balances.

Cash	1,500
Accounts Receivable	5,000
Prepaid Insurance	500
Equipment	30,000
Accumulated Depreciation	6,000
Accounts Payable	3,000
Notes Payable	1,000
Capital Stock	10,000
Retained Earnings	?
Revenue	40,000
Salary Expense	21,000
Insurance Expense	1,000
Rent Expense	6,000
Other Expense	5,000

REQUIRED:

(a) Prepare the necessary closing entries
(b) Prepare an income statement and a balance sheet.

4. The trial balance before adjustment of Dole Co. at December 31, 19X9, is presented below.

DOLE CO.
Trial Balance
December 31, 19X9

Account	Debit	Credit
Cash	$ 2,000	
Accounts Receivable	5,000	
Supplies	3,000	
Prepaid Insurance	1,000	
Equipment	20,000	
Accumulated Depreciation		$ 8,000
Accounts Payable		4,000
Deferred Revenue		2,000
Capital Stock		10,000
Retained Earnings		4,000
Revenue		21,000
Wage Expense	6,000	
Rent Expense	9,000	
Miscellaneous Expense	3,000	
	$49,000	$49,000

Additional Data:
1. Accrued wages at December 31 amounted to $500.
2. A physical count indicated that $1,000 of supplies were on hand at December 31.
3. The balance in the Prepaid Insurance account resulted from a two-year insurance policy purchased on June 30, 19X9.
4. The equipment was purchased on January 1, 19X5 for $20,000.00. It had an estimated useful life of 10 years, zero residual value, and straight-line depreciation was used.
5. One-half of the deferred revenues were earned as of December 31.

REQUIRED:
  (a) Prepare a worksheet.
  (b) Prepare an income statement and a balance sheet.
  (c) Prepare the necessary closing entries.

5. The Trial Balance before adjustment of the Hart Co. at December 31, 19X9, is presented below.

HART CO.
Trial Balance
December 31, 19X9

Account	Debit	Credit
Cash	$ 6,000	
Accounts Receivable	7,500	
Supplies	600	
Prepaid Rent	1,200	
Equipment	12,000	
Building	24,000	
Accumulated Depreciation on		
Building and Equipment		$ 6,000
Accounts Payable		4,000
Deferred Revenue		400
Notes Payable		1,000
Salaries Payable		500
Capital Stock		15,000
Retained Earnings		13,000
Revenue		19,900
Insurance Expense	4,000	
Salaries Expense	2,000	
Miscellaneous Expense	2,500	
	$59,800	$59,800

Additional Data:
1. Depreciation on the buildings and equipment is calculated under the straight-line method. Estimated life of both is six years, with no residual value.
2. Rent for the year amounted to $1,200.00, which had been paid on January 1, 19X9 and debited to Prepaid Rent.
3. Exactly $500.00 of supplies were still on hand on December 31.
4. Annual interest on the note payable dated January 1, 19X9 is 10 per cent. Interest has not been paid during 19X9.
5. One-half of the deferred revenue was earned during the year.

REQUIRED:
(a) Prepare a worksheet to reflect appropriate adjustments.
(b) Prepare income statement and balance sheet.
(c) Prepare necessary closing entries.

6. Listed below are financial data extracted from the records of Boyd and Sons Service Company for calendar year 19X5:
(a) Depreciation expense of $2,100 has not been recorded.
(b) The Supplies on Hand account has a balance of $600. A count of supplies on hand shows only $200 actually on hand at year-end.

(c) Utilities expense of $80 has been incurred but no formal bill had been received by year-end.

(d) Rent Expense for three months was prepaid on December 1, 19X5, totaling $1,500.

(e) Wages of $900 have been earned by employees but unpaid at year-end.

(f) Customers' fees totaling $1,000 have been received by the firm for services to be performed in January and February of next year. They were recorded as revenues.

REQUIRED:

Prepare general journal entries to record these adjustments.

7. The Ohio Company has completed one year of operations and has the following (normal) ledger balances before adjustments:

Accounts Receivable	$ 3,000
Accounts Payable	1,000
Cash	2,600
Equipment	8,000
Prepaid Advertising	1,000
Prepaid Rent	1,200
Notes Payable	1,000
Sales	18,200
Wages Expense	7,800
Utilities Expense	800
Supplies Expense	2,600
Owner's Equity	6,800

The financial records of the firm disclose the following additional data:

(a) All supplies acquired were recorded as Supplies Expense. Actually, $550 in supplies are still on hand at year-end.

(b) The Prepaid Advertising relates to newspapers ads for October, November, and December, 19X3, the last three months of their year.

(c) Prepaid Rent was debited for three months rent paid in advance on December 1, 19X3.

(d) Wages earned but unpaid to employees at year-end totaled $300.

(e) The Equipment account reflects the cost of two machine owned by the firm:

Machine	Life	Cost	Salvage
A	6	$3,200	$200
B	8	4,800	0

Depreciation for this year has not been recorded. The firm will use the straight-line method.

(f) Sales include $400 in fees that have been received for services to be provided in the future.

REQUIRED:

(a) Set up T accounts and enter the unadjusted balances as shown above.

(b) Prepare general journal entries to record the necessary adjusting entries.

(c) Post the adjusting entries to the T accounts.

(d) Prepare an adjusted trial balance.

8. The trial balance before adjustment for Coker Company at December 31, 19X6, is shown below:

COKER COMPANY
Trial Balance
December 31, 19X6

Cash	$ 2,400	
Accounts Receivable	1,800	
Supplies on Hand	320	
Equipment	8,000	
Accounts Payable		$ 3,520
Owner's Equity		8,600
Sales		9,000
Wages Expense	3,200	
Advertising Expense	900	
Insurance Expense	600	
Utilities Expense	600	
Rent Expense	3,300	
	$21,120	$21,120

An analysis of Coker's financial records disclose the following data:

(a) December rent of $300 was unpaid due to oversight.

(b) Straight-line depreciation of $1,200 for 19X6 is unrecorded.

(c) Supplies on hand at December 31, 19X6, total only $100.

(d) Revenues of $600 have been earned but are unrecorded at December 31. 19X6: Invoices to customers will be mailed in January 19X7.

(e) The $600 insurance premium was paid on June 27, 19X6, for a two-year fire insurance policy, expiring on the same date in 19X8.

REQUIRED:

(a) Prepare a worksheet and enter the trial balance in the trial balance columns.

(b) Enter all required adjustments on the worksheet.

(c) Complete the worksheet by extending the balances from the adjusted trial balance column to the balance sheet and income statement columns.

□ 5
THE INCOME STATEMENT: REVENUES AND REALIZATION

□ OBJECTIVES

AFTER STUDYING THIS CHAPTER, YOU SHOULD BE ABLE TO DO THE FOLLOWING:

1. DISCUSS THE MEANING AND METHODS OF MEASURING BUSINESS INCOME.

2. PREPARE THE REVENUE SECTION OF AN INCOME STATEMENT.

3. DEFINE REALIZATION AND DISCUSS ALTERNATIVE CHARACTERISTICS OF THE EARNING PROCESS THAT CAN INDICATE WHEN REALIZATION OCCURS.

4. CALCULATE TRADE AND CASH DISCOUNTS.

5. CONTRAST THE MULTIPLE STEP AND THE SINGLE STEP FORM OF AN INCOME STATEMENT.

Businesses, like most organizations, prepare reports, or disseminate information, about the success or failure of their operations. The purpose of this reporting activity is to inform owners, creditors, and other interested parties about the organization and its accomplishments. Success can be measured in a variety of ways depending on the purpose of the evaluation. A baseball team, for example, may achieve success if it wins more games than its rivals. From another perspective, the baseball team may be evaluated on the profitability of its operations: Do the fans pay more for admission to see the team play than management pays the players and other suppliers of goods and services?

The investment of owners, the funds loaned by a bank, and the salaries of employees are examples of the financial interest that many individuals have in a business. The income statement is periodically prepared by accountants to report on the financial consequences of activities undertaken by a business within a certain period of time. If the enterprise has earned a profit, it has more resources available to it at the end of the period than were available at the beginning of the period. If a loss has been incurred, the converse is true, or the business consumed more resources in its operations than it generated during the period.

Profit and loss relate to business income, which is widely used as a measure of effectiveness and performance. However, there are alternative definitions of income.

Business Income

Economists have often viewed income as a measure of well-being relative to an enterprise. Income has been described as the maximum value that could be distributed to owners during a period and still leave the business as well off at the end of the period as it was at the start of the period. While conceptually appealing, the application of this definition becomes virtually impossible. Many assumptions must be made to measure how "well off" a business is at any point in time.

Another approach to income determination is to use a total venture concept. In this sense, the value of all investment inputs in a business venture are determined and accumulated over its life. At the end of the venture, the residual value, plus the value of all distributions made to owners are also accumulated. The difference between the inputs and the final value is deemed to be income. The total venture approach is very objective and accurate. However, income cannot be determined until the venture ends. Investors in most businesses require timely, ongoing feedback and could not wait for this type of information.

The Matching Concept. Accountants measure business income by *matching,* or relating, revenues and expenses for a specific time period. Since revenues and expenses are quantified by using historical data, the resulting income is deemed to be historical also. Accounting income does not, necessarily, reflect current values or determinations of how well off a business is. It does provide for a timely, objective, periodic report.

Fundamentally, the accountant realizes, or isolates, revenue that relates to a specific time period. Normally, revenue realization follows a specific transaction with a customer of the organization. Once the revenues have been identified, the accountant determines the expenses that the business incurred to generate the revenues. The expenses and revenues are matched, or related, by the accountant. The difference between revenues and expenses is termed income or loss.

Accounting Income. When goods or services are sold by a business an expense is incurred. The expense represents an *outflow* of cost associated with the product or service that was sold. The business entity also receives an *inflow* as a part of the sale transaction. The form of the inflow is an asset, and it also increases the owner's claim through the recognition of revenue. The revenue is measured by the value of the asset received. Both revenues and expenses are valued by using the historical cost of specific assets received and given in the transaction.

Through a focus on revenues and expenses, accounting income produces a historical measure. The results are quantifiable and objective. The income statement is the reporting device used by accountants to disclose this information.

Most businesses prepare annual financial reports that include an income statement. Many organizations are also required to provide interested users with quarterly reports. Special income statements can be prepared for varying time periods to satisfy the information needs of creditors or management.

The Income Statement

The income statement provides a summary of revenues and expenses for a specific period of time. Revenue and expense items are grouped by type or by class to condense the report and to make it readable. Thus, a single line entitled "Sales Revenue" may be shown instead of 2,000 lines bearing such titles as "Revenue from Sale to Andy Barnes" and "Revenue from Sale to Betty Benett."

Although specific formats can vary among organizations, industries, or uses, a functional classification system is most popular. A functional system will isolate the expenses that relate to major activities. These normally include the cost of the product that was sold, the expenses incurred to sell (or market) the product, and the expense of administrating the organization. These classifications tend to follow major areas of interest to statement users.

An Illustration. Exhibit 5-1 presents a classified income statement for the

EXHIBIT 5-1
A CLASSIFIED INCOME STATEMENT

MORRIS MERCHANDISING COMPANY
Income Statement
For the Year Ended December 31, 19X0

Sales			
Sales revenue		$412,900	
Less Sales Returns and Allowances	$ 7,400		
Sales Discounts	4,200	11,600	
Net Sales			$401,300
Cost of Goods Sold			
Beginning Inventory, January 1, 19X0	38,700		
Purchases during 19X0	252,300		
Cost of Goods Available for sale		291,000	
Less Ending Inventory, December 31, 19X0		42,800	
Cost of Goods Sold			248,200
Gross Margin on Sales			$153,100
Operating Expenses			
Selling Expenses			
Sales Salaries and Commissions	21,200		
Advertising	16,100		
Travel	5,200		
Telephone	2,100		
Supplies	900		
Depreciation on Sales Equipment	1,800		
Total Selling Expense		47,300	
Administrative Expenses			
Salaries	25,900		
Telephone	2,900		
Legal and Professional Fees	3,000		
Supplies	1,200		
Depreciation Expense—Building	5,000		
Depreciation Expense—Equipment	3,700		
Miscellaneous	400		
Total Administrative Expense		42,100	
Total Operating Expense			89,400
Net Income from Operations			63,700
Other Revenue:			
Rental Income		7,300	
Other Expense:			
Interest Expense		5,100	2,200
Net Income Before Taxes			65,900
Income Tax Expense			26,400
Net Income			$ 39,500
Earnings Per Share			$ 5.10

Morris Merchandising Company. The statement contains four major sections and several subsections. The major sections include the following:

1. *Sales.* The total revenue relating to normal operations of the business is reported in this section. Various deductions are considered in arriving at the net sales revenue.
2. *Expenses.* A variety of expenses that relating to the sales revenue are considered in this section. The expense items have been subclassified into cost of goods sold, selling expenses, and administrative expenses.
3. *Other Revenue and Expense.* The results of normal, ongoing operations are separated from revenue and expense items that relate to activities not directly associated with the principal operations of the firm.
4. *Earnings Per Share.* This is a required part of the income statement for most corporations. The goal is to provide additional user information by relating net income on a per share basis.

This chapter focuses on the sales or slaes revenue section of the income statement, while the next chapter deals with the expense sections.

Revenue Realization

Business operations are based on a series of exchanges. Products and services are acquired, combined in a marketable form, and exchanged for other assets, or resources. For example, the Morris Merchandising Company acquired products, facilities, and personnel. These resources were initially valued at their cost to the firm.

When the product was resold by the firm, the customers paid for the product and the service provided by the company. Thus, the customers paid for the combination of product, facility, and personnel. This combination is valued at the amount received by the firm in exchange for the resource given up. The acquisition value of the resources becomes an expense, and the resale value is a revenue.

To the extent that revenue exceeds expense, income results. Income then suggests a positive market reaction to the activities of the firm. If expense exceeds revenue, a loss results and indicates that the market reacted in a negative way to the activities of the firm.

In determining periodic income, the accountant first identifies those revenue items that relate to the time period in question. This identification process is governed by the **realization principle.**

Revenue is realized, or recorded in the accounts and income statement, when an exchange has taken place and when the earning process is essentially complete. Realization provides the accountant with an objective means of determining when revenue should be included in the income statement.

Consider the following revenue-related situations in terms of the realization principle:

Situation 1: Goods or services are sold for $1,000 and the customer pays cash.

Analysis: This is a common situation that clearly fits the constraints of the realization principle; an exchange has taken place, and the earning process is complete. Revenue in the amount of $1,000 is recognized by the following entry:

Cash	$1,000	
Sales Revenue		$1,000

Situation 2: Goods or services are sold for $1,200 on account.

Analysis: In this situation a sale was made, but cash was not received. Accounting practice treats this as a transaction, recognizing the account receivable as an asset. The other realization constraints have been met, and the following entry is made:

Accounts Receivable	$1,200	
Sales Revenue		$1,200

Situation 3: A future service contract is sold to a customer for $800.

Analysis: This situation does not meet the realization constraints. Although a transaction has taken place, the earning process is far from complete, since the service has not been provided. The company has acquired cash, and it has incurred a liability to provide a future service. The liability may be called "unearned revenue" and reported in the liabilities section of the balance sheet.

Cash	$800	
Unearned Sales Revenue		$800

Realization is an extremely important accounting principle. It governs which transactions result in revenue attributable to a specific time period. The revenue items, in turn, lead to an identification of the periodic expenses through the matching concept. Revenue and expense together result in the periodic income or loss reported by a firm.

Sales

The sales, or sales revenue, section of the income statement sets out the revenue for the period that is related to normal, ongoing business operations. Nonrecurring or extraordinary items are disclosed in another part of the statement.

In most situations, a sale results in the immediate recognition of revenue. The accountant relies upon *source documents* to provide evidence of a sale and uses them as the basis for recording revenues. Source documents can include cash register summary tapes, receipts for credit sales, or special agreements between a buyer and seller.

THE INCOME STATEMENT:
REVENUES AND
REALIZATION

Cash Sales. Cash sales result in an outflow of cash to the firm in exchange for the product or service provided. The cash inflow is used to value the revenue. If daily cash sales of $2,900 were made, the following entry is used to recognize the revenue:

Cash	$2,900	
Sales Revenue		$2,900

While an entry could be made to record each cash sale, there is no need for information in that much detail. Therefore, summary totals are normally recorded. Sometimes, management will use sales information about particular departments, locations, or products. To provide this information, the accountant can accumulate sales data in separate revenue accounts. For example, the previous sales of $2,900 could have come from three products and been recorded as follows:

Cash	$2,900	
Sales Revenue, Product A		$1,200
Sales Revenue, Product B		800
Sales Revenue, Product C		900

When the income statement is prepared, the three sales revenue accounts are merged into a single revenue item. However, by recording the sales data separately, the accountant was able to facilitate additional product information reporting at limited added cost.

Credit Sales. When credit sales are made, the firm receives a promise of payment from their customers. The promise of payment is termed an account receivable. The accountant must record the name of the customer who owes the firm money. However, there is no real need to differentiate revenue by customer name. Periodically, generally on a daily basis, the amount of the credit sales will be totaled, and a summary entry will be made.

If a company had $3,300 of credit sales, the revenue would be recorded as follows:

Accounts Receivable	$3,300	
Sales Revenue		$3,300

Accounts Receivable is an asset account reflecting the debts owed by customers. The accountant also maintains a set of subsidiary accounts, one for each customer, showing the individual amounts owed. The total of the subsidiary account balances equals the balance of the control, or summary, account—Accounts Receivable.

In the construction of an income statement, sales revenue is normally reduced by two types of items—returns and allowances and discounts—to arrive at net sales revenue.

Sales Returns and Allowances

Many businesses allow their customers to return damaged, defective, or unwanted items of merchandise. Depending upon the company's policy, such returns result in the firm's refunding cash to the customer, reducing the customer's account receivable balance, or issuing a credit allowance for future redemption. In all of these cases, the amount of revenue associated with the original sale should be reduced; to the extent that goods have been returned, revenue has not been earned.

One way to adjust revenue correctly is to reverse the original entry. For example, if the Dee Company sold $2,750 of merchandising on account, it would make the following entry:

Accounts Receivable	$2,750	
Sales Revenue		$2,750

If the customer subsequently returns $150 of the merchandise for credit, the Dee Company could make the following entry:

Sales Revenue	$150	
Accounts Receivable		$150

After the latter entry has been made, the balance of the sales revenue account is correctly stated at net sales of $2,600 ($2,750 credit less $150 debit).

The amount of returns and allowances is an extremely important type of management information. Excessive amounts of returns and allowances could indicate production or procurement problems relative to quality, extremely liberal return policies, a "too agressive" sales force, or "problem" customers. To provide management with information concerning the volume of sales adjustments and returns, a separate account titled "Sales Returns and Allowances" is generally used.

The *Sales Returns and Allowances* account is used to accumulate the revenue reductions that result from customer returns and adjustments. The account is used as an offset against the Sales Revenue, or gross revenue, account to derive the amount of net revenue.

In the previous example of the Dee Fective Company, the entry to record the return would be:

Sales Returns and Allowances	$150	
Accounts Receivable		$150

Sales Returns and Allowances will be deducted from Sales Revenue to derive the net sales revenue reported on the income statement.

Sales Discounts

Many times, especially in wholesale operations, customers will be quoted prices that are lower than the list or catalog prices of the selling firm. Also, customers can often secure an added discount, or price reduction, either by paying cash or by paying within a specified time period. Reductions from list price are called *trade discounts,* and prompt payment reductions are called *cash discounts.* Both must be considered in deriving the proper amount of sales revenue.

Trade Discounts. Trade discounts are reductions from a list price or a catalog price that are granted to a purchaser. The use of trade discount has certain advantages to the seller, including the following:

☐ Catalogs can be printed at a suggested retail selling price. The trade discount can be used to reduce the catalog price for wholesale purchases.
☐ Reprinting costs of the catalog prices can be saved by adjusting the amount of the trade discount instead of the list price.
☐ Special sales situations, for quantities or types of products, can be priced without prepublishing a price structure for every possible circumstance.

The Robinson-Patman Act and other pieces of federal legislation impose limits on some types of special trade discounts.

Trade discounts are expressed as a percentage reduction of the list price. A 15 percent trade discount means that the actual sale price will be 85 percent (100% − 15%) of the list price. Frequently, several trade discounts will be given on a single purchase. The discounts may relate to several characteristics of the sale—quantity, type of product, type of customer—or they may relate to a single characteristic. Multiple discounts are treated in a cumulative fashion.

For example, if a company sold goods having a list price of $5,000 subject to trade discounts of 25, 20 and 10 percent, the actual sale price will be $2,700, computed as follows:

List Price	$5,000
Less 25%	1,250
	3,750
Less 20%	750
	3,000
Less 10%	300
Actual Price	$2,700

Normal accounting practice is to deduct any applicable trade discounts and to bill customers for the net amount, or the actual sale price. Revenue will be realized at the net amount, and no separate disclosure of trade discounts is made in the income statement. Trade discounts are a part of the firm's pricing policy and, as such, the net sales price is the relevant information.

Cash Discounts. Many businesses will grant discounts for cash sales or for credit sales paid promptly. Cash discounts and credit terms are placed on the sales invoice to fully inform the customers and to avoid any misunderstandings. Generally, these terms are expressed as:

"*n/20*"—which means that the net amount of the sale is due no later than 20 days from the date of the sale.

"*2/10, n/30*"—which means that a 2 percent discount may be deducted from the net amount if payment is made within 10 days of the date of sale and that if the discount is not taken, the net amount is due within 30 days of the date of the sale.

Cash discounts are normally offered because of industry practice or a desire to speed up customer payments and thus increase the cash flow for the firm. The discount terms will normally motivate purchasers to pay within the discount period. Purchasers can evaluate the discount in terms of an annual interest rate.

If a sale is subject to terms of 3/10, *n/30*, the purchaser will receive a 3 percent reduction up through the 10th day and no reduction from the 11th through the 30th day. Thus, by not paying within the discount period, the purchaser will lose 3 percent for withholding payment until the 30th day. This represents 3 percent for a 20-day period ranging from day 11 through day 30. There are roughly eighteen, 20-day periods in a year ($360 \div 20$) and at the rate of 3 percent per period, these discount terms translate into an annual rate of 54 percent.

When discounts are taken, the revenue attributable to the sale should be reduced to reflect the cash actually received from the sale. This reduction is reflected in an account called Sales Discounts.

A company sold $15,000 of merchandise subject to terms of 2/10, *n/30*. At the time of the sale, the following entry would be made:

Accounts Receivable	$15,000	
Sales Revenue		$15,000

If the customer does not pay until the 30th day, the net amount—$15,000—must be remitted. The company would record this receipt as follows:

Cash	$15,000	
Accounts Receivable		$15,000

However, if the customer pays within the discount period, $14,700 will be received by the company [$15,000 - (0.02 \times 15,000)$]. Thus cash of $14,700 must be recorded, because it was received. Accounts Receivable must be reduced by $15,000 since this debt was satisfied by the customer's payment. The difference is $300 and it represents a reduction in sales revenue because of a cash discount. To update this information, Sales Discounts is debited and subsequently used as an offset against revenue in the income statement. The entry appears as follows:

Cash	$14,700	
Sales Discounts	300	
Accounts Receivable		$15,000

Sales discounts will be reported on the income statement as a reduction in sales revenue to arrive at net sales. This information is included in the report to provide interested users with some indication of the cost of the firm's credit terms.

Most of the income statement is generally devoted to information concerning the normal, ongoing operations of the entity, as opposed to special or secondary items. This follows from an assumption that the ongoing operations provide the basis for the long-term success or failure of the enterprise. The results of ongoing operations are presented in the operating section of the income statement that ends with the calculation of net income from operations.

Other Income Elements

The next part of the statement is the nonoperating section, which presents other income and other expense. These items summarize revenues and expenses resulting from the secondary activities of the firm.

Other Revenue. The other revenue section of the income statement lists revenue, net of related expenses, resulting from nonoperating transactions. That is, the total received from these activities is reduced by expenses relating to them and the result is reported. This category often includes interest income, gains on sales of plant and equipment, and rental income. Several revenue and expense accounts may be summarized in a single disclosure of other revenue.

Other Expense. Like other revenue, other expense relates to nonoperating items. This section of the income statement summarizes expenses or losses incurred, net of any related revenue. Again, the total loss, less any related revenue is reported. Examples of other expenses include interest expense from financing operations and losses on the disposal of plant and equipment items.

Extraordinary Items. Sometimes, firms will add a section to the income statement after the other income and other expense section. *Extraordinary gains or losses* are set out to inform statement users of highly unusual events that occurred during the period and influenced net income.

Accountants use a twofold test to determine if a transaction is extraordinary:

1. *Unusual nature.* The event or transaction must be clearly abnormal and unrelated to the ordinary and typical activities of the entity.
2. *Infrequency of occurrence.* The event or transaction should not be reasonably expected to recur in the future.

These criteria establish parameters on the types of items subject to classification as extraordinary.

Normally, losses relating to fire, flood, earthquakes, or other acts of nature are extraordinary. Likewise, unexpected gains, such as the discovery of oil under farm land, can qualify as extraordinary items.

An Illustration

To review the process of revenue realization and disclosure, consider the following transactions of Save-T Stores, Inc.:

1. Cash sales of $12,400 were made.
2. Credit sales of $18,200 subject to trade discounts of 20 and 10 percent were made.
3. $8,300 of the credit invoices were collected.
4. Credit sales of $9,800 were made and were invoiced with terms of 2/10, *n*/30.
   (a) $5,200 of these invoices were paid within 10 days.
   (b) $4,600 of these invoices were paid after the discount period.
5. Merchandise that was sold for $800 cash was returned.
6. Rent of $1,000 on a vacant lot was collected.
7. Store equipment that cost $1,800 was deemed inappropriate and was resold one week later for $1,400.
8. Merchandise that cost $2,000 was destroyed in an uninsured fire.

Recording the Information. Journal entries for these transactions are presented in Exhibit 5-2. The transaction numbers relate to the explanations presented below.

1. Cash sales meet the realization criteria and will lead to recording revenue.
2. Revenue may also be realized on credit sales. The amount of the sale is deemed to be net of applicable trade discounts. In this case that value is $13,104 \ (18,200 - (0.20 \times 18,200) = 14,650 - (0.10 \times 14,560) = 13,104)$.
3. The collection of credit sales does not affect revenue. The collection transaction would be recorded as it does affect two asset accounts.
4. Credit sales again give rise to the realization of revenue. These sales may be recorded at their gross value and adjusted later for any cash discounts that are taken.
4a. Invoices paid within the discount period are reduced by 2 percent. Thus, the firm will receive $5,096 in cash ($5,200 - (0.02 \times 5,200)$) as

EXHIBIT 5-2
RECORDING REVENUE ITEMS

1.	Cash	$12,400	
	Sales Revenue		$12,400
2.	Accounts Receivable	13,104	
	Sales Revenue		13,104
3.	Cash	8,300	
	Accounts Receivable		8,300
4.	Accounts Receivable	9,800	
	Sales Revenue		9,800
4a.	Cash	5,096	
	Sales Discounts	104	
	Accounts Receivable		5,200
4b.	Cash	4,600	
	Accounts Receivable		4,600
5.	Sales Returns and Allowances	800	
	Cash		800
6.	Cash	1,000	
	Rent Revenue		1,000
7.	Cash	1,400	
	Loss on Sale of Equipment	400	
	Equipment		1,800
8.	Fire Loss	2,000	
	Merchandise Inventory		2,000

full payment. Sales discounts of $104 are recognized and will subsequently be used as a revenue reduction.

4b. Payments made after 10 days are not subject to discount. Revenue is unaffected by this transaction.

5. Merchandise returns are set out in a special account. This entry will reduce sales revenue to the extent of the returned merchandise.

6. The receipt of rent gives rise to a revenue item. Since rental income is not a part of the firm's operations, it will be disclosed as other revenue.

7. The sale of store equipment also falls outside the normal operations. The resulting loss will be reported as another expense item. Other expenses relate to potentially recurring events that are not part of the normal business operations.

8. A fire loss is generally an extraordinary event. This loss will be reported as an extraordinary item.

Reporting the Results. The above transactions relate primarily to items of revenue for Save-T Stores, Inc. The partial income statement shown in Exhibit 5-3, below, has omitted the expense elements and focused on revenue.

The revenue elements included in the income statement were derived

EXHIBIT 5-3
PARTIAL INCOME STATEMENT

SAVE-T STORES, INC.
Income Statement
For the Year Ended December 31, 19X3

Sales:			
Sales Revenue		$35,304	
Less: Sales Returns and Allowances	$800		
Sales Discounts	104	904	
Net Sales			$34,400
Cost of Goods Sold			XX
Gross Margin on Sales			XX
Operating Expenses			XX
Net Income from Operations			XX
Other Income:			
Rental Income		1,000	
Other Expense:			
Sale of Equipment		400	600
Net Income Before Taxes			XX
Income Tax Expense			XX
Net Income Before Extraordinary Items			XX
Extraordinary Loss:			
Fire loss		2,000	
Income Tax Effect		XX	XX
Net Income			XX

from the preceding transactions. The account balances resulting from these transactions provided the data for inclusion in the report.

Forms of the Income Statement

The purpose of the income statement is to convey meaningful economic information to users of the statement. To provide for consistency among firms and organizations, the income statement generally is laid out, or arranged in a predetermined form. However, the accountant does have the option to alter the statement to meet particular reporting needs.

The general format of the income statement follows the logic of computing net income; revenues, expenses, and income are reported in sequence. The statements illustrated in this chapter follow a *multiple-step form.* This multiple-step income statement has two main characteristics:

1. Operating and nonoperating results are separated and shown in different parts of the statement.

EXHIBIT 5-4
SINGLE-STEP INCOME STATEMENT

MORRIS MERCHANDISING COMPANY Income Statement For the Year Ended December 31, 19X0	
Sales Revenue	$401,300
Other Revenue	7,300
Total Revenue	408,600
Expenses	
Cost of Goods Sold	248,200
Selling Expenses	47,300
Administrative Expenses	42,100
Interest Expense	5,100
Total Expenses	342,700
Net Income Before Taxes	65,900
Income Tax Expense	26,400
Net Income	$ 39,500
Earnings Per Share	$ 5,10

2. Expenses are separated and classified by function, such as cost of goods sold, selling expense, and administrative expense.

The *single-step income statement* uses revenues and expenses as major classifications but does not provide the detail found in the multiple-step form. Exhibit 5-4 recasts the Morris Merchandising Company's income statement (Exhibit 5-1) in a single-step format. Recognize that the amount of net income remains the same; only the amount of disclosure and the arrangement have changed.

Other variations of the income statement are prepared for special needs. A condensed income statement may be prepared by using just the major captions of the multiple-step statement and eliminating the subclassifications of the expense data. A divisionalized income statement will use multiple columns and separate income data by various segments of the organization. The accountant's judgment must be used to select the proper reporting format.

Summary

There are various ways to define and measure business income. Accountants use a historical cost approach and relate revenues and expenses to derive periodic income for a business organization. Income is reported on the income statement, which most businesses must prepare regularly. The income statement sets out a variety of revenue and expense information. The format of the statement depends on the final use for which it is intended.

Income measurement is based on matching revenues and expenses. Revenue is recognized on the income statement after it is deemed to be realized. Realization takes place when an exchange has occurred and the related earning process is essentially complete. The matching process identifies items of expense that are related to the revenues.

Sales revenue results from an organization selling a product or service. Revenue may be reduced if some of a customer's purchase is returned for credit. Trade discounts and cash discounts will also reduce the amount of net revenue during a period.

In the multiple-step form of the income statement, operating income is separated from nonoperating income and expense elements. The goal of this disclosure is to provide users and analysts with additional information on the source of income. Extraordinary items, which are unusual and occur infrequently, are disclosed in another, separate section of the income statement.

In recent years, many business analysts have placed significant importance on the income statement and its contents. The information derived from this statement has profound effects on stock market prices, loan agreements, and employee wage settlements. All accountants, business managers, stockholders, and interested parties must be familar with this statement and its contents.

Income determination begins with the realization process. Revenue, then, is a vital element in the process. This chapter provided the basis for revenue measurement. In the next chapter, the expense elements of income are considered.

A Supplementary Discussion: Special Journals and Subsidiary Ledgers

The accounting system must be effective and efficient to be of maximum service to an organization. An effective accounting system processes all data of accounting relevance into reports that are both useful and that conform with generally accepted accounting principles. Efficiency is concerned with the relationship between inputs and outputs; system efficiency relates to the manner in which tasks are performed and the methods employed to process data. Special journals and subsidiary ledgers can be integrated into the accounting data processing sequence to increase processing efficiency.

Subsidiary Ledgers

Subsidiary ledgers are books of secondary entry composed of a group of similar accounts. For example, a group of accounts receivable listing the names of each credit customer would comprise the Accounts Receivable subsidiary ledger. Subsidiary ledgers are designed to maintain detailed information about any general class of accounts. Subsidiary ledgers can be created to maintain detailed information on any asset, liability, owners' equity, revenue, or expense account. The listing of amounts owed to trade creditors would represent the Accounts Payable subsidiary ledger, while a listing of stockholders' equity interests would represent the Common Stock subsidiary ledger. The subsidiary Sales Revenue ledger might maintain a separate account for each sales department, cash register, or general class of merchandise.

Subsidiary ledgers are linked to the general ledger through corresponding _control accounts._ A control account is established to represent each subsidiary ledger. The control account maintains a summary balance equal to the sum of the individual balances in the subsidiary ledger. For example, the Accounts Receivable Control account will have a balance equal to the sum of the balances of accounts contained in the Accounts Receivable subsidiary ledger. Whenever a subsidiary ledger is established, one control account is substituted in the general ledger for many accounts. The general ledger is composed of control accounts that provide summary information used in preparing financial statements, while the subsidiary ledgers provide detailed information needed in day-to-day operations of the business.

Special Journals

Special journals are books of original entry used to record information about a single type of recurring transaction. Sales journals, cash receipts journals, purchases journals, and cash disbursement journals are examples of special journals.

All transactions can be recorded in a general journal. However, general journals are organized so that each and every entry must be individually posted to the general ledger accounts. In contrast, special journals do not require that each and every entry be individually posted. Furthermore, special journals provide for a separation of duties so that several people can perform the journalizing task at one time. Task simplification through the use of special journals allows specialization, which in turn encourages greater speed and accuracy for greater control. The increased speed, accuracy, and control are each part of the increased efficiency associated with use of special journals and subsidiary ledgers.

Sales Journals. The simplest form of a sales journal only records transactions involving the sale of merchandise on account. This type of transaction is characterized by entries to two accounts:

1. A debit (increase) in Accounts Receivable.
2. A credit (increase) in Sales Revenue.

The design of a sales journal is illustrated in Exhibit 5-5. Journal columns are used to record information on the date, invoice (sales slip) number, customer name, and dollar amount, all of which can be obtained from the sales slip. In nonelectronic accounting systems, sales clerks batch the sales slips and then transmit a batch to the accounting department, where entries are made in the appropriate columns of the sales journal. Advanced Electronic systems can generate a sales journal entry automatically when the sales slip is created by the terminal at the point of sale (a posterminal).

The "Post. ref." (posting reference) column of the sales journal is used to reflect

EXHIBIT 5-5
SALES JOURNAL

Date	Invoice No.	Account Debited	Post. Ref.	Acct. Rec. Dr. Sales Rev. Cr.
6/1	213	Kaupp, Inc.	X	$ 295
6/2	214	Markell Company	X	1,025
6/2	215	Tiani & Minsley	X	65
6/2	216	R & R Construction	X	175
6/3	217	Kaupp, Inc.	X	950
6/3	218	R & R Construction	X	640
6/4	219	Frank Rogg	X	495
6/4	220	Tiani & Minsley	X	895
6/5	221	J. Knott, Inc.	X	1,200
6/5	222	Kaupp, Inc.	X	105
				$5,845

the posting activity that transcribes data from the journal to the ledger. Individual customer account numbers may be listed in the "Post. ref." column as entries are posted to the individual customer's account. These numbers serve as a control reference to ensure that entries have been made to the correct account. Alternately, a "X" or check mark may be placed in the "Post. ref." column simply to indicate that a posting has occurred. Some electronic accounting systems automatically post credit sales to the customer's account when the sales slip is created by the terminal at the point of sale. In nonelectronic systems, the posting must be done as a separate operation.

Dollar amounts in the last column of the sales journal are periodically totaled, and the column total is posted to both the Accounts Receivable Control account and to the Sales Revenue account. Individual transaction entries are not posted to these accounts, only the column totals. Thus, the credit to Sales Revenue will be reflected as one entry rather than as several entries.

While the Accounts Receivable Control account will reflect the summarized debit, individual customer account balances must be maintained.

Information from the previous sales journal are posted to individual accounts in the Accounts Receivable subsidiary ledger. The total of these accounts equals the total in the Accounts Receivable account appearing in the general ledger. These relationships are shown in Exhibit 5-6.

Information from a source document (Sales Invoice) is entered into the special sales journal. Individual account data from this journal is posted to corresponding accounts in the subsidiary accounts receivable ledger. Page totals from the sales journal are posted to the Sales Revenue and Accounts Receivable Control accounts in the general ledger. The total balance in the subsidiary ledger accounts should equal the balance in the general ledger Accounts Receivable control account.

EXHIBIT 5-6

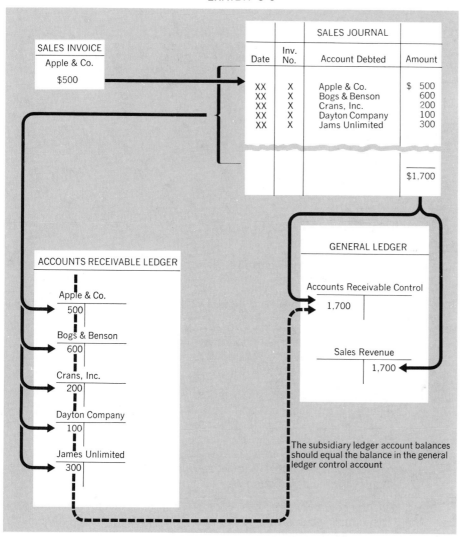

Cash Receipts Journal

The cash receipts journal is designed to expedite the process of recording cash receipt transactions. All cash receipts will result in a debit to, or an increase in, the account cash. The special journal provides for the more common types of cash receipt, including cash sales and the collection of accounts receivable.

A cash receipts journal sample is shown below.*

CASH RECEIPTS JOURNAL

Date	Account Credited	Post. Reference	Sales Credit	Accounts Receivable Credit	Sales Discount Debit	Sundry Credit	Cash Debit
6/15	Markell Company	X		$1,025			$1,025
	Sales	X	$ 650				650
	Kaupp, Inc.	X		105	2		103
6/16	Sales	X	725				725
6/17	Purchase/Returns	15				50	50
	Sales	X	810				810
6/18	Supplies	28				1,000	1,000
6/19	Sales	X	450				450
			$2,635	$1,130	$2	$1,050	$4,813

The recording process can best be explained by analyzing some selected transactions:

June 15   Markell Company. The Markell Company paid an account receivable resulting in a debit to Cash and a credit to Accounts Receivable.

June 15   Sales. Cash sales are recorded by a debit to Cash and a credit to Sales.

June 15   Kaupp, Inc. Kaupp, Inc., paid an account receivable within the company's discount period and deducted $2 from their payment. The transaction is recorded by debiting Cash and Sales Discounts and crediting Accounts receivable.

June 17   Purchases. Your company returned some merchandise that did not meet your specifications and the seller granted you a cash refund. The Purchase account (account number 15) is credited, and Cash is debited. Because the special journal did not specifically provide for this transaction, the credit is entered in the Sundry, or miscellaneous, column. The posting reference column shows the specific number of the account to be credited.

Periodically, the columns of the cash receipts journal are footed. The totals for Sales, Sales Discounts, and Cash are posted directly to the general ledger. Accounts Receivable totals are posted to the general ledger control account, and specific accounts are credited in the subsidiary ledger. Sundry amounts are posted individually to the accounts involved in the general ledger.

* The specific form of special journals may be altered to fit specific circumstances. For example, the cash receipts journal could be reorganized so that the debits—Cash and Sales Discount—appear first, followed by columns for the credits—Sales, Accounts Receivable, and Sundry.

Other Special Journals

Purchases journals are structured in a similar manner to the sales journal. The goal is to recognize that most purchase transactions require similar entries. The purchases journal normally provides for a credit to Accounts Payable and a debit to the Purchases and/or the Supplies accounts.

The construction of *cash disbursement* journals parallel that of cash receipts journals. Normally, these journals provide for a credit to the Cash account, a credit to the Purchase Discount account, and a debit to Accounts Payable.

Although some special journals and subsidiary ledgers are used more in practice than others, there is no set number or format that should be employed. The purpose of both special journals and subsidiary ledgers is to improve the efficiency of the recording process. In each particular organization, the accountant must decide which special journals and subsidiary ledgers fit the information flows and benefit the data processing effort.

The design of special journals and subsidiary ledgers is not fixed. Formats may be altered to fit any enterprise. While the format of special journals and subsidiary ledgers may vary from organization to organization, the ultimate purpose of these devices is to increase the efficiency of the accounting system.

Key Terms

Matching
Realization principle
Source Documents
Sales returns and allowances
Trade discounts
Cash discounts
Extraordinary gains
Extraordinary losses
Multiple-step form
Single-step income statement

Questions

1. How does the economist measure income?

2. Describe the total venture concept of income measurement. Why is this concept not useful for periodic financial reporting?

3. Explain the matching concept.

4. Relate the terms "revenue" and "expense" to the conventional income determination process.

5. How is accounting income measured?

6. What is meant by the realization principle?

7. Explain what is meant by the term, "sales returns and allowances." How are they reported in the financial statements?

8. Explain the difference between trade discount and cash discounts.

9. What is an extraordinary item? What are some examples of extraordinary items, and how are they reported in the income statement?

10. Describe the difference between the multiple-step and the single-step income statement? Will the net income figure be the same using the two different types of statement?

11. A company sells a product with a list price of $10,000 subject to a trade discount of 10 percent and terms of "2/10, n/30." What amount of revenue should be recorded on the sale, and how should the transaction be accounted for if the customer pays within the discount period?

12. Define the term, "gross margin on sales".

13. What items of income might be reported on the income statement as "other income?"

Exercises

1. Prepare the journal entries to record the following transactions for King Co.:
(a) Sold a product for $500, and the customer paid cash.
(b) Sold a product to a customer for $600 on account.
(c) Collected the account receivable from the customer, described in (b) above.
(d) Received an advance payment of $300 from a customer for services to be performed in the future.

2. The Jones Co. sold merchandise to a customer for $4,000 on January 15 with terms of "2/10, n/30". The customer returned a portion of the goods on January 17 with a cost of $500. The customer received credit from Jones Co. for these goods, which were damaged in shipment. On January 23, the customer paid Jones Co. the balance of the account receivable. Prepare the journal entries to record the above events, and show how the sales revenue from these transactions would be reflected in the income statement.

3. The Longhorn Company sold merchandise with a list price of $1,000 on April 10. Trade discounts of 20 and 10 percent were allowed, and the credit terms were 2/10, n/30. On April 12, the customer requested and received on allowance for $200 (list price) of merchandise that had been destroyed in transit. The company received full payment from the customer on April 18.
Record all the entries required on the books of Longhorn Co.

4. The following account balances after adjustment were taken from the books of the Phillips Co. at December 31, 19X0:

Sales Revenue	50,000
Cost of Goods Sold	25,000
Rental Revenue	2,000
Sales Returns and Allowances	3,000
Selling Expenses	10,000
Administrative Expenses	5,000
Interest Expense	2,500
Income Tax Expense	3,000
Sales Discounts	1,000

From the above information, prepare a single-step income statement.

5. Refer to the information in Exercise 4 above and prepare a multiple-step income statement.

6. A company sold merchandise with a list price of $20,000. The customer was granted trade discounts of 25, 20, and 10 percent, and the cash discount terms are 2/15, n/60. How much will the company receive if the account is paid within 15 days? How much will the company receive if the account is paid after 15 days?

7. Listed below is selected information from the accounts of Richards Co. at December 1, 19X0.

Inventory, 1/1/X0	$10,000
Sales Revenues	200,000
Purchases	100,000
Sales Returns and Allowances	5,000
Sales Discounts	4,000

Inventory at December 31 was $12,000. Compute the following, as shown in Exhibit 5-1:
(a) Net sales.
(b) Cost of goods sold.
(c) Gross margin on sales.

8. On October 1, the following entry was made to record the sale of merchandise on account:

Accounts Receivable   1,000
     Sales Revenue   1,000
To record a sale on which the terms were 2/10, n/60.

Give the necessary journal entry if the customer paid on (1) October 9, (2) October 27.

9. On April 1, 19X0, the Alexander Co. sold merchandise to a customer with a $10,000 list price. The terms of the sale provided trade discounts of 20 and 10 percent and a cash discount of 2/10, n/30. On April 5, the customer returned $100 (at list price) of the merchandise that had been damaged in transit. The remaining balance was paid by the customer on April 10. Prepare the journal entries required on the books of Alexander Co.

10. Provide the missing amounts in the four income statements listed below.

	A	B	C	D
Sales Revenue	100,000	100,000	100,000	100,000
Sales Returns and Allowances	5,000	6,000	6,000	6,000
Sales Discounts	———	3,000	4,000	4,000
Net Sales	92,000	———	———	90,000
Beginning Inventory	———	15,000	12,000	5,000
Purchases	60,000	———	50,000	———
Cost of Goods Available to Sell	70,000	80,000	———	———
Ending Inventory	———	20,000	———	6,000
Cost of Goods Sold	58,000	———	52,000	———
Gross Margin on Sales	———	———	———	22,000
Operating Expenses	20,000	20,000	———	———
Net Income from Operations	———	———	13,000	2,000
Other Revenues (Expense)	(4,000)	5,000	0	2,000
Net Income Before Extraordinary Item	———	———	———	———
Extraordinary Gain (Loss)	(2,000)	0	5,000	———
Net Income Before Taxes	———	———	———	———
Tax Expense	4,000	2,000	———	0
Net Income (Loss)	———	———	8,000	(5,000)

11. Classify the following revenue items as (1) operating income, expense, or loss, (2) other income, expense, or loss, or (3) extraordinary income or loss, for purposes of presentation on the income statement.
(a) An uninsured fire loss.
(b) Interest income to a bank.
(c) Interest income to a shoe shop.
(d) Gain on the sale of a machine recognized by a manufacturer who uses the machine in a trade or business.
(e) Sale of a machine by the manufacturer of the machine who sells it as inventory.
(f) Rental income recognized by a firm that rented a portion of an unused warehouse temporarily.
(g) Income from sale of groceries in a supermarket.

12. Prepare a partial income statement similar to Exhibit 5-3, to report the following events for Hayes Manufacturing Company for the year ended March 31, 19X6:
(a) Revenue from sales of manufactured goods, $78,520; sales returns and allowances, $2,650; sales discounts, $610.
(b) Interest income, $350.
(c) Rental income from renting unneeded warehouse space, $2,000; related expenses, $240.
(d) Sales of equipment at a loss, $300.
(e) Loss from fire, $9,000; insurance recovery, $7,800.

13. Brandon Company sold an item of inventory with a list price of $1,200 on November 1, 19X7. In each independent case below, determine (1) the amount to be recorded as a sale, and (2) the appropriate amount of cash to be received.

Case	Trade Discount	Credit Terms	Payment Date
(a)	10%	2/10, n/30	November 9
(b)	10%, 10%	n/30	November 26
(c)	10%, 5%	2/15, n/30	November 18
(d)	30%	3/10, n/30	November 8
(e)	5%, 10%, 10%	n/30	November 30

14. Gross billings for merchandise sold by Baker Company to customers last year amounted to $5,260,000; sales returns and allowances reduced the amounts owed by $160,000. How much were net sales last year for Baker Company? (AICPA adapted).

15. Management is considering a change in the discount terms offered by the firm. One proposal is to change the firm's credit terms from 2/10, n/60 to 2/10, n/30. If adopted, what effects will this change probably have on the firm's average collection and sales? (CMA adapted.)

16. Tackle Company sells football helmets. In 19X9 Tackle discovered a defect in the helmets that will lead to future lawsuits if the helmets are sold. The current Inventory balance of helmets is $900,000. Should the $900,000 of helmets be reflected on the income statement or on the balance sheet at the end of 19X9? Explain.

Problems

1. The following information was reflected in the accounts of Welker Co. on December 31, 19X0:

Sales Revenue	$100,000
Purchases	40,000
Sales Discounts	1,000
Selling Expenses	17,000
Inventory, January 1	6,000
Administrative Expenses	15,000
Interest Expense	2,000
Sales Returns and Allowances	3,000
Rental Revenue	4,000
Income Tax Expense	8,000
Fire Loss (Extraordinary Item)	10,000

From the periodic physical inventory, it was determined that the ending inventory amounted to $8,000.

REQUIRED:
Based on the above information, prepare a multiple-step income statement for Welker Co.

2. The following list of transactions was selected from the records of Drexel Co. for the year ended December 31, 19X0.
   (a) Cash sales of $55,000 were made.

(b) Credit sales of $40,000 were made subject to trade discounts of 20 and 10 percent with credit terms of 2/10, *n*/30.

(c) One-half of the invoices from (b) were collected within 10 days.

(d) One-half of the invoices from (b) were collected after the discount period.

(e) Rent of $1,200 on office space was collected. The rent was for the period from January 1 to December 31, 19X0.

(f) Purchased merchandise for $40,000 cash.

(g) Credit sales of $5,000 were made with credit terms of 2/10, *n*/30.

(h) The customer from (g) requested and received an allowance of $500 on merchandise damaged in transit.

(i) The customer from (g) paid the remainder of the account within the discount period.

(j) Land that was purchased for $10,000 as a possible building site was sold for $11,000.

(k) Equipment that cost $1,500 was destroyed in an uninsured fire one week after it was purchased.

REQUIRED:

(a) Prepare the journal entries to record the above transactions.

(b) Prepare an income statement for the year ended December 31, 19X0, using multiple-step form (see Exhibit 5-1) and assuming the following information.

Inventory, 1/1/X0	$7,000
Inventory, 12/31/X0	5,000
Operating Expenses	24,000
Income Tax Expense	10,000

3. The following trial balance after adjustment taken from the ledger of Moore Co. at December 31, 19X6:

THE MOORE COMPANY
Trial Balance After Adjustment
December 31, 19X6

	Debits	Credits
Notes Payable		$ 60,000
Retained Earnings		52,200
Cash	$ 11,000	
Land	10,000	
Interest Revenue		3,000
General Administrative Expenses	12,400	
Sales Discounts	11,700	
Purchases	271,000	
Accounts Receivable	45,200	
Common Stock		175,000
Interest Expense	6,000	
Inventory, January 1, 19X6	42,000	
Telephone, Office	7,100	
Office and Officers' Salaries	95,000	
Accounts Payable		9,000
Notes Receivable	30,000	
Sales Salaries and Commissions	51,000	
Income Tax Expense	20,000	
Prepaid Insurance	1,600	
Extraordinary Loss	40,000	
Building and Equipment	200,000	
Advertising	12,000	
Supplies Expense	700	
Rental Revenue		24,000
General Selling Expenses	23,000	
Sales		530,000
Accumulated Depreciation		42,000
Interest Payable		500
Sales Returns and Allowances	6,000	
	895,700	895,700

The inventory on hand December 31, 19X6, had a cost of $63,000.

REQUIRED:
From the above data, prepare an income statement using (a) the single-step form, and (b) the multiple-step form.

4. Some account balances of the Hanson Corporation at December 31, 19X5, are presented below:

	Debit	Credit
Sales		$1,200,000
Sales Returns and Allowances	$ 20,000	
Purchases	600,000	
Flood Loss (Extraordinary Item)	50,000	
Loss on Sales of Equipment	5,000	
Sales Office Salaries	25,000	
Salesmen's Commissions	75,000	
Travel Expense	15,000	
Interest Revenue		6,000
Conventions and Entertainment (Selling)	11,000	
Telephone and Telegraph—Sales Department	7,300	
Depreciation of Sales Equipment	3,400	
Miscellaneous Selling Expenses	2,100	
Officers' Salaries	50,000	
Administrative Salaries and Wages	32,000	
Office Supplies Expense	3,300	
Telephone and Telegraph—Administration	2,500	
Depreciation of Office Furniture and Equipment	2,700	
Miscellaneous Office Expenses	4,100	
Discounts on Sales	31,000	
Rental Income		12,000
Interest Expense	9,000	
Income Tax Expense	135,000	
Merchandise Inventory—December 31, 19X4	65,000	

The merchandise inventory at December 31, 19X5, amounted to $73,000.

REQUIRED:
(a) Prepare an income statement for the year ended December 31, 19X5, using the multiple-step form.
(b) Prepare an income statement for the year ended December 31, 19X5, using the single-step form.

5. The Kingsbery Co. had the following transactions for the year ended December 31, 19X3:
(a) Cash Sales of $100,000 were made.
(b) Land, which was purchased for $25,000 as a possible building site, was sold for $28,000.
(c) Cash Sales of $35,000 were made.
(d) Credit sales of $25,000 were made subject to trade discounts of 20 and 5 percent with credit terms 1/10, n/30.
(e) Building in South America that cost $21,000 was totally destroyed by an earthquake one day after it was constructed. Unfortunately, the building was not insured.

(f) All but $5,000 of the net sales in (d) were collected in less than 10 days.

(g) The rest of the credit sales were collected before the 30 days was up.

(h) A company leased from Kingsbery the mineral royalties on the land in South America for $20,000 for the year of 19X3, and paid in cash.

(i) Merchandise purchased for $40,000 on account.

REQUIRED:

(a) Prepare journal entries to record the above transactions.

(b) Prepare an income statement for the year ended December 31, 19X3, using the multiple-step form and assuming the following:

Inventory 1/1/X3	$120,000
Inventory 12/31/X3	60,000
Administrative Expense	19,000
Operating Expenses	28,000
Selling Expenses	14,000

6. Morris Sales Company's account balances are shown below for the year ended December 31, 19X1:

Sales	$620,000
Sales Returns and Allowances	18,500
Sales Discounts	7,400
Inventory (1/1/X1)	59,000
Purchases	405,000
Sales Salaries and Commissions	71,000
Advertising Expenses	18,000
Administrative Salaries	38,000
Administrative Supplies Expenses	9,700
Miscellaneous Administrative	
Expenses	8,400
Interest Income	2,000

Other Data: Ending inventory was found to be $91,400.

REQUIRED:

Prepare a single-step income statement for Morris Sales Company.

7. A portion of the worksheet for Webb Company is shown below for calendar year 19X8.

| | Income Statement | | Balance Sheet | |
	Debit	Credit	Debit	Credit
Owner's Equity				$62,000
Sales		$108,000		
Sales Returns and Allowances	2,600			
Sales Discounts	1,050			
Cost of Goods Sold	42,500			
Wages Expense	21,000			
Selling Expenses	12,600			
Utilities Expense	1,900			
Depreciation Expense	16,200			
Loss on Sale of Equipment	800			
Loss on Fire	5,000			

REQUIRED:

1. Prepare a single-step income statement for Webb Company for calendar year 19X8.
2. Prepare the necessary closing entries in general journal format.

8. The unadjusted trial balance of Dill Service Company on December 31, 19X4, is shown below:

DILL SERVICE COMPANY
Trial Balance
December 31, 19X4

	Debit	Credit
Cash	$ 6,000	$
Accounts Receivable	8,200	
Supplies	14,200	
Prepaid Insurance	1,200	
Equipment	16,500	
Accumulated Depreciation		3,200
Accounts Payable		4,700
Owner's Equity		20,100
Sales		103,000
Sales Discounts	1,000	
Wage and Salary Expense	59,000	
Rental Expense	12,000	
Insurance Expense	1,800	
Utilities Expense	2,100	
Advertising Expense	9,000	
	$131,000	$131,000

These additional financial data are also available:

(a) An Inventory of supplies showed only $3,600 on hand at year-end.

(b) Depreciation of $2,400 was unrecorded at year-end.

(c) The insurance shown as prepaid on the trial balance was a 12-month fire insurance policy dated April 1, 19X4.

(d) Wages of $1,400 were earned by employees but not paid at year-end.

REQUIRED:

1. Prepare a worksheet for the Dill Company for December 31, 19X4.

2. From the income statement columns of the worksheet, prepare a multiple-step income statement in good form.

□ 6
THE INCOME STATEMENT: EXPENSES

□ OBJECTIVES

AFTER STUDYING THIS CHAPTER, YOU SHOULD BE ABLE TO DO THE FOLLOWING:

1. PREPARE A COMPLETE, DETAILED INCOME STATEMENT.
2. CONTRAST THE PERPETUAL AND PERIODIC INVENTORY SYSTEMS.
3. RECORD INVENTORY DATA.
4. ESTIMATE UNCOLLECTABLE ACCOUNTS RECEIVABLE AND BAD DEBT EXPENSE.
5. CONSTRUCT A RETAINED EARNINGS STATEMENT.

Virtually all income-producing activity requires some consumption of resources. Accountants maintain that, to the extent these resources have an economic value, their cost must be included in the calculation of income. Therefore, revenue is reduced by related expenses, or the cost of resources consumed, or because it no longer has the future service potential to derive net income.

Business operations require a variety of expense items. The expenses related to operating a movie theater, for example, include employee salaries, film rentals, heat, power, maintenance, janitorial services, and the use of the building, its furnishings, and projection equipment. Some of these expense elements are more clearly identified and quantified than others.

If monthly income is to be calculated, the accountant can usually determine the salary, film rental, heat, power, and janitorial costs that were incurred during the month. These items were also consumed during the month, so they can be expensed. The use of the building, furnishings, and projection equipment also represents an expense to be charged against the month's operations. However, it is difficult to determine how much of the $2,000,000 cost of a theater building was used during a month. The accountant must determine *which* resources were consumed, the *extent* to which they were consumed, and their *value* as a part of the income determination process.

This chapter focuses on some major elements of expense as they relate to income measurement. Expenses must be properly measured and matched with reported revenues for income to be accurately determined.

Cost of Goods Sold

Income statements that follow a functional classification begin by isolating the expense of products sold during the period. In most manufacturing and merchandising operations, this cost of products sold is a significant expense item. As products are purchased or manufactured by a firm, their costs are accumulated in an *inventory* account. There are a variety of techniques available for determining the cost of inventory. Many of these are considered in Chapter 8. As inventory items are sold or consumed, their cost flows as an expense to the income statement and is reported as cost of goods sold.

Most businesses will begin a period with some quantity of merchandise on hand. This is termed the *beginning inventory*. Throughout the period, additional quantities of merchandise will be purchased (or manufactured) and added to the inventory.

The beginning inventory plus the purchases represents the amount of merchandise *available for sale* during the period. This is the most that is possible for the firm to sell. Typically, sales will be less than the total quantity available and the firm will end the period with remaining merchandise, termed the *ending inventory*. Logically, the ending inventory of one period becomes the beginning inventory of the next period.

These relationships are used in calculating the cost of goods sold:

> Cost of Beginning Inventory
> +Cost of Purchases (Net of Returns)
> =Cost of Goods Available for Sale
> −Cost of Ending Inventory
> =Cost of Goods Sold

Cost of goods sold results from deducting the ending inventory from the cost of goods available for sale; items available for sale will either be sold during the period or will remain at the end of the period.

If a firm began the period with an inventory valued at $125,000, purchased an additional $319,000 of merchandise during the period but returned $1,000 as damaged and ended the period with $98,000 of remaining inventory, its cost of goods sold is $345,000, calculated as follows:

> $125,000 Cost of Beginning Inventory
> +318,000 Cost of Purchases (Net of Returns)
> =443,000 Cost of Goods Available for Sale
> − 98,000 Cost of Ending Inventory
> =345,000 Cost of Goods Sold

Cost of goods sold is reported as an expense in the income statement. Ending inventory is an asset and will appear on the balance sheet. In this example, $98,000 is reported as the inventory value at the end of the period. It is also the beginning inventory value for the next accounting period.

Statement Presentation. The cost of goods sold calculation is often included in the income statement. This provides the reader with an overview of inventory and product cost flows during the period. Cost of goods sold is deducted from net sales revenue to determine the gross margin on sales.

Net sales		$1,945,000
Cost of Goods Sold:		
Beginning Inventory	$ 113,000	
Purchases	1,206,000	
Cost of Goods Available for Sale	1,319,000	
Less: Ending Inventory	152,000	
Cost of Goods Sold		1,167,000
Gross Margin on Sales		$ 778,000

The *gross margin* on sales is the difference between the net sales revenue and the cost of the merchandise that was sold during the period. It reflects the average markup applied to the merchandise to derive the sales price. In the preceding example, the gross margin in percentage terms was 40 percent of the selling price, calculated as follows:

$$\text{Gross Margin Percentage} = \frac{\text{Gross Margin}}{\text{Net Sales Revenue}}$$

$$= \frac{\$ \ 778,000}{\$1,945,000}$$

$$= 0.40 \text{ or } 40\%$$

Thus, 60 cents of each sales dollar generated by the firm was used to acquire the merchandise that was sold. The remaining 40 cents, or the gross margin, is available to provide for the operating and administrative expenses and for profit.

Inventory Systems The Cost of Goods Sold calculation is dependent upon the ending inventory and the purchases made during the period. There are two major systems that can be used to measure inventories—periodic and perpetual. A well-designed inventory system will provide for valuing the inventory and for effective inventory control.

Control ensures that proper valuations, measurements, and determinations have been made relative to the inventory. This ranges from monitoring inventory levels for decision-making purposes to verifying the existence of inventory items through periodic physical counts. Inventory controls require adequate records and information flows about inventory levels and certain physical safeguards relating to the custody of the items. Accounting systems focus on the information flows.

Periodic Measurement. Periodic inventory systems rely on physical counts of merchandise to determine the ending inventory value. On a regular basis, usually annually, the inventory quantity is determined through actual observation. The number of units observed during the physical count is multiplied by the firm's purchase cost per unit to determine the inventory value. This value becomes the ending inventory and is used in calculating the cost of goods sold.

Under a periodic system, the inventory value for accounting purposes is only available after the physical count. Many businesses that require inventory information for decision-making activities will supplement the accounting records with other inventory data such as: estimations of quantities sold, ordering models, and point-of-sale data accumulation. The annual physical count will serve to verify the inventory subsystem.

Perpetual Measurement. Perpetual inventory systems use physical counts to *confirm* the inventory balance. However, an ongoing, continuous determination of inventory quantity and value is maintained in the accounts. The inventory account is updated each time an item is purchased or sold. Perpetual inventory systems provide management with up-to-date information about quantities and costs throughout the period.

Obviously, a perpetual inventory system will involve more clerical effort and related cost than a periodic system. However, the perpetual data is usually used to support a variety of decision-making activities. Computers and other types of data processing equipment have been used extensively in maintaining perpetual inventory data.

Periodic inventory systems must provide an inventory valuation for the balance sheet and sufficient data to calculate cost of goods sold for presentation on the income statement. To facilitate this process, purchase information is collected throughout the period, and inventory cost is determined at the end of the period, after a physical count has been made. **Recording Periodic Inventory Data**

Throughout the period, the cost of all merchandise acquired for resale is accumulated in an account called **Purchases**. This information is normally recorded at the same time that the cash payment or credit liability is entered into the records.

For example, if a company purchased $10,000 worth of merchandise on account and, subsequently, purchased $2,000 worth of merchandise for cash, the following entries would be made:

Purchases	$10,000	
Accounts Payable		$10,000
Purchases	$ 2,000	
Cash		$ 2,000

A purchase return is recorded in the journal as an inverse of the original entry: Cash or Accounts Payable are debited and Purchases is credited. Alternatively, a Purchase Returns and Allowances account receives the debit and is considered as a contra to the account Purchases. At the end of the accounting period, a determination of the ending inventory value must be made and entered into the accounts. Prior to this entry, the Inventory account reflects the prior period's inventory value. These two values—the prior and the current—are used in determining the cost of goods sold.

Assume that in the preceding case, the beginning inventory value was

$15,000 and that the physical count reveals an ending inventory of $11,000. Cost of goods sold will be calculated as follows:

$15,000	Cost of Beginning Inventory
12,000	Cost of Purchases
27,000	Cost of Goods Available for Sale
11,000	Cost of Ending Inventory
$16,000	Cost of Goods Sold

The $16,000 cost of goods sold will appear on the income statement and the ending balance of $11,000 will be reported as the inventory value on the balance sheet.

Closing Entries. When a periodic inventory system is used, the closing process, relative to ledger accounts, has four distinct objectives:

1. Remove the prior period inventory from the accounts.
2. Place the current inventory in the accounts.
3. Remove any balance in the Purchases account.
4. Isolate the cost of goods sold.

These objectives can be accomplished through the closing entries.

Income Summary is a temporary account, used in the closing process to compute net income and to transfer it to owner's equity (see Chapter 3). Revenue items are transferred by crediting Income Summary and expense items are debited to this account. A single compound entry, using Income Summary, will accomplish all of the inventory closing objectives.

The preceding example will lead to the following closing entry:

Inventory (as of 12/31/X2)	$11,000	
Income Summary	16,000	
Inventory (as of 12/31X1)		$15,000
Purchases		12,000

The ending inventory value (12/31/X2) is placed in the accounts by a debit. The prior period inventory value (12/31/X1) is removed from the records by a credit. The Purchases account is cleared (or closed) by crediting it for its balance. The difference between these debits and credits is reflected by a debit to Income Summary and represents the cost of goods sold.

Recording Perpetual Inventory Data

In perpetual systems, the Inventory account is continually updated to record additions to or deletions from the merchandise inventory. Purchases are immediately reflected in the account balance by debiting (increasing) the inventory account and crediting accounts payable or cash, as appropriate. For example, if a firm purchased $15,000 of merchandise on account, the following entry would be made:

Inventory	$15,000	
Accounts Payable		$15,000

A purchase return can be recorded as the reverse of this entry. Similarly, when a sale is made, the inventory account is immediately reduced to reflect the outflow of merchandise. The cost of the merchandise that was sold is moved from the inventory account to the Cost of Goods Sold expense account. At the end of the period, Cost of Goods Sold will be used in the determination of income.

If a company sold merchandise costing $9000, the following entry would be made:

Cost of Goods Sold	$9,000	
Inventory		$9,000

Therefore, at any given time, the perpetual system will provide an inventory account that contains the cost of the merchandise available for sale at that time. On a regular basis, a physical count should be taken to confirm the inventory balance.

At the end of the accounting period, the perpetual inventory account contains the ending inventory balance. The cost of goods sold account also contains the cost of merchandise sold during the period. Additional calculations relative to these accounts are unnecessary. The perpetual system leads to a basic closing entry as follows:

Income Summary	$9,000	
Cost of Goods Sold		$9,000

In most product-related businesses, inventory is a significant item. It is essential for the accountant to use a system that will facilitate the accurate determination of cost of goods sold. This item of expense is extremely important in calculating periodic income. In selecting an inventory system, the accountant must weight the costs and benefits of the alternatives. Management uses of inventory data throughout the period and effective control over the items in inventory are factors to be considered.

Operating Expenses

After the gross margin on sales has been determined, the income statement sets forth operating expenses that relate to the reported revenues. Operating expenses are those elements of cost that were consumed during the period and were directly related to the production or distribution of the product or service that was sold. Administrative expenses and selling expenses may be set apart in separate subsections of the income statement.

Selling expense items normally include cost elements related to merchandising capacity and operations. Examples of these expenses include rent, depreciation of sales facilities and equipment, wages, and the cost of a credit policy. Most of these expenses will be recorded as they are incurred. Depreciation expense is a charge to reflect asset utilization. In accordance with accounting theory, depreciation is calculated using a reasonable and systematic method. Various depreciation techniques are discussed in Chapter 9.

Some operating expenses must be estimated by the accountant. These relate to situations where it is reasonable to expect that an expense has been incurred, but at the time the income statement is to be prepared, the exact amount of the expense is not determinable. Bad debt expense is an example of such a situation.

Bad Debt Expense

Companies offer their customers credit for a variety of reasons. One of these is to stimulate additional sales and, thus, additional profits. Credit policies will lead to some additional expenses for the firm.

When credit is extended, additional record keeping is necessitated. The firm must maintain information about who owes it money. Also, many organizations will establish credit departments to decide which customers should receive credit and what limits should be placed on their credit purchases. Both of these functions will have a cost and will comprise part of the expense of a credit policy.

When customers buy on credit, it is reasonable to expect that some of them will be unable or unwilling to pay their debts. In these cases, the seller must absorb the loss as a bad debt expense. Recognizing the expense is essential to maintain the integrity of the accounting records.

If the Watson Company purchased $17,000 of merchandise on account, the seller would recognize this promise to pay as an asset.

Accounts Receivable—Watson Co.	$17,000	
Sales Revenue		$17,000

Subsequently, if the debt was not paid, the seller must remove the asset from the books and treat the $17,000 as an expense.

Bad Debt Expense	$17,000	
Accounts Receivable—Watson Co.		$17,000

Bad debt expense is another cost of a credit policy. In most cases, the profit resulting from additional sales will more than offset the expenses involved in granting customers credit. Organizations generally monitor their bad debt losses so that credit granting policies can be geared to acceptable levels of risk.

If credit is granted during an accounting period, it is reasonable to expect that some bad debt losses will occur. At the end of the period, it may be impossible to determine which debts in particular will not be paid in the future. However, bad debts are an expense that relates to current sales revenue, revenue that resulted from the credit policy that has led to some bad debts. Therefore, the accountant must estimate future bad debt losses and include them as an expense in the current period.

Past experience is usually the basis for estimating bad debt losses. One widely used technique relates the estimate to sales volume. Another technique relates the estimate to the age of customer debt. Both methods are acceptable means of relating expected future losses to current income. However, the latter method usually provides better estimations although the bookkeeping costs are higher.

Estimating Bad Debts

Sales Volume. Past experience and accounting data may reveal that bad debt losses follow in some constant or predictable relationship to the total dollar value of credit sales. In these cases, a percentage will be applied to the current sales revenue to derive an estimate of bad debt expense. Experience and knowledge of current business conditions enable management to make these estimates. Current sales are the base and set the parameters for the calculation.

The Markel Company has determined that about 1.4 percent of its past sales have resulted in uncollectable debts. During the current period, sales totaled $237,000. The firm will use $3,318 ($237,000 × 0.014) as an estimation of its current bad debt expense.

Age of Accounts. Sometimes, the amount of time that a debt has been outstanding will closely correlate with its probability of collection. Analysis of outstanding accounts receivable may be undertaken to provide an estimation of bad debt expense. Such an analysis is generally referred to as *aging the receivables*.

The aging process begins by classifying accounts into groups based on the length of time that they have been outstanding. The number of groups used will depend on previous experiences by the company. After the accounts have been grouped, percentages reflecting past experience will be applied to each group to determine the current amount of estimated bad debts.

The aging process is illustrated below:

Customer Balance		Age of Account			
		1–30	31–90	91–180	Over 180
Apple and Company		$ 390			
Bunt and Punt					$265
Clothier Limited			$ 120		
Zebra Stripe, Inc.				$ 225	
Total		$9,200	$7,300	$2,500	$940

Age Group	Total	Estimated Uncollectable	
		Percentage	Amount
1–30 days	$9,200	2%	$ 184
31–90 days	7,300	5%	365
91–180 days	2,500	20%	500
Over 180 days	940	80%	752
Total			$1,801

In contrast, the sales volume method usually relies on current sales while the aging method applies to all outstanding receivables. Thus, aging tends to encompass more historic data than does percentage estimation. Either method is acceptable and both are used in practice.

Recording Bad Debt Estimations

At the end of an accounting period, the accountant must enter the estimated amount of bad debt expense in the accounts to properly match revenues and expenses. However, while the amount of bad debts can be estimated from prior experience, the specific customer accounts that will be uncollectable cannot be identified. Therefore, a contra account is used to facilitate reporting the desired information.

The contra account, *Allowance for Doubtful Accounts* is normally used to reflect bad debt estimations. This account will always be reported with the Accounts Receivable account and the net difference between the two will be disclosed as the receivable balance.

Assume that a company has made $102,000 of credit sales in its first year. These receivables have been directly entered in the Accounts Receivable account as follows:

| Accounts Receivable | $102,000 | |
| Sales | | $102,000 |

At the end of the accounting period, the company estimates that $4500 of these accounts will be uncollectable. The following entry will be made:

| Bad Debt Expense | $4,500 | |
| Allowance for Doubtful Accounts | | $4,500 |

The effect of this entry is to properly recognize an expense and to provide for the valuation of accounts receivable. The estimated expense of $4,500 will appear on the income statement and balance sheet will report accounts receivable as shown below:

| Accounts Receivable | $102,000 | |
| Less: Allowance for Doubtful Accounts | 4,500 | $97,500 |

Recording Aged Information.   When aging analysis is used, the result is an estimation of the total allowance balance to date. To determine the amount of current expense, the difference between the current and prior allowance balances must be determined.

For example, assume that a company estimates from an aging schedule that the total allowance for doubtful accounts should be $28,300. If the prior balance in this account was $25,200, a current period expense of $3,100 ($28,300 − $25,200) will be recognized.

| Bad Debt Expense | $3,100 | |
| Allowance for Doubtful Accounts | | $3,100 |

Bad Debts.   When a specific account is deemed to be uncollectable and the allowance method has been used, the account is written off through the allowance account. If the Fox Company debt of $2,050 is uncollectable, the following entry will be made to remove this receivable from the books:

| Allowance for Doubtful Accounts | $2,050 | |
| Accounts Receivable—Fox Company | | $2,050 |

This entry reduces accounts receivable by the amount of the bad debt. When using an allowance account, bad debt expense was estimated in the period when the sale was made; an adjustment to the allowance account is all that must be recorded now. In the very unusual case where an account that has been written off as uncollectable is collected, the Cash account is debited and the Allowance for Doubtful Accounts is credited for the amount received.

Administrative expenses are normally set apart from selling expenses in the income statement. This is done to call attention to different types of expense elements. Selling expenses relate somewhat directly to the market-

Administrative Expenses

ADMINISTRATIVE
EXPENSES

ing of the product a service provided by the organization. By contrast, _ad-ministrative expenses_ relate to the organization in general and to the cost incurred and consumed to provide for an administrative and supervisory capacity.

Examples of administrative expenses include the salaries of corporate officers and the supplies, equipment, personnel, and facilities to support their work. Most of these items will be directly recorded in expense accounts as they are incurred.

Completing the Income Statement

Selling and administrative expenses are deducted from the gross margin on sales to derive the net income from operations. Operating income is adjusted for other revenue and expense and any extraordinary items to provide net income before taxes. After taxes have been deducted the net income is presented.

To enhance the usefulness of the income statement to stockholders, earnings per share must be calculated and reported on the face of the statement. Earnings per share relates the total reported Income of a corporation to an individual by expressing earnings on the basis of the smallest unit of ownership interest—one share of stock.

Depending on the ownership and debt structure of a corporation, the earnings per share calculation can be quite simple or quite complex. In its simplest form earnings per share involves dividing net income by the average number of outstanding shares of stock:

$$\text{Earnings per share} = \frac{\text{Net income}}{\text{Average number of shares of outstanding stock}}$$

Retained Earnings Statement. The income statement is often supplementedwithanoptionalstatementcalledtheStatementofRetainedEarnings. This statement relates to corporations and explains increases and decreases in the retained earnings account during the period. Usually, net income and dividends are included in the statement and explain the changes. An example of such a statement is presented below:

TIANI COMPANY, INC.
Statement of Retained Earnings
For the Year Ended December 31, 19X3

Beginning Retained Earnings Balance (1/1/X3)	$190,250
Add Net Income 19X3	25,850
	216,100
Less Dividends Paid 19X3	24,300
Ending Retained Earnings Balance (12/31/X3)	$191,800

EXHIBIT 6-1
RECORDING EXPENSE ITEMS

Original Entry			Closing Entry		
1. Accounts Receivable	$118,500		Sales Revenue	$118,500	
Sales Revenue		$118,500	Income Summary		$118,500
2. Purchases	14,000		Inventory	51,000	
Accounts Payable		14,000	Income Summary	25,000	
			Inventory		62,000
			Purchases		14,000
3. Salary Expense	19,500		Income Summary	25,300	
Advertising Expense	2,800		Salary Expense		19,500
Supplies Expense	1,800		Advertising Expense		2,800
Cash		24,100	Supplies Expense		1,800
Depreciation Expense	1,200		Depreciation Expense		1,200
Accumulated Depreciation		1,200			
4. Bad Debt Expense	1,896		Income Summary	1,896	
Allowance for Doubt-			Bad Debt Expense		1,896
ful Accounts		1,896			
5. Salary Expense	21,000		Income Summary	22,700	
Supplies Expense	1,700		Salary Expense		21,000
Cash		22,700	Supplies Expense		1,700
6. Income Tax Expense	21,802		Income Summary	21,802	
Income Tax Payable		21,802	Income Tax Expense		21,802
7.			Income Summary	21,802	
			Retained Earnings		21,802

The Harrison Company has been in existence for several years. During the current period, the following income related activities occurred:

An Illustration

1. Net sales revenue was $118,500. All sales were made on credit.
2. Beginning inventory was $62,000. Purchases during the period were $14,000. A physical count revealed an ending inventory of $51,000.
3. Operating expenses during the year included sales salaries, $19,500; advertising, $2,800; promotional supplies, $1,800; and depreciation, $1,200.
4. Bad debts are estimated to be 1.6 percent of current sales.
5. Administrative expenses that were incurred during the year included: administrative salaries $21,000 and supplies $1,700.
6. The company is subject to a 50 percent federal and local tax rate on its earnings.
7. Since the firm is incorporated all income or loss will be closed to Retained Earnings.

Recording the Information. Journal entries for these transactions are presented in Exhibit 6-1. End-of-period closing entries are also shown for each transaction. The transaction numbers relate to the information given above and the explanations offered below.

1. Credit sales lead to a realization of revenue. Revenue will be closed to the Income Summary account.
2. Under a periodic inventory system, purchases are recorded as they are made. At the end of the period, the beginning inventory is removed from the accounts, the ending inventory is entered in the accounts and the Purchases account is cleared through the closing process. The cost of goods sold is isolated in the Income Summary account.
3. Salary, advertising, and supplies expenses are recognized as they are incurred. At the end of the period, depreciation expense is estimated and recorded. All of the expense accounts are closed to Income Summary.
4. The annual amount of bad debt expense results from an estimate based on past experience. In this case, the amount $1896 resulted from applying 1.6 percent to the total sales revenue ($118,500 × 0.016). Bad debt expense is closed to the Income Summary account.
5. Administrative expenses are recorded in the appropriate expense accounts as they are incurred. These expense accounts are also closed to Income Summary.
6. Income taxes are levied on the firm's taxable income. In this case, taxable income is the difference between revenues and expenses—$43,604. By applying the 50 percent rate to the income, tax expense is determined. Like all expenses, Income Tax Expense will be closed to the Income Summary account.
7. The balance in the Income Summary account is closed to Retained Earnings to complete the recording and the closing process.

Statement Presentation. The transactions considered above focus primarily on the expenses of the Harrison Company. The income statement shown in Exhibit 6-2 illustrates the disclosure of this information. Earnings per share were calculated on the assumption that 10,000 shares of stock are outstanding.

Summary

To properly compute income, accountants must identify and measure expenses related to the reported revenues. Expenses result from the sale or consumption of resources that had an acquisition cost to the firm. Some expense elements can be measured directly, others must be estimated.

Cost of goods sold is an expense item that represents the cost of products that were sold during the period. The calculation of cost of goods sold depends on the inventory system in use. A periodic inventory system accounts for purchases and relies on an ending physical count to calculate

EXHIBIT 6-2
REPORTING NET INCOME

HARRISON COMPANY
Income Statement
For the Year Ended December 31, 19X9

Sales Revenue			$118,500
Cost of Goods Sold			
Beginning inventory, January 1, 19X9	$62,000		
Purchases during 19X9	14,000		
Cost of goods available for sale		$76,000	
Less: Ending inventory, December 31, 19X9		51,000	
Cost of Goods Sold			25,000
Gross Margin on Sales			93,500
Operating Expenses			
Selling Expenses			
Salaries	19,500		
Advertising	2,800		
Supplies	1,800		
Depreciation	1,200		
Bad Debts	1,896		
Total Selling Expense		27,196	
Administrative expenses			
Salaries	21,000		
Supplies	1,700		
Total Administrative Expense		22,700	
Total Operating Expenses			49,896
Net Income from Operations			43,604
Income Tax Expense			21,802
Net Income			$ 21,802
Earnings per Share			$ 2.18

cost of goods sold. Perpetual inventory systems maintain a continuous balance and accumulate cost of goods sold data on an ongoing basis.

Operating expenses include all those costs that were consumed in selling activities and in providing for the administration of the organization. Bad debt expense results from uncollectable credit accounts. This expense item is usually considered to be part of the cost of maintaining a credit policy for customers of the firm.

Bad debt expense is usually estimated periodically based on the past experience of the firm. The estimations may be related to the total sales volume or to the age of the outstanding debts. A valuation or contra account is used to provide a reduction in the Accounts Receivable balance without specifically identifying the doubtful accounts.

The income statement includes income tax effects and a calculation of earnings per share. The income statement is also used in preparing the optional retained earnings statement. The statement of retained earnings explains changes in this account during the period under consideration.

A Supplementary Discussion: Nonprofit Organizations

Managers of nonprofit organizations have as great a need for information to help them in planning, control, and decision making as do managers of private, profit-seeking business enterprises. Although nonprofit organizations do not pursue traditional profit goals, other organizational goals such as growth, survival, and social service apply equally to both profit and nonprofit organizations. The primary characteristics of nonprofit organizations are the absence of private ownership and the elimination of the opportunity for private profits.

A not-for-profit organization is one in which:

1. There is no deliberate or conscious profit motive.

2. There are no personally or individually owned equity shares or interests.

3. Equity interest may not be sold or exchanged.

4. There is no usual or required direct or proportionate financial benefit to contributors of capital or to the patrons.

This definition encompasses the more common types of nonprofit organizations, such as colleges, churches, hospitals, charitable organizations, and governmental units, all of which share many common problems of accounting and control, but it excludes such organizations as cooperatives, trade unions, and private clubs, which operate for the personal and collective benefits of their members.

There are an exceedingly large number of nonprofit organizations in the United States, although a definitive census has not been taken recently. At last count, there are over 78,000 local government organizations (counties, municipalities, townships, special service districts, and school districts), 29,000 libraries, 7,000 hospitals, 25,000 foundations, 21,000 nursing homes, 10,000 nonpublic schools, 8,000 noncollegiate, postsecondary schools, according to the *Statistical Abstract of the United States*.

Nonprofit organizations are created to provide goods and services that are considered socially desirable, but which might not be provided at all, as efficiently, or in the quality or quantity deemed necessary if the decision to provide the goods or services were determined by supply and demand in a competitive market. Thus, the quality, quantity, and mix of goods and services provided by nonprofit organizations are determined without benefit of those competitive market factors that regulate the allocation of resources in private enterprises. A nonprofit organization's resources are commonly limited by its fundraising ability: the amount of tax assessments for governmental units, contributions for charitable organizations, donors' support for churches, and the fee structures for hospitals.

However, the accounting needs of nonprofit organizations are the same as those for any organization. Adequate reports are needed for the organization, its managers, directors and other interested parties, to monitor the operations and their results. The accountability demanded from nonprofit directors has increased the concern for proper accounting.

Historically, nonprofit organizations had wide latitude in reporting. Recently, regulations imposed by funding agencies have demanded compliance with generally accepted accounting principles. These principles require nonprofit organizations to use accrual accounting as do profit oriented firms. While some few differences exist, fundamental accounting concepts apply equally to all organizations.

Key Terms

Inventory
Beginning inventory
Cost of goods available for sale
Ending inventory
Gross margin
Purchases
Bad debt expense
Aging the receivables
Administrative expense

Questions

1. How are expenses and assets related?

2. Why is it important for the accountant to determine the extent of consumption and the value of resources that a business consumes?

3. Many income statements include a section called cost of goods sold. What does cost of goods sold measure, and how is it calculated?

4. Explain how beginning inventory, purchases, and ending inventory are related in determining the amount of cost of goods sold.

5. The term gross margin is included in the income statement. What does it represent, and why is it set out for special attention?

6. A well-designed inventory system will provide the accountant with a value for the inventory. What else will the system provide?

7. Describe two major types of inventory systems, and identify their similarities and differences.

8. Why are two inventory systems available to the accountant? Would one system be sufficient for most business ventures?

9. Describe the objectives of the closing process when a periodic inventory system is used.

10. Explain the term operating expenses. Give three examples of items that probably would be operating expenses.

11. Why is bad debt expense considered part of the expense of a credit policy for the firm?

12. What happens if an overdue account is written off as a bad debt and the customer subsequently pays?

13. Discuss two techniques for estimating bad debt expense.

14. If bad debt expense is estimated, will imprecision creep into the financial statements of a company?

15. What is the purpose of the retained earnings statement? Describe the basic structure of the statement.

Exercises

1. The Taylor Clothing Company wishes to determine the amount of cost of goods sold at the end of an accounting period. The inventory at the start of the period was $250,000. During the period, the Company purchased $125,000 of merchandise, and the ending inventory disclosed that $225,000 of stock was still on hand. What is the cost of goods sold for the period? What is the amount of inventory that will be disclosed on the balance sheet?

2. The following three situations relate to different components involved in calculating cost of goods sold or inventory values. In each case, evaluate the data presented, and complete the calculation.
(a) Beginning inventory was $210,000. Inventory at the end of the period was $60,000 and cost of goods sold was reported to be $330,000. What is the value of purchases made during the period?
(b) At the end of an accounting period, the income statement disclosed that cost of goods sold was $73,000, and the balance sheet reported an inventory value of $10,000. Management indicates that $51,000 of merchandise was purchased during the period. What was the beginning inventory?
(c) A firm began the period with $13,000 of inventory. During the period purchases totaled $18,000. Cost of goods sold expense is reported to be $14,500. What is the value of the ending inventory?

3. If the beginning inventory and the ending inventory values are the same, then the firm's cost of goods sold must equal what amount? Similarly, if periodic purchases equal the ending inventory, then the cost of goods sold must equal what amount?

4. The Mark Up Company recorded sales of $1,228,000 during the month of October. The cost of goods sold for October was $921,000. What was the gross margin on sales for the month? What was the gross margin percentage, and what does it mean?

5. The income statement of the Sampson Company reported that the gross margin on sales for the year was $273,000. The gross margin percentage for this company is 35 percent. What was the cost of goods sold for the Sampson Company for the year? What was the total annual sales revenue generated by this company?

6. A firm had net sales of $587,500. At the beginning of the period, the inventory was $278,000, and at the end of the period the inventory was $252,000. Merchandise purchases during the period totaled $315,000. Construct in good form an income statement which reports the gross margin on sales for this company.

7. The following transactions were made during a recent accounting period:
(a) Merchandise of $208,000 was purchased on credit.

(b) Sales totaling $302,000 were made. Cash sales accounted for $180,000 of the total, and the remainder were on credit.

(c) Cash purchases of merchandise equaled $73,500.

(d) Credit sales of $37,500 were made.

(e) The merchandise purchased on credit in (a) was paid for in cash.

(f) The merchandise inventory at the beginning of the period was $102,000, and at the end of the period it was $167,500.

Assuming that the company uses a periodic inventory system, give the journal entries that would have been made for each of the events described above. Prepare an income statement that reports the gross margin on sales.

8. A company made purchases of $125,000, $250,000, and $375,000, respectively. At the start of the period, the inventory was $650,000, and at the end of the period the inventory level had fallen to $550,000. Assuming that all of the purchases were made on credit, prepare journal entries to record these purchases (the company uses a periodic inventory system). Make the appropriate entries to close the purchase account at the end of the period and adjust the ending inventory balance.

9. The Continual Corporation uses a perpetual inventory system. During the year of 19X4, the company made two purchases of $234,000 and $412,000, respectively. The inventory at the beginning of the period was $718,000 and cost of goods sold equaled $650,000. Assume that the purchases were made on credit. At the end of the period, what entries will be necessary to update the inventory account.

10. The following three cases relate to estimations of uncollectable accounts receivable. In each case, make the appropriate journal entry to properly reflect the information in the accounts.

(a) Amos Apple & Company estimates that $12,500 of this year's credit sales will be uncollectable.

(b) Brown, Bear, and Son age accounts receivable. As a result of this process, they determine that the allowance for doubtful accounts should equal $48,000. The current credit balance in the account is $33,000.

(c) C & D Company estimates that $2,500 of current sales will result in uncollectable accounts.

11. Mitchell Corporation made sales of $410,000 during 19X9. The Allowance for Doubtful Accounts currently has a credit balance of $16,200. Prepare appropriate journal entries to reflect the following events:

(a) An account receivable from a prior year was determined to be uncollectable. It amounted to $1,700 and was written off immediately.

(b) Bad debt losses for the current year were estimated to be 2 percent of the current sales.

(c) An account of $200, which was previously deemed to be uncollectable and written off, was unexpectedly paid in full.

12. The Key Company reported net income for the year 19X6 of $43,600. Retained earnings on January 1, 19X6, were $23,400. During the year, the firm paid dividends of $35,700. Prepare a retained earnings statement in good form for the Key Company.

13. The Toe Towel Company makes the following information available:

Administrative expenses	$412,000
Beginning inventory, January 1, 19X9	112,000
Ending inventory, December 31, 19X9	100,000
Purchase during 19X9	815,000
Sales revenue	1,426,000
Selling expenses	318,000
Total outstanding shares of stock	10,000

Using this information, prepare an income statement for this company in good form. Make certain that the statement isolates the gross margin, net income from operations, net income, and earnings per share.

14. Calculate the gross margin percentage for the following independent cases:

	A	B	C
Sales	$282,000	$192,000	$66,500
Sales Returns and Allowances	16,000	9,000	500
Sales Discounts	3,000	2,000	0
Beginning Inventory	47,000	31,000	6,000
Purchases	180,000	201,000	40,000
Purchases Returns and Allowances	6,000	11,000	0
Ending Inventory	51,000	88,000	12,000

15. Fill in the missing data in the following independent case situations:

	A	B	C
Sales	$100,000	$_____	$200,000
Sales Returns and Allowances	1,000	3,000	_____
Sales Discounts	2,000	1,000	3,000
Net Sales	_____	_____	196,000
Beginning Inventory	_____	35,000	_____
Purchases	65,000	_____	105,000
Purchases Returns and Allowances	1,000	0	2,000
Purchase Discounts	1,000	1,000	0
Goods Available for Sale	90,000	_____	170,000
Ending Inventory	_____	20,000	_____
Cost of Goods Sold	60,000	_____	_____
Gross Margin on Sales	_____	40,000	_____
Gross Margin Percentage	_____	40%	30%

16. From the data below, prepare an aging of accounts receivable and make the necessary general journal entry to reflect your estimate of bad debts in the accounts:

Customer	Receivable Amount	Age of Account
A	$100	44
B	210	3
C	400	21
D	50	10
E	80	80
F	240	191
G	200	50
H	50	38
I	600	2
J	150	7

Estimated Uncollectable	
Age Group	Percentage
1–30 days	1%
31–60 days	5%
61–90 days	12%
91–120 days	20%
over 121 days	80%

A $200 balance is in the Allowance for Doubtful Accounts account before the adjustment.

Problems

1. The Light Company operates a retail lighting business in Wattville. Information about the Company for the year of 19X8 is provided below:

(a) During the year, total sales were $2,052,165. Of this amount, $425,745 were made for cash, and the remainder were made to regular customers who purchased on credit.

(b) The company made several purchases during the year. Credit purchases amounted to $673,810, and $105,485 of merchandise was purchased for cash. Light Company uses the periodic inventory method.

(c) Selling expenses for the year included: salaries, $78,340; wages, $104,480; rent, $26,745; and supplies, $35,700.

(d) Depreciation on equipment owned by the company totaled $15,495 for the year.

(e) Administrative expenses included the following items: salaries, $147,695; supplies, $4,890; and miscellaneous, $6,710.

(f) On January 1, 19X8, the inventory was valued at $357,260, and at the end of the year, on December 31, 19X8, the inventory remaining equaled $298,750.

(g) The company is subject to a combined 50 percent rate for federal, state, and local taxes.

(h) The company has 20,000 shares of stock outstanding.

REQUIRED:

(a) Prepare a set of summary journal entries to record the information given in items (a) through (e) above.

(b) Prepare a complete set of closing entries for this company. Be sure that the inventory information presented in item (f) above is included.

(c) Prepare an income statement for the Light Company for 19X8.

2. During 19X5, the Johnson Corporation generated $147,260 of sales revenue. Of this amount, $102,620 of sales were made on account. The company began the year with an inventory, at cost, of $48,620. On December 31, 19X5, a physical count was made and the inventory cost was determined to be $50,700. During the year, the company made four major purchases of merchandise. All of the purchases were paid for in cash and were for the following amounts: January, $18,750; June, $17,580; August, $10,270; and November, $15,350.

Selling expenses, excluding depreciation and bad debt expense, were $14,270. Administrative expenses totaled $12,830. The annual depreciation charge was calculated to be $3,720. Bad debt expense was estimated to be 2 percent of current credit sales. The company is subject to a 40 percent income tax rate. Johnson has 1,000 shares of stock outstanding. At the beginning of the year, retained earnings were reported to be $43,820. During the year, dividends of $3.25 per share were declared and paid by the company.

(a) Prepare an income statement for the Johnson Corporation for 19X5.

(b) Prepare a retained earnings statement for the Johnson Corporation as of December 31, 19X5.

3. The Walker Company is concerned about the adequacy of its allowance for doubtful accounts. Historically, the Company has estimated bad debt expense as a percentage of sales volume. However, their accountant has suggested that an aging of accounts receivable could provide a better estimate. At the present time, Allowance for Doubtful Accounts has a credit balance of $7,000.

The following information was summarized from the financial records of the Walker Company. It was decided to base the percentage uncollectable on past experience.

| Age Group | Past Experience | | Outstanding Receivables |
	Total Receivables	Total Collected	
1–30 days	$1,764,500	$1,746,855	$465,800
31–90 days	985,600	965,888	323,850
91–180 days	415,200	394,440	156,700
Over 180 days	158,300	66,486	12,400

Using this information, prepare an aging schedule for the current accounts receivable for the Walker Company. Determine the balance of the Allowance for Doubtful Accounts account. Prepare the journal entry that would be made to adjust the account balance to reflect the use of aging information. Discuss what effect this adjustment will have on current income for the Company.

4. The Brenner Company operates several wholesale outlets in the State of Nevada. Income-related information from the year of 19X7 has been summarized below. Although the Company collected and summarized the information, none of it was entered into their accounting records.

(a) Net sales revenue was $367,950. Of this amount, $312,400 was sold on credit, and the balance resulted from cash sales.

(b) The Company began the year with an inventory valued at $41,250. During the year, the Company made several purchases for cash. Total purchases for the year totaled $174,450. At the end of the year, a physical count of the inventory was taken. The ending inventory value was determined to be $53,675. The periodic inventory method was used.

(c) Operating expenses incurred during the year included salaries, $31,260; advertising, $2,750; rent, $12,675; supplies, $1950; and depreciation, $2,975.

(d) The Company uses an estimating process to determine the current charge for uncollectable accounts. Based on past experience, the firm estimates uncollectables to be 2 percent of current credit sales.

(e) Annual administrative expenses included the following items: salaries $25,980; depreciation $1,250; and supplies $2,975. The firm is a corporation, and at the present time there are 1,000 shares of common stock outstanding. Because of its earnings, the Company is subject to a combined 50 percent rate for federal and local taxes. All income or loss for the period will be closed to Retained Earnings. Beginning Retained Earnings balance for the year was $66,000.

REQUIRED:

(a) Prepare summary journal entries to record all of the transaction information presented above.

(b) Prepare closing entries for this information, and complete the process through closing the Income Summary account.

(c) Prepare an income statement in good form for the Brenner Company.

(d) Prepare a retained earnings statement for the Company.

5. The Wattsun Company merchandises imported desk and table lamps. During the year 19X8, 5,000 shares of the Company's common stock were outstanding. The Company uses a periodic inventory system to record information about the cost of the products it sells. At the end of the year, a physical count of the inventory is made and is used for control purposes and to value the ending inventory. The following information was taken from the general ledger on December 31, 19X8:

	Debit	Credit
Cash	$ 51,605	
Accounts Receivable	102,750	
Allowance for Doubtful Accounts		5,278
Inventory, January 1, 19X8	68,500	
Plant and Equipment	278,790	
Accumulated Depreciation—Equipment		157,983
Accrued Salaries Payable		12,850
Accounts Payable		53,575
Mortgage Loan		125,000
Capital Stock		100,000
Retained Earnings, January 1, 19X8		32,854
Sales		587,325
Sales Returns and Allowances	11,125	
Selling Expenses	183,230	
Administrative Expenses	151,125	
Income Tax Expense	8,570	
Purchases	219,170	
	$1,074,865	$1,074,865

The Company uses an estimating procedure to determine its provision for bad debts. Based on previous experience, the current provision is 0.8 percent of current net sales. The physical count resulted in a final inventory cost of $67,250.

REQUIRED:
(a) Bad debt expense has not been recorded for the current year. Make the entry to record it on December 31, 19X8.
(b) Make the necessary journal entries to record the ending inventory value and to close out the books for the year.
(c) Construct an income statement for the Wattsun Company.
(d) Prepare a retained earnings statement for the year. Assume that no dividends were paid.

6. The unadjusted trial balance of the Helvering Company is shown below:

HELVERING COMPANY
Trial Balance
December 31, 19X4

	Debit	Credit
Cash	$ 3,000	$
Accounts Receivable	5,000	
Inventory (1/1/X4)	18,000	
Prepaid Insurance	1,200	
Supplies	1,100	
Machinery and Equipment	8,000	
Accumulated Depreciation		2,600
Accounts Payable		7,500
Helvering, Capital		15,000
Sales		128,800
Sales Returns and Allowances	900	
Purchases	80,000	
Purchases Returns and Allowances		400
Wages Expense	29,000	
Rental Expense	7,000	
Miscellaneous Expense	500	
Utilities Expense	600	
	$154,300	$154,300

Adjustment data from Helvering's financial records are as follows:
(a) Ending inventory at December 31 was $15,000.
(b) Prepaid insurance was for a one-year fire insurance policy dated July 1, 19X4.
(c) An inventory of supplies showed only $300 in supplies on hand at year-end.
(d) Depreciation expense for the year is $1,300.
(e) Wages of $900 have been earned by employees but have not been paid at December 31, 19X4.
(f) Bad debts expense of $300 is estimated.

REQUIRED:
(a) Prepare a worksheet for the Helvering Company.
(b) Prepare a multiple-step income statement for the year ending December 31, 19X4.

7. The Zinnie Wholesale Boutique sells high-fashion women's clothing. Beginning inventory had a cost of $2,000. Transactions for the month of July include the following involving inventory:
(a) Purchased merchandise for $26,000 on account at terms 2/10, n/30.
(b) Paid for merchandise within the discount period.
(c) Sold merchandise costing $8,000 for $14,000 in cash.
(d) Sold merchandise costing $3,000 for $4,700 on account at terms n/30.

(e) Sold merchandise costing $4,000 for $6,000 on account at terms 2/10, *n*/30.
(f) Received payment for sale noted in (e) after the discount period.

REQUIRED:
Prepare the necessary general journal entries to account for the above transactions assuming that (a) the firm uses a periodic inventory system, and (b) the firm uses a perpetual inventory system.

8. Bimson Corporation's unadjusted trial balance at October 31, 19X8, the corporation's fiscal year end, is shown below:

BIMSON CORPORATION
Trial Balance
October 31, 19X8

	Debit	Credit
Cash	$ 4,000	$
Accounts Receivable	8,000	
Inventory	10,000	
Equipment	9,000	
Accumulated Depreciation		3,000
Accounts Payable		6,000
Common Stock ($5 par)		5,000
Retained Earnings		14,000
Sales		44,200
Sales Discounts	1,000	
Cost of Goods Sold	25,000	
Salary Expense	8,000	
Rental Expense	7,200	
	$72,200	$72,200

Adjusting data are shown below:
(a) The firm uses a perpetual inventory system.
(b) Bad debts expense of $200 is estimated.
(c) Straight-line depreciation is used. Expected life of assets in the account is nine years with no expected salvage value.
(d) Wages of $400 have been earned but not paid to employees as of October 31.

REQUIRED:
(a) Prepare the necessary general journal entries to make the necessary adjustments.
(b) Prepare a single step income statement for Bimson Corporation for the year ended October 31, 19X8.
(c) Calculate earnings or loss per share assuming 1000 shares of stock are outstanding during the year.
(d) Prepare a Retained Earnings Statement as of December 31, 19X8.
(e) Make the necessary closing entries for Bimson Corporation.

□ 7
CASH, TEMPORARY INVESTMENTS, AND RECEIVABLES

□ OBJECTIVES

AFTER STUDYING THIS CHAPTER, YOU SHOULD BE ABLE TO DO THE FOLLOWING:

1. DESCRIBE THE CHARACTERISTICS OF CURRENT ASSETS.

2. DISCUSS CONTROL PROCEDURES FOR CASH.

3. PREPARE A BANK RECONCILIATION STATEMENT.

4. RECORD THE ACQUISITION AND DISPOSITION OF TEMPORARY INVESTMENTS, AND DESCRIBE HOW TEMPORARY INVESTMENTS WOULD BE DISCLOSED ON A BALANCE SHEET.

5. CALCULATE THE INTEREST OR DISCOUNT ASSOCIATED WITH NOTES RECEIVABLE.

Cash is a fundamental financial resource. As the most common medium of exchange, it serves as the measurement standard for all other financial items. Because of this, cash measurement problems are minimal. However, cash is volatile—it can be lost, stolen, misplaced, or misused easily. Therefore, many accounting procedures relating to cash focus on areas of control and cash utilization. This chapter discusses the valuation, reporting, and control of the most liquid assets of an enterprise: cash, temporary investments, and short-term receivables.

Cash

All resources classified as cash must be negotiable and immediately available for use and exchange without any restrictions. The classification *cash* usually includes coin, currency, bank deposits, checks, and money orders. Some judgment must be used by the accountant in classifying items as cash. Technically, since banks retain the right to require notice prior to withdrawals, savings account deposits should not be classified as cash. As a practical matter, however, banks normally do not exercise this requirement, and savings deposits are generally reported as cash.

Control over the assets of a business is important to protect against loss, misappropriation, or inefficiency. Because of the volatility of cash, its control is fundamental to a good accounting system. The control of assets is based on a set of generally accepted concepts referred to as *internal control.* Internal control relates to policies, procedures, and activities designed to safeguard the assets of an enterprise and to promote their effective utilization.

Control of Cash

While there are various means of obtaining good internal control, the American Institute of Certified Public Accountants has specified that good internal control should include at least the following characteristics:

1. A *plan of organization* that provides appropriate separation of functional responsibilities—those involved with receiving cash should be separate from those disbursing cash; those involved with handling cash should be separate from those recording cash.
2. A *system of authorization and recording* adequate to provide accounting control over assets, liabilities, revenues, and expenses—predetermined routines and procedures should be established; all flows of cash should be properly authorized, and the accounting system should be able to detect exceptions to these procedures.
3. *Sound practices* to be followed in all organizational functions involving resources—cash receipts should be deposited daily in a bank; cash on hand should be secured.
4. *Quality of personnel* should be commensurate with responsibil-

ities—authority should match with responsibility; individual ability should be equivalent with the position held.

Control Procedures. Because cash is very transferable and not easily identified, it is very susceptible to misappropriation. Therefore, it is important to provide detailed controls over the receipt and disbursement of cash. The objectives of a system of cash control are to assure that all cash that should be collected is collected and properly recorded and that all disbursements are for valid business purposes and accounted for properly. While the specific procedures may vary depending on the characteristics of the entity, basic principles for controlling cash and cash transactions include the following:

1. Predetermined procedures for handling cash and recording cash transactions should be established.
2. Cash receipts should be deposited daily in a bank account, and disbursements should be made by prenumbered checks.
3. All cash receipts and disbursements should be recorded immediately.
4. Separation of duties relating to the handling of cash and recording cash transactions and receiving cash and disbursing cash should be enforced.
5. Physical safeguards, such as cash registers, check protectors, and prenumbered business forms, should be used.
6. Disbursements should be made only for purposes authorized by a limited number of designated persons.
7. The responsibility for authorizing a disbursement and the responsibility for signing checks should be separated, and all checks should require the signatures of two authorized persons.
8. Periodic audits should be made to determine that cash is being accounted for properly.

Specific methods of achieving good internal control must be developed for and adapted to a specific business enterprise. Also, the cost of each part of the control system must be weighed against the benefit derived from the control. Generally, only those procedures that provide for benefit in excess of their cost should be implemented. Cash control usually involves significant interaction with banks.

An important element of the cash control system is the requirement that daily cash receipts be deposited promptly and intact in a bank checking account. Checking accounts provide certain additional documentation about the receipt and disbursement of cash. When a bank deposit is made, the depositor details the information on a form provided by the bank. The de-

Bank Checking Account

BANK CHECKING ACCOUNT

posit slip is usually prepared in duplicate, with one copy serving as the depositor's receipt for the transaction.

Disbursements from a checking account are authorized by checks. A check is a written legal instrument, signed by the maker, ordering the bank to pay a specified sum of money from the maker's account to the order of a person or entity designated on the check. Checks are normally printed bank forms that are sequentially numbered and contain the depositor's name, address, and account number. The sequential numbering can assist the accountant in determining that all checks have been recorded.

Banks provide their customers with periodic statements about the status of and changes in their accounts. These bank statements list deductions (withdrawals) from the account (debits) and additions (deposits) to the account (credits) that occurred during the period. The bank will usually return source documents along with the statement, including checks paid, deposit receipts, and memorandums relating to other account activities. A *debit memorandum* indicates that the account has been charged, or reduced, by the bank. This may result from account service charges, or from checks that were accepted by the bank as deposits but subsequently returned because of insufficient funds. A *credit memorandum* indicates that the account has been increased by the bank. For example, a bank may collect an outstanding note for the depositor and credit the amount to the depositor's account. A typical bank statement is shown in Exhibit 7-1.

Bank Reconciliation

The cash balance shown on the bank statement normally will not equal the cash balance shown in the company's ledger account. The difference results from timing differences and/or errors in recording transactions by either the bank or the company. These differences can be classified into the following four types.

1. Amounts that have been charged to the depositor's account by the bank but are not yet recorded by the depositor. Such items include bank service charges and NSF (not sufficient funds) checks returned to the bank.
2. Amounts that have been added to the depositor's account by the bank but are not yet recorded by the depositor. Examples of these items are the proceeds of notes or drafts collected by the bank for the depositor.
3. Amounts that the depositor has deducted from his cash account but have not yet been deducted by the bank. Normally, this results from checks issued by the depositor that have not yet been presented to the bank for payment.
4. Amounts that the depositor has added to his cash account but have not yet been added by the bank. This generally occurs when deposits are in transit at the date of the bank statement. The depositor will record the deposit when it is transmitted, but the bank will record it after it is received.

EXHIBIT 7-1
A BANK STATEMENT

CITY NATIONAL BANK

Henderson Company
1217 Ring Street
Brian, Texas 77840

Account Number	Page Number
02038001	1
5-31-X9	6-30-X9
From	To
Statement Period	

Date	Debits		Deposits	Balance
5-31				$1,116.08
6-1	100.00			1,016.08
6-3	50.00	425.00		541.08
6-6	181.00	163.20		196.88
6-8			1,431.62	1,628.50
6-12	145.00NF			1,483.50
6-14	274.36	191.17		1,017.97
6-15	371.15	22.60		624.22
	13.45	173.62		437.15
6-17			1,763.19	2,200.34
6-21	545.40	317.71		1,337.23
6-23	41.00	63.27		1,232.96
6-24			1,020.00CM	2,252.96
6-25	317.13	267.41		1,668.42
6-27	5.00SC	63.42		1,600.00

Beginning Balance	No. Of Credits	Total Credits	Ending Balance	
$1,116.08	3	$4,214.81	$1,600.00	
	No. Of Debits	Total Debits	Code Explanation	
	20	$3,730.89	CC certified check	
			CM credit memo	
			NF nonsufficient funds	
			LC late charges	
			SC service charge	
			XC certified check	

As a part of the control process, a **_bank reconciliation statement_** should be prepared to explain differences between the cash balance in the ledger account and the cash balance on the bank statement. Control is enhanced, because the bank statement provides an independent record of the company's cash-related transactions. Reconciliation provides a mechanism for isolating errors made by the bank or the company in recording cash transactions and yields data necessary to adjust the company's cash records.

The bank reconciliation statement includes four distinct parts. The goal is to reconcile both the bank balance and the ledger balance to the correct cash balance at the end of the period. Accordingly, the bank balance is adjusted for additions and deductions by the depositor not shown on the bank statement, and the ledger balance is adjusted for additions and deductions by the bank not recorded in the books of the company. The illustration presented below relates to the bank statement for the Henderson Company, shown in Exhibit 7-1.

Illustration. The City National Bank statement to the Henderson Company indicates a balance of $1,600.00 as of June 30, 19X9. On the same date, the company's ledger balance for cash in bank was $1,757.00. The following additional data relate to information about the company's cash balance and are relevant in preparing a bank reconciliation statement:

1. Deposit mailed to the bank on June 30, but not recorded on the bank statement. $1,500.00
2. Checks written during the month of June but not recorded by the bank as of June 30 (check 527 for $122.71, 531 for $167.19, and 532 for $310.10). $ 600.00
3. A credit memorandum included with the bank statement indicated that a note receivable of $1,000 plus $20 interest ($1,020.00 in total) had been collected by the bank and credited to the Henderson Company account. $1,020.00
4. A debit memorandum was forwarded by the bank and indicated that a check deposited by the Henderson Company (received from a customer) was being returned because of insufficient funds (NSF). $ 145.00
5. A debit memorandum was also included with the bank statement for service charges for the month of June. $ 5.00
6. An examination of the canceled checks returned by the bank revealed that a check written by the Hinson Company had been erroneously charged against the Henderson Company account. $ 100.00
7. A comparison of the canceled checks with the firm's accounting records indicated that check 511 for $41.00 to the Acme Supply Company had incorrectly recorded in the books as $14.00, indicating an error of $27.00.

The bank reconciliation statement consists of two sections. The first adjusts the balance presented in the bank statement to the correct cash bal-

EXHIBIT 7-2
BANK RECONCILIATION STATEMENT

HENDERSON COMPANY
Bank Reconciliation
June 30, 19X9

Balance per Bank Statement, June 30		$1,600
Add Deposit in Transit	$1,500	
Check of Hinson Co. incorrectly charged to Henderson account	100	1,600
		$3,200
Less Outstanding checks (#527, #531, #532)		600
Correct Cash Balance		$2,600
Balance per Books, June 30		$1,757
Add Note collected by the Bank for the Company		1,020
		$2,777
Less Bank service charges	5	
NSF check—Smith Company	145	
Error in recording check #511	27	177
Correct Cash Balance		$2,600

ance. The second adjusts the balance presented in the depositor's books to the correct cash balance. If the two adjusted balances do not agree, an additional examination for undetected errors must be made. A bank reconciliation statement for the Henderson Company is presented in Exhibit 7-2.

The deposit made by the Henderson Company on June 30 should be a part of the cash balance. Because it was in transit when the bank statement was made, it was not included. Consequently, it is added to the balance per bank statement as a part of the reconciliation process. In certain situations, control procedures will require that a follow-up contact be made with the bank to ensure that the deposit was received.

A check prepared by the Hinson Company was erroneously charged against the Henderson Company account by the bank. To adjust for this error, $100—the amount of the check—is added to the balance reported by the bank. The bank should be notified promptly of the error.

Three checks were outstanding when the bank statement was prepared. Because they were not presented to the bank for payment, they have not been deducted from the Henderson Company account. They should be deducted from the bank balance to derive the proper cash balance. There is no reason to expect that all checks written by a company will be presented promptly for payment. Consequently, adjustments for the same outstanding check may be made for many periods. The first part of the Henderson Company reconciliation statement indicates that the correct cash balance is $2,600.00.

The bank reconciliation statement continues by focusing on the cash balance reported in the company's ledger on June 30. The bank statement notified the company that a note of $1,000 plus $20 interest was collected on its behalf by the bank and included in its account balance. This collection would be added to the reported cash balance since it had not previously been included by the firm. The bank also notified the company of three deductions from its cash balance.

Service charges during the month totaled $5. While these could be anticipated, service charges are usually not recorded until they are confirmed by notification from the bank. Henderson Company had previously deposited a check that it had received from the Smith Company. Deposits are accepted subject to collection of checks or other financial instruments. In this case, the check of the Smith Company was not supported by adequate funds and it was returned. Consequently, the $145 was not added to the account of the Henderson Company by the bank and should be deducted from the reported bank balance. Finally, an error of $27 was made in recording check 511. This amount should be deducted from the bank balance to properly derive the cash balance. The second part of the reconciliation agrees with the first—that the adjusted cash balance is $2,600. Agreement does not assure correctness, but it does imply consistency.

The first part of the bank reconciliation dealt with adjustments to the balance reported by the bank. In cases where corrections are not automatic, (such as deposits in transit) the bank should be notified to make the necessary adjustments. The second part of the reconciliation relates to the company's books. Adjustments and corrections here should be reflected in the cash account through an appropriate journal entry. In this case, four adjusting entries would be necessary.

Cash	$1,020	
Notes Receivable		$1,000
Interest Revenue		20

To record the collection of an outstanding note plus interest

Miscellaneous Expense	$5	
Cash		$5

To record the payment of bank service charges for June

Accounts Receivable	$145	
Cash		$145

To record the return of an NSF check:

Accounts Payable	$27	
Cash		$27

To record an error correction for recording payment to Acme Supply

After the entries have been made, the cash balance in the ledger will be $2,600. This amount is in agreement with the balance derived in the bank reconciliation statement and would be reported as the cash in bank on a balance sheet for June 30.

For control purposes, it is useful to have all cash disbursements made by check. However, it is impractical to issue checks for various small payments for items such as postage, miscellaneous supplies, and other minor expenditures. To allow such payments to be made in cash and at the same time to maintain control over these disbursements, many firms establish petty cash funds. A *petty cash fund* is a regulated quantity of cash under the control of an employee to be used for making minor payments.

The petty cash fund is established by cashing a check and placing the cash under the control of the employee who will have charge of the fund. As disbursements are made, the recipient is required to sign a voucher indicating the purpose and amount of the payment. Thus, at any time, the sum of the cash and the vouchers should equal the amount originally placed in the fund. Periodically, the fund is replenished by writing a check on the general bank account for the sum of the petty cash vouchers. The check is cashed and the proceeds are returned to the petty cash fund. When the petty cash fund is replenished, various expense accounts are debited (increased) as indicated by the vouchers and cash is credited (reduced). The fund is also replenished at the end of an accounting period so that the expenses reflected by the vouchers will be included in the financial statements.

To illustrate the use of a petty cash fund, assume that a company establishes a fund on January 1 by cashing a check for $500. The entry reflects the reclassification of cash within the firm:

Petty Cash $500
    Cash $500
To establish a petty cash fund

Various disbursements are made by the cashier during January, and the following list of disbursements is presented for reimbursement on January 25:

Postage	$ 70
Office Supplies	180
Miscellaneous Selling Expenses	125
	$375
Cash on Hand	125
	$500

The following entry would be made to record the reimbursement:

Postage Expense	$ 70	
Office Supplies Expense	180	
Miscellaneous Selling Expense	125	
Cash		$375
To reimburse the petty cash fund		

Notice that no entry is made directly to the petty cash account at the time of reimbursement. The only entries to petty cash are on establishing the fund and on increasing or decreasing the amount of cash authorized for the fund.

The basic control over the petty cash fund is at the time of reimbursement, since all disbursements must be supported by vouchers. An additional control may be provided by periodic unannounced counts of the fund. When financial statements are prepared, the balance in the petty cash fund will be combined with other forms of cash and reported on the balance sheet as a single entry entitled "Cash."

Cash that is restricted in any way is reported separately from the account *Cash.* Usually, such items will be treated as a noncurrent asset and reported as funds held for some specific purpose. For example, cash that is set aside for redeeming outstanding bonds would be disclosed on the balance sheet as follows:

Noncurrent Assets:
    Funds for Bond Redemption $100,000

Temporary Investments

Businesses frequently have cash that is not currently needed in the operations of the organization. In such cases, it is economically wise for the firm to invest its cash and earn a return rather than leaving the balances idle and unproductive. In cases of a short-term cash surplus, temporary investments will be made. These **temporary investments** are normally in liquid securities that can easily be converted to cash, such as certificates of deposit, commercial paper, government securities, and corporate bonds and stock.

If the cash surplus is deemed to be other than temporary, a more permanent commitment of the resources will be made. The company will invest in growth, facilities, or another organization; the prospects of a quick conversion of these investments into cash is reduced. Consequently, for accounting and reporting purposes, a distinction is made between temporary investments and long-term investments. Temporary investments are shown as current assets, while long-term investments are included in the noncurrent asset section of the balance sheet.

For securities to be classified as temporary investments, they must satisfy the following two criteria.

1. The security must be readily marketable at a determinable price. In this test, marketable means that a sales price is currently available on an organized securities exchange or that there is an established market for the security.
2. It is the intention of management to convert the securities into cash within one year (or the operating cycle of the business if it is longer than one year).

Long-term investments are those securities that do not meet the marketability criterion or that are acquired for some long-range objective such as exercising control over the operations of another company. Thus, a specific security that is readily marketable could be classified as either a temporary investment or a long-term investment depending on the intentions of management. Long-term investments are discussed in Chapter 9.

The accountant primarily deals with three aspects of the temporary investment: acquisition, income, and valuation. Temporary investments are initially valued at their acquisition cost. This includes the purchase price of the security plus additional acquisition costs, such as broker's commissions. For example, assume that the Anderson Company purchased 100 shares of F and C Corporation common stock as a temporary investment. The stock was purchased at $48 per share plus a brokerage commission of $200. The following journal entry would be made by Anderson Company:

Accounting for Temporary Investments

```
Temporary Investments      $5,000
     Cash                                  $5,000
To record the acquisition of 100 shares of F and C common stock
```

Investment Income.   Temporary investments are made to earn a return on otherwise idle cash. The return can be in the form of interest on bonds and notes and dividends on corporate stock. As it is earned, income from temporary investments is included in appropriate revenue accounts and recognized in the income statement. Measurement problems are the same as other assets earning a similar type of return.

As discussed in Chapter 4, interest revenue is earned with the passage of time and therefore must be recorded with an adjusting entry if the interest collection date and the end of the accounting period do not coincide. To illustrate this process, assume that the Anderson Company purchased $100,000 of Porter Company 8 percent bonds on July 1 for $100,000 plus a $1,000 brokerage commission. The bonds pay interest annually on June 30. The purchase would be recorded by increasing (debiting) temporary investments and reducing (crediting) cash for $101,000. If the bonds are still held on December 31, the end of the company's accounting period, the following adjusting entry must be made to properly state income for the year:

Accrued Interest Receivable $4,000
     Interest Revenue $4,000
To recognize interest revenue earned on temporary investments

By contrast, common stock dividends are not earned until they are declared by the board of directors of the corporation. Normally, dividend income would be recognized when it is received by the firm. However, if a dividend is declared in one year, with payment to take place in the following accounting period, the revenue would be accrued and recognized in the period when the declaration was made.

Valuation of Investments. Many times, the market value of temporary investments will change during the accounting period when the investment is being held. If the market price exceeds the acquisition cost of the investment, no adjustment is made. This is consistent with the accounting principle of conservatism; no gains are recorded until they are realized through the act of sale. However, if the market price falls below the acquisition cost, an adjustment must be made. If the market price has declined, financial statements which report temporary investments at their acquisition cost could be misleading by implying a higher value for the securities than is realizable. In these cases, the value of the temporary investment will be lowered to the market value and a corresponding *holding loss* will be recognized. This valuation practice is known as the **lower of cost or market principle.**

Lower of cost or market is applied by comparing the total acquisition cost of all temporary investments with the total market value of these investments at the end of the accounting period. If the market value is lower than the cost, a loss is recognized, and the asset account Temporary Investments is reduced by the difference. Normally, the asset is reduced by means of a valuation or contra account, which is subsequently offset against the asset in the financial statements.

To illustrate this process, assume that the Derek Company had the following portfolio of temporary investments as of December 31:

	December 31, 19X9		
Security	Cost	Market	Increase (Decrease)
A	$10,000	$11,000	$ 1,000
B	7,000	4,000	(3,000)
C	5,000	3,000	(2,000)
Total	$22,000	$18,000	$(4,000)

At the end of the year, the market value of these securities is less than their acquisition cost. Consequently, a loss of $4,000 will be recognized and the value of the securities will be reduced by that amount.

While the account, Temporary Investments, could be reduced directly, usually, a separate valuation account is used so that the historical cost of the investments is preserved in the resulting reports. In this case, the following journal entry would be made:

Loss on Temporary Investments	$4,000	
Allowance for Decline in Value of		
Temporary Investments		$4,000
To value temporary investments at the lower of cost or market		

The reported loss will be included in the income statement for the period. The allowance account will be reported on the balance sheet as an offset against the historical cost balance for temporary investments as follows:

Current Assets:		
Temporary Investments	$22,000	
Less: Allowance for Decline in Value	4,000	$18,000

In subsequent accounting periods, increases in the value of temporary investment portfolio up to the amount of the original cost could be recognized by decreasing (debiting) the allowance account and increasing (crediting) a corresponding gain account. Because of the short-term nature of temporary investments, it is unlikely that offsetting gains will be recognized.

When a temporary investment is sold, the gain or loss to be recognized on the sale is the difference between the original acquisition cost and the selling price. Previous valuation adjustments do not enter into the calculation. This follows the view that lower of cost or market is applied to the entire portfolio rather than to specific parts of the portfolio. However, if the whole portfolio of marketable securities is liquidated, the gain or loss will be determined with reference to the net book value of the portfolio.

Disposition of Temporary Investments

If, in the previous example, security C was sold for $3,500, a loss of $1,500 would result and would be recognized through the following entry:

Cash	$3,500	
Loss on Sale of Temporary Investments	1,500	
Temporary Investments		$5,000
To record the sale of Security C		

Accounting for the sale of temporary investments follows that procedure used for the sale of any other assets (except, of course, for inventory); the asset account is written down, the receipt is recognized, and any resulting gain or loss is reported.

DISPOSITION OF TEMPORARY INVESTMENTS

Receivables

Receivables are claims held by the business against others for money or goods and services. Receivables are generated primarily from the sale of goods and services on credit, but they also result from transactions involving loans made to others, rentals, leases, or various types of refunds. Receivables that are collectable within one year or the normal operating cycle of the business are classified as current assets; all other receivables are listed as investments in the noncurrent assets section of the balance sheet. Receivables which result from the sale of goods and services in the course of normal operations are called *trade receivables*. Other types of receivables would be identified by the specific purpose of the transaction, such as loans to employees or interest on loans.

Trade receivables that are not supported by a written promissory note are normally short-term in duration (30 to 90 days) and do not have an explicit interest rate. As discussed in Chapter 5, many receivables bear an implicit interest in the terms of the invoice—such as 2/10, *n*/30 (2 percent discount if paid within 10 days but the net amount is due in 30 days).

In contrast, notes receivable are supported by a formal written promise to pay a certain sum (principal) of money at a fixed or determinable future time. Trade notes receivable are often used with goods and services with a high selling price or an extended payment period and for settling outstanding accounts receivable balances. Nontrade notes receivable may arise from transactions involving loans or the sale of noncurrent assets. Most notes provide for a specific interest rate to be charged for the period that the note is outstanding. Notes that do not specify a provision for interest are referred to as noninterest bearing and only the principal amount is due at maturity. Normally, an interest charge is implicitly provided in the terms of such a note. That is, the face amount of the note is higher than the cash value of a comparable transaction; the interest has been added.

Interest terms are usually specified in terms of an annual rate (for simplicity, interest will be calculated on the basis of 360 days per year) and is applied to the principal amount. Interest is calculated by the formula:

$$\text{Interest} = \text{Principal} \times \text{rate} \times \text{time}$$

Thus, the interest on a $2,000, 9 percent, 90-day note would be computed as follows:

$$\text{Interest} = \$2,000 \times 0.09 \times 90/360$$
$$= \$45$$

In this case, the amount due at the maturity of the note would be $2,045—the principal plus the interest. Terms specified by the creditor determine whether the computation of interest includes a day for the date that the note was originated and/or the date of replacement.

In the case of interest-bearing notes, the interest revenue accrues, or is earned, over the period of the note. When a note originates in one accounting period and matures in another, an adjusting entry must be made to properly reflect the interest earned during each period. When a note originates and matures in the same period, the interest revenue is recorded at maturity.

Accounting for Notes Receivable

To illustrate, assume that on November 1, 19X9, Hawsey Company accepted a $2,000, 9 percent, 90-day note from a customer in settlement of an open, or outstanding, account receivable. Hawsey Company would record the receipt of the note as follows:

Notes Receivable	$2,000	
Accounts Receivable		$2,000
To record the transfer of an open account to a note		

As discussed in Chapter 4, if the note extends beyond the end of an accounting period, an adjusting entry is necessary to record the interest revenue earned during the period and to record the interest receivable at the end of the period. If the Hawsey Company's accounting period ended on December 31, the following adjusting entry would be made:

Accrued Interest Receivable	$30	
Interest Revenue		$30
(Calculated as $2,000 \times 0.09 \times 60/360$)		

The entry at the date of collection of the note and interest would be[1]:

Cash	$2,045	
Notes Receivable		$2,000
Accrued Interest Receivable		30
Interest Revenue		15
To record the collection of an interest-bearing note		

If the holder of the note is unable to collect from the maker at maturity, the note is termed *dishonored*. Since the holder still has a legal claim to the principal and interest, an entry should be made to record the dishonored note receivable at its maturity value. For example, if the note held by the

---

[1]If the period of the note had not extended beyond the end of the period, no adjusting entry would have been made. The following entry would have been made on the collection date:

Cash	$2,045	
Notes Receivable		$2,000
Interest Revenue		45

Hawsey Company proved to be uncollectable, the following entry would be made on the maturity date:

Notes Receivable—Dishonored	$2,045	
Notes Receivable		$2,000
Accrued Interest Receivable		30
Interest Revenue		15
To record a dishonored note		

If the note is subsequently collected, the Notes Receivable–Dishonored account is eliminated. If the note is ultimately determined to be uncollectable, the amount would be moved from Notes Receivable–Dishonored and written off against Bad Debt Expense or Allowance for Doubtful Accounts.

Discounting Notes Receivable

A promissory note is a legally negotiable instrument that can be readily transferred between parties. For various reasons, a business may transfer a note receivable to a bank or other financial institution to obtain funds. The transfer is facilitated by the holder of the note endorsing it over to the bank. The process is similar to transferring a check by endorsement. The bank charges interest at a specified interest rate (referred to as the *discount rate*) for the use of its money on the maturity value of the note (principal plus interest). The bank will collect from the maker of the note at maturity. The proceeds received by the business are determined by deducting the amount of interest charged by the bank from the maturity value of the note.

Normally, notes transferred are endorsed with recourse. Recourse means that the endorser is liable to the bank if the maker of the note does not pay the bank at maturity. A contingent, or possible, liability results from discounting notes receivable, and it must be disclosed in the financial statements. A footnote is normally used to make the disclosure. The contingent liability is eliminated at the maturity of the note, when it is paid, or dishonored. If dishonored, the liability will become actual, rather than contingent.

When notes receivable are discounted, the payee receives proceeds calculated in the following manner:

1. Compute the maturity value of the note:
   Maturity value = principal + (principal × rate × time)
2. Compute the discount on the maturity value:
   Discount = maturity value × discount rate × time to maturity
3. Compute cash proceeds:
   Proceeds = maturity value − discount

An Example. To illustrate the accounting procedures related to discounting, assume that the Hawsey Company discounted a $2,000, 9 percent, 90-day note receivable at a bank after 30 days have elapsed at a 12 percent discount rate. The proceeds received by the Hawsey Company are computed as follows:

$$\text{Maturity value} = \$2{,}000 + (\$2{,}000 \times 0.09 \times 90/360)$$
$$= \$2{,}045$$
$$\text{Discount} = \$2{,}045 \times 0.12 \times 60/360$$
$$= \$40.90$$
$$\text{Proceeds} = \$2{,}045.00 - \$40.90$$
$$= \$2{,}004.10$$

This process may be viewed as a set of financial transactions involving two loans. First, the Hawsey Company loaned $2,000 to a customer for 90 days at 9 percent interest. Subsequently, the Hawsey Company borrowed funds from the bank for 60 days at 12 percent interest. The difference between the initial note and the amount borrowed is the net proceeds received by the Hawsey Company.

When a note is discounted, the payee records the transaction by a debit (increase) to cash and a credit (decrease) to notes receivable. A balancing debit or credit will be made to interest expense or to interest revenue. The Hawsey Company would record the discounting as follows:

Cash	$2,004.10	
Notes Receivable		$2,000.00
Interest Revenue		4.10

To record discounting a 90 day, 9 percent note for 60 days at 12 percent

The interest revenue recorded at the time of discounting is actually the net difference between the interest revenue accrued on the note through maturity less the interest expense charged by the bank from the date of discount to maturity. In some cases (depending on the relationship between the interest rate on the note, the bank discount rate, and the time to maturity), the interest expense charged by the bank may exceed the accrued interest on the note. In these instances, the payee records the net interest on discounting the note. For example, if the Hawsey Company discounted the note on the same date, but the bank discount rate was 15 percent, the proceeds would be $1,993.88 and the transaction would be recorded as follows:

Cash	$1,993.88	
Interest Expense	6.12	
Notes Receivable		$2,000.00

To record discounting a 90 day, 9 percent note for 60 days at 15 percent

Because the payee of the note is contingently liable for the note a footnote disclosure would be made until the note matures. If the note is paid by the maker, the footnote would be removed. However, if the note is dishonored, and the payee must fulfill the liability, the following entry would be made:

Notes Receivable-Dishonored $2,045
    Cash $2,045
To record payment on a dishonored note

Summary

Cash, temporary investments, and receivables are fundamental financial resources of the firm. By its nature, cash is volatile and must be controlled to ensure its effective utilization and its security. Internal controls are an important part of the accounting system and relate to policies, procedures, and activities that are intended to safeguard assets and promote their effective utilization.

One control process requires all cash to be deposited in checking accounts and properly endorsed checks to be used for all disbursements. This action adds to the firm's system of control over cash. Periodically, the bank will report an account balance which, along with the balance shown in the firm's books, must be reconciled to derive the correct cash balance. As a part of the bank reconciliation process, items that should be brought to the attention of the bank will be found along with items that should be recorded in the books of the company. Notifications and adjusting entries should be made.

Many organizations will maintain an accessible supply of cash in a petty cash fund. The purpose of this fund is to pay for incidental items that require cash. The fund is limited in size and is controlled by periodic counts of the cash balance and the voucher receipts.

Temporary investments are made to earn a return on otherwise idle cash balances. The managerial intention is to convert these investments back to cash in the near future. Consequently, they are disclosed as a current asset rather than as a long-term investment. Income is recorded as earned and is accrued at the time of statement preparation. Many times, temporary investments are valued at the lower of cost or market to ensure conservatism in the financial statements.

Receivables represent claims against others that are due in the near future. They are reported as current assets on the balance sheet. Notes receivable represent a formal written document in support of the promise to pay. Notes normally are recorded at their principal amount, and interest is recognized as earned. Notes may be discounted, or sold, to a bank or other financial institution. In these cases, the original holder, or payee, usually is held liable for the payment until it is actually made.

A Supplementary Discussion: Fund Accounting

The accounts of most nonprofit organizations are divided into several *funds,* each of which is a self-balancing accounting entity, designed to measure the fiscal responsibility for particular activities within a multifunction nonprofit organization. Each fund maintains a complete set of accounts, Assets, Liabilities, Fund Balance (equity), Revenues, and Expenditures, and these are used to record data solely concerned with that particular fund. For example, the accounting systems of governmental units have general funds to account for receipts and expenditures of general purpose (not restricted) resources, special funds to account for receipts and disbursements of resources earmarked for particular purposes, such as education and libraries, revolving or self-sustaining funds to account for operations that are self-sustaining once they are established, such as motor pools and centralized purchasing, and trust funds to account for resources held in trust for specified purposes in accordance with donor or legal specifications. Hospitals have similar funds with titles such as operating fund, special purpose fund, plant fund, endowment fund, and construction fund. Colleges, churches, and charitable organizations use general funds, trust funds, and others as appropriate to their operations.

A second attribute of nonprofit fund accounting is the integration of budgetary accounts into the accounting system, a feature that is absent from accounting systems of profit-oriented organizations. Accounts are created for budgeted Revenue, Budgeted Expenditure, and the accompanying Budgeted Liabilities, and financial estimates from approved budgets are formally journalized and posted to the budgetary accounts. This integration makes possible the comparison by funds of actual results with budgeted expectations. Although an automatic comparison does not assure that resources were used efficiently, it does indicate the effectiveness of the budgeting process, as well as giving some assurance that expenditures were properly authorized and that resources were used only for authorized purposes. Assurance that expenditures are authorized is particularly important in accounting for governmental units because budgeted expenditures, when approved by a legislative body, become legal authorizations to spend. An excess expenditure would therefore constitute a violation of a spending ordinance.

A third feature of fund accounting for nonprofit organizations is an inordinate concern about the flow of resources into and through each fund. Attention thus focuses on *expenditures* rather than *expenses* in a shift toward cash-basis accounting rather than the common-accrual-basis accounting used by commercial organizations. Cash-basis accounting recognizes revenue when it is collected and cost when it is paid, in contrast to accrual accounting that recognizes revenue when it is earned and expense when it is incurred. That is, revenue may be received in a period other than when it is earned, and cost may be paid in periods different than when it is incurred. Under the typical nonprofit cash-basis accounting, capital expenditures receive the same accounting treatment as current expenditures, and depreciation is not recognized as a cost of operations. There are exceptions to this generalization for particular types of nonprofit organizations. Hospitals, for example, use many accrual accounting procedures as do particular funds within most nonprofit organizations, including governmental units.

For an example of the interrelationships between funds of a nonprofit organization, consider the financial statements for Display City, presented in Exhibit 7-3. The municipality expects to receive and spend $113,000 from all sources during the coming fiscal year. Legal, legislative, and administrative restrictions prohibit the $113,000 from being spent for unauthorized purposes. Four funds are maintained: the General Fund, the School Fund, the Motor Pool, and the Cemetery Trust Fund.

EXHIBIT 7-3
STATEMENT OF REVENUES AND EXPEDITURES:
Display City

	Total	General Fund	School Fund	Motor Pool	Cemetery Trust Fund
Revenue					
Taxes	$108,000	$50,000	$58,000	$ 0	$ 0
Investment Income	2,000	0	0	0	2,000
Interfund Charges	3,000	0	0	3,000	0
	$113,000	$50,000	$58,000	$3,000	$2,000
Expenditures					
Salaries	$ 61,200	$20,000	$40,000	$1,000	$ 200
Supplies and Materials	19,700	7,500	10,000	1,000	1,200
Contractual Services	18,100	10,000	7,600	0	500
Capital Outlays	11,000	10,000	0	1,000	0
Interfund Charges	3,000	2,500	400	0	100
	$113,000	$50,000	$58,000	$3,000	$2,000

The operations of the motor pool are financed from charges made against other funds that use motor pool services, and therefore, $3,000 of the total amount shown involves double counting. For example, the $1,000 salaries expenditure in the motor pool is also counted as part of the $400 interfund charges assigned to the school fund and the $2,500 assigned to the general fund. A separate fund for the motor pool is created as an administrative control to improve services and provide an equitable means of allocating the cost of motor pool facilities to common users of those facilities.

The actual accounts for each fund should follow the format established in the budget. Comparing actual results with budgeted authorizations by funds provides the following assurances: (1) trust fund income has not been used to finance police operations or local schools, (2) taxes levied for education have not been spent for capital improvements, and (3) amounts appropriated for teachers' salaries have not been spent for sanitation.

Key Terms

Cash
Internal control
Bank reconciliation statement
Petty cash fund
Temporary investments
Lower of cost or market principle
Trade receivables
Discount rate

1. Identify the individual accounts that may be grouped together on the financial statements under the caption Cash.

2. Why is restricted cash reported separately from the account *Cash*? What are the implications of failing to classify restricted cash separately?

3. What is meant by internal control? Why is this of concern to the accountant dealing with cash?

4. Identify the characteristics of a good internal control system. Give an example of each characteristic.

5. In what way can a bank checking account assist in providing internal control?

6. What is the purpose of a bank reconciliation? Describe the major sections of the reconciliation statement.

7. Discuss the nature of journal entries made as a result of completing a bank reconciliation statement.

8. For what purpose is a petty cash fund usually established? Describe the nature of controls used to monitor the petty cash fund.

9. Temporary investments are made for what purpose? Is there a difference in managerial intent between temporary investments and long-term investments?

10. Describe the valuation practice of lower of cost or market as applied to temporary investments. Explain the rationale for applying lower of cost or market to information that will appear on the financial statements.

11. Why are notes receivable sometimes discounted? Discounting has sometimes been equated to borrowing. Explain why this is true.

12. Cash has been described as a fundamental financial resource. Why is this description used?

13. Is the bank reconciliation process different for business organizations and individual people? Discuss any major differences or similarities.

14. Alternatives are available to the accountant in valuing temporary investments. How can meaningful reports result if the information can be influenced by the accountant's judgment?

15. Notes and accounts receivable can be discounted, or sold, to financial intermediaries called factors. Explain how the factoring business can be profitable.

1. Several financial resources are listed below. Identify which ones would be classified as *Cash*. Explain why items not classified as Cash were so identified.
(a) Coin and currency.
(b) A promissory note.
(c) Checks.
(d) Funds restricted for paying employee bonuses.
(e) Savings account deposits.

2. A check is a negotiable financial instrument. Identify how each of the following characteristics or features of a check contribute to internal control.

(a) Sequential numbering.
(b) Printed address of maker.
(c) Numerical and written amount.
(d) Name of bank.
(e) Date.

3. The general form of a bank reconciliation statement has four parts as shown below:

Balance Bank Statement
Add: Type A items
Less: Type B items
Correct Cash Balance
Balance per Books
Add: Type C items
Less: Type D items
Correct Cash Balance

Using the letters A through D, as appropriate, identify where each of the following items would appear in a reconciliation statement.
(a) Deposit in transit.
(b) Collection of a note by the bank.
(c) Outstanding checks.
(d) Service charges.
(e) NSF check that was returned.
(f) Debit memorandum.
(g) Credit memorandum.

4. Make the necessary journal entries to record the following petty cash activity:
(a) Fund of $1,000 is established.
(b) $100 is paid for postage.
(c) $200 is paid for supplies.
(d) The fund is reimbursed for $300, and vouchers for $100 and $200 are available.
(e) The fund is permanently reduced to $500.

5. Management of the Key Company decided to invest some surplus cash until it was needed later in the year. Make the necessary journal entries to record the events described below:

Jan. 15   Bought 100 shares of Lock Company common stock at $12 per share plus $40 brokerage commission.
Jan. 20   Received $10 (10 cents a share) as a dividend on the stock.
Feb. 1   Sold 50 shares at $11 per share. No brokerage commission was paid on the sale.

6. The Vest Company has a portfolio of temporary investments. The original cost of these securities including brokerage commissions is as follows: Security G—$7,500; Security M—$20,000; Security C—$15,000. On December 31, the market values of these securities are calculated and used to determine the reported

value of temporary investments. The Company uses the lower of cost or market valuation method.

Determine the total value of Marketable Securities to be reported on the balance sheet in each case given below:

	Security		
Case	G	M	C
A	$6,000	$21,000	$13,000
B	5,000	18,000	20,000
C	7,500	19,000	16,000
D	7,000	18,000	14,000

7. The Watson Printing Company accepted a $5,000, 12 percent, 90-day note from one of its customers on June 1, 19X7.

(a) Prepare the journal entries that Watson would make on June 1 to record the acceptance of the note and 90 days later to record its collection.

(b) Assume that the Watson Printing Company's fiscal year ends on June 30, 19X7. Prepare the entries that would be made on June 1, June 30, and August 30 relative to this note.

8. The Leaf Company accepted a $1,000, 6 percent, 60-day note from Ted Bates on January 1. On February 1, the Company discounted the note at Watt's Bank and Trust Company. The bank charged an 8 percent discount rate. On March 1, Leaf was informed that Ted Bates had defaulted on the note. On April 1, Ted Bates settled with Leaf for the full value that was owed. Prepare the journal entries that Leaf Company would make on each date above.

9. On November 1, several notes received from customers of AAA Company were discounted at the First Bank. The bank discount rate was 10 percent. Calculate the net proceeds paid by the bank for each note described below:

(a) A $10,000, 90-day note with 9 percent interest dated October 1.

(b) A $4,000, 12 percent, 120-day note dated September 1.

(c) A 10 percent, $1,000, 60-day note dated November 1.

10. Jones Company received a bank statement indicating a balance of $1,250. The company's books indicated a balance of $1,000.

(a) Using the supplemental information shown below, prepare a bank reconciliation:

Deposits in transit were $300.

A $20 check for supplies had been erroneously recorded in the journal as $200 by the company.

Checks totaling $400 were not cleared through the bank.

Bank service charges were $30 for the month.

(b) What journal entries should be made by the Jones Company?

11. Determine the unknown data in each of the following independent situations

using your knowledge of bank reconciliations, assuming that in each case the amounts do reconcile:

	A	B	C
Balance per books	$600	$14,170	$1,950
Balance per bank	937	13,650	————
Outstanding checks	————	755	640
NSF Checks	110	300	220
Notes Collected by Bank	0	500	100
Bank Service Charge	10	25	10
Deposit in Transit	60	————	370

12. Calculate the proceeds to be received in discounting the following notes receivable:

	Terms of Note			Discount	
Note	Principal	Term	Rate	Rate	Time to Maturity
A	$3,000	90 days	10%	9%	60 days
B	500	60 days	6%	9%	30 days
C	8,000	180 days	8%	8%	30 days
D	1,000	60 days	9%	8%	45 days
E	700	120 days	6%	10%	60 days

13. Record general journal entries for the following transactions involving a petty cash fund.
(a) Created the fund for $100.
(b) Increased the amount of the fund to $200.
(c) Reimbursed the fund for the following expenses:

Postage $ 28
Freight Fees   108
Supplies   21

(d) Reimbursed the fund for the following expenses:

Postage $ 31
Freight Fees   68
Supplies   39

(e) Reduced the fund balance to $150.

14. Lingham Company's fiscal year ends on April 30, and the company's certified public accountant, Sanders & Stein, conducts the annual audit during May and June. Sanders & Stein has prepared audit procedures for the different phases of the audit engagement with Lingham. Included in the audit program is a step calling for obtaining a bank confirmation and a statement directly from the Union State Bank. This is part of the audit program relating to cash on deposit in the bank. Why is it necessary for the auditor to secure a statement directly from the bank? Could this

procedure provide any information not available through the review of the company's monthly bank reconciliation (CMA adapted)?

1. The following independent situations relate to the cash controls of various businesses. In each situation, comment on the reasonableness of the procedures and their adequacy in providing internal control over cash. In cases where a control problem might exist, suggest procedures that could rectify the situation.

   (a) Able Company has expanded rapidly. No specific procedures for handling cash have been developed. "When a problem arises, we'll solve it then" says the president.

   (b) Because Baker Company is fairly small, the bookkeeper rotates his duties. About once every two weeks, he records cash receipts and disbursements.

   (c) The Denver Disbursing Company does not use prenumbered checks or a check protector to imprint the amount. The Company feels that the bookkeeper has a distinctive handwriting.

   (d) Mildred Adams, president of a medium-sized firm, opposes any cash audits throughout the year. "Our business depends on our employees. To audit their cash would suggest that we don't trust them. We cannot afford to do this."

   (e) Frank's Bargain Store is very concerned about cash controls. Bank deposits are made five times a day as a part of company policy.

2. The Morris Company receives a monthly statement from the National Bank. On June 30, the bank reported a balance of $102,750. On the same date, the Company's books showed a balance of $133,460. The following information relates to the reconciliation process:

   (a) A deposit of $23,000 was mailed to the bank on June 29. It does not appear on the bank statement.

   (b) A deposit of $11,000 was taken to the bank on June 30. It does not appear on the bank statement.

   (c) The bank statement included a credit memorandum for $2,200, resulting from the collection by the bank of a note receivable. The note was for $2,000 and provided for $200 interest at maturity.

   (d) A debit memorandum with the bank statement reported a $20 fee for collecting the note described in (c).

   (e) Twelve checks, totaling $1,730, were not included in the bank statement.

   (f) The bank notified the Company a check for $300, included in a deposit, had been returned because of insufficient funds.

   (g) Check 619 included with the bank statement was made payable to Jones Company for supplies. The check had been incorrectly journalized by Morris as $210, but it was actually written for $21.

   (h) The bank statement showed that three checks written by the Marris Company had been deducted from the Morris Company account. The checks totaled $480.

   (i) The bank adjusted the account for service charges of $29 for the month.

(1) Prepare a bank reconciliation statement for the Company as of June 30.

(2) After reviewing the reconciliation statement, prepare any appropriate journal entries for Morris Company. Should Morris take additional actions?

3. The Zebra Company established a petty cash fund to provide a source of cash for small recurring expense items. Each disbursement from the fund required a voucher; vouchers were accumulated and recorded when the fund was replenished. Prepare the three general journal entries that would be made for the following petty cash activities during January:

1/2 Petty cash fund of $300 is established.

1/3 $30 paid for postage; $20 for office supplies.

1/4 Shipping supplies of $40 were purchased.

1/5 $10 paid for postage.

1/6 $25 was paid for office supplies.

1/9 The petty cash fund was replenished.

1/10 $50 was spent for office supplies and $40 for shipping supplies.

1/11 $20 paid for postage; a miscellaneous item of $10 was also paid.

1/12 $15 was paid to the Post Office for special handling mail.

1/13 Stationary costing $30 was purchased. $20 was paid for service on the office water cooler.

1/16 The petty cash fund was replenished.

4. On February 1, Johnson Company invested surplus cash in two temporary investments. The firm bought 100 shares of A Company stock for $5,000 and 100 shares of B Company stock for $4,000. Brokerage costs were $400 on the first purchase and $300 on the last.

B Company declared a dividend of $2 per share which was paid on March 1. The Johnson Company's fiscal year ends on March 31. On that date, A Company stock was selling for $40 per share and B Company stock for $30 per share.

On April 15, Johnson Company sold its stock in company A for $60 per share and its B Company Stock for $50 per share.

REQUIRED:

(a) Prepare the journal entries that would be made by the Johnson Company on each of the dates identified above.

(b) Show how temporary investments would be disclosed on the company's balance sheet on March 31.

(c) If the stock in A Company and B Company was not sold on April 15, but held for another year when the market prices were $90 and $30 per share, respectively, how would they be reported and valued on the balance sheet?

5. The Take Company accepted several notes from customers in exchange for food delivery equipment that they sell. Prepare the proper journal entries to record the transactions described below:

January 10	Accepted a $2,000, 8 percent note from Albert Adams due in 30 days.
January 15	Accepted a $5,000, 10 percent note from Buddy Baker due in 30 days.
February 9	Collected Adams note plus interest.
February 14	Collected Baker note plus interest.
March 1	Accepted a $10,000, 6 percent note from Charles Case due in 90 days.
April 30	Discounted the Charles Case note at the Jones Bank. The discount rate was 9 percent.
June 10	Jones Bank informed Take that Charles Case has defaulted on the note.
June 15	The Charles Case note is deemed to be uncollectable.

6. The tables shown below present information about a series of notes. Complete the missing information in each table:

Note	Date Originated	Period	Date Due	Interest Rate	Face Amount	Amount Received
A	March 1	30 days	March 31	?	$1,000	$1,005
B	April 1	60 days	?	12%	2,000	?
C	May 1	?	July 30	10	5,000	?
D	June 1	120 days	?	12	?	1,040

					Discount		
Note	Date Originated	Period	Interest Rate	Face Amount	Date	Rate	Proceeds
E	June 1	60 days	6%	$1,000	July 1	12%	?
F	July 1	120 days	10	2,000	July 31	5%	?
G	May 1	60 days	8	3,000	May 1	8%	?

7. The Quantum Company has reported the following items in its cash account as of December 31, 19X6:
   (a) Cash balance in checking account, $6,947.00.
   (b) Cash balance in savings account, $1,000.00. The bank reserves the right to require 30 days notice of withdrawal, but has never required such notice for balances below $10,000.
   (c) Petty cash on hand for office use, $200.
   (d) Cash balances of $50 in each of six cash registers in its retail store.

(e) Postage stamps costing $40.

(f) A one-year bank Certificate of Deposit, costing $5,000, maturing two months after year end and paying $300 in interest. The bank does not permit withdrawal of the funds prior to maturity.

(g) $500 in cash are currently on deposit in a Mexican bank and are temporarily frozen (i.e., may not be withdrawn) because of a local legal dispute.

(h) The firm has $8,000 in a fund for use in paying off a long-term liability that falls due in two years. The creditor required these funds to be accumulated in a "sinking" fund.

REQUIRED:

(a) What is the correct balance of cash for the Quantum Company on December 31, 19X6?

(b) What adjusting entry would be required to properly report these amounts?

(c) How would the noncash items be classified on the balance sheet—Current Assets, Noncurrent Assets, or some other classification?

8. On August 31 the cash account of the AAA Corporation totaled $680. On that date the bank statement received by the firm indicated a balance of $1,040. An analysis of the firm's cash records and the bank statement reveals the following:

(a) Deposits in transit on August 31 total $290.

(b) Outstanding checks on August 31 total $705.

(c) The bank accidentally charged the firm's account with a $110 check drawn on the AA Corporation.

(d) Service charges of $5 are shown on the bank statement but unrecorded on the books of the firm.

(e) The bank has charged the firm's account for a $90 NSF check.

(f) The bank statement also shows that the bank collected a note for the firm, totaling $140 in principal and $10 in interest, and has credited the account for those amounts.

REQUIRED:

(a) Prepare a bank reconciliation as of August 31.

(b) Make the necessary general journal entries to adjust the cash account to its appropriate balance.

(c) What other actions should be taken in light of this reconciliation?

9. The Ash Company finds itself with substantial amounts of cash on hand during certain times of the year, and normally invests these funds. The Ash Company had the following transactions involving termporary investments during the year:

(a) Acquired 100 shares of Terminal, Inc., common stock at a total cost of $3,100.

(b) Acquired 200 shares of Aileen, Inc., for $1,000.

(c) Received $50 dividend from Terminal, Inc.

(d) Acquired 100 shares of IBM for $25,000.

(e) Sold the Terminal, Inc., stock for $3,600.

(f) Sold the Aileen, Inc., stock for $900.

(g) Received a dividend of $250.

(h) Acquired 100 shares of Technology, Inc., for $6,000.

REQUIRED:

(a) Prepare general journal entries to record these transactions.

(b) The IBM stock has a fair market value of $23,800 and the Technology stock is worth $5,000 at year-end. Prepare any adjusting entries needed to value these temporary investments at lower of cost or market *and* show the balance sheet presentation of these items.

□ 8
INVENTORY MEASUREMENT AND REPORTING

PHYSICAL FLOWS

PERPETUAL INVENTORY SYSTEMS

PERIODIC INVENTORY SYSTEMS

THE VALUATION PROCESS

SPECIFIC IDENTIFICATION

AVERAGE COST METHOD

FIRST-IN, FIRST-OUT METHOD

LAST-IN, FIRST-OUT METHOD

COMPARISON OF COST FLOW ASSUMPTIONS

COST FLOW IN PERPETUAL SYSTEMS

AVERAGE COST METHOD

LIFO METHOD

INVENTORY ON THE BALANCE SHEET

LOWER OF COST OR MARKET

INVENTORY ESTIMATION

SUMMARY

A SUPPLEMENTARY DISCUSSION: INVENTORY CONTROL SYSTEMS

INTERNAL CONTROL SYSTEMS

MANAGEMENT CONTROL SYSTEMS

☐ OBJECTIVES

AFTER STUDYING THIS CHAPTER, YOU SHOULD BE ABLE TO DO THE FOLLOWING:

1. DESCRIBE THE DIFFERENCES IN RECORD KEEPING ASSOCIATED WITH USE OF THE PERPETUAL AND PERIODIC INVENTORY SYSTEMS, AND DEFINE THE ABBREVIATION, FOB.

2. DETERMINE INVENTORY VALUES THAT RESULT FROM USE OF FIFO, LIFO AND OTHER COST FLOW ASSUMPTIONS.

3. RELATE INVENTORY VALUES TO REPORTED INCOME.

4. DESCRIBE THE LOWER OF COST OR MARKET PROCEDURE.

5. PREPARE ESTIMATES OF INVENTORY VALUES.

Inventory is a significant component of current assets for most merchandising and manufacturing businesses. In a merchandising firm, *inventory* generally includes all of the goods that are available for sale to customers in the normal course of business. Manufacturing organizations usually maintain three types of inventories: raw materials, partially completed production, and finished merchandise ready for sale to customers. In addition, all businesses normally hold quantities of supplies for future use within the organization rather than for sale to customers. From an accounting point of view, inventory represents the dollar *balance* in the inventory accounts.

Business inventories are maintained to provide continuity of operations. Merchandise inventories link the acquisition or manufacturing functions and the customer; customer demand can be satisfied with goods from inventory, thus averting delays that would result if customers had to wait for goods to be acquired or manufactured. While customer satisfaction can be increased by stocking large quantities of a variety of goods, the maintenance of such stocks requires a significant investment. Inventory management involves the balancing of opposing forces—increased inventories to satisfy demand and reduced inventories to minimize costs. Inventory accounting systems are designed to provide management with information needed to make intelligent decisions affecting inventory policy. In particular, management must be able to understand the physical flow of inventory items, the accounting flow of costs, and the relationship between inventory value and cost of goods sold.

The impact of inventories on the financial statements is not limited to the balance sheet. As noted in Chapter 6, inventory plays an important role in the measurement of income. Beginning Inventory combines with net purchases to equal Goods Available For Sale, most of which becomes Cost of Goods Sold, as shown in Exhibit 8-1. Measurements of inventories at year-end not only affect the inventory account on the balance sheet, but

EXHIBIT 8-1
RELATIONSHIPS BETWEEN BEGINNING AND ENDING
INVENTORY AND COST OF GOODS SOLD

	19X1	19X2	19X3
Beginning Inventory	$ 40	$ 20	$ 30
Net Purchases	+ 60	+ 140	+ 150
Goods Available for Sale	100	160	180
Ending Inventory	− 20	− 30	− 25
Cost of Goods Sold	$ 80	$ 130	$ 155

also Cost of Goods Sold, and, ultimately, Net Income. Because ending inventory in one year becomes beginning inventory in the next year, as shown by the arrows in Exhibit 8-1, inventory balances relate to the income statements of a firm for two consecutive years. As a result, the proper determination of inventory has long been recognized by accountants as critical to both the balance sheet and the income statement.

The inventory measurement process involves two steps: first, the physical quantity of each inventory item must be determined and second, the physical quantity must be translated into dollar terms. The discussion in this chapter will focus on these two critical steps in measuring inventory for financial statement purposes.

Most organizations acquire stocks of merchandise or raw materials from external suppliers. The acquisition process usually starts when the seller receives a *purchase order.* Purchase price, credit terms, and delivery schedules are determined by negotiation, and a firm contract is established. Typically, the inventory of a business includes only those items to which the firm has *legal title.* In most cases, delivery of merchandise is the critical event that indicates passage of title. Thus, the point of delivery is usually used in accounting to determine when a purchase has occurred.

Physical Flows

Provisions in the agreement between buyer and seller indicate when legal title has passed between them. Unless otherwise specified, the point of delivery hinges on who has responsibility for delivering the purchased goods. If the seller has this responsibility, the purchase does not occur until the goods are received. This condition is commonly referred to as "F.O.B. destination," where F.O.B stands for "free on board." If the purchaser has the responsibility for delivery, termed "F.O.B. shipping point," legal title passes as soon as the carrier picks up the goods from the seller.

Once received, the merchandise becomes part of the inventory balance of the buyer and it remains in inventory until it is sold. Several accounting periods may elapse during that time, and physical counts of inventory stocks may be taken at the end of each period to validate the inventory levels. Physical counts and financial values are reconciled in the accounting inventory system. One of two major systems is generally used to account for inventory. The appropriateness of a perpetual or a periodic system will depend on the organization, its inventory characteristics, and its information needs.

Some companies desire data on the inventory balances at any moment in time. A *perpetual inventory system* facilitates this by providing a running count of the number of units and unit costs of each inventory item. At the heart of such systems are perpetual inventory cards or files. The card for an

Perpetual Inventory Systems

PERPETUAL INVENTORY SYSTEMS

EXHIBIT 8-2
PERPETUAL INVENTORY CARD

Part No.: A703			Weight	Class	Reorder Point	Reorder Quantity
Description: Leg Assembly			2.5 lbs.	A761	200	1,000

	Received (Purchased)		Shipped (Sales)		Balance (Inventory)		
Date	Units	Unit Cost	Units	Unit Cost	Units	Unit Cost	Total Cost
1/1	Balance				700	$5	$3,500
1/6			200	$5	500	$5	2,500
1/10	Ordered	1,000					
			300	$5	200	$5	1,000
1/15			100	$5	100	$5	500
1/17	1,000	5.50			100	$5	
					1,000	$5.50	6,000
1/18			100	$5			
			100	$5.50	900	$5.50	4,950

inventory item usually shows the units and dollar value of each purchase, each sale or transfer, and the balance on hand. The perpetual inventory card produces a timely update of inventory activity, including the beginning balance, purchases, sales (at cost), and the current balance. This continuous record is maintained for every transaction involving the inventory item, thus providing a complete activity history. A perpetual inventory card is illustrated in Exhibit 8-2.

This card relates details concerning inventory activity of part A703, a leg assembly. A balance of 700 units was available at the beginning of the year. Issues of 200, 300, and 100 units were made on January 6, 10, and 15, respectively. An order for 1,000 units was placed on January 10 and received on January 17. An additional 200 units were shipped out on January 18; these units consisted of the remaining 100 units of the beginning balance and 100 units from the newest acquisition. Data about the four shipments during January would be determined from sales invoices, while information about the delivery would be obtained from a receiving report and supported by a copy of the purchase order.

Perpetual inventory records may be maintained manually, mechanically, or by means of a computer. Whatever the means, preparing such records is relatively costly, so they are usually reserved for use with expensive, low-balance inventory items. Perpetual records can be used to monitor inventory balances and trigger the reorder procedure. For example, the illustrated card designates a reorder quantity; when the balance falls below this point, an inventory clerk would initiate a purchase order.

Perpetual inventory cards also represent subsidiary inventory accounts. That is, the sum of the balances on the individual perpetual inventory cards will equal the balance in the Inventory control account. Formal journal entries would reflect the same information as appeared on the perpetual inventory cards. A summary entry to reflect the four decreases in inventory that accompany transfers of goods to customers would appear as follows:

```
Cost of Goods Sold      4,050
     Inventory                   4,050
     To record issuance of 700 units @ $5.00 and 100 units @ $5.50
```

A summary entry to reflect the acquisition of inventory would appear as follows:

```
Inventory                   5,500
     Accounts Payable              5,500
     To record the acquisition of 1,000 units @ $5.50
```

Periodic physical counts may be taken to verify the perpetual inventory records. Usually, an annual count will be made before the financial statements are prepared.

Periodic inventory systems do not require detailed records on specific inventory items. No ongoing count is kept of the actual usage of these items. Instead, *periodic inventory measurement* is based on physical counts of the goods on hand at the end of each period. The number of units on hand is multiplied by the purchase cost per unit (determined from the accounting records) to compute the total dollar value of inventory. Thus, the balance of goods on hand is not known until the last day of the period. The data in Exhibit 8-2 would be recast as follows if a periodic system was used:

Periodic Inventory Systems

Beginning Inventory	$3,500
+ Purchases	5,500
Available for Sale	$9,000
− Ending Inventory	4,950
Cost of Goods Sold	$4,050

Once the ending inventory is measured by a physical count, the cost of goods sold can be determined through deduction.

Remember that the journal entries used with a periodic inventory system differ from those used with a perpetual system. Purchases are recorded in separate account. Using the example data from above, the following entry would be made:

Purchases	$5,500	
Accounts Payable		$5,500

The Inventory account is not changed during the period and therefore it continually reflects the beginning inventory. At the end of the year, a physical count is taken, and the Inventory account is adjusted via the process of closing journal entries as follows:

Income Summary	$3,500	
Inventory		$3,500
To close out the beginning inventory		
Inventory	$4,950	
Income Summary		$4,950
To record the ending inventory in the accounts		

The purchases account is also closed out to income summary, as follows:

Income Summary	$5,500	
Purchases		$5,000
To close the purchases account		

The Valuation Process

Inventory value is determined by multiplying the physical quantity of goods in inventory by a per unit dollar amount. Accountants generally value assets on the balance sheet at their cost to the firm, and inventory is no exception. In theoretical applications of the cost principle, the term *cost includes all expenditures incurred to bring an item to its existing condition and location.* Thus, in addition to the invoice price of the merchandise, inventory costs should include transportation charges, transit insurance costs, material handling, and assembly labor costs.

As a practical matter, many businesses use separate accounts to retain information on each element of cost. The invoice cost of inventory enters the Inventory account in perpetual systems (or the Purchases account in periodic systems) while accounts titled Freight-in, Transit Insurance, Materials Handling, and Assembly Labor collect information on other cost elements. These separate accounts provide management with information useful for control and decision-making purposes (e.g., should purchases be air-freighted or trucked in). Often these costs are classified as expenses and are reported in the income statement for the period in which they were incurred. Thus, they are not always included in the inventory as an asset.

Although the concept of cost valuation is relatively simple, its application is not without complications. No difficulty exists if the cost of inventory items is constant. If 40 units were sold and 50 units remained in inventory, the constant cost would be multiplied by the units to determine the cost of goods sold and the ending inventory value. However, if costs change during the period, the accountant must decide which value to assign to which units. In a competitive economy, it is unusual for unit costs to remain constant over time.

To address changing prices, accountants have developed cost-flow methods and assumptions, including:

1. Specific identification.
2. Average cost.
3. First-in, first-out (FIFO).
4. Last-in, first-out (LIFO).

Each method assigns a different dollar amount to a given physical quantity of goods under conditions of changing prices. The computation of inventory values using each of these methods is described and explained below. The objective of each method is to value the ending inventory and, as a consequence, the cost of goods sold.

Accuracy is greatest if actual unit costs are accumulated and associated with specific units. *Specific identification* requires that a record is made of the acquisition cost of each inventory item by coding the cost on the item itself or by maintaining a perpetual record of items by serial number. As a sale is completed, the specific unit cost is identified and recorded as a cost of sales, thus excluding it from inventory.

Specific Identification

For example, a car dealer might purchase an automobile and prepare an inventory card identifying it by the manufacturer's serial number. In addition to the cost, the card could list other useful sales information, such as optional equipment. If the car remains unsold at the inventory date, its cost is easily determinable for valuation purposes. When it is eventually sold, the cost of a specific automobile will become part of the cost of goods sold and the inventory card will be placed in a reference file.

In contrast to the above situation, a supermarket could not begin to maintain adequate records for the thousands of items it maintains in its inventory. Normally, the specific identification method is practical where:

1. A relatively few number of items are included in inventory.
2. The units are readily identifiable by a serial number or other unique characteristics.
3. Unit costs are high.

The expense of keeping detailed records must be evaluated in terms of benefits. Usually, minimum benefit results from extensive detail about low unit-cost items.

**Average
Cost Method**

One cost-flow assumption that may be used in determining inventory cost is the average annual unit cost to the firm. The *average cost method* allocates the cost of goods available for sale between sales (cost of goods sold) and the ending inventory on a weighted average basis. Assume that there are ten units available for sale and that five different prices were paid for them ($70, 70, 60, 60, 50, 50, 40, 40, 30, 30) for a total cost of $500. If there are three units remaining in inventory, the pro rata distribution of cost would be:

$$\text{Inventory} = 3/10 \times \$500 = \$150$$
$$\text{Cost of sales} = 7/10 \times \$500 = \$350$$

This result is usually achieved using the following computational process:

1. Average unit cost is:

$$\frac{\text{Cost of goods available for sale}}{\text{Units available for sale}} = \frac{\$500}{10} = \$50$$

2. Total average cost is:

Cost of sales 7 × $50	=	$350
Ending inventory 3 × $50	=	150
Cost of goods available for sale	=	$500

The average unit cost of $50 is a weighted average, since it is based on total cost and total units involved for the period.

Exhibit 8-3 presents information about the inventory of the Redfern Corporation. If a periodic inventory system were used, inventory calculations would be made once a year. The average unit cost for the year would be calculated as follows:

$$\frac{\text{Cost of goods available for sale}}{\text{Units available for sale}} = \frac{\$1,280}{200} = \$6.40$$

This result becomes part of the cost of goods sold calculation. During the year, 50 units were sold. Their value is as follows:

$$\text{Average unit cost} \times \text{Units sold}$$
$$= \$6.40 \times 50$$
$$= \$320.00$$

EXHIBIT 8-3
REDFERN CORPORATION
Inventory Cost Information

Date		Units	Unit Cost	Total Cost
January	Beginning Inventory	100	$5	$ 500
February	Purchase	50	7	350
June	Purchase	20	8	160
October	Purchase	30	9	270
	Available for Sale	200		$1,280
	Sales (at cost)	50		A*
December	Inventory	150		B*

*The determination of unit cost and total sales cost is a function of the cost flow assumption.

The ending inventory is calculated as follows:

Average unit cost × Units in inventory
= $6.40 × 150
= $960.00

Together, the cost of goods sold ($320) and the ending inventory ($960) account for the total cost of units available for sale ($1,280).

First-in, First-out Method

The first-in, first-out, or *FIFO,* method makes the assumption that the first costs into the inventory (the oldest costs) are the first costs out of the inventory. Thus, the earliest costs incurred during the year are attached to the earliest units sold. Consequently, the ending inventory is priced at the most recent or latest unit costs paid by the firm. Some justification for using FIFO is that inventory values reported on the balance sheet should approximate current costs.

Many times, FIFO will approximate the actual flow of goods through the firm. The first units placed in stock are often the first units sold. However, the method is used to measure *cost flows* and is applicable regardless of the physical flow of goods. Thus, the cost-flow assumption, not the actual physical flow, determines the measurement method to be used.

In the Redfern Corporation example, FIFO assumes that the $5 units are sold first and the $9 units last. Consequently, the cost of goods sold would be $250; 50 units valued at $5 per unit. Ending inventory can be determined by deduction [goods available for sale less cost of goods sold

($1,280 − $250 = $1,030)] or by accumulating the costs of the *last* 150 units acquired (30 @ $9 + 20 @ $8 + 50 @ $7 + 50 @ $5 = 150 units at a total cost of $1,030).

Last-in, First-out Method

The last-in, first-out, or *LIFO* method makes the cost-flow assumption that the units costs paid most recently (last) are the first ones to be attached to the goods sold. This supports the view that the cost of sales should be measured at the most recent costs paid during the period for purchases. This is the opposite view of FIFO. Even though the LIFO cost-flow assumption rarely reflects the physical flow of goods, it is a widely used method because it often results in a realistic matching of current inventory costs with sales revenue. In doing this, however, it does distort the balance sheet value of inventory, reporting the oldest costs as inventory value.

In the preceding example, LIFO assumes that the costs associated with the latest acquisitions should be used to determine the cost of goods sold. Fifty units were sold with a LIFO cost of $430; included in the calculation are 30 units at $9 and 20 units at $8. Again, ending inventory can be determined by deduction ($1,280 − $430 = $850) or by accumulating the costs of the first 150 units acquired (100 @ $5 + 50 @ $7 = 150 units at a total cost of $850).

Comparison of Cost Flow Assumptions

The four cost flow assumptions discussed above are all acceptable methods for valuing inventories. Firms can generally choose whichever method they prefer since all are generally accepted. However, they will produce different results whenever unit costs vary over time.

The Redfern Corporation example has shown that the cost-flow assumption will influence both the ending inventory and the cost of goods sold calculation. This impact will be carried through to the income statement and the balance sheet. Exhibit 8-4 illustrates this effect for three of the methods.

Note that the FIFO method, in a period of *rising prices,* results in the highest net income. LIFO yields the lowest net income, while the average cost method falls in the middle. The differences in gross profit are equal to the differences in values assigned to ending inventory. That is, the FIFO cost of goods sold is $180 *lower* than the LIFO cost of sales, and the FIFO inventory is $180 *higher* than the LIFO inventory. Thus, the FIFO method defers some cost to future accounting periods. In this example, FIFO states the inventory at the most recent prices, which are higher, whereas the LIFO method includes the most recent costs in the cost of sales and prices the inventory at the older unit costs, which are lower. FIFO includes the more current costs of doing business on the balance sheet while LIFO tends to place these costs on the income statement. The average method tends to be in the middle of these extremes.

EXHIBIT 8-4
REDFERN CORPORATION
Cost Flow Comparisons

	Partial Income Statements Using		
	Average Cost	FIFO	LIFO
Sales (50 units @ $12)	$ 600	$ 600	$ 600
Cost of Sale			
Beginning Inventory	$ 500	$ 500	$ 500
Purchases	780	780	780
Available for Sale	$1,280	$1,280	$1,280
Ending Inventory*	960	1,030	850
Cost of Sales	$ 320	$ 250	$ 430
Gross Profit	$ 280	$ 350	$ 170

*Ending inventory will be reported as a current asset on the balance sheet.

In periods of *falling prices,* the distinction between LIFO and FIFO will reverse. FIFO, using older, higher costs, will result in the lowest net income, while LIFO will yield a higher income amount.

Perpetual inventory systems require a continuous determination of unit costs to facilitate updating the inventory records. The average cost method and the LIFO method can result in differences if a perpetual, instead of a periodic, system is used. Consider the following set of transactions:

Cost Flow in Perpetual Systems

Date	Transaction	Units	Unit Cost	Total Cost
Jan 10	Purchase	50	$4	$200
12	Purchase	50	$6	$300
14	Sale	(60)		
17	Purchase	40	$7	$280
18	Sale 2	(20)		

Average Cost Method. The average cost method will generally produce different results under a perpetual system than under a periodic system. Because costs are determined currently on a perpetual system, the average can consider only those costs incurred to date.

Two rules govern the assignment of costs to inventory and goods sold under the average cost method for perpetual inventory systems:

1. A new average cost is calculated *each time* new units are purchased.

EXHIBIT 8-5
PERPETUAL INVENTORY AND AVERAGE COST

Date	Received (Purchased)		Shipped (Sales)		Balance (Inventory)		
	Units	Unit Cost	Units	Unit Cost	Units	Unit Cost	Total Cost
1/10	50	$4			50	$4	$200
1/12	50	$6			100	$5*	500
1/14			60	$5	40	$5	200
1/17	40	$7			80	$6†	480
1/18			20	$6	60	$6	360

```
* Average cost = Total Cost/Total Units
              = $500/100
              = $5

† Average cost = Total Cost/Total Units
              = $480/80
              = $6
```

2. The cost of goods sold is determined by multiplying the number of units sold by the *current average cost per unit.*

This method is frequently called the *moving weighted average* method when applied to a perpetual inventory system.

The illustrated data would result in two calculations and different unit valuations for the two sales. These calculations and the results are illustrated in the perpetual inventory card shown in Exhibit 8-5.

On January 12, a weighted average was taken, and the unit cost was revised up to $5 per unit. Sales before this date would have been costed at $4 per unit. On the date of the next purchase, January 17, a new average is made and the per unit cost is revised to $6 per unit.

LIFO Method. The LIFO method of determining inventory cost will differ between the periodic and perpetual inventory systems. This results from LIFO values being based on the cost of the most recent acquisitions. Under a perpetual system, sales are valued at the most recent *costs to date,* instead of the most recent *costs incurred during the year.*

The example data is used to illustrate perpetual valuations in Exhibit 8-6. Cost of goods sold totals $480, and the ending inventory is valued at $300. If a periodic system were used, cost of goods sold would be $520 (40 @ $7 and 40 @ $6), and the ending inventory would be valued at $260.

Although the inventory system can lead to differences if LIFO is being used, FIFO will not differ under a periodic or a perpetual inventory system.

EXHIBIT 8-6
PERPETUAL INVENTORY AND LIFO

Date	Received (Purchased)		Shipped (Sales)		Balance (Inventory)		
	Units	Unit Cost	Units	Unit Cost	Units	Unit Cost	Total Cost
1/10	50	$4			50	$4	$200
1/12	50	$6			50	$4	
					50	$6	500
1/14			50	$6			
			10	$4	40	$4	160
1/17	40	$7			40	$4	
					40	$7	440
1/18			20	$7	40	$4	
					20	$7	300

Based on the earliest costs in the inventory, FIFO valuations will use the same data regardless of the inventory systems.

Merchandise inventory is reported in the current asset section of the balance sheet, typically after accounts receivable. As with all financial statement presentations, it is important to provide users with sufficient information. Consequently, balance sheet disclosures of inventory usually include a description of the cost flow assumption employed and the valuation method used. This information may be noted parenthetically or included in a footnote.

Inventory on the Balance Sheet

For example; the illustration below extracts part of the balance sheet of the Redfern Corporation:

REDFERN CORPORATION
Balance Sheet
Dec. 31, 19X6

Assets
Current Assets:
Cash		$570
Accounts Receivable	$129	
Less Allowance for Bad Debts	19	110
Merchandise Inventory (at cost using LIFO method)		850

If inventory is pledged as collateral for loans (or subject to other restrictions) that may have an impact on the decisions of financial statement users, full disclosure should be made.

Most valuations reported on the balance sheet are based on the *historical cost* of the particular item. The inventory valuation methods discussed so far are based on the historical cost of the inventory items. However, accountants became concerned that a reduction in the *fair market value* (selling price) of inventory below its *historical cost* (acquisition cost) to the firm could cause the financial statements to be misleading. Inventory could be valued on the balance sheet at a cost that exceeds the expected selling price. This assures that a loss from sale will result. However, the recognition of the loss would be deferred until a sale is actually made.

To respond to this concern, a *__lower of cost or market convention__* was developed as an alternative valuation technique. Lower of cost or market results in inventory reported on the balance sheet at the lower of its cost or fair market value. This leads to the recognition of losses at the time the loss occurs, instead of in later periods when the inventory is sold.

The adjustment is calculated by comparing the cost of individual items, groups of items, or the entire inventory, with the market price or replacement cost of those inventory items. Replacement cost is the amount that the firm must pay now to acquire similar goods. Thus, it is an acquisition cost, not a selling price. This process is shown below, comparing individual inventory items, which is the most common approach in practice.

Item	Original Cost	Market Value	Number of Units in Ending Inventory	Total Cost	Total Market Value	Total Lower of Cost or Market
A	.20	.25	100	$ 200	$ 250	$ 200
B	1.00	.80	100	100	80	80
C	5.00	6.00	200	1000	1,200	1000
D	4.00	3.00	300	1200	900	900
E	6.00	8.00	100	600	800	600
Total Lower of Cost or Market				$3,100		$2,780

In this case, inventory would be valued at $2,780 on the balance sheet. The difference between the cost ($3,100) and the lower of cost or market valuation ($2,780) would be reported on the income statement of separate cost item and identified as "Loss from Reduction of Inventory to the Lower of Cost or Market" ($320). As with other valuation methods, lower of cost or market provides a full accounting of all inventory costs; they are included in the balance sheet or reported on the income statement.

Some accountants argue that the lower of cost or market convention can confuse financial statement users by suggesting that the balance sheet reports the fair market values of assets. They maintain that the balance sheet should use either fair market values or historical costs and should not mix methods.

Lower of cost or market is defended on the grounds that it results in conservative financial statement presentations and is not unreasonably difficult to apply. It is commonly used in current financial accounting practice.

Periodic inventory systems are dependent on a physical count of the goods on hand to properly value the inventory. Physical counts are time-consuming and costly and often are taken only once a year to prepare the annual financial statements. However, many companies using periodic inventory systems need inventory data on an interim basis. Inventory valuation estimates can be made for these interim statements rather than making a physical count of all inventory. The most common estimating technique is the *gross profit method.*

This method makes use of the ratio of gross profit to sales:

$$\text{Gross profit ratio} = \text{gross profit} \div \text{sales}$$

The basic assumption underlying the gross profit method is that the gross profit ratio of the immediately preceding period is a reasonable approximation of the current period's ratio. The estimated ratio is used to compute the total gross profit, given a level of total sales. The cost of sales and ending inventory are then calculated, in that order.

To illustrate, assume that a firm's accounting records indicate the following account balances at the end of January:

	January	Prior Year
Sales	$200,000	$2,200,000
Purchases	$125,000	
Beginning Inventory	24,000	
Gross Profit		660,000
Operating Expenses	22,000	

These amounts can partially complete the following income statement:

Sales		$200,000
Cost of Sales:		
Beginning Inventory	$24,000	
Purchases	$125,000	
Available for Sale	$149,000	
Ending Inventory	?	
Cost of Sales		?
Gross Profit		$ 660.
Operating Expenses		$ 22,000
Net Income		$?

Last year, the firm earned a gross profit of $660,000 on sales of $2,200,000. Consequently, the gross profit ratio is:

$$\text{Gross profit ratio} = \$660,000 \div \$2,200,000 = .30$$

By assuming that the gross profit ratio is consistent, current estimations may be made. The income statement will be completed as follows:

Sales		$200,000
Cost of Sales:		
Beginning Inventory	$24,000	
Purchases	125,000	
Available for Sale	$149,000	
Ending Inventory	9,000 (3)	
Cost of Sales		140,000 (2)
Gross Profit		60,000 (1)
Operating Expenses		22,000
Net Income		$ 38,000

These amounts were determined by the following steps.

1. Gross profit $= \text{gross profit ratio} \times \text{sales}$
   $= .30 \times \$200,000$
   $= \$60,000$
2. Cost of sales $= \text{sales} - \text{gross profit}$
   $= \$200,000 - \$60,000$
   $= \$140,000$
3. Inventory $= \text{available for sale} - \text{cost of sales}$
   $= \$149,000 - \$140,000$
   $= \$9,000$

These calculations are estimates. If the gross profit percentage changes greatly, or if the inventory mix is composed of items with varying gross profit percentages, adjustments may be required to produce reliable estimates of the results of operations for the interim period.

Summary

Inventories are important items on the financial statements of most firms. By virtue of their size in relation to total assets and their role in the measurement of net income, proper accounting for inventory is critical if the firm's financial statements are to be meaningful.

There are two aspects of inventory measurement: (1) determining the physical quantity and (2) assigning a dollar value. Merchandise should be included in inventory only if the firm has legal title. The most common inventory system in use—the periodic system—determines inventory balances at year end only, by taking a physical count and adjusting the account balance for items in transit. A perpetual inventory system maintains a continuous count of inventory on hand.

Inventory is valued at either its cost or the lower of its cost or market value. Because a specific identification of costs of units sold is often impractical, the assignment of costs goods sold may be made on the basis of several inventory cost-flow assumptions—weighted average, FIFO, and LIFO. The weighted average method assigns average costs to sales, while the FIFO method assigns the earliest incurred costs to goods sold and the LIFO method assigns the latest incurred costs to goods sold. These methods may be used with either periodic or perpetual inventory systems.

In accounting for a periodic inventory system, merchandise acquired during the year is recorded in a purchases account. No attempt is made to keep the inventory account balance current. A perpetual system maintains a current inventory account balance, increasing the account for purchases and decreasing it for the cost of goods sold as these events occur.

The balance sheet presentation of inventory requires full disclosure of all relevant information about the inventory, including valuation technique and flow assumptions. For interim financial statement purposes, firms using a periodic inventory system often estimate inventory balances using the gross profit method, instead of counting all units each month or quarter.

Inventory is a major asset in most businesses. Because of its importance to the business and its constant movement in and out of the organization, inventory controls are especially critical to the firm. There are two major kinds of controls or control systems commonly found in business: *internal control systems* and *management control systems.* As applied to inventory, internal control systems are designed to safeguard the inventory of the firm, prevent fraud, theft, or damage to physical units, and protect the integrity of the inventory records. Management control systems are designed to minimize the costs of maintaining inventory by determining optimum inventory levels.

A Supplementary Discussion: Inventory Control Systems

INTERNAL CONTROL SYSTEMS

Internal controls for inventory include physical control systems to protect inventory from loss and records control systems to insure the accuracy of inventory of inventory records. Physical control systems for inventory include a broad array of system design elements. The critical factors in physical and records control are strict determination of responsibility for inventory as it flows through the firm, and separation of personnel involved with handling inventory or processing information about it.

An individual should have strictly determined responsibility for the inventory and its condition at each stage of its movement through the firm. By clearly establishing that an individual is accountable for the inventory and its condition, the chances that damaged inventory will go unnoticed or inventory will be stolen should be reduced. A typical system of controls might have the receiving department assume the responsibility for checking the quality and quantity of inventory that is received.

The signature of the person responsible for the inventory in the receiving department on bills or invoices indicates that the person assumes responsibility for the inventory and attests to the accuracy of the bills and invoices.

If goods are to be stored, the warehouse manager assumes responsibility for goods transferred from the receiving department by signing transfer documents, attesting to the number and condition of the inventory items received. The transfer report should be independent of the reports sent by the receiving department to the firm's accounting department. This provides a means of comparing the number of units reported received with the number of units reported transferred to the warehouse.

Goods should be taken from the warehouse only on receipt of properly authorized requisitions, and the accounting department of the firm should be notified directly of the transfer. In this fashion, the warehouse is relieved of responsibility for the goods and the selling, manufacturing, or shipping departments assume the responsibility. In each of these departments, responsibility implies the general burden of protecting the inventory from damage resulting from fire or other abuse, as well as protecting it from theft or pilferage and properly accounting for each item. Fire control systems, alarm systems, guards and night watchmen, and other protective devices become integral systems elements in inventory control.

The separation of duties in handling and accounting for inventory is critical to the integrity of a system of internal controls. The general principle is that at no time should an individual control the records for inventory and the physical units themselves. This necessary step prevents that individual from stealing inventory from the firm and making fictitious entries in the accounting records. For example, the receiving department should sign the bills and invoices on receipt of inventory, attesting to the quality and quantity of inventory, but those records should be delivered directly to the accounting department by the shipping agent, not by the receiving department. If the receiving department has control over the invoices and the inventory, the documents could be altered to cover units stolen by people in that department. Similarly, the accounting department personnel should never have access to inventory units. At each step in the transfer of responsibility for inventory, the party assuming responsibility should report this to the accounting department directly as well as giving a receipt to the previous department, signifying the release of responsibility. Without these systems controls, inventory would be easy prey to theft, fraud, and pilferage.

MANAGEMENT CONTROL SYSTEMS

Management control systems for inventory are designed to determine the optimum quantity of inventory to be purchased or manufactured and the optimum price to purchase or manufacture that inventory. Without proper management controls over inventory levels, the firm would run the risk of carrying excessive inventory and incurring substantial unneeded carrying costs. Likewise, the firm could carry too little inventory and lose sales and customers. Excessive inventory levels lead to higher property taxes, higher insurance premiums, higher handling and storage costs, other administrative costs, and increase the risk that internal control system will break down, leading to damage, pilferage, or obsolescence of inventory.

A number of mathematical models have been designed by businessmen and scholars to identify the economic order point (that period of time or level of inventory that triggers a new order) and the economic order quantity (the amount to be ordered to minimize order and handling costs but take advantage of quantity discounts and other savings). The result of these calculations is an optimum inventory level—neither too little nor too much inventory. While the use of these models must be carefully monitored to insure that the model selected is appropriate and does not require modification, using such techniques is an important aid in managing inventory levels. Advanced studies in accounting and management will expose the student to a number of such modeling techniques.

Perpetual inventory system
Periodic inventory system
Specific identification
Average cost method
FIFO
LIFO
Lower of cost or market
Gross profit method

1. What constitutes "inventory" for financial statement purposes?

2. Is the impact of the measurement of year-end inventory balances felt on the balance sheet, income statement, or both? Explain.

3. At what point in the process of purchasing merchandise are these goods considered inventory of the firm for financial statement purposes?

4. What do the terms "FOB shipping point" and "FOB destination" mean, and what role do they play in inventory measurement?

5. Identify two steps in determining end-of-year inventory balances for accounting purposes?

6. Describe a perpetual inventory system.

7. What is a periodic inventory system?

8. What cost-flow methods are used to value inventory for financial statement purposes?

9. Relate the cost-flow assumption to the inventory valuation process.

10. List and describe the major cost-flow assumptions.

11. Which cost-flow assumption generally results in *higher* net income being reported during a period of consistently rising prices: FIFO, LIFO, or weighted average? Why?

12. For which of the following inventory cost-flow assumptions are identical costs assigned to ending inventory under periodic and perpetual inventory systems?
(a) Specific identification.
(b) Weighted average.

(c) FIFO.

(d) LIFO.

13. What information about inventories should be reported on the balance sheet?

14. Why do accountants abandon the historical cost principle in allowing ending inventory to be valued at lower cost or market?

15. If a periodic inventory system is used, how can the firm prepare monthly or quarterly financial statements?

Exercises

1. Which of the following items would be included in Bakely Corporation's inventory for June 30, 19X5?

(a) 100 units of part A106, ordered on June 21, 19X5, from a supplier, at terms F.O.B destination. Shipping documents show the units were shipped on June 29 and received July 7.

(b) 200 units of part A200, ordered on June 28, 19X5, from a supplier at terms F.O.B shipping point. Shipping documents show the units were shipped on July 6 and received on July 19.

(c) 300 units of Bakely Corporation's product, sold to customer at terms F.O.B shipping point. Bakely shipped the goods on June 29 and the goods were received by the customer on July 5.

2. Anson Brothers uses a periodic inventory system. Give the journal entries necessary to adjust the balance in inventory and close the purchases account *at year-end*, given the following data:

Beginning inventory	$102,000
Purchases	400,000
Ending Inventory	88,000

3. A summary of perpetual inventory cards for Jake's Auto Service shows the following totals for the month:

Cost of Sales	$15,800
Purchases	$16,200

Give the summary entries to record these totals in the firm's general journal.

4. Which of the following costs are properly considered costs of inventory for a retail clothing store?

(a) Cost of merchandise purchased from supplier.

(b) Salesman's salary.

(c) Freight cost in delivering merchandise to retail store.

(d) Insurance charge made by delivery firm for coverage of inventory in transit to retail outlet.

(e) Materials handling costs.

(f) President's salary.

(g) Insurance on retail building.

5. How can the cost of the following items be maintained in using the specific identification method to determine the cost of inventory?
(a) Color television sets.
(b) Auto parts in a repair shop.
(c) Wine in bottles.

6. Assume the following data for the month:

Beginning Inventory and Purchases	Date	Unit Cost	Total Cost
100	June 1	$3.00	$ 300
200	June 19	3.20	640
300	June 26	3.50	1050

Calculate the cost of goods sold if 400 units were sold, a periodic inventory system is used, and the FIFO inventory cost-flow assumption is used.

7. Using the same data in Exercise 6, calculate cost of goods sold under a perpetual inventory system assuming all sales were made on June 28.

8. Calculate the weighted average cost of units in inventory for the following data, assuming no sales were made this month.

Date	Beginning Inventory and Purchases	Unit Cost	Total Cost
Aug. 1	200	$300	$60,000
Aug. 12	300	330	99.000
Aug. 26	100	350	35,000

9. Determine the cost of goods sold and the cost of ending inventory for the firm data shown in Exercise 8, assuming the firm sells 270 units during the period and uses a weighted average cost-flow assumption and a periodic inventory system.

10. Complete the blanks in the following perpetual inventory card assuming that the weighted average cost-flow assumption is in use.

	Purchases		Sales		Balance		
Date	Units	Cost	Units	Cost	Units	Unit Cost	Total Cost
Beginning					10	$3.00	$30.00
1/6	30	$4.00			40	_____	_____
1/8			5	_____	35	_____	_____
1/9			15	_____	20	_____	_____
1/10	20	$4.25			40	_____	_____

11. Calculate the cost of goods sold and ending inventory from the following data

assuming that a periodic inventory system is in use and the following cost-flow assumptions are used: (a) LIFO (b) FIFO.

	Units	Unit Cost	Total Cost
Beginning Inventory	110	$3.00	$330
Sold (1/5)	70		
Purchased (1/8)	200	4.00	800
Sold (1/9)	100		
Purchased (1/15)	200	4.50	900
Sold (1/20)	150		
Purchased (1/27)	100	4.80	480

12. Fill in the blanks in the following perpetual inventory card, assuming that the LIFO cost-flow assumption is used by this firm:

	Purchases		Sales		Balance		
Date	Units	Unit Cost	Units	Unit Costs	Units	Unit Costs	Total Costs
1/1					200	$3.00	$600
1/6			20	___	180	___	___
1/8	100	$3.25			___	___	___
1/10			30	___	___	___	___
1/18			70	___	___	___	___
			10	___	___	___	___

13. Fill in the blanks for the cost of goods sold section of three income statements, given the data below.

	Firm X	Firm Y	Firm Z
Beginning Inventory	$ 3,500	$175,000	$ 620,000
Purchases	____	$600,000	$1,380,000
Ending Inventory	$ 5,000	____	$ 260,000
Cost of Goods Sold	$20,500	$710,000	____

14. Calculate the lower of cost or market valuation for the following independent cases.

Inventory Item	Number of Units	Unit Cost	Unit Fair Market Value
A	200	$ 1.10	$ 2.00
B	300	1.00	1.20
C	150	2.10	1.50
D	400	10.00	12.00
E	300	9.00	8.00
F	100	8.00	6.00

15. Estimate ending inventory using the gross profit method. The firm's gross profit ratio is 30 percent and the following data are available:

Net Purchases	$300,000
Sales	480,000
Beginning Inventory	80,000

16. In the following independent situations, calculate the lower of cost or market valuation for inventory, comparing individual inventory items, and give any general journal entries necessary to properly report the lower of cost or market valuation:

Case A

Item	Number of Units	Unit Cost	Unit Fair Market Value
A	300	$3.00	$6.00
B	140	8.00	7.00
C	110	9.00	8.00

Case B

Item	Number of Units	Unit Cost	Unit Fair Market Value
A	110	$ .60	$ .85
B	160	3.50	5.00
C	210	4.00	6.00

Case C

Item	Number of Units	Unit Cost	Unit Fair Market Value
A	60	$1.00	$3.00
B	70	2.00	1.50
C	80	3.00	4.00

17. Calculate ending inventory and cost of goods sold for the following perpetual inventory data, assuming a LIFO inventory flow assumption is used:

	Beginning Inventory and Purchases		Sales
Date	Units	Cost	Units
Dec. 1	100	$5.00	
Dec. 7	400	6.00	
Dec. 10			50
Dec. 12			70
Dec. 16	200	7.00	
Dec. 21			500
Dec. 28	50	8.00	

18. Prepare the necessary general journal entries to account for the following transactions and to properly report inventory and cost of goods sold at year end assuming (1) a perpetual inventory system is used, and (2) a periodic inventory system is used.

(a) Beginning inventory balance was $12,000.
(b) Acquired inventory costing $2,500 on account.
(c) Sold inventory costing $6,000 for $9,000 in cash.
(d) Acquired inventory costing $15,000.
(e) Sold inventory costing $3,000 for $4,500.

19. The following information was available from the inventory records of the Alexander Company for January 19X7:

	Units	Unit Cost	Total Cost
Balance at January 1, 19X7	2,000	$ 9.775	$19,550
Purchases:			
January 6, 19X7	1,500	10.300	15,450
January 26, 19X7	3,400	10.750	36,550
Sales:			
January 7, 19X7	1,800		
January 31, 19X7	3,200		
Balance at January 31, 19X7	1,900		

(a) Assuming that Alexander maintains perpetual inventory records, what should be the inventory at January 31, 19X7, using the weighted moving average inventory method, rounded to the nearest dollar?

(b) Assuming that Alexander does *not* maintain perpetual inventory records, what should be the inventory at January 31, 19X7, using the weighted average inventory method, rounded to the nearest dollar? (AICPA adapted)

Problems

1. The following data is taken from the financial records of Columbia Company for 19X1 and 19X2:

19X1

(a) Net Sales	$180,000
(b) Beginning Inventory	21,000
(c) Net Purchases	158,000
(d) Ending Inventory	31,000
(e) Operating Expenses	29,000

19X2

(a) Net Sales	$226,000
(b) Net Purchases	165,000
(c) Ending Inventory	30,000
(d) Operating Expenses	35,000

REQUIRED:

Prepare the income statements for Columbia Company for 19X1 and 19X2 in good form.

2. The following financial data were abstracted from the records of Fern Company, which uses a periodic inventory system:

Beginning Inventory	$ 306,000
Purchases	1,140,000
Cash	261,000
Accounts Receivable	300,000
Prepaid Expenses	19,000
Allowance for Bad Debts	3,000
Ending inventory determined by physical count, valued at cost using LIFO	$ 280,000

REQUIRED:

(a) Give the necessary closing entries to account for the above data.

(b) Establish T accounts and post the entries.

(c) Prepare the current asset section of the balance sheet in good form for Fern Company, year 19X7.

3. Flint is in the retail sporting goods business and uses a periodic inventory system. During the current year Flint had the following transactions for sailboats.

	Units	Unit Price
Beginning Inventory	20	$395/ea.
Sold 1/6	10	
Purchased 2/7	40	429/ea.
Purchased 5/9	50	445/ea.
Sold 5/3	50	
Purchased 7/17	40	455/ea.
Sold 8/8	50	
Purchased 9/14	20	470/ea.

REQUIRED:

Calculate the cost of the ending inventory of sailboats, using these cost flow and system assumptions:

(a) FIFO, periodic.

(b) Weighted Average, periodic.

(c) LIFO, perpetual.

4. Justin is a small wholesaler who currently deals in just two products, using a periodic inventory system. There are 350 units of product A and 350 units of prod-

uct B on hand at year end. Beginning inventories and purchases of these products during the year were as follows:

	Product A		Product B	
	Units	Unit Cost	Units	Unit Cost
Beginning Inventory	100	$500	200	$260
Purchase One	200	520	300	240
Purchase Two	500	550	400	230
Purchase Three	200	570	200	220
Purchase Four			100	200
Total	1,000 units		1,200 units	

REQUIRED:
(a) Calculate cost of goods sold and ending inventory for product A and product B separately, using these cost flow assumptions:
   1. FIFO.
   2. Weighted Average.
   3. LIFO.
(b) What general conclusions can you draw about the relative effects of LIFO and FIFO on reported net income in a period of rising prices and a period of falling prices?
   5. Hornbeck Company uses a perpetual inventory system. The beginning balance, purchases, and sales for one of its products are given below:

Flywheel, Type B				
Date	Transaction	Units	Unit Cost	Total Cost
Beginning Balance		200	$3.00	$ 600
January 22	Sold	100		
February 14	Purchased	400	4.00	1600
March 15	Sold	300		
May 9	Purchased	200	4.00	800
May 15	Sold	200		
July 22	Purchased	300	5.00	15.00
August 18	Sold	200		
October 15	Purchased	200	6.00	1200
November 18	Sold	200		

REQUIRED:
(a) Calculate cost of goods sold for this product using the (1) FIFO and (2) LIFO cost flow assumptions.
(b) Recalculate the cost of goods sold, assuming that a periodic inventory system was used.
(c) Explain any differences you found in parts (a) and (b).

6. Quentin Fabricating Company uses a perpetual inventory system to account for its inventory. Below is data from a perpetual inventory record for one of its products:

Date	Purchases		Sales		Balance		
	Units	Unit Cost	Units	Unit Cost	Units	Unit Cost	Total Costs
Beginning Inventory					200	$20.00	$4000
3/16			80	___	120	___	___
4/8	120	$30			240	___	___
4/22			140	___	100	___	___
7/10	100	$35			200	___	___
8/10			120	___	80	___	___
11/15	120	$40			200	___	___

REQUIRED:
(a) Fill in the blanks on the perpetual inventory record assuming a weighted average cost flow assumption is used.
(b) Give the necessary general journal entries to account for these purchases and sales, assuming that the sales price is $50 per unit.

7. Bedly Company has three products in its wholesale inventory:

Product	Unit Cost	Unit Value	Units in Ending Inventory
X	$29	$26	3,000
Y	$40	$60	4,700
Z	$59	$80	2,600

Bedly uses a periodic inventory system to account for its inventory.

REQUIRED:
(a) Calculate the lower of cost or market valuation for these items in inventory.
(b) How will the accountant report the lower of cost or market adjustment on the financial statements?

8. McGarity Enterprises is applying for a loan from a bank. The bank has asked the firm to present to it financial statements for the previous year and an income statement for the first two months of the current year. McGarity has received the approval of the bank to estimate inventory rather than incur the expense of

taking a complete physical inventory for the two month income statement. McGarity's adjusted trial balance is given below as of February 28, 19X3:

	Debit	Credit
Cash	$ 2,100	
Accounts Receivable	13,000	
Allowance for Bad Debts		$ 200
Merchandise Inventory	23,000	
Prepaid Expenses	300	
Equipment	18,000	
Accumulated Depreciation		8,000
Furniture and Fixtures	6,000	
Accumulated Depreciation		600
Accounts Payable		6,100
Notes Payable (9%, due in 30 days)		10,000
McGarity, Capital		36,450
Sales		29,000
Purchases	26,000	
Depreciation Expense	500	
Selling Expenses	200	
Salaries and Wages	1,000	
Interest Expense	150	
Other Expenses	100	
	90,350	90,350

REQUIRED:

Prepare an income statement for the two months ended February 28, 19X3, using the gross profit method of estimating ending inventory for the two month period. Assume the gross profit ratio for McGarity was 42 percent in the previous year.

9. Winston Sales Company had its retail outlet completely destroyed by fire. A balance sheet for the day of the fire is shown below:

WINSTON SALES COMPANY
Trial Balance
March 9, 19X8

	Debit	Credit
Cash	$ 2,400	
Accounts Receivable	2,100	
Merchandise Inventory, Jan. 1, 19X8	11,000	
Prepaid Insurance	200	
Supplies on Hand	400	
Office Furniture and Fixtures	6,000	
Accumulated Depreciation		$ 1,400
Accounts Payable		4,000
Capital Stock		9,000
Retained Earnings		5,100
Sales		64,000
Purchases	46,600	
Salaries Expense	12,000	
Rent Expense	1,500	
Delivery Expense	100	
Utilities Expense	1,200	
	$83,500	$83,500

The insurance company has asked Winston Sales to determine the cost of its inventory destroyed in the fire.

REQUIRED:

Using the gross profit method and a gross profit percentage of 35 percent, estimate the amount of inventory on hand at March 9, 19X8.

10. Una Sales Company accounts for its inventory using a perpetual inventory system. Below is partial data from the perpetual inventory records for its major product:

	Purchases		Sales		Balance		
Date	Units	Unit Cost	Units	Unit Cost	Units	Unit Cost	Total Cost
1/1					200	$20.00	$4,000
1/26	200	$22.00			___	___	___
3/9			300	___	___	___	___
5/16	400	25.00			___	___	___
6/13			450	___	___	___	___
6/18	400	25.00			___	___	___
8/10			420	___	___	___	___
11/16	200	28.00			___	___	___

REQUIRED:

(a) Fill in the blanks in this perpetual inventory record, assuming the LIFO inventory flow assumption is used.

(b) Calculate cost of goods sold and ending inventory for this item at year end.

11. Earnhardt Company sells a single line of commercial solar heating units it purchases from a manufacturer. During the year it has the following inventory transactions:

(a) Beginning inventory was 10 units costing $16,000 each.

(b) Purchased 20 units for $16,500 each.

(c) Sold 9 units for $24,000 each.

(d) Sold 12 units for $25,000 each.

(e) Purchased 10 units for $18,000 each.

(f) Sold 6 units for $27,000 each.

REQUIRED:

Assuming all sales were for cash, calculate the cost of goods sold and ending inventory for Ernhardt Company, given that the firm uses:

(a) Periodic inventory system and LIFO.

(b) Periodic inventory system and FIFO.

(c) Periodic inventory system and weighted average.

(d) Perpetual inventory system and LIFO.

(e) Perpetual inventory system and FIFO.

(f) Perpetual inventory system and weighted average.

□ 9
NONCURRENT ASSETS

LAND

PLANT AND EQUIPMENT

MEASUREMENT OF COST OF PLANT AND EQUIPMENT

MEASURING COST EXPIRATIONS

DEPRECIATION ACCOUNTING AND REPORTING

DEPRECIATION METHODS

STRAIGHT-LINE DEPRECIATION METHOD

DOUBLE-DECLINING-BALANCE DEPRECIATION METHOD

SUM-OF-THE-YEAR'S-DIGITS DEPRECIATION METHOD

COMPARISON OF METHODS MEASURING LIFE IN YEARS

OTHER METHODS

PARTIAL YEAR'S DEPRECIATION

CONSISTENCY

MAINTENANCE

DISPOSITION OF PLANT AND EQUIPMENT

NATURAL RESOURCES

INTANGIBLE ASSETS

LONG-TERM INVESTMENTS

DEFERRED CHARGES

SUMMARY

SUPPLEMENTARY DISCUSSION: THE INVESTMENT TAX CREDIT

☐ OBJECTIVES

AFTER STUDYING THIS CHAPTER, YOU SHOULD BE ABLE TO DO THE FOLLOWING:

1. DEFINE "NONCURRENT" AND DESCRIBE THE MAJOR CATEGORIES OF NONCURRENT ASSETS.

2. DETERMINE THE COST OF ASSETS ACQUIRED IN A LUMP-SUM PURCHASE OR IN A TRADE-IN TRANSACTION.

3. PREPARE A NONCURRENT ASSET SECTION OF A BALANCE SHEET.

4. CALCULATE DEPRECIATION AND AMORTIZATION EXPENSE FOR FULL AND PARTIAL YEARS USING DIFFERENT METHODS.

5. RECORD THE SALE AND DISPOSITION OF NONCURRENT ASSETS.

6. DESCRIBE THE FINANCIAL STATEMENT PRESENTATION OF LONG-TERM INVESTMENTS.

Preceding chapters have discussed current assets and inventory. This chapter deals with all *other* assets, the noncurrent ones. These assets are also referred to as fixed assets or long-term assets because they have long lives and appear on several consecutive balance sheets of the firm. Major categories of noncurrent assets are land, plant and equipment, natural resources, intangible assets, long-term investments, and deferred assets. The investment in these types of assets depends on the nature of the business, but frequently is substantial.

A large public utility, such as an electric company, requires enormous investment in production facilities including generating plants, power lines, and maintenance equipment. A retailer may require a smaller percentage investment in noncurrent assets, and relatively higher investment in current assets, such as inventory. The investments of service businesses in long-lived assets varies widely, from the barber who rents his shop and has little investment in plant and equipment to the computer service bureau that owns its computers, and has a major investment.

This chapter is devoted to the problems of accounting for plant and equipment. These assets are commonly held by almost all businesses and generally make up the most significant part of the noncurrent assets. Primary accounting problems relate to the nature of assets, the valuation methods used for financial statement presentations, the methods of matching the costs of long-lived assets with the revenues they help to generate, and the appropriate financial statement presentation for each class of noncurrent assets.

Land

Land is unique among the tangible, long-lived, productive resources of an entity because it has an unlimited life. The major accounting problem involved with land is the measurement of the cost of land. The cost of an asset is defined as the cash or cash equivalent paid or incurred to acquire the asset and prepare it for its intended use. Items frequently included in the cost of land besides the purchase price are title insurance, legal fees, costs of recording the deed, and local taxes on the transfer.

Some special problems can arise in acquiring land. For example, if a firm acquires land for use as a parking lot that currently has a derelict building on it, what accounting treatment is given the building? Then, how do we account for the demolition of the building? As a general rule, the entire cost of the property is considered the cost of the land. In addition, the net cost (cost of demolition less any salvage receipts) of removing the building is treated as an additional cost of the land. In summary, the entire cost of acquiring the property and preparing it for its intended use is treated as the cost of the land.

Because land has an unlimited life, the accounting problem of measuring the expiration of the land's service potential and matching this expense with the revenues it helps to generate is solved easily. Since the land has unlimited service potential because of its unlimited life, none of the cost of the land is treated as an expense on the income statement. Consequently, the land account measures the cost of land acquired and is not reduced as the land is used. Likewise, the cost base is rarely adjusted upward regardless of changing land values. Increases in potential market value of the land are not recorded in the accounts. Restatements of value are made in extraordinary situations, such as the discovery of oil under a parking lot. Discussion of such restatements are beyond the scope of this book.

Plant and equipment consists of the tangible, long-lived, productive assets that a firm will use in its operations. Common examples are buildings, machinery, office furniture and equipment, delivery trucks, and automobiles.

Plant and Equipment

Three major problems in the accounting for plant and equipment are (1) measurement of the cost, (2) measurement of cost expirations and allocation of the depreciation expense to the appropriate time periods, and (3) presentation on the financial statements. Plant and equipment items represent unexpired costs that will provide future benefits. When a machine is purchased for $500, the cost of the machine represents an unexpired resource of the firm. As the machine is used, its service potential is reduced by wear and age. The accountant must report the reduction in its service potential—the expiration of a part of the original cost of the machine—as an expense on the income statement. The expiration of part of the cost must then be reflected on both the balance sheet and income statement.

Maintenance costs must also be considered by the accountant. Distinctions exist between ordinary upkeep and major repairs and renovations. Treatments of these items will affect reported income and will provide the basis for valuing the asset.

Measurement of Cost of Plant and Equipment. The measurement of the cost of plant and equipment is similar to that of other assets. The original acquisition cost is defined as all reasonable and necessary expenditures to acquire the asset and place it in operating condition in the desired location at the appropriate time. By this definition, cost includes such expenditures as sales tax, transportation charges, handling charges, and installation charges. Allowable discounts should be deducted in arriving at the cost of an asset.

The materiality concept must be applied in the determination of asset costs. For example, if machine is purchased and installed by the employees of the firm instead of paying someone outside the entity to install the machine, the cost of the machine should include the cost of the employees' time. The cost of the employees' time is based on the hourly rate and the appropriate portion of the cost of fringe benefits. If the employees take just a few minutes to install the machine, installation cost may be ignored since it is immaterial.

To illustrate these principles, suppose The Smith Manufacturing Company orders a new machine for the plant. The price is $8,000 but a cash discount of 5 percent is allowed if the amount due is paid within ten days. A four percent sales tax is added to the price of the machine. Freight charges are $27 and an outside firm is paid $75 to uncrate and install the machine. The cost of the machine is computed as follows regardless of whether the discount is actually taken:

Invoice price	$8,000
Sales tax	320
Freight	27
Installation charges	75
	$8,422
Less 5% discount (8,000 × .05)	400
Total Cost	$8,022

Productive assets are sometimes acquired in a group by a lump-sum expenditure without a breakdown of the cost of each item. The total acquisition cost must then be allocated to the various assets on some systematic basis, usually on the basis of the relative fair market value of each asset. For example, suppose Jones Corporation acquires land and a building at a total price of $120,000. There is no indication in the agreement of how the total of $120,000 should be allocated to the two assets—land and building. This allocation is especially important because the building has a limited life, and a part of its cost will be charged as depreciation expense each period; the land has an unlimited life and none of its cost will be treated as an expense. To allocate the cost of $120,000 between the land and building, the relative fair market values of each asset must be determined. If the land is appraised at a value of $30,000 and the building is appraised at $95,000, we now have a basis for allocating the $120,000 between the two assets, as follows.

Fair Market Values:

Land	$ 30,000
Building	$ 95,000
Total fair market value	$125,000

Cost to be Allocated:

$120,000

Allocation to Land:

$$\frac{\text{Fair market value of land}}{\text{Total fair market value of purchase}} \times \text{Cost to be allocated}$$
$$= \text{Cost allocated to land}$$

$$\frac{\$30,000}{\$125,000} \times \$120,000 = \$28,800$$

Allocation to Building:

$$\frac{\text{Fair market value of land}}{\text{Total fair market value of purchase}} \times \text{Cost to be allocated}$$
$$= \text{Cost allocated to land}$$

$$\frac{\$95,000}{\$125,000} \times 120,000 = \$91,200$$

The land account would be debited for $28,800 and the building account is debited for $91,200. Note that the historical cost concept does *not* allow us to record these assets at their individual fair market values. They are recorded at their allocated portion of the total historical cost.

Sometimes productive long-lived assets are acquired in exchange for other assets or the firm's stock, but not cash. The accountant is faced with a problem of determining the cost of these assets so they may be properly recorded in the accounts and reported on financial statements. As a general rule, the cost of an asset acquired in an exchange is the fair market value of the asset given up, or the fair market value of the asset received, whichever is more readily valued. For example, if a corporation issues 1,000 shares of stock for land, and the stock has recently sold for $15 per share, the land would reasonably be valued at $15,000. On the other hand if the land is appraised at $22,000 and there have not been recent sales of the stock to establish its value, the land is properly recorded at $22,000. If the values of both assets are equally determinable and different, accountants use the value of the asset given as the measure of the cost of the asset received.

Assets may be purchased that require additional expenditures before they are ready for use. If there are necessary expenditures to place the asset in operating condition, they are treated as part of the cost of the asset. These are especially common when used assets are acquired. For example, it may be necessary to incur expenditures to renovate and repair a building before it can be occupied by a new owner. These expenditures are treated as part of the cost of the building.

Measuring Cost Expirations

Once the acquisition cost of an item of plant and equipment is determined, the next major accounting problem is measuring the cost expiration that occurs as a result of wear and age. The accountant faces this allocation problem: If a machine is acquired for $5,000 and will last five years, after which it will have no value, which year or years' net income should be charged with this $5,000 expense? It seems inequitable to charge the earnings of any one year with the full cost of the machine since it was used by the firm during all five years. Accountants will attempt to match an estimate of each year's cost expirations with the revenues that were generated. These cost expirations, resulting from reductions in asset's service lives caused by wear and age, are called *depreciation expense* on the income statement.

Calculating depreciation expense involves three factors:

1. Acquisition cost.
2. Service life.
3. Residual value.

The service life of a fixed asset is the time period over which the firm expects to use the asset. The service life is an estimate. If a firm plans to use an asset until it has no value, the service life would be the estimated useful life of the asset. Often, a firm plans to sell or trade in an asset before all its service potential is gone. For example, cars and trucks are often traded in while there is still some service potential. Under these circumstances, the service life would be the number of years the firm expects to keep the truck or car before it is traded.

Residual value of a fixed asset is the expected value of the asset at the end of its service life. It represents that part of the asset's cost that is not expected to expire. The residual value of an asset is normally reduced for estimated disposition costs of the asset at the end of its service life. For example, if a building is expected to have a 40-year life with a salvage value of $4,000 at the end of its life and the costs of disposing of the building are expected to be $3,000, then its residual value is calculated to be $1,000 ($4,000 − $3,000).

The allocation of cost over time periods as depreciation expense lacks exactness. It is based on estimates of both the service life and the residual value of the asset. For example, assume The Ace Corporation purchases a delivery truck to be used in its business activity for $8,200. No one can know for certain just how long the delivery truck will be used, so an estimate must be made. Suppose management estimates that the truck will be used for four years. Next, an estimate must be made of the value (residual value) of the truck at the end of that four-year period. The estimate may take into consideration relevant information such as the "blue-book" value of a similar truck that is already four years old and projected supply and demand for used trucks. Assume that the residual value is estimated at $2,200. If management decides to recognize an equal amount of depreciation expense each year, then it will allocate part of the asset's cost as depreciation expense, calculated as follows:

$$\frac{\text{Cost} - \text{Residual value}}{\text{Estimated service life}} = \text{Annual depreciation expense}$$

$$\frac{\$8,200 - \$2,200}{4} = \$1,500$$

Note that changes in the estimate of residual value or service life can have a material impact on the calculation of annual depreciation expense.

The allocation of the cost of a fixed asset over its estimated service life is not an attempt to measure the market value of the asset. Depreciation is the allocation of part of the cost of an asset as a period expense over the time periods benefited. The book value of the asset (cost minus total depreciation taken) may have no resemblance to the market value of the asset. As an extreme illustration, a building may, for a time, actually appreciate in market value because of its favorable location while it is being depreciated for accounting purposes. Depreciation is an attempt to match the expiring cost of an asset with the revenues derived from the asset. The cost is allocated over the period of time during which the service potential of the asset is used. It usually results in values quite different from an appraisal of fair market value.

Depreciation Accounting and Reporting

Allocating the cost expiration of a long lived asset over the period of time it benefits the firm is accomplished by calculating depreciation expense. Once calculated, the depreciation expense is normally recorded as an adjusting entry at the end of the accounting period. It may also be recorded during the accounting period if there is a need to bring the account balances up to date. For example, if an asset is sold during the year, depreciation should be recorded up to date of sale. The entry to record depreciation expense is illustrated below:

| Depreciation Expense: Auto | $500 | |
| Accumulated Depreciation: Auto | | $500 |

Note that the credit in this entry is to a contra asset account, entitled Accumulated Depreciation, rather than a direct reduction of the asset account. By this approach, the asset account continues to reflect the original cost of the asset and the contra account shows the cumulative effect of depreciation for all periods since the asset was placed into service.

The balance sheet presentation of fixed assets and their related accumulated depreciation is shown below:

Fixed Assets		
Equipment	$ 9,000	
Less Accumulated Depreciation	3,600	$ 5,400
Office Furniture and Fixtures	1,800	
Less Accumulated Depreciation	600	1,200
Trucks	15,000	
Less Accumulated Depreciation	9,000	6,000
Total Fixed Assets		$12,600

Footnotes to the financial statements normally describe the accounting methods used to prepare the financial statements, and should describe the depreciation methods used to calculate depreciation expense.

Depreciation Methods

The estimate of annual depreciation expense may be calculated several ways. Each of the generally accepted techniques provides a systematic method for allocating part of the cost of a long-lived asset to an expense. Each method makes a basic presumption about the rate at which the cost of the asset "expires," or should be recognized as an expense. In this chapter we discuss four depreciation methods:

1. Straight-line method.
2. Double-declining-balance method.
3. Sum-of-the-years'-digits method.
4. Units-of-production method.

The straight-line method assumes that the reduction in the service life of an asset occurs at an even, constant rate, and therefore charges each year that an asset is used with an equal amount of depreciation expense. The sum-of-the-years'-digits and double-declining-balance methods are referred to as accelerated methods. They hypothesize that an asset is more productive in its early years of use. Consequently, these methods charge higher depreciation expense to the earlier years of an asset's life, and lower amounts to the later years. This matches higher depreciation expense with higher revenues generated in the early, more productive years of the asset's life. The units-of-production method measures the life of an asset in output units or expected life in hours, instead of in an expected life in years.

Straight-line Depreciation Method. The formula for *straight-line depreciation* is:

$$\frac{\text{Cost} - \text{Residual value}}{\text{Useful life}} = \text{Annual depreciation expense}$$

If a building is acquired at a cost of $80,000, and is expected to have a useful life of 20 years with no residual value at the end of the 20 years, the annual depreciation is computed as follows:

$$\frac{\$80,000 - 0}{20 \text{ years}} = \$4,000 \text{ per year}$$

If this building is expected to have a residual value of $8,000 at the end of the 20 years, the annual depreciation would be computed as follows:

$$\frac{\$80,000 - \$8,000}{20 \text{ years}} = \$3,600 \text{ per year}$$

If this building is expected to have a service life of 25 years instead of 20 years and has an estimated residual value of $8,000, the annual depreciation would be computed as follows:

$$\frac{\$80,000 - \$8,000}{25 \text{ years}} = \$2,880 \text{ per year}$$

Using this last example, the adjusting entry for the first year (and each year for 25 years) would be:

Depreciation Expense—Building	$2,880	
Accumulated Depreciation—Building		$2,880

The balance sheet at the end of the first year would contain the following information:

Plant and Equipment		
Building	$80,000	
Less Accumulated Depreciation	2,880	$77,120

Like all expense accounts, the Depreciation Expense account is closed at the end of the year. Thus, Depreciation Expense will have no balance after the closing entry has been made, but the Accumulated Depreciation account is not closed and will be carried forward to the next year. The Depreciation Expense on the income statement each year will be the current year's depreciation expense, but the asset contra account, Accumulated Depreciation, will include the total depreciation recognized on the asset over its life to date and will be shown on the balance sheet.

For the building illustrated above, the entry to record depreciation for the second year would be the same as for the first year:

Depreciation Expense—Building	$2,880	
Accumulated Depreciation—Building		$2,880

Depreciation expense on the income statement for the second year will be

$2,880, the same as the first year. The relevant portion of the balance sheet will appear as follows:

Plant and Equipment
Building $80,000
Less Accumulated Depreciation   5,760 $74,240

Although residual value is used in the calculation of the annual depreciation expense, it does *not* appear as a separate item on the balance sheet. It is assumed that the reader of the statements is interested in total cost and total accumulated depreciation, but not the exact calculations or estimates of residual value.

If the building is used for 25 years as estimated, the depreciation adjustment for the twenty-fifth year would be the same as for other years:

Depreciation Expense—Building $2,880
Accumulated Depreciation—Building $2,880

The income statement would include Depreciation Expense on the building of $2,800 and the balance sheet would be as follows:

Plant and Equipment
Building $80,000
Less Accumulated Depreciation   72,000 $8,000

The book value of the building at this point—$8,000—is the residual value estimated at the time the building was acquired. Even if the building continues to be used, no additional depreciation expense would be taken. The building would be reported on the balance sheet at its residual value as shown above.

So far, this illustration has made the assumption that the business owns only one item of plant and equipment. When several items are owned, the balance sheet normally reports these items grouped together in a few asset classes, such as machinery, delivery equipment, office furniture and fixtures, land, and so on. This condenses the information into a more readable format for the financial statement user.

Double-Declining-Balance Depreciation Method. Accelerated depreciation methods recognize larger increments of cost in the earlier part of the asset life and smaller increments in the latter part of the life. *Double-declining balance* is one of these accelerated methods.

Annual depreciation expense using the double-declining-balance method of depreciation is computed by the following formula:

$$\text{Book value} \times \frac{2}{\text{Useful life}} = \text{Annual depreciation expense}$$

The book value of an asset is the cost of the asset less the accumulated depreciation to date. Book value and cost are the same at the date of acquisition, but the book value decreases each accounting period because of depreciation taken in prior periods.

Suppose a machine is purchased for $12,000, has an estimated service life of five years, and an estimated residual value of $2,000. Using the double declining balance method, how do we calculate depreciation expense?

Depreciation for the first year is computed as follows:

$$\$12,000 \times \frac{2}{5} = \$4,800$$

Depreciation for the second year is computed as follows:

$$(\$12,000 - \$4,800) \times \frac{2}{5} = \$2,880$$

Depreciation expense and the book value at the end of each year for this asset are shown below:

Year	Depreciation Expense	Book Value	Accumulated Depreciation
0		$12,000	
1	$4,800	7,200	$ 4,800
2	2,880	4,320	7,680
3	1,728	2,592	9,408
4	595	2,000	10,000
5	—	2,000	10,000

Note that the formula for calculating double declining balance depreciation does not consider the residual value of the asset in calculating the annual depreciation expense. But also note that the asset is *not* depreciated below its salvage value. For example, depreciation in year 4 in our illustration above is limited to $592, even though the formula calculated $1,037 in depreciation expense for that year. To take more depreciation than that would result in reporting the asset on the balance sheet below its salvage value. That would be inappropriate.

This depreciation method resulted from an income tax law that limits the annual depreciation expense to twice the depreciation expense that would be determined by the straight-line method, ignoring residual value. In effect, the double-declining-balance method uses a *rate* of depreciation that is double the straight-line rate. In our illustration of a machine with a five year life, the straight-line rate is 20 percent per year (100 percent divided by five years). The double-declining-balance method uses twice the straight-line rate (2/5 or 40 percent in this illustration) but applies that rate to the book value, not original cost.

Sum-of-the-Years'-Digits Method. The *sum-of-the-years'-digits method* of depreciation is another consistent approach to recognizing larger amounts of depreciation in early years and less in later years as compared with the straight-line method. Its formula is:

$$(\text{Cost} - \text{Residual value}) \times \frac{\text{Year's digit}}{\text{Sum-of-the-years' digits}}$$
$$= \text{Annual depreciation expense}$$

In this formula, the sum of the years' digits is the sum of the estimated life of the asset and each integer below that number, down to one. For example, if the useful life of the asset is 5, the sum of the years' digits would be calculated as follows:

$$5 + 4 + 3 + 2 + 1 = 15$$

Since it would be rather time-consuming to calculate the sum of the years' digits for a building with a life of 30 years, the sum of the year's digits may be calculated using this formula:

$$n\left(\frac{n + 1}{2}\right)$$

where n = estimated useful life.
For a useful life of five years, we could calculate the sum of the years' digits as follows:

$$5\left(\frac{5 + 1}{2}\right) = 15$$

The numerator in the depreciation formula is the years of service life remaining. This number is the year's digit taken in declining order. This, for an asset with an estimated useful life of five years, the years' digits are 5, 4, 3, 2, and 1 in declining order. In year 1, the numerator of the fraction would be 5. In year 2, the numerator would be 4, and so on.

Using the same illustration as before, what is the depreciation expense for a machine with a cost of $12,000, a five-year estimated service life, and an estimated residual value of $2,000, using the sum-of-the-years'-digits method of depreciation?

Depreciation for the first year is computed as follows:

$$(12,000 - \$2,000) \times \frac{5}{15} = \$3,333 \text{ (rounded to nearest dollar)}$$

Depreciation for the second year is computed as follows:

$$(\$12,000 - \$2,000) \times \frac{4}{15} = \$2,667$$

The following table shows the depreciation expense for each of the five years along with accumulated depreciation and book value for each year.

Year	Depreciation Expense	Accumulated Depreciation	Book Value
0			$12,000
1	$3,333	$ 3,333	8,667
2	2,667	6,000	6,000
3	2,000	8,000	4,000
4	1,333	9,333	2,667
5	667	10,000	2,000

Both the double-declining-balance method and the sum-of-the-years'-digits method of depreciation are consistent ways to compute larger amounts of depreciation during the early years than in the later years as compared with the straight-line depreciation method. The double-declining-balance method generally provides for faster depreciation than the sum-of-the-years' digits method because mathematically it is more accelerated and because residual value is not considered in the double-declining-balance calculation, whereas the formula for the sum-of-the-years'-digits calculation does consider salvage values.

Comparison of Methods Measuring Life in Years. Exhibit 9-1 compares the depreciation calculation for the straight-line, double-declining balance, and sum-of-the-years' digits methods, using the example discussed previously: cost, $12,000; life, five years; residual value, $2,000.

In all three methods, a total of $10,000 in depreciation expense is allocated over the time periods. The difference occurs because of the timing of the cost allocation. The accelerated methods result in larger allocations of expense to earlier years and less to later years as compared to straight-line depreciation. This means that the income statement will include a larger depreciation expense and a smaller net income (com-

EXHIBIT 9-1
COMPARISON OF DEPRECIATION METHODS

Case: Asset with cost of $12,000, life of five years and estimated residual value of $2,000

	Straight-line			Double-declining balance			Sum-of-the-years'-digits		
	Depreciation Expense	Accumulated Depreciation	Book Value	Depreciation Expense	Accumulated Depreciation	Book Value	Depreciation Expense	Accumulated Depreciation	Book Value
			$12,000			$12,000			$12,000
	$ 2,000	$ 2,000	10,000	$ 4,800	$ 4,800	7,200	$ 3,333	$ 3,333	8,667
	2,000	4,000	8,000	2,880	7,680	4,320	2,667	6,000	6,000
	2,000	6,000	6,000	1,728	9,408	2,592	2,000	8,000	4,000
	2,000	8,000	4,000	592	10,000	2,000	1,333	9,333	2,667
	2,000	10,000	2,000	—	10,000	2,000	667	10,000	2,000
	$10,000			$10,000			$10,000		

pared to the straight-line method) during approximately the first half of the service life of an asset. The opposite is true during approximately the second half of the service life—depreciation expense will be lower and net income would be higher as compared with the straight-line method.

From the standpoint of the balance sheet, accelerated depreciation methods would result in a lower book value of the fixed assets and lower retained earnings during approximately the first half of the service life, as compared with the straight-line method.

The straight-line depreciation method is simple, rational, and systematic. Accelerated methods are appropriate when there is reason to allocate larger amounts of the cost to early years of the service life of the asset. This is generally true when obsolescence of the asset is a factor and when repair expenses become greater in the later years of the asset life.

Other Methods. There are a number of other depreciation methods that are generally accepted, though much less frequently used. Generally, these methods do not measure estimated useful life in years of expected service—they use some other measure. Two alternative methods are the units-of-production method and the machine-hour method.

The *units-of-production method* measures the useful life of a productive machine in terms of the number of units the machine can produce during its life. The formula for units of production depreciation expense is as follows:

$$\frac{\text{Cost} - \text{Residual value}}{\substack{\text{Number of units machine} \\ \text{can produce}}} \times \substack{\text{Number of units} \\ \text{produced this year} \\ \text{by this machine}} = \substack{\text{Annual depreciation} \\ \text{expense}}$$

The annual depreciation is based on utilization of the productive output potential of the machine.

For example, if a machine costs $9,000, has a $1,000 salvage value, an estimated useful productive capacity of 40,000 units, and actual produces 6,000 units this year, depreciation would be calculated as follows:

$$\frac{\$9,000 - \$1,000}{40,000 \text{ units}} \times 6,000 \text{ units} = \$1,200$$

The formula for calculating units of production depreciation expense is very similar to the formula for calculating straight-line depreciation, except estimated useful life is measured in terms of units of productive capacity instead of number of years. Note that it is also similar to straight-line depreciation in that it assigns the same amount of depreciation expense—20¢ per unit in the case above—to each unit produced.

The machine-hour method of depreciation is very similar to the units of production method, except that it measures useful life in terms of the number of hours the machine is expected to operate. The formula is as follows:

$$\frac{\text{Cost} - \text{Residual Value}}{\begin{array}{l}\text{Number of expected}\\ \text{operating machine}\\ \text{hours over its life}\end{array}} \times \begin{array}{l}\text{Number of hours}\\ \text{operated this year}\end{array} = \begin{array}{l}\text{Annual depreciation}\\ \text{expense}\end{array}$$

To illustrate, if a machine costs $9,000, has a estimated $1,000 in salvage value and an estimated productive life of 20,000 hours, and actually operates 8,000 hours this year, depreciation would be calculated as follows:

$$\frac{\$9,000 - \$1,000}{20,000} \times 8,000 \text{ hrs.} = \$3,200$$

Again, note that the formula assigns the same rate of depreciation to each hour the machine operates and otherwise is very similar to both the units of production and straight-line methods.

Partial Year's Depreciation. If an asset is acquired or disposed during the year rather than at the beginning or end of the year, depreciation must be calculated for the partial year. One practical approach to this problem is to calculate depreciation to the nearest whole month. For example, if the straight-line depreciation expense would have been $2,400 for a whole year, and a machine is acquired on April 6 by a business using a calendar year, depreciation to the nearest whole month would count April (the asset was acquired in the first half of the month) and the first partial year's depreciation is calculated as follows:

$$\frac{9}{12} \times 2,400 = \$1,800$$

Many firms have elected to use other methods to calculate partial year's depreciation. One way would be to calculate one-half year's depreciation for all assets in the year they are acquired, and one-half year's depreciation in the year of disposal. Another way would be to calculate a full year's depreciation on assets acquired in the first half of the year, and none on assets acquired in the second half. Similarly, asset disposals in the second half of the year would have a full year's depreciation calculated, while none would be calculated on asset disposals in the first half. Although these "year-of-purchase, year-of-sale" conventions are much less exact than the nearest month method, the differences in total depreciation are unlikely to be material.

When accelerated depreciation methods are used, the calculation of partial depreciation follows the same logic. Also, annual depreciation charges are sometimes adjusted to reflect the inclusion of two partial years in the calculation. Assume that a company bought a machine for $18,000 on July 1, 19X6, and that the machine has no expected salvage value at the end of its life. If the sum-of-the-years'-digits method is used, annual depreciation for this asset is as follows:

Year	Calculation	Depreciation
1	3/6 × $18,000	$9,000
2	2/6 × $18,000	6,000
3	1/6 × $18,000	3,000

If the firm reports on a calender year basis, $4,500 of depreciation would be reported in 19X6. This is one-half of the first year depreciation on the machine. Depreciation of $7,500 would be reported in 19X7. This includes the remaining half of the first year depreciation added to one-half of the second year depreciation ($\frac{1}{2} \times \$9,000 + \frac{1}{2} \times \$6,000$). Likewise, the depreciation expense recorded in 19X8 would be $4,500 calculated as follows: ($\frac{1}{2} \times \$6,000 + \frac{1}{2} \times \$3,000$).

Consistency. An individual asset may be depreciated using any acceptable depreciation method. If three assets are acquired, each may be depreciated using a different method. Once a method is selected, however, that method should generally be used consistently throughout the life of the asset.

Maintenance. Periodically, repairs and other maintenance activities are undertaken to keep buildings, equipment, and other assets in proper operating condition. Usually, a certain amount of recurring service is necessary for all facilities. Those expenditures that provide for normal operating repairs and maintenance are treated as an expense and are charged to income immediately.

For example, the annual cost of overhauling a manufacturing plant is $14,200, which includes the necessary materials and labor. Because of its annual nature, the overhaul is related to activities of the current period. This cost would be recorded as an expense.

Maintenance Expense	$14,200	
Cash		$14,200

Some maintenance and repair activities will alter or improve a facility. In the case of improvement, the benefit of the maintenance activity may extend for several periods in the future. It would not be appropriate to write off this cost by charging it to expense immediately. Instead, the cost is treated as a capital improvement and is recorded as an asset. The asset may be depreciated over its expected useful life as would any other resource owned by the organization.

For example, suppose a company decides to replace the wiring in its manufacturing plant with a new system costing $45,600. If the new wiring system does more than replace regular recurring wear and tear, it should be treated as an asset and recorded as such. In this case, the expenditure would probably be included in the total cost of the plant and depreciated as it is used in the future.

Plant	$45,600	
Cash		$45,600

Disposition of Plant and Equipment. The disposition of plant and equipment may occur through sale, trade-in on another asset, or scrapping the asset. No matter which method is used, the results of the disposition should be reflected in the accounting records of the firm. The first step in accounting for the disposition of an asset is to bring the depreciation on the asset up to date by recording depreciation for a partial year, if necessary. This ensures that the appropriate amount of depreciation expense is recorded and that the accumulated depreciation account is current.

If the asset is sold, and depreciation has been recorded up to the date of sale (as we will assume in the remaining illustrations), the next step is to account for the sale itself. For purposes of illustration, assume the sale of the machine used in previous examples: cost $12,000; life, five years; salvage value, $2,000. If this machine is depreciated using the straight-line method and sold at the end of year 2 for $8,500 cash, we would make the following calculations:

Cost	$12,000
Less: Accumulated Depreciation	4,000
Book Value	$ 8,000

Because the cash received exceeds the book value of the asset sold, a gain of $500 is recognized on the sale:

Cash Received	$8,500
Book Value	8,000
Gain	$ 500

The journal entry to record the sale of the machine for $8,500 cash is as follows:

Cash	$8,500	
Accumulated Depreciation Machine	4,000	
Machine		$12,000
Gain on Sale of Machine		500

If the machine had been sold for less than its book value, a loss would be recognized. For example, if the machine were sold for $7,000, a loss of $1,000 would be recognized by the following entry:

Cash	$7,000	
Accumulated Depreciation Machine	4,000	
Loss on Sale of Machine	1,000	
Machine		$12,000

The purpose of the journal entry is to:

1. Record the amount of assets received (cash, accounts receivable, and notes receivable are examples).
2. Remove the cost of the asset sold from the asset account.
3. Remove the accumulated depreciation.
4. Recognize a gain or loss, if any.

Accounting for a trade-in requires recognition of the newly acquired asset as well as an entry for the disposition of the old assets. The cost of an asset includes all reasonable and necessary expenditures to acquire the asset and place it in operating condition in the desired location at the appropriate time. In a trade-in, the cost basis of the new asset is measured by the fair market value of the assets given or the assets received, whichever is more readily determined. Frequently, it is easier to establish the fair market value of the asset received in trade-in situations because the asset is usually new and its value more readily determined.

Suppose a machine originally acquired for $80,000 with accumulated depreciation of $60,000 is traded for a machine with a fair market value of $100,000. The firm is allowed a trade-in allowance of $15,000 on the old machine, reducing the cash required to $85,000.

This is the general journal entry made to record the trade-in:

Machinery (new)	$100,000	
Accumulated Depreciation	60,000	
Loss on Disposition of Assets	5,000	
Cash		$85,000
Machinery (old)		80,000

The purpose of the entry is to:

1. Record the new machine at its fair market value (the most easily determinable)—$100,000.
2. Remove the cost of the old machine—$80,000.
3. Remove the accumulated depreciation on the old machine—$60,000.
4. Record the payment of $85,000 cash.
5. Record the loss of $5,000 as the difference between the book value of the machine ($20,000) given and the fair market value of the old machine—the trade-in allowance ($15,000).

If the fair market value of the old machine had been equal to its book value, no gain or loss would be recognized. However, if the fair market value of the old machine had been greater than the book value, no gain would be recognized according to current authoritative pronouncements.

The tax law provides that *no gain or loss* may be recognized for tax purposes on the trading of an asset for a similar asset. Many companies prefer to use this "tax method" to simplify their accounting. Using the tax method, the example just described would be recorded as follows:

Machine (new)	$95,000	
Accumulated Depreciation	60,000	
Cash		$75,000
Machine (old)		80,000

No gain or loss is recognized under the tax method, and the asset acquired is recorded at the book value of the old asset ($20,000 in our illustration) plus the cash paid.

If a depreciable asset is scrapped, or abandoned, a loss is recognized in the amount of the book value. If the book value is zero, there would be no gain or loss. Assume a machine costing $12,000 has Accumulated Depreciation of $10,000. If the machine is abandoned, a loss of the book value (i.e., $2,000) is recognized by the following entry:

Accumulated Depreciation—Machine	$10,000	
Loss on Abandonment of Fixed Asset	2,000	
Machine		$12,000

The recognition of losses on asset dispositions may be viewed as simply allocating additional asset expirations as expenses (though called losses) to the income statement, suggesting that insufficient depreciation was taken in the past.

Natural Resources

Natural resources are those assets of the firm such as timber, coal and oil. Like land, they are provided by nature—unlike land, their service potential expires when they are exhausted. Accounting for natural resources involves problems of determining the cost of the natural resource, separate from the cost of the land that may bear the resource, separate from the cost of the land thay may bear the resource, and accounting for the extraction of the natural resource, called *depletion.*

The accounting records of the firm must separate the cost of minerals, which will be extracted and whose cost expiration should be recorded as depletion expense, from the land that bears the resources, which will not be used up. As noted earlier, if the purchase contract fails to specify how this division is to be made, accountants normally allocate a lump-sum purchase price between land and a natural resource on the basis of their relative fair market values. If $400,000 is paid for timberland and timber, and 3/4 of the value of the property is attributable to the land and 1/4 attributable to the timber, the following entry would be made:

Land	$300,000	
Timber	100,000	
Cash		$400,000

As the resource is used, the accounting records should report the cost expiration associated with the mining or cutting. For example, if one-half of the timber is cut and sold during the first year after acquisition, the following entry would be made to record the depletion expense:

Cost of timber sold	$50,000	
Timber		$50,000

Note that the asset account, timber, is reduced directly rather than indirectly through a contra asset account as with depreciation of plant and equipment. From a theoretical standpoint, the credit could be to either Timber or Accumulated Depletion—Timber. Conventionally, the asset account is reduced directly.

Depletion is almost always calculated on a unit of production basis, assigning and equal amount of depletion expense (cost expiration) to each unit mined or harvested.

Intangible Assets

Intangible assets are noncurrent rights or privileges acquired or developed by a firm to which costs may be assigned. Common examples of intangible assets are patents, franchises, copyrights, and goodwill. The primary problems in accounting for intangible assets are the same as for natural resources—accounting for the cost of the asset and determining the appropriate cost expiration.

A patent is the exclusive right to produce and sell an item. A copyright is the exclusive right to print and sell a literary or musical creation, such as a book, play, song, or symphony. Both are granted by the government to encourage creativity. A franchise is an exclusive right to market a product or service within a specified geographical region. Many motels and fast-food restaurants are franchises, acquired by contract with the creator of the product or service.

Intangible assets are recorded at the cost of the asset. Cost is defined as all the necessary and customary expenditures to acquire the asset and have it ready for use in the entity. If a patent is purchased, the asset Patents is measured at the entire cost, or expenditure, to acquire the Patent. This definition would include any legal fees involved in acquiring the patent or defending its integrity in court.

Goodwill poses some rather thorny problems for accountants. Goodwill is a purchased intangible asset. It has been described as a master valuation account for a business—that additional cost of acquiring a business above the fair market value of its physical assets, attributable to its potential to earn an unusually high rate of return because of location, reputation, or a combination of other factors. Although some accountants argue that goodwill is imaginary and should not be recognized, it is recognized only when purchased and valued as the excess of the total purchase price of the business over that value directly attributable to the physical and other intangible assets of the firm. In other words, it is a residual value. If $400,000 is paid for a business, and the fair market value of its identifiable assets is $350,000, goodwill would be valued at $50,000. See Chapter 15 for an extended discussion of goodwill that is associated with the purchase price of a business.

The cost expiration associated with the reduction in the service life of intangible assets is recognized and called *amortization* or amortization expense. Amortization of intangible assets is the same as depreciation of plant and equipment. Amortization is usually calculated on a straight-line basis over the expected useful life of the asset. If a patent has a maximum legal life of 17 years, but is expected to benefit a firm for only 10 years, and it cost $100,000, the following entry would be made:

Amortization of Patent	$10,000	
Patent		$10,000

Note again that the asset account is usually reduced directly rather than through a contra account.

Intangible assets are reported on the balance sheet at their net amount. For example, at the end of the first year, the patent recorded above would be reported as follows on the balance sheet:

Intangible Assets:
Patents $90,000

Again, goodwill poses problems for accountants. How long does goodwill remain an asset? Does the cost of goodwill expire, and if so, how fast? The

Accounting Principles Board requires that goodwill be amortized over its estimated useful life. This period of time should not exceed 40 years in the Board's opinion. Many firms—uncertain as to how long goodwill lasts—simply amortize the cost over 40 years.

Marketable securities were defined in Chapter 7 as investments in securities (e.g., stocks, bonds) for which there is a ready market and the securities are not held in order to control or influence another firm, or for some other long-term benefit. Securities held for some long-term benefit or for which there is no ready market are classified in accounting as long-term investments. This is a noncurrent category on the balance sheet. Other assets of an investment nature that management intends to hold for long-term benefit should also be reported as a long-term investment. For example, if the firm invests in land with the intention of possibly developing the land several years in the future, that land should be reported as a long-term investment.

Long-term Investments

Long-term investments usually are recorded and reported in accordance with the historical cost principle. For example, if a firm acquires a subsidiary corporation by purchasing 80 percent of its voting stock for $3,200,000, and pays $32,000 in brokerage fees and $6,000 additional transfer costs, the purchase would be recorded as follows:

Long-term investment in Stock	$3,238,000	
Cash		$3,238,000

The exact content of financial statement disclosures for long-term investments in common stock depends upon the relative size of the stockholding, the purpose for making the investment, and the nature of the business being conducted. Further discussion of accounting for long-term investments in corporate common stock is found in Chapter 15.

Long-term investments in bonds pose an unusual accounting problem. A bond is really a long-term loan. Bonds pay a fixed or stated rate of interest printed on the bond certificate and determined at the time the bonds are issued. Without intervention, resale of the bond from one investor to another would be difficult if the market rate of interest for new bonds was higher than that paid on older bonds. To adjust for variations in the market rate of interest and to keep older bonds marketable, the purchase price of the bond adjusts. If the current rate of interest is 8 percent and a bond only pays 6 percent, the price of the bond *drops* so that the new investor receives a yield on his investment that is approximately 8 percent. Similarly, if a bond pays 9 percent and the current rate of interest is 7 percent, the price of the bond will be driven up by investors to a price that allows the investor to yield approximately 7 percent—the current rate of interest—on the investment. The difference between the maturity value of a bond and its purchase price is called a *premium* if purchased for more than the maturity value of the bond, and a *discount* if purchased for less than the bond's maturity value. The accounting problem is how to account for the premium or discount.

Premiums or discounts adjust the stated rate of interest to the market rate. For example, if a bond is purchased for $90,000, and at maturity in 10 years it will pay $100,000, plus 6 percent interest until maturity, how much return does the investor receive for a $90,000 investment? It can be calculated as follows:

Amount Received at Maturity	$100,000
Interest to be Received in Cash	
($6,000/yr. × 10 yrs.)	60,000
Total Received	$160,000
Original Investment	− 90,000
Total Return on Investment	$ 70,000

Accountants have concluded that the entire return from an investment in a bond held to maturity is interest. An approximation of the total interest income earned each year on this bond can be calculated by dividing the total return on the bond by the number of years the bond is to be held ($70,000 ÷ 10 = $7,000/year).

How does the accountant report $7,000 per year in interest income when the bond only pays $6,000 interest each year? The answer is by "amortizing" the bond discount—increasing interest income and increasing the reported value of the bond. The following entries illustrate the acquisition of the bond and amortization of the discount:

1. Purchase of $100,000 Bonds for $90,000 at beginning of year:

Long-term Investment in Bonds	$90,000	
Cash		$90,000

2. Received semiannual interest on June 30:

Cash	3,000	
Interest Income		3,000

3. Received semiannual interest on Dec. 31:

Cash	3,000	
Interest Income		3,000

4. Amortization of bond discount on Dec. 31:

Long-term Investment in Bonds	1,000	
Interest Income		1,000

The amount of discount amortized each year would be calculated by dividing the total discount ($10,000) by the number of years over which it is to be amortized (10). Note that the result of the amortization process is that interest income is adjusted over time for the amount of premium or discount, and the book value of the bond at maturity exactly equals the maturity value of the bond.

If bonds are acquired at a premium instead of a discount, the book value of the bonds is reduced over time, and interest income is reduced by the amortization of the premium. The entry to amortize bond premium of $1,000 this year would be as follows:

Interest Income	$1,000	
Long-term Investment in Bonds		$1,000

Again, it results in adjusting interest income and reducing the book value of the bond to its maturity value at maturity.

Premiums and discounts are amortized on a regular basis so that they will be properly included as an interest adjustment, rather than shown as a gain or loss at maturity. For purposes of illustration, the straight-line method of amortization was used in the previous discussion. However, this method is limited in practice by its conceptual basis. A superior technique is the *effective-interest method* of amortization. The effective-interest method provides for an accurate determination of periodic income and a proper statement of the asset balance by basing the amortization process on compound interest techniques and the time value of money. Compound interest and present value methods are discussed in the Supplementary Discussion at the end of Chapter 10 and the effective-interest method of allocation is illustrated in Chapter 11.

Deferred Charges

Deferred charges sometimes appear on a balance sheet as noncurrent assets. *Deferred charges* are prepaid expenses that are long-term; they cannot appropriately be included in the current assets. An example of a deferred charge would be organization costs. These are costs incurred to organize a business. Obviously, these costs will benefit the business as long as it functions and they therefore cannot be classified as current assets. Deferred charges should be recognized as expenses as they benefit the firm. This asset expiration is normally recognized by reducing the asset account and debiting an appropriate expense.

Summary

Noncurrent assets are also called fixed or long-term assets. The primary problems in accounting for noncurrent assets are measuring the cost of the assets, measuring their cost expiration, matching the expired cost with revenues, and accounting for the ultimate disposal of the assets.

The historical cost principle is used to value noncurrent assets at acquisition. All reasonable and necessary expenditures incurred to acquire, install, and prepare the assets for use become part of the cost of the assets. Adjustment entries are made to reflect the expiration of the service potential through age, wear, use, or consumption, but the name for the expired costs, depreciation, depletion, or amortization, depends upon whether the asset is classified as plant and equipment, natural resources, or intangibles and deferred charges. Several systematic depreciation methods are currently in use, including the straight-line method, the sum-of-the-years'-digits method, the double-declining method, and the units of production method. Depletion usually is calculated under the units of production method. Amortization is calculated under the straight-line method. Disposal of noncurrent assets includes sales, trade-ins, or abandoment, and gains or losses on disposal usually are reflected in the income statement for the year of disposal. Accounting for trade-ins, deferred charges, and long-term investments was also discussed.

Supplementary Discussion: The Investment Tax Credit

Federal income tax law has a number of diverse objectives in addition to simply providing revenues for the federal government. Among these objectives are the stimulation of business and the economy to provide jobs and create economic growth and stability. In creating income tax laws, the U.S. Congress has provided a number of special provisions dealing with the business acquisition and use of plant and equipment. These provisions are so important that most businesses carefully study them and their impact in making purchase decisions. In this discussion we examine one of the most important of these provisions: the investment tax credit.

To encourage firms to acquire and use plant and equipment, thereby stimulating the economy, Congress gives an income tax credit for part of the cost of acquiring the assets. An income tax credit reduces the tax bill of a taxpayer one dollar for each dollar of credit. Note that this is more beneficial than an income tax deduction. A deduction saves less than one dollar of tax for each dollar of deduction because it reduces the amount of taxable income, not the tax itself. Thus, if a taxpayer is in a 40 percent income tax bracket, a one dollar deduction saves only 40¢ in tax—instead of the $1 saved by the credit of $1.

The investment tax credit is allowed generally for tangible, personal (not land or building) property used in a trade or business. The amount of the credit is 10 percent of the cost of such property if the property has a life of at least seven years; 10 percent of two-thirds of the cost of property with a life of five but less than seven years; and 10 percent of one-third of the cost of property with a life of three but less than five years. Taxpayers are allowed to offset the first $25,000 of income tax liability completely, and one-half of the liability above $25,000. If these limits do not allow the full use of the credit in a year, the excess credit can be used in other years.

The essential effect of the investment tax credit is to take dollars that would normally become tax revenues to the government and allow businesses to spend these dollars on long-lived assets to expand their businesses and replace worn and less productive equipment. In substance, the Federal government allows the taxpayer to elect to reinvest these funds in their businesses instead of paying them in taxes. This credit effectively reduces the cost of new equipment to a business, thereby encouraging businesses to acquire more equipment. Congress even allows up to $100,000 in used equipment to qualify for the investment tax credit!

Congress did feel the need to protect the government's revenues by preventing manipulation of the investment tax credit by unscrupulous taxpayers. First, the law does not generally allow an investment tax credit on assets acquired from related parties. This prevents a corporation and its subsidiary from trading assets back and forth to receive the credit, without really replacing the equipment. Second, the law requires that the credit or part of it be recaptured—added back as additional tax liability—if disposal of the asset occurs prior to serving the necessary period to earn the full credit claimed. For example, if the taxpayer claimed the asset has a three year life and paid $27,000 for it, he could have claimed a credit of $900 ($10\% \times \frac{1}{3} \times \$27,000$). But if the taxpayer sells the asset after only two years—which should make the asset not qualified for the credit because its life is too short—the credit claimed would be required to be recaptured in the year of disposition as $900 added tax liability. Of course, if the asset had been held three years, no recapture would have been necessary. If the taxpayer claimed that the asset has a life of seven years, he would have been entitled to claim a credit of $2,700 ($10\% \times \$27,000$). If the asset was disposed in its sixth year, the taxpayer would be required to recapture the part of the credit not properly claimed. In this case, the taxpayer should have claimed only $1,800 ($10\% \times \frac{2}{3} \times \$27,000$). So $900 would be required to be recaptured.

Clearly the amount of the investment tax credit is so material that it has had an important impact on business expansion and asset acquisition. In this and other ways, Congress hopes to stimulate the economy. With proper asset management and purchasing decisions, businesses can help Congress accomplish its objectives of sustained growth and prosperity—and save taxes!

Key Terms

Depreciation expense
Residual value
Straight-line method
Double-declining balance method
Sum-of-the-years'-digits method
Units-of-production method
Depletion
Amortization
Premium
Discount
Effective-interest method
Deferred charges

Questions

1. What are noncurrent assets?

2. List the major classes of noncurrent assets.

3. How do accountants value noncurrent assets at the time of their acquisition for balance sheet purposes?

4. How is land unique from most other longlived, noncurrent assets? What is the accounting impact of this difference?

5. If several assets are purchased for a single price, how should the total price paid be allocated to the various individual assets?

6. Why should the lump-sum purchase price of a group of assets be allocated to the individual assets?

7. How should a long-lived asset be valued if it is acquired in an exchange for assets other than cash?

8. Does the balance sheet presentation of plant and equipment reflect their fair market value?

9. Why do accountants recognize depreciation expense for part of a year?

10. What three factors must be known or estimated to calculate depreciation expense?

11. What is the residual value of an asset?

12. Identify the elements used in both the calculation of straight-line depreciation and units-of-production depreciation.

13. What does the account Accumulated Depreciation measure?

14. Why are the double-declining-balance and sum-of-the-years'-digits methods of depreciation called accelerated depreciation methods?

15. Is depreciation expense related to depletion expense? Explain.

16. Distinguish between tangible and intangible assets.

17. How do accountants calculate the cost expiration associated with the reduction in the service life of an intangible asset?

18. Describe the difference between marketable securities and long-term investments.

19. Why do accountants amortize bond premiums or discounts?

20. Define deferred charge.

Exercises

1. Classify the following as current assets or noncurrent assets:
(a) Cash.
(b) Rent prepaid for five years.
(c) Treasury bills maturing in 91 days held as a temporary investment.
(d) Land and building used in manufacturing.
(e) Stock in a company that supplies parts.
(f) Patents to a process developed by the firm.
(g) Inventory.
(h) Coal in a coal mine operated by the firm.

2. Consider the following data:

Purchase price of land and building	$225,000
Cost to demolish building	32,000
Cost of constructing new building on land	72,000

Determine (a) the cost of the land, and (b) the cost of the building.

3. Five machines of varying sizes are purchased for a bargain $27,000. Estimates of their individual fair market values are as follows:

Machine A = $ 5,000
Machine B =   5,000
Machine C =   6,600
Machine D =   9,000
Machine E = 12,400

What cost is allocated to each machine?

4. Calculate the first full year straight-line depreciation expense for a machine acquired on January 2 of the current year for $6,000. The machine is estimated to have a residual value of $500 and a useful life of five years.

5. Give the entry to record a $3,000 depreciation expense on an automobile.

6. Calculate the depreciation expense to the nearest whole month for a truck purchased on March 28 by a calendar year business for $8,000, using an estimated residual value of $2,000, a useful life of three years, and the straight-line method.

7. Calculate depreciation expense for the *second* full year on a truck purchased for $8,000 with a residual value of $500 and an estimated useful life of five years; using the sum-of-the-years'-digits method.

8. Calculate depreciation expense for the *second* full year in the life of a machine acquired for $40,000 with a residual value of $4,000 and an estimated life of eight years, using the double-declining-balance method.

9. Calculate and compare the depreciation expense for each complete year in the life of an automobile with a cost of $8,000, a residual value of $2,000, and a life of three years, using the straight-line and double-declining-balance methods.

10. A machine is estimated to be able to produce 40,000 units during its productive life, costs $16,000, and has no estimated residual value. Calculate the depreciation expense for the machine if it produces 2,940 units this year.

11. A particular pneumatic press can be operated 8,000 hours during its estimated productive life. A time clock attached to the machine indicates that it was operated 1,800 hours this year. Calculate the depreciation expense for the press, assuming it cost $26,000 and has an estimated residual value of $2,000.

12. Prepare a journal entry necessary to record the sale of a machine that originally cost $6,200, has depreciation recorded to date of $4,800, and is sold for $1,500.

13. Prepare the journal entries necessary to account for the trade-in of an automobile. The old automobile originally cost $4,200, the new automobile has a fair market value of $7,000, the accumulated depreciation on the old automobile to date is $3,700, and $6,600 cash is required along with the old automobile. Use both the accounting and income tax methods of valuing the new auto.

14. A coal mine is estimated to contain 1,500,000 tons of coal reserves and the cost allocated to the reserves is $6,000,000. (a) Prepare a journal entry to record depletion expense on 125,000 tons of ore removed and sold during the year. (b) Present the balance sheet disclosure of the coal mine at the end of the year.

15. Determine the amount of the amortization expense for one year for a patent developed by the firm at a cost of $380,000, assuming the firm estimates the patent to have a useful life of 12 years.

16. Prepare the entries necessary to report the annual interest income received on an 8 percent $100,000 bond purchased for $98,000 and properly reported as a long-term investment, assuming the bond matures eight years from the date of its purchase. Remember to amortize the bond discount.

17. Prepare the entries needed to record the annual interest income reportable on a 7.5 percent $100,000 bond purchased for $105,000 and properly reported as a long-term investment, assuming the bond matures in 10 years. Be sure to amortize the premium.

18. Classify the following investments of a manufacturing firm as temporary or long-term investments:
(a) Land that management intends to hold as an investment for appreciation in value.
(b) Common stock of a firm listed on the New York Stock Exchange that management plans to sell when the price goes up.
(c) Common stock of a local corporation for which there is no established market.
(d) Common stock of a supplier that is acquired to insure a constant supply.
(e) A two-year note evidencing a loan to a valuable customer who is in temporary financial difficulty.
(f) Land in a developing tract that management expects will appreciate rapidly and they will soon sell.
(g) Bonds acquired to earn interest on excess funds available in the business.
(h) Stock of a subsidiary corporation.

19. Prepare the general journal entries necessary to record these transactions involving bonds acquired as a long-term investment:
(a) Acquired a $1,000, 8 percent bond maturing in 7.5 years for $1,075 on January 1, 19X6.
(b) Received semiannual interest of $40 on June 30.
(c) Acquired a $1,000, 9 percent bond for $980 maturing in five years on July 1.
(d) Received semiannual interest on both bonds on December 31.
(e) Amortized premium and discount on December 31.
(f) Sold the 8 percent bond on January 1, 19X7, for $1,090.

20. Prepare a section of a balance sheet to reflect the following events associated with patents of the Ross Development Co.
(a) Developed a patent costing a total of $120,000. Estimated life is eight years.
(b) Purchased a patent for $160,000. This patent is estimated to have a 10-year useful life to the firm.
(c) Amortized the cost of both patents for one full year.

21. The Token Company sold some of its fixed assets during 19X7. The original cost of the fixed assets was $750,000, and the allowance for accumulated depreciation at the date of sale was $600,000. The proceeds from the sale of the fixed assets

were $210,000. Prepare the journal entry to record the sale of the fixed assets by the Token Company (AICPA adapted).

22. On February 1, 19X7, the Reflection Corporation purchased a parcel of land as a factory site for $50,000. An old building on the property was demolished, and construction began on a new building that was completed on November 1, 19X7. Costs incurred during this period are listed below:

Demolition of old building	$ 4,000
Architect's fees	10,000
Legal fees for title investigation and purchase contract	2,000
Construction costs	500,000
(Salvaged materials resulting from the demolition of the old building were sold for $1,000)	

Reflection Corporation would report the value of the land and the value of the new building at what amounts on their year-end financial statements (AICPA adapted)?

23. On July 1, 19X6, the Carol Corporation purchased factory equipment for $25,000. Salvage value was estimated to be $1,000. The equipment will be depreciated over 10 years using the double-declining-balance method. Counting the year of acquisition as one half year, calculate the amount of depreciation expense that the Carol Corporation should record in for 19X6 and 19X7 (AICPA adapted).

24. On January 1, 19X6, the Kent Corporation purchased a machine for $50,000. Kent paid shipping expenses of $500 and installation costs of $1,200. The machine was estimated to have a useful life of 10 years and an estimated salvage value of $3,000. In January 19X7 additions costing $3,600 were made to the machine in order to comply with pollution control ordinances. These additions did not prolong the life of the machine or add anything to the estimated salvage value. If the Kent Corporation records depreciation under the straight-line method, depreciation expense for 19X7 is how much (AICPA adapted)?

25. The Flood Corporation purchased a machine on January 1, 19X1, for $150,000. At the date of acquisition, the machine had an estimated useful life of 10 years, with no salvage value. The machine is being depreciated on a straight-line basis. Prepare a portion of a balance sheet to reflect the machine as of December 31, 19X5.

26. The Mann Company does not carry insurance on its office machines. On December 27, 19X6 Machine A was totally destroyed by fire. The book value of Machine A, depreciated to the date of the fire, was $62,000. Disposal costs were $3,000. What is the total amount of losses that should be charged to income in 19X6? Does the accountant have any discretion in preparing the income figure (AICPA adapted)?

27. On December 1, 19X6, the Hobart Company acquired a new delivery truck in exchange for an old delivery truck that it had acquired in 19X3. The old truck was purchased for $7,000 and had a book value of $2,800. On the date of the exchange

the old truck had a market value of $3,000. In addition, Hobart paid $3,500 cash for the new truck, which had a list price of $8,000. Prepare the journal entry to record this exchange, using the income tax method (AICPA adapted).

Problems

1. The Retsin Company engaged in the following transactions involving noncurrent assets during the year.
(a) Retsin purchased 20 acres of land for $40,000, paid $2,200 in expenses associated with the purchase and $1,600 to have the land prepared for construction.
(b) Retsin incurred $20,000 in costs to purchase rights to a patented process. Additional attorney's fees to close the transaction were $3,000.
(c) Retsin purchased on earth mover for $26,000. Additional sales taxes on the purchase were $1,030.
(d) Retsin abandoned as worthless a truck that had originally cost $11,000 but had a related accumulated depreciation account balance of $9,600. Depreciation for the partial year up to the date of abandonment has not been recorded and is $600.
(e) Retsin paid $6,000 to a firm going out of business to acquire an automobile and a truck. The automobile and the truck each had a fair market value of $4,000.

REQUIRED:
Prepare general journal entries necessary to record these transactions.

2. Moscowitz and Sons is trading in a printing press for a larger, newer model on September 28, 19X7. The old press was purchased on January 6, 19X1, for $27,000. It was estimated to have a $2,000 salvage value and a useful life of 10 years. Straight-line depreciation was used by the firm. The new press has a market value of $68,000, and a $6,000 trade-in allowance is given for the old press.

REQUIRED:
(a) Give the entry to bring the depreciation up to date on the old machine, assuming the firm takes a ½ year depreciation on assets in the year of purchase or sale.
(b) Give the entries necessary to account for the trade-in using both the accounting method and the tax method of accounting for the trade-in.

3. Corbin and Company has the following land, plant, and equipment account balances in 19X5. Depreciation is determined to the nearest half year.

Item	Date of Purchase	Cost	Life	Residual Value
Automobile	1/6/X3	$ 3,600	4 years	$ 600
Office Equipment	1/3/X3	9,000	8 years	1,000
Printing Press	1/3/X3	13,000	6 years	0
Building	6/28/X3	48,000	30 years	3,000
Land	6/28/X3	10,000	—	—

REQUIRED:
(a) Calculate depreciation expense for Corbin and Comany for 19X5, assuming the building is depreciated using the straight-line method and the double-declining-balance method is used for all other depreciable assets.

(b) Give the entries to record depreciation expense.

(c) Show the balance sheet presentation of these assets at year end, December 31, 19X5.

4. Lohman Enterprises acquired an air-conditioning unit this year, paying $18,000 for the unit on September 23, 19X2. Management estimates that the unit has a useful life of 10 years and will have no residual value thereafter.

REQUIRED:
Calculate straight line depreciation expense for 19X2 on this air-conditioning unit, based on (a) the nearest whole month, and (b) the half year "year-of-purchase, year-of-sale" alternative.

5. Reynard Clothiers has remodeled its shop, installing movable clothing racks costing $17,500. The racks are chrome plated and estimated to have a useful life of five years and a residual value of $2,500. They were installed during the second week of the firm's fiscal year.

REQUIRED:
Construct a depreciation schedule for these racks showing annual depreciation for each of the five years of its expected life, using the straight-line method, the sum-of-the-years'-digits method, and the double-declining-balance method.

6. Rothchild Industries produces corduroy cloth for the apparel industry. The production process is completed in two steps, utilizing two different machines, A and B. Machine A cost $26,000 and has an estimated productive capacity of 1,600,000 yards of cloth. Machine B cost $39,000 and has an estimated productive life of 12,000 machine hours.

REQUIRED:
Calculate depreciation expense for 19X3, assuming that Machine A produced 243,000 yards of cloth in 19X3 and Machine B operated 2,120 hours. Neither machine is expected to have residual value at the end of its life.

7. Hamm Company is curtailing its operations due to a reduction in the demand for its product. To carry out this process, Hamm disposed of the following equipment during 19X4:

Item	Date of Acquisition	Cost	Depreciation Method	Life	Accumulated Depreciation	Residual Value	Date of Disposition	Sales Price
Leather Cutter	1/5/X1	$2,200	Straight Line	5 Years	$1,200	200	6/20/X4	Abandoned
Wood Roller	1/5/X1	3,800	Straight Line	6 Years	1,800	200	8/26/X4	$ 600
Truck	4/3/X1	5,600	Straight Line	3 Years	4,200	1400	9/3/X4	$1,000
Packing Machine	1/6/X3	3,000	Double Declining Balance	5 Years	1,200	500	12/20/X4	1,500

REQUIRED:

Present general journal entries to account for these dispositions during 19X4. Assume the firm uses the nearest half of a year method of recognizing depreciation expense on dispositions during the year.

8. The Greenbriar Coal Company has the following intangible assets and natural resources during 19X8:

Patent on Coal Extraction Process
Cost: $150,000; Life: 12 years;
Year of Development: 19X5

Coal in Lucky Dollar Coal Mine
Cost: $220,000; Total Coal at
Time of Discovery: 800,000 Tons;
Coal Removed and Sold in 19X8: 136,000 Tons

Coal in Greenbriar Coal Mine
Cost: $60,000; Total Coal at Time
of Discovery: 1,200,000 Tons;
Coal Removed and Sold in 19X8: 155,000 Tons

REQUIRED:

Give the adjusting entries needed at year end to record depletion expense and patent amortization.

9. The Marston Company purchased a long-term investment in corporate bonds. At the end of last year Marston bought 30 $1,000 corporate bonds as follows:

Bond	Number Acquired	Rate of Interest	Annual Interest Payment Due	Amount Paid for Each Bond	Time to Maturity from Date of Purchase
Corporation X	8	7%	6/30	$ 975	5 Years
Corporation Y	8	9%	3/31	1,030	20 Years
Corporation Z	14	8%	9/30	1,002	4 Years

REQUIRED:

(a) Prepare adjusting entries necessary to recognize the annual amortization of bond premium or discount on these long-term investments as of December 31, 19X2.

(b) Determine the amount of interest income recognized on the long-term investments during 19X2.

(c) Present the balance sheet disclosure at year-end of the bond investments, and the income statement disclosure of the interest income for the year.

10. The unadjusted trial balance for the Glen Company is shown below:

GLEN COMPANY
Trial Balance
December 31, 19X4

	Debit	Credit
Cash	$ 12,400	
Accounts Receivable	29,000	
Inventory	45,000	
Prepaid Insurance	2,100	
Supplies	1,400	
Furniture and Fixtures	17,000	
Accumulated Depreciation		$ 1,200
Patent	12,000	
Goodwill	6,000	
Long-Term Investment in Bonds	10,300	
Accounts Payable		10,750
Owners' Equity		85,600
Sales		305,000
Sales Discounts	3,750	
Purchases	196,000	
Salary Expense	40,000	
Delivery Expense	6,000	
Advertising Expense	6,000	
Rent Expense	12,000	
Utilities Expense	3,600	
	$402,550	$402,550

Financial data for adjustments include the following:
(a) The Furniture and Fixtures account and supporting financial records show the following:

Asset	Cost	Date of Acquisition	Life	Salvage	Accumulated Depreciation
Desks	$3,000	7/1/19X3	6 Years	None	$250
Calculators	5,000	7/1/19X3	10 Years	$1,000	500
Sales Equipment	9,000	9/30/19X3	10 Years	None	450

Straight-line depreciation is used for the desks. The double-declining-balance method is used for the other assets.

(b) The patent was acquired on January 9, 19X4, at a cost of $12,000 and estimated useful life of eight years.
(c) The goodwill was acquired with the purchase of the business on January 1, 19X0, and is being amortized over 20 years.

(d) Bonds were acquired on January 1, 19X4. They pay interest of 8 percent on December 31. The check has not been received yet. The bonds will mature six years from the date of acquisition.

(e) Ending periodic inventory has a balance of $38,000.

REQUIRED:
1. Prepare a worksheet for the Glen Company.
2. Prepare an income statement and balance sheet from the work sheet.
3. Prepare general journal closing entries.

11. The following accounts are found in the general ledger of Simpson, Inc., before year end adjustment, December 31, 19X7:

Delivery Equipment	$25,000
Machinery	45,000
Building	60,000
Land	60,000
Patents	30,000
Goodwill	20,000
Accumulated Depreciation—Delivery Equipment	0
Accumulated Depreciation—Machinery	18,000
Accumulated Depreciation—Building	10,000

Additional data about these assets are shown below:

Asset	Date of Acquisition	Depreciation of Amortization Method	Salvage	Life, in Years
Delivery Equipment	7/6/19X7	Double Declining Balance	$5,000	3
Machinery	1/3/19X6	Double Declining Balance	5,000	5
Building	1/8/19X2	Straight Line	0	30
Patents	1/8/19X2	Straight Line	0	10
Goodwill	1/8/19X2	Straight Line	0	10

REQUIRED:
(a) Prepare general journal adjusting entries to bring these accounts up to date on December 31, 19X7, Simpson's year end.
(b) Prepare the long-term asset section of the balance sheet.

12. The Lightfoot Company acquired a new delivery truck on April 3, 19X4, paying the amounts shown here:

List price	$ 8,000
Options	1,300
Taxes	460
	9,760
Less Dealer Discount	(1,000)
	$ 8,760

In addition, the firm added storage racks and decorative lettering to the truck. Costs of these additions were $420 for the racks and $120 for the lettering. All of this work was completed on April 10, 19X4.

REQUIRED:

(a) Present general journal entries necessary to reflect these activities.

(b) Prepare a four-year depreciation schedule using the sum-of-the-years'-digits method, assuming a life of four years and a salvage value of $1,300.

(c) Give the general journal entry needed to record the trade-in of this truck on April 12, 19X7, on a new truck costing $10,600, given a $4,000 trade-in allowance on the old truck. Use both the "tax method" and the normal accounting method of accounting for the trade-in. Remember to bring depreciation up to date.

□ 10
CURRENT LIABILITIES

☐ OBJECTIVES

AFTER STUDYING THIS CHAPTER, YOU SHOULD BE ABLE TO DO THE FOLLOWING:

1. IDENTIFY THE CHARACTERISTICS OF LIABILITIES AND DESCRIBE THEIR FINANCIAL STATEMENT DISCLOSURE.

2. PRESENT PROCEDURES FOR EFFICIENT LIABILITY MANAGEMENT.

3. DESCRIBE THE ACCOUNTING AND REPORTING OF DEFERRED REVENUE.

4. SPECIFY JOURNAL ENTRIES AND FINANCIAL STATEMENT DISCLOSURES RELATED TO PAYROLL COSTS AND LIABILITIES.

5. CALCULATE THE EFFECTS OF PURCHASE DISCOUNT ON ACCOUNTS PAYABLE.

6. DETERMINE INTEREST EXPENSE AND DESCRIBE DISCLOSURE OF RELATED LIABILITIES.

Creditors are one of the most important sources of economic resources for businesses. They provide a firm with the use of goods, services, or direct loans of cash. Claims by creditors of the business are called *liabilities;* the business is required to convey assets or perform services of a reasonably definite amount at a specific future date or dates for obligations resulting from past or current transactions. A broad variety of transactions may give rise to liabilities. Direct loans of cash from banks or other sources are common transactions that cause the recognition of liabilities. Credit may also be extended by suppliers who allow the firm to pay for goods or services after the date of purchase. The very nature of some transactions automatically generates a liability. For example, employees are rarely paid at the end of each workday. To avoid the time and expense of drawing daily payroll checks, employees ordinarily are paid weekly, biweekly, or monthly. Because each employee extends services to the business for which he will be compensated on payday, he is a creditor for that period of time.

Characteristics of Liabilities

The following characteristics of liabilities deserve particular notice: the presence of a specific obligation that is measureable or definite in amount and that calls for satisfaction on or before specific future dates.

Specific Obligation. By its very nature, a liability is an obligation of the firm. All legally enforceable obligations constitute accounting liabilities. However, the accounting definition of liability is broader than the legal concept. Liabilities include all future obligations for assets or services that arise from past events or transactions and can be measured or closely estimated in monetary terms.

Most liabilities require the payment of cash to satisfy an obligation. Some liabilities, however, require the provision of specific goods or services to satisfy an obligation. Advances from customers, for example, are called *deferred revenues*. They represent the value of goods or services that the firm is obligated to provide. Even though they do not require the payment of cash, deferred revenues are properly classified as liabilities because they represent an obligation of the firm.

Definite Obligation. The amount of a future obligation must be known or subject to reasonable estimation before it can be classified as an accounting liability. A bank note indicates exactly how much principal and interest must be paid on the loan. An invoice indicates exactly how much the firm must pay for the purchase of goods. The exact amount of some liabilities may not be known, however. For example, the extent of liability to perform under warranty contracts is unknown at the time of the sale of the merchandise. Although the firm knows that some warranty claims will be made, it does not know exactly how many or what the cost of those claims will be. If the firm can estimate the amount of future warranty claims, this reasonably definite amount should be recorded as a liability. If the uncertainty of the amount of the liability is great or if there is material uncertainty as to the existence of the liability, no liability should be recorded.

For example, a lawsuit may impose substantial liabilities to pay damages if the suit is lost, but no liability at all if it is won. Such liabilities are called _contingent liabilities_. They are potential future obligations whose existence will be resolved when one or more future events occur. If their occurrence is not considered probable, if the amount is not subject to reasonable estimation, or if the amount is not material to the firm, contingent liabilities are not recorded as liabilities. Normally, however, the accountant will include a footnote to the financial statements describing the nature of the contingent liability in order to provide the financial statement user with this information.

Specific Due Date. Almost all liabilities require satisfaction on or by a specific date. This date is usually specified in a contract, by a law, or as a matter of business custom. For example, the contract between a lender and borrower usually specifies when the borrower must repay the loan. Tax laws indicate exactly when taxes must be paid. Business custom in a particular industry may determine when a supplier is paid for goods purchased. Some liabilities, however, do not have specific due dates. For example, deferred income taxes, discussed in Chapter 11, may have indeterminate due dates. Nonetheless, they are generally classified as liabilities for lack of a better classification.

The proper measurement and reporting of liabilities helps the financial statement user to evaluate the financial position of the firm. Of particular importance in assessing the impact of a liability on the firm is the date on which the obligation must be satisfied; this is called the *maturity date*. A great deal of confusion would exist if those liabilities, which must be paid within one week, are combined with long-term liabilities, which may not be repaid for several years. To aid the financial statement user in assessing the impact of liabilities with greatly varying maturity dates, all liabilities are divided into two separate balance sheet classifications: current liabilities and long-term liabilities.

Current liabilities are obligations of the firm that must be satisfied within one year or one operating cycle, whichever is longer. Also, it must be reasonable to expect them to be satisfied by the use of current assets or by the incurrence of additional current liabilities. All other liabilities are classified as long-term liabilities. This classification system produces a balance sheet presentation of liabilities that highlights the impact of differences in maturity dates.

Classification of Liabilities

This chapter discusses the measurement and reporting problems of current liabilities, including accounts payable, notes payable, payroll liabilities, accrued liabilities, and deferred revenues. In addition, the supplementary discussion to this chapter will describe important concepts in the measurement of all liabilities: compound interest and present value. Chapter 11 completes the presentation of liabilities with a discussion of long-term liabilities.

Objectives in Accounting for Current Liabilities

There are two broad objectives in accounting for current liabilities: to provide for the efficient internal management of current liabilities and their costs and to provide relevant information about current liabilities for financial statement users.

Efficient Internal Management

The efficient internal management of current liabilities is aimed at controlling the costs of using short-term credit and establishing a system of internal controls over the payments made to satisfy current liabilities.

Costs of Credit. If management is to evaluate alternative sources of funds properly, it must have accurate information about differences in costs. The cost of using borrowed funds is the interest charged by the creditor. Interest rates for current liabilities vary widely. Some current liabilities have no cost, while others bear extremely high rates of interest. For example, there is no interest cost associated with paying employees weekly instead of daily. Nor is there any interest expense associated with trade credit, as long as payments are made within the discount period. If the firm fails to pay within the discount period, however, the cost of using trade credit may become very high. For example, if merchandise costing $1,000 is purchased at terms of 2/10, n/30, the firm gets a 2 percent discount if it pays for the merchandise within 10 days of the invoice date. Otherwise, the firm must pay the full $1,000 instead of only $980 [1,000 − (1,000 × 0.02)]. The 2 percent discount expressed as an annual rate of interest for the use of the credit for an additional 20 days is very high—approximately 36 percent.[1] The rates of interest charged by banks or other commercial lending institutions vary from a low in past years of 6 percent to rates that are more than twice as high.

Timely Payment. Providing management with information about the relative cost of using credit in various forms is an important function of the accountant. After management has considered costs and established liability

[1] Two percent (rate for using money for 20 days) times 18 (approximate number of 20-day periods in a year) equals 36 percent. The difference between paying on the tenth day and the thirtieth day is 20 days. The cost of holding funds for this period is 2 percent, thus the 36 percent annual rate.

policies, the accountant plays an active role in implementing these policies. Trade credit poses a special problem for the firm. Many businesses elect to make all payments within the discount period to avoid the high rates of interest associated with the use of trade credit beyond the discount period. If the payment is delayed, the discount is lost. To insure that discounts are taken, many firms file invoices that require payment in a "tickler file" by discount payment date instead of by vendor's name. All invoices that require payment on a particular day to get the discount are kept in the same file. The use of tickler files reduces the chance that discounts may be accidentally lost.

Some firms also modify their accounting systems to highlight the amount of discounts lost. As we noted in Chapter 5, a purchase normally is recorded at cost:

Purchases	$1,000	
Accounts Payable		$1,000

If a discount of 2 percent is taken, the entry to record the payment is:

Accounts Payable	$1,000	
Cash		$980
Purchase Discounts		20

But if the discount is lost, this accounting system fails to note this additional interest cost:

Accounts Payable	$1,000	
Cash		$1,000

By recording the purchase "net of discount," the accountant creates the vehicle for highlighting lost discounts. Consider these entries to record a purchase, a payment within the discount period, and a payment after the discount period:

Purchase Recorded "Net of Discount"

Purchases	$980	
Accounts Payable		$980

Payment Within Discount Period

Accounts Payable	$980	
Cash		$980

Payment After the Discount Period

Accounts Payable	$980	
Purchases Discounts Lost	20	
Cash		$1,000

Management is continually advised about the consequences of failure to adhere to their discount policy. Since this method separates interest charges from the purchase price of merchandise, it is also theoretically more acceptable. It does not group these dissimilar items together under one label.

Voucher System. Another problem faced by all business is the problem of establishing control over cash disbursements. Management wishes to insure that employees do not embezzle funds by writing checks to themselves and that errors in disbursements are minimized. One common system of controls over cash disbursements is the **voucher system.** It provides that each cash disbursement must be accompanied by a properly approved voucher, similar to the one illustrated in Exhibit 10-1. Before a check may be drawn, a voucher must be completed. Ideally, a voucher must be completed before a liability is recorded. The voucher will detail the reason for the disbursement and will be accompanied by supporting documentation and signatures of persons authorized to approve disbursements. The voucher system is integrated directly into the accounting system of the firm. A Vouchers Payable account replaces the Accounts Payable account. A separate voucher register is maintained to record the details of each voucher. The voucher register is a special journal used to record original entries about current purchase liabilities. The entry to record the purchase shown in Exhibit 10-1 would be:

> Purchases (or Inventory) $150
>   Vouchers Payable $150
> (To record Voucher 1948, due 7/15/X5)

A voucher is prepared at the time the purchase transaction occurs. Until its due date, the unpaid voucher is filed in a Vouchers Payable File, usually by date of payment. When it is time to prepare the check, the approved voucher and supporting documentation is sent to the appropriate officer, who approves payment and orders a check prepared. Payment of the voucher is recorded as follows and noted on the voucher itself:

> Vouchers Payable $150
>   Cash $150
> (To pay Voucher 1948, Check 673)

The payment information on the voucher, which may be accompanied by the word "PAID" stamped on the face of the voucher, insures that this voucher is not accidentally used again.

Like any system of internal control, the voucher system should be designed to meet the specific needs of each individual firm. Consequently, the specific form of a voucher and the voucher system may vary greatly from firm to firm. Requiring a properly completed, supported, and authorized voucher before issuing a check significantly reduces the chances of error or theft.

EXHIBIT 10-1
VOUCHER

JEM, Incorporated		Voucher No. 1948
Norwark, Virginia		
		Date Payment Due July 15, 19X5
Date of Voucher June 15, 19X5		
Payee Acme, Inc.		
213 W. 68th St.		
Los Angeles, California		

Date of Purchase	Explanation (Attach all supporting documents)	Amount
June 12, 19X5	No. 5 Socket wrenches, Invoice No. 1087, *n*/30	$150.00
	Total	$150.00

Approved by _B.B. Davis_
Signature
June 15, 19X5
Date

Account Distribution		Payment:
Account(s) Debited	*Amount*	Check No. 673
Purchases	$150.00	Check Date July 15, 19X5
		Amount Pd. $150.00
Credited to Vouchers Payable	$150.00	Approved _W. W. Kellogg_ Signature
		July 15, 19X5
		Date

Two questions are posed by the objective of providing relevant information about current liabilities for external financial statement users: how do we measure current liabilities, and how do we report them on the balance sheet?

The Measurement Issue.   To answer the measurement question, current liabilities are initially measured and recorded in accordance with the cost principle. Thereafter all liabilities should, in theory, be reported on the bal-

Information for Financial Statement Users

INFORMATION FOR FINANCIAL STATEMENT USERS

ance sheet as the current cash equivalent amount of the liability, which is often called the present value of the liability. This means that the liability should be reported at the amount for which the liability could be paid off, or liquidated, on the balance sheet date. A valuation problem is created when the initial cost valuation of the liability differs from the amount that must be paid at maturity. If the obligation, for example, could be satisfied for $1,000 today or $1,050, 90 days from today, such a valuation problem would be created for a balance sheet that had to be prepared 30 days from today. An implicit interest charge explains the difference in these two values. In the case of current liabilities, however, this valuation problem rarely exists because of the short time period involved before payment of the liability. Generally, the initial cost value placed on a current liability is also the amount that must be repaid later. As a result, accountants run into few valuation problems in valuing current liabilities. Where the problem does arise, it is resolved using present-value techniques. The concepts of compound interest and present value will be discussed at the end of this chapter. Their importance in valuing liabilities will be discussed in the context of long-term liabilities in Chapter 11, where they are more applicable.

The Reporting Issue. The question of how to report current liabilities should be answered in terms of the information needs of the financial statement users. How do users evaluate the impact of current liabilities? Financial statement users perceive the relationship between current assets and current liabilities to be an important measure of the ability of the firm to meet its financial obligations. The term *liquidity* refers to the ability of the firm to pay current debts when they become due. The proper classification of liabilities as either current or long term provides important information about liquidity to financial statement users. The primary reporting problems in reporting liabilities lie in proper classification of an item as a liability and then in proper classification as a current or long-term liability.

There are two major measures of liquidity that financial statement users calculate to help them assess the relationship between current assets and current liabilities. One measure of this relationship is *working capital,* which is defined as the difference between total current assets and total current liabilities. This relationship may also be expressed as a ratio, commonly called the *current ratio.* It is calculated as current assets divided by current liabilities. Exhibit 10-2 illustrates the calculation of these two measures.

A $300,000 working capital balance tells the financial statement user that the firm has $300,000 more in current resources to meet current obligations than it requires. Viewed another way, this is the amount of current assets that is available for investment or other purposes without impairing the ability of the firm to pay its current liabilities. Expressed as a ratio, the

EXHIBIT 10-2
CALCULATION OF LIQUIDITY

Working Capital Calculation	
Total Current Assets	$500,000
Less Total Current Liabilities	− 200,000
Working Capital	$300,000

Current Ratio Calculation

$$\frac{\text{Total current assets}}{\text{Total current liabilities}} = \frac{\$500,000}{\$200,000} = 2.5$$

firm has 2.5 times as many resources to meet current obligations as it has current obligations. Improper classification of current liabilities could mislead the financial statement user by causing him to calculate working capital or the current ratio incorrectly. To avoid this error, special care should be taken to classify liabilities appropriately.

Not only should the accountant properly identify and classify all of the liabilities of the firm, but the financial statements should also disclose all relevant details about the current liabilities of the firm that a financial statement user would need to evaluate the impact of the liability on the firm. Due dates, rates of interest, and other relevant information should be presented parenthetically or in footnotes to the financial statements.

Types Of Current Liabilities

Accounts Payable

Accounts Payable are claims against the firm that generally arise from the purchase of merchandise or supplies on account. An account payable is less formal than a note payable. Generally, no legal debt instrument signed by the parties supports the debt. Instead, the purchase order, invoices, and shipping documents serve as evidence that merchandise was shipped and received by the firm. Two ways of recording the incurrence and payment of accounts payable have been described in this chapter. One involved recording the liability at the full amount of the purchase price. The more theoretically accurate method recorded the liability "net of discount." If the discount was not taken, the additional amount to be paid was reported as "Purchases Discounts Lost." This system more accurately characterizes the interest element as Purchases Discounts Lost and reports the liability at the amount for which it may be satisfied on the day it is incurred.

Notes Payable

A note is a legal debt instrument representing a written promise to pay a stated sum at one or more dates in the future. A note usually provides for the payment of interest. Notes are more formal evidences of obligations than accounts payable. They are legal evidence of the debt and are more easily processed in court in the event of a controversy over the obligation. For these reasons, traditional accounting practice separates classifications for short-term notes payable and accounts payable. The current liability section of the balance sheet should reflect all Notes Receivable that are due within one year, including that portion of the longer term liabilities that are currently falling due.

The party promising to pay the amount of the note is called the *maker* of the note; the party to be paid is called the *payee.* If a note requires the maker to pay interest for the extension of credit, the note is called an *interest-bearing note.* If the note requires payment of its face amount and no more, the note is called a *noninterest-bearing note.* The accounting treatment for interest-bearing notes differs from noninterest-bearing notes.

Interest-Bearing Notes. The interest terms on interest-bearing notes are always stated as annual rates of interest. The amount of interest to be paid on a short-term note can be calculated by using this formula:

$$\text{Principal} \times \text{Rate} \times \text{Time} = \text{Interest}$$

For example, interest would be calculated on a $1,000, 90-day note charging 6 percent interest per year as follows:

$$\$1,000 \times 0.06 \times 90/360^2 = \$15$$

Because this was only a 90-day note and the interest rate is stated as a rate per year, the time element in the formula adjusts for the actual part of a year the money was used.

When merchandise is purchased and a note is given for the purchase, the maker of the note should record it as follows:

Purchases (or Inventory)	$1,000	
Notes Payable		$1,000
Gave Ace, Inc., 30-Day 6% note dated 6/15/X8		

Note that the liability is recorded at its principal or face amount, which corresponds to the cost of the purchases. When the note is repaid on July 15, $5 of interest ($100 × 0.06 × 30/360 = $5) is also due and would be recorded as follows:

Notes Payable	$1,000	
Interest Expense	5	
Cash		$1,005

---

² Interest will be calculated on a 360-day year.

Interest expense is incurred over the period of the note, even though it does not have to be paid until the time specified in the note. Therefore, when the accounting period ends during the term of the note, an adjusting entry must accrue the interest expense that has been incurred but has not yet been paid. This accrual is required to match interest expense with the revenues that the interest expense helps to generate. If the firm's fiscal year ends on June 30, the note given Ace, Inc., in the previous illustrations would require this entry:

```
Interest Expense          $2.50
    Interest Payable                $2.50
Adjusting entry to accrue interest expense on
Ace, Inc., note ($1,000 × 0.06 × 15/360 = $2.50)
```

When this note is paid on July 15, the entry to record the payment would be as follows:

```
Notes Payable         $1,000.00
Interest Payable           2.50
Interest Expense           2.50
    Cash                          $1,005.00
Paid Ace, Inc. note; Recognized $2.50 in additional
interest expense. ($1,000 × 0.06 × 15/360 = $2.50)
```

Noninterest-Bearing Notes. A noninterest-bearing note is one that requires that the maker pay only the principal, or face amount, of the note. There are actually two types of noninterest bearing notes: discounted notes and true noninterest-bearing notes. A *discounted note* is a note on which interest is subtracted from the principal amount of the note in advance. For example, if a $1,000, 60-day note is drawn by the maker for a bank loan in the form of a noninterest-bearing note with 6 percent interest on the face discounted, the maker would only receive $990—$10 in interest would be taken in advance. The maker would record the note as follows:

```
Cash                      $990
Discount on Notes Payable   10
    Notes Payable                 $1,000
Borrowed from First State Bank on discounted 60-day
note due March 3 ($1,000 × 0.06 × 60/360 = $10)
```

The Discount on Notes Payable account is a contraliability account. If a balance sheet were prepared on the day this note was made, it would report the note as follows:

```
Current Liabilities:
    Accounts Payable                       $5,000
    Notes Payable            $1,000
    Less Discount on
        Notes Payable            10          990
```

Payment of the note on March 3 would be recorded as follows:

Notes Payable	$1,000	
Interest Expense	10	
Discount on Notes Payable		$ 10
Cash		1,000

Describing a discounted note as noninterest bearing is misleading. Although no interest is charged above the face of the note, the maker does pay interest, and at a higher rate than the stated discount rate of interest. In the preceding example, the stated rate of interest used in discounting was 6 percent. But note that the effective interest rate is actually 6.06 percent, because $10 in interest was paid for the use of only $990—not $1,000—for 60 days:

Rate of Discount:	6%
Effective Rate of Interest:	
Interest/Principal = Rate for 60 days	
$10/$990 = 1.01%	
Annual Rate = (6 × Rate for 60 days)	
Annual Rate = (6 × 1.01%)	

A true noninterest-bearing note is one on which no interest is charged or discounted. Even in this case, professional standards do require that interest be imputed on the note. This means that a portion of the note payable must be recognized and treated as interest, even though none is provided in the note itself.

Payroll Liabilities

Wages and salaries are frequently the largest single expense incurred by a firm. Accurate accounting for wages and salaries is extremely important. Errors in accounting for wages certainly would destroy employees' confidence in the firm. In addition, employers are legally obligated to withhold certain taxes from the pay of employees, as well as other deductions if the employee consents. The law also requires that employers pay certain payroll taxes. Consequently, accurate accounting for payrolls, payroll deductions from employees, and payroll taxes for the employer, is essential if the firm is to meet its obligations to employees and to the government.

When an employee is hired by the firm, certain information about the employee is gathered for the company's payroll records: the employee's full name; the employee's address; social security number (for proper crediting of social security taxes to the employee's account with the Social Security Administration); number of withholding exemptions claimed for purposes of income taxes to be withheld; the classification of the job to be performed and rate of pay; other deductions to be made by the employer such as union dues, U.S. Savings Bonds, life or health insurance premiums, pension contributions; and other information that may be helpful to the firm. From this information and a record of the time worked by employees, the accountant prepares the payroll. An understanding of payroll accounting requires a brief review of the various deductions withheld from employees' paychecks and the payroll taxes assessed by the employer.

Payroll Deductions. The most common payroll deductions from employees paychecks are federal and, sometimes, state income taxes, and FICA (Social Security) taxes. Employers are required by law to withhold and remit periodically to the government income taxes out of each employee's paycheck. In this fashion employees pay their income tax gradually throughout the year instead of in one lump sum at the end of the year. The amount of the payroll deduction for income taxes is determined by reference to a set of tables published by the Internal Revenue Service. Withholdings are based on the amount of the employee's pay for the period covered (weekly, monthly, etc.) and the number of withholding exemptions claimed by the employee. The withheld taxes must be remitted to the government by the employer. Employers with small payrolls are allowed to send these withheld taxes to the government every three months. Larger employers must send withholdings more often. During the time between withholding money from the employees' paychecks and sending it to the government, a liability to pay these amounts must be recorded on the employer's books.

Under the terms of the Federal Insurance Contribution Act, employers or their family members who are qualified receive pension benefits at retirement and other benefits such as Medicare and Survivors and Disability Insurance. To receive these benefits, employees must meet the specific requirements of the law and make contributions to pay for the benefits. The contributions are withheld from each covered employee's paycheck. The employer is required to match this amount, paying a sum equal to that withheld from the employee's wage as an additional payroll expense.

Many other payroll deductions are frequently withheld from employee's pay. A contract with a union may require the employer to withhold union dues from the employee's check and periodically pay them to the union. The employee may elect to take advantage of pension plans, life or health insurance plans, stock purchase plans, or other fringe benefits that require him to bear some cost of the benefits. These amounts are usually withheld periodically. The employee may also elect to become involved in savings plans. He may have a specific sum withheld from his paycheck and directly deposited with a private savings institution or invested in U.S. Savings Bonds.

The entry to record wage and salary expenses and related liabilities for employee deductions is illustrated as follows:

Wage and Salary Expense	$20,000	
Liability for Federal Income Taxes Withheld		$ 3,500
Liability for State Income Taxes Withheld		500
Liability for FICA Taxes Withheld		1,170
Liability for Pension Contributions Withheld		500
Wages Payable		14,330

Each of the liability accounts would be debited when the employer sends the withheld funds to the government, as follows:

Liability for Federal Income Taxes Withheld	$3,500	
Liability for State Income Taxes Withheld	500	
Liability for FICA Taxes Withheld	1,170	
Cash		$5,170

(Paid employee withholdings to U.S. government at Federal Reserve Bank in Atlanta)

Liability for Pension Contributions Withheld	$500	
Cash		$500

(Paid employee withholdings for pensions to pension trust)

Wages Payable	$14,330	
Cash		$14,330

Employer Payroll Taxes. In addition to the taxes that must be withheld from the paychecks of employees, the law imposes certain additional taxes on the employer. The employer must pay the Social Security Administration a sum equal to the FICA taxes withheld from employees' paychecks. In accordance with the terms of the Federal Unemployment Tax Act (FUTA), employers are required to pay 0.5 percent of the first $4,200 in wages paid each employee each year to the federal government to support a program of federal unemployment insurance. Furthermore, each state operates an unemployment compensation program and charges a tax of up to 3 percent of the first $4,200 in wages paid each employee each year to fund state unemployment compensation plans. Each of these taxes is imposed on the employer—not withheld from the wages of employees[3]—and is a tax expense to be recognized by the firm, as shown:

Payroll Tax Expense	$1,870	
FICA Taxes Payable		$1,170
FUTA Taxes Payable		100
State Unemployment Taxes Payable		600

The liability accounts for payroll taxes would be debited when payments of taxes are made to the federal and state governments.

[3]Except in some states.

Accrued liabilities result from end-of-period accounting adjustments for the acquisition of goods or services that remain unpaid. Full disclosure requires that these liabilities be reported on the balance sheet and that related expenses be recognized on the income statement. As a result, the accountant must search for unrecorded business transactions and recognize accrued liabilities. As discussed in Chapter 4, this recognition takes the form of an adjusting entry made at year end. Common accrued liabilities include wages payable, income taxes payable, and property taxes payable. The Hornblower Corporation would make the following entry to accrue $105,000 in federal income taxes, which are properly the expense of calendar year 19X8 but not payable until May 15, 19X9:

Accrued Liabilities

Income Tax Expense	$105,000	
Income Taxes Payable		$105,000
Accrued income tax expense for 19X8		

When advances are received from clients or customers, the standard entry is similar to the following entry for rental income:

Deferred Revenues

Cash	$1,200	
Rental Income		$1,200

Care must be made to ensure that all receipts recorded in this manner have been earned by year end. For example, if the entry just illustrated related to cash recieved on October 1, 19X5, for 12 months rental paid in advance, financial statements prepared on December 31, 19X5, would also fail to show that the firm has a current liability to perform under the rental contract. An adjusting entry would recognize the deferred revenue and reduce the revenue account:

Rental Income	$900	
Deferred Rental Income		$900

Financial statements will now report $300 in earned rental income and $900 in deferred rents to be earned in the next accounting period.

This chapter considered the major accounting problems of current liabilities. A liability is an obligation to convey specific assets or perform specific services of definite or measurable amount on or by specific future dates. Once having determined that an obligation is a liability, its classification as a current liability or a long-term liability is critical to the proper interpretation of the balance sheet. Failure to classify current liabilities properly can obscure the calculation of working capital and the current ratio, two

Summary

liquidity measures used by financial statement users to determine the ability of the firm to meet its obligations.

The primary objectives in accounting for current liabilities are promoting efficient internal management of current liabilities, minimizing their costs, and providing information for financial statement users. Efficiency is accomplished by providing management with the information it needs to establish policies for the use of current liabilities, by implementing these policies, and by establishing controls over disbursements of cash. Cost information is perhaps the most critical in establishing policies about current liabilities. By using tickler files for accounts payable and recording purchases net of discount to highlight discounts lost, the accountant can help to insure that management policies are fully implemented. The voucher system is commonly used to establish controls over cash disbursements.

Providing information to financial statement users requires that the current liabilities of the firm—accounts payable, notes payable, payroll liabilities, accrued liabilities, and deferred revenues—be accounted for in accordance with generally accepted principles. Current liabilities should be initially recorded at cost and thereafter reported at their present values.

A Supplementary Discussion: The Time Value of Money: Compound Interest and Present Value

Given the opportunity to receive $1 today or $1 in one year, most people choose to receive $1 today. They do so because they have a *time preference for money.* Money has time preference, or value, because its early possession opens opportunities for investment or early consumption. For example, $1 invested at 6 percent simple interest per year is worth $1.06 at the end of one year. Clearly, $1.06 received at the end of one year is preferable to $1 received at the end of one year. If consumption rather than investment is the individual's objective, $1 received today would be preferable to $1 to be received at the end of one year, if all other factors are unchanged, because it allows immediate instead of postponed consumption. As a result of the time preference for money, money may be said to have *time value.*

The concept of the time value of money is very important in accounting. It is used by the accountant to calculate the amount of periodic payments needed to repay debt, the recorded value of noninterest-bearing notes, the recorded value of assets acquired for debt, and many other value measurements. Measuring the time value of money requires that an individual's *time-value preference rate for money* be determined. This is the rate of interest at which an individual is indifferent to receiving $1 today or $1 *plus interest* at some future date. The time value of money is, therefore, expressed as an interest rate. For example, suppose an individual were faced with these situations:

1. Receive $1 today or $1.09 one year from today.
2. Receive $1 today or $1.10 one year from today.
3. Receive $1 today or $1.11 one year from today.

If the individual in situation 1 preferred to receive $1 today instead of $1.09 in one year, in situation 2 the individual was indifferent to receiving $1 today or $1.10 in one year, and in situation 3 the individual preferred to receive $1.11 in one year instead of $1 today, we know that this individual's time preference rate for money is 10 percent. This is the rate of interest at which the individual is indifferent to receiving $1 today or $1 plus interest at some future date. It is calculated as follows:

$$\frac{\text{Amount of interest}}{\text{Amount of principal}} = \text{Rate of interest}$$

$$\frac{\$0.10}{\$1.00} = 10\%$$

After determining the time-value preference rate for money, the accountant is now able to calculate the time value of a specific amount of money. Two kinds of problems can be solved: (1) we can take a sum of money today and determine its value at some future point in time, or (2) we can take a sum of money in the future and determine its value today. In the first kind of problem we calculate the future amount of money. For example, we can calculate the future amount that would be available at the end of four years, assuming that $100 was invested in a bank at 6 percent interest. In the second kind of problem we calculate the present value of money. This, for example, would allow an accountant to determine how much must be invested in a bank at 6 percent interest to have $100 available in four years. The remainder of this supplementary discussion will demonstrate the techniques for calculating the future amount and present value of money.

FUTURE AMOUNT AND COMPOUND INTEREST

Compound interest extends the concept of simple interest beyond one year. Using compound interest, accountants can evaluate decisions that extend two, four, or more years into the future. Thus, once an accountant has determined the rate of interest at which the firm will cease to be indifferent, he can determine the trade-off amount on any given sum for any future period of time. For example, an accountant with a 10 percent time value of money and an opportunity to receive $100 now or some money in three years could calculate the indifference values as $100 now or $110 a year from now; $100 now or $121 two years from now; or $100 now and $133 three years from now. To determine the second- and third-year amounts, consider each year as a separate proposition. For example, at the end of the first year, the payoff would have to be $110 for the accountant to be indifferent. At the end of the second year, he would require 10 percent more than $110, or $121. At the end of the third year, he would require 10 percent more than $121, or $133 (rounded to the nearest whole dollar). The first year's interest would amount to $10, the second year's interest would amount to an additional $11, and the third year's interest would be an additional $12. In other words, each year's interest is calculated on both the interest from prior years and the original $100.

Interest accumulated as just described is called *compound interest*. A simple formula can be used to determine the indifference amount that an individual would demand after any number of future years in return for $1 given up initially at any rate of interest. Let r represent the decimal equivalent of the rate of interest and let n represent the number of years before payoff. The amount an individual would require in return for an initial $1 given up for n years at r rate of interest is equal to $1 times $(1.0 + r)^n$. Applying the formula to the previous example of a three-year indifference situation and a 10 percent rate of interest, the payoff at the end of three years equals $1 times $(1.0 + 0.10)^3$, or $1.33 (rounded). Since the initial investment was $100 and not $1, the payoff is calculated by multiplying the $100 by the results determined from the formula, or $133. The initial investment is commonly called *principal* and is abbreviated as P. The compound interest formula to yield some future value for any amount, P, for n years at r rate of interest is $P(1.0 + r)^n$.

For any given n and r, the compound interest formula will produce only one answer, thus allowing a compound interest table to be drawn. Table 10-1 is a compound interest table. To use Table 10-1, select the desired interest rate in one of the columns. Next select a row that corresponds to the number of periods during which the compounding is to occur. Then find the intersection of the row and the column to find the compounded value of principal and interest for $1 for that rate and period of time. For example, the value of $1 to be invested for five years at 6 percent interest is $1.3382; for six years at 8 percent interest it is $1.5869. For original amounts other than $1, simply multiply the principal by the factor from the table.

If the accountant is attempting to calculate the future amount of several deposits to a bank account, the procedures just described are followed; *each* deposit is treated separately. For example, if $100 is deposited on the first day of the year; $200 in year 2, and $300 in year 3, the accumulated balance of the account compounded annually at 6 percent interest is calculated in this fashion:

$$[\$100(1.06)]^3 + [\$200(1.06)]^2 + [\$300(1.06)] = \$661.82$$

This problem could be alternatively solved by using Table 10-1, as follows:

Amount		Future Amount Factor, n periods at 6%	Total
$100	×	1.1910 Where $n = 3$	= $119.12
$200	×	1.1236 Where $n = 2$	= 224.72
$300	×	1.0600 Where $n = 1$	= 318.00
			$661.82

If the stream of payments is an **annuity,** a great deal of simplification is possible. An annuity is a series of equal sums of money to be received or paid at regular intervals. The payment or receipt may occur at either the beginning or the end of the period, but compound interest applies only to sums covered by the full period; that is, no interest accrues on principal invested at the end of the period or withdrawn at the beginning of the period. A table can be constructed to display the growth of an annuity, much as compound interest tables display the growth of a single amount.

TABLE 10-1
FUTURE VALUE AMOUNT OF $1.00 DUE IN n PERIODS $V = (1 + r)^n$

				Rate of Interest, %					
n	1.0	2.0	3.0	4.0	5.0	6.0	8.0	10.00	15.00
1	1.0100	1.0200	1.0300	1.0400	1.0500	1.0600	1.0800	1.1000	1.1500
2	1.0201	1.0404	1.0609	1.0816	1.1025	1.1236	1.1664	1.2100	1.3225
3	1.0303	1.0612	1.0927	1.1249	1.1576	1.1910	1.2597	1.3310	1.5209
4	1.0406	1.0824	1.1255	1.1699	1.2155	1.2625	1.3605	1.4641	1.7490
5	1.0510	1.1041	1.1593	1.2167	1.2763	1.3382	1.4693	1.6105	2.0114
6	1.0615	1.1262	1.1941	1.2653	1.3401	1.4185	1.5869	1.7716	2.3131
7	1.0721	1.1487	1.2299	1.3159	1.4071	1.5036	1.7138	1.9487	2.6600
8	1.0829	1.1717	1.2668	1.3686	1.4775	1.5938	1.8509	2.1436	3.0590
9	1.0937	1.1951	1.3048	1.4233	1.5513	1.6895	1.9990	2.3579	3.5179
10	1.1046	1.2190	1.3439	1.4802	1.6289	1.7908	2.1589	2.5937	4.0555
11	1.1157	1.2434	1.3842	1.5395	1.7103	1.8983	2.3316	2.8531	4.6524
12	1.1268	1.2682	1.4258	1.6010	1.7959	2.0122	2.5182	3.1384	5.3502
13	1.1381	1.2936	1.4685	1.6651	1.8856	2.1329	2.7196	3.4523	6.1528
14	1.1495	1.3195	1.5126	1.7317	1.9799	2.2609	2.9372	3.7975	7.0757
15	1.1610	1.3459	1.5580	1.8009	2.0789	2.3966	3.1722	4.1772	8.1370
16	1.1726	1.3728	1.6047	1.8730	2.1829	2.5404	3.4259	4.5950	9.3576
17	1.1843	1.4002	1.6528	1.9479	2.2920	2.6928	3.7000	5.0545	10.761
18	1.1961	1.4282	1.7024	2.0258	2.4066	2.8543	3.9960	5.5599	12.375
19	1.2081	1.4568	1.7535	2.1068	2.5270	3.0256	4.3157	6.1159	14.232
20	1.2202	1.4859	1.8061	2.1911	2.6533	3.2071	4.6610	6.7275	16.366
21	1.2324	1.5157	1.8603	2.2788	2.7860	3.3996	5.0338	7.4002	18.821
22	1.2447	1.5460	1.9161	2.3699	2.9253	3.6035	5.4365	8.1403	21.645
23	1.2572	1.5769	1.9736	2.4647	3.0715	3.8197	5.8715	8.9543	24.891
24	1.2697	1.6084	2.0328	2.5633	3.2251	4.0489	6.3412	9.8497	28.625
25	1.2824	1.6406	2.0938	2.6658	3.3864	4.2919	6.8485	10.834	32.919
26	1.2953	1.6734	2.1566	2.7725	3.5557	4.5494	7.3964	11.918	37.856
27	1.3082	1.7069	2.2213	2.8834	3.7335	4.8223	7.9881	13.110	43.535
28	1.3213	1.7410	2.2879	2.9987	3.9201	5.1117	8.6271	14.421	50.065
29	1.3345	1.7758	2.3566	3.1187	4.1161	5.4184	9.3173	15.863	57.575
30	1.3478	1.8114	2.4273	3.2434	4.3219	5.7435	10.062	17.449	66.211
35	1.4166	1.9999	2.8139	3.9461	5.5160	7.6861	14.785	28.102	133.17
40	1.4889	2.2080	3.2620	4.8010	7.0400	10.285	21.724	45.259	267.86
45	1.5648	2.4379	3.7816	5.8412	8.9850	13.764	31.920	72.890	538.77
50	1.6446	2.6916	4.3839	7.1067	11.467	18.420	46.901	117.39	1083.7

Table 10-2 parallels the compound interest table (Table 10-1), except that each factor in Table 10-2 represents the vertical summation of all preceding Table 10-1 factors. For example, consider the following situation.

One thousand dollars are deposited in a savings account at the beginning of each year for four years. If the account pays 6 percent interest compounded annually, what is the balance of the account at the end of the fourth year? Deposits such as these would result in $1,000 accruing interest for four years, another $1,000 accruing interest for three years, another $1,000 for two years, and so on. To calculate appropriate compound interest rates for this problem, we could go to the fourth row in the 6 percent column of Table 10-1, then to the third row in the 6

$$\left(1 + r\right)^n$$

A SUPPLEMENTARY
DISCUSSION: THE TIME
VALUE OF MONEY:
COMPOUND INTEREST
AND PRESENT VALUE

TABLE 10-2

FUTURE VALUE OF AN ANNUITY OF $1.00 RECEIVED PER PERIOD, $V = \sum_{i=1}^{n} (1 + r)^i$

				Rate of Interest. %					
n	1.0%	2.0	3.0	4.0	5.0	6.0	8.0	10.0	15.0
1	1.0100	1.0200	1.0300	1.0400	1.0500	1.0600	1.0800	1.1000	1.1500
2	2.0301	2.0604	2.0909	2.1216	2.1525	2.1836	2.2464	2.3100	2.4725
3	3.0604	3.1216	3.1836	3.2465	3.3101	3.3746	3.5061	3.6410	3.9934
4	4.1010	4.2040	4.3091	4.4163	4.5256	4.6371	4.8666	5.1051	5.7424
5	5.1520	5.3081	5.4684	5.6330	5.8019	5.9753	6.3359	6.7156	7.7537
6	6.2135	6.4343	6.6625	6.8983	7.1420	7.3938	7.9228	8.4872	10.0668
7	7.2857	7.5830	7.8923	8.2142	8.5491	8.8975	9.6366	10.4359	12.7268
8	8.3685	8.7546	9.1591	9.5828	10.0266	10.4913	11.4876	12.5795	15.7858
9	9.4622	9.9497	10.4639	11.0061	11.5779	12.1808	13.4866	14.9374	19.3037
10	10.5668	11.1687	11.8078	12.4864	13.2068	13.9716	15.6455	17.5312	23.3493
11	11.6825	12.4121	13.1920	14.0258	14.9171	15.8699	17.9771	20.3843	28.0017
12	12.8093	13.6803	14.6178	15.6268	16.7130	17.8821	20.4953	23.5227	33.3519
13	13.9474	14.9739	16.0863	17.2919	18.5986	20.0151	23.2149	26.9750	39.5047
14	15.0969	16.2934	17.5989	19.0236	20.5786	22.2760	26.1521	30.7725	46.5804
15	16.2579	17.6393	19.1569	20.8245	22.6575	24.6725	29.3243	34.9497	54.7175
16	17.4304	19.0121	20.7616	22.6975	24.8404	27.2129	32.7502	39.5447	64.0751
17	18.6147	20.4123	22.4144	24.6454	27.1324	29.9057	36.4502	44.5992	74.8364
18	19.8109	21.8406	24.1169	26.6712	29.5390	32.7600	40.4463	50.1591	87.2118
19	21.0190	23.2974	25.8704	28.7781	32.0660	35.7856	44.7620	56.2750	101.4436
20	22.2392	24.7833	27.6765	30.9692	34.7193	38.9927	49.4229	63.0025	117.8101
21	23.4716	26.2990	29.5368	33.2480	37.5052	42.3923	54.4568	70.4027	136.6316
22	24.7163	27.8450	31.4529	35.6179	40.4305	45.9958	59.8933	78.5430	158.2764
23	25.9735	29.4219	33.4265	38.0826	43.5020	49.8156	65.7648	87.4973	183.1678
24	27.2432	31.0303	35.4593	40.6459	46.7271	53.8645	72.1059	97.3471	211.7930
25	28.5256	32.6709	37.5530	43.3117	50.1135	58.1564	78.9544	108.1818	244.7120
26	29.8209	34.3443	39.7096	46.0842	53.6691	62.7058	86.3508	120.0999	282.5688
27	31.1291	36.0512	41.9309	48.9676	57.4026	67.5281	94.3388	133.2099	326.1041
28	32.4504	37.7922	44.2189	51.9663	61.3227	72.6398	102.9659	147.6309	376.1697
29	33.7849	39.5681	46.5754	55.0849	65.4388	78.0582	112.2832	163.4940	433.7451
30	35.1327	41.3794	49.0027	58.3283	69.7608	83.8017	122.3459	180.9434	499.9569

percent column, then to the second row, and so on. We would multiply each year's deposit by its corresponding factor and add all the products:

$$($1,000 \times 1.2625) + ($1,000 \times 1.1910) + ($1,000 \times 1.1236)$$
$$+ ($1,000 \times 1.06)$$
$$= $4,637.10$$

Alternately, we could go to the 6 percent column, fourth row in Table 10-2 and find the factor 4.6371, which represents the future amount of an annuity of $1. This factor is the simple summation of all the factors found in Table 10-1. Finally, to find the balance at the end of the fourth year, multiply the factor by the principal: $4.6371 \times $1,000 = $4,637.10$.

DISCOUNTED PRESENT VALUE

Compound interest allows us to calculate the future unknown amount of some currently known amount of money. The original problem can be reversed by asking, "How much would we be willing to pay now in order to receive $106 one year from today or $112.36 two years from today, assuming a 6 percent rate of interest?" Based on our prior calculation, we know that the amount would be $100. What we have done, however, is to discount some future amount back to its present value—hence the name discounted present value.

Discounted present value is the amount of current cash that is equivalent to some specified amount of cash to be received or given in some specified future period. Calculation of a discounted present value requires data on the amount of the future flow, the date of the flow, and the interest rate. For example, we can readily calculate that $100 is the discounted present value of $106 one year from today and $112.36 two years from today, assuming a 6 percent rate of interest compounded annually. A formula for discounted present value can be easily calculated, since it is nothing more than the reciprocal of the compound interest formula. That is, for compound interest we were willing to pay out $1 now in order to receive $1 multiplied by $(1.0 + r)^n$ at some future date. Under the present-value assumption, we would be willing to receive $1 in the future only if the amount that we had to pay out now were $1 multiplied by $1/(1 + r)^n$. For example, consider the following. How much would you be willing to pay now (discounted present value) in order to receive $100 (P) in three years (n = 3) if the rate of interest we require is 10 percent (r)? The terms in the brackets equal 0.751.

$$P\left[\frac{1}{(1 + 0.1)^3}\right]$$

To find the discounted present value of $100, multiply $100 times 0.751; the answer is $75.10.

For any given n and r, the discounted present value formula will produce only one answer, thus allowing a precalculation of present-value tables. Table 10-3 is a present value table. To use Table 10-3, select an interest rate corresponding to your time value-of-money preference. Next select a row corresponding to the number of future periods that will pass before the future flows will occur. Then find the intersection of the row and the column to find the discounted present value of $1 for that rate and period of time. For example, the discounted present value of $1 to be received in five years at 6 percent interest is $0.7473; in six years at 8 percent interest it is $0.6302. If the principal were some amount other than $1, simply multiply the principal by the factor found in the table. Table 10-3 can be used to determine the present value of a stream of cash flows simply by multiplying the appropriate factors from the table by the corresponding amount of cash flow for each year. For example, if the amount to be received at the end of one year equals $100, at the end of two years equals $200, and at the end of three years equals $300, what is the discounted present value of this flow of cash, given a time value-of-money preference of 6 percent? Using Table 10-3, the solution to this problem is as follows:

Amount		Present Value Factor, n Periods at 6%	Total
$100	×	0.9434 Where $n = 1$	$ 94.34
200	×	0.8900 Where $n = 2$	178.00
300	×	0.8396 Where $n = 3$	251.88
			$524.22

If the stream of payments is an annuity, the calculation is once again simplified.

TABLE 10-3

PRESENT VALUE OF $1.00 $PV = (1 + r)^{-n} = \dfrac{1}{(1 + r)^n}$

	Rate of Interest, %								
n	1.0	2.0	3.0	4.0	5.0	6	8	10	15
1	.990099	.980392	.970874	.961538	.952381	0.9434	0.9259	0.9091	0.8696
2	.980296	.961169	.942596	.924556	.907029	0.8900	0.8573	0.8264	0.7561
3	.970590	.942322	.915142	.888996	.863838	0.8396	0.7938	0.7513	0.6575
4	.960980	.923845	.888487	.854804	.822702	0.7921	0.7350	0.6830	0.5718
5	.951466	.905731	.862609	.821927	.783526	0.7473	0.6806	0.6209	0.4972
6	.942045	.887971	.837484	.790315	.746215	0.7050	0.6302	0.5645	0.4323
7	.932718	.870560	.813092	.759918	.710681	0.6651	0.5835	0.5132	0.3759
8	.923483	.853490	.789409	.730690	.676839	0.6274	0.5403	0.4665	0.3269
9	.914340	.836755	.766417	.702587	.644609	0.5919	0.5002	0.4241	0.2843
10	.905287	.820348	.744094	.675564	.613913	0.5584	0.4632	0.3855	0.2472
11	.896324	.804263	.722421	.649581	.584679	0.5268	0.4289	0.3505	0.2149
12	.887449	.788493	.701380	.624597	.556837	0.4970	0.3971	0.3186	0.1869
13	.878663	.773033	.680951	.600574	.530321	0.4688	0.3677	0.2897	0.1625
14	.869963	.757875	.661118	.577475	.505068	0.4423	0.3405	0.2633	0.1413
15	.861349	.743015	.641862	.555265	.481017	0.4173	0.3152	0.2394	0.1229
16	.852821	.728446	.623167	.533908	.458112	0.3936	0.2919	0.2176	0.1069
17	.844377	.714163	.605016	.513373	.436297	0.3714	0.2703	0.1978	0.0929
18	.836017	.700159	.587395	.493628	.415521	0.3503	0.2502	0.1799	0.0808
19	.827740	.686431	.570286	.474642	.395734	0.3305	0.2317	0.1635	0.0703
20	.819544	.672971	.553676	.456387	.376889	0.3118	0.2145	0.1486	0.0611
21	.811430	.659776	.537549	.438834	.358942	0.2942	0.1987	0.1351	0.0531
22	.803396	.646839	.521893	.421955	.341850	0.2775	0.1839	0.1228	0.0462
23	.795442	.634156	.506692	.405726	.325571	0.2618	0.1703	0.1117	0.0402
24	.787566	.621721	.491934	.390121	.310068	0.2470	0.1577	0.1015	0.0349
25	.779768	.609531	.477606	.375117	.295303	0.2330	0.1460	0.0923	0.0304
26	.772048	.597579	.463695	.360689	.281241	0.2198	0.1352	0.0839	0.0264
27	.764404	.585862	.450189	.346817	.267848	0.2074	0.1252	0.0763	0.0230
28	.756836	.574375	.437077	.333477	.255094	0.1956	0.1159	0.0693	0.0200
29	.749342	.563112	.424346	.320651	.242946	0.1846	0.1073	0.0630	0.0174
30	.741923	.552071	.411987	.308319	.231377	0.1741	0.0994	0.0573	0.0151
35	.705914	.500028	.355383	.253415	.181290	0.1301	0.0676	0.0356	0.0075
40	.671653	.452890	.306557	.208289	.142046	0.0972	0.0460	0.0221	0.0037
45	.639055	.410197	.264439	.171198	.111297	0.0727	0.0313	0.0137	0.0019
50	.608039	.371528	.228107	.140713	.087204	0.0543	0.0213	0.0085	0.0009

Table 10-4 gives the present value of an annuity of $1 per period. The factors shown in Table 10-4 illustrate the algebraic summation of the present-value factors (previously shown in Table 10-3) for the appropriate interest rate and number of periods. The date of valuation of the annuity is the beginning of the first period and is constructed to answer questions such as: "What single sum must be deposited in a fund on the first of every year to permit five annual withdrawals of $1,000 each, beginning on the last day of each year, assuming that the fund pays 6 percent inter-

TABLE 10-4

PRESENT VALUE OF AN ANNUITY OF $1.00 RECEIVED PER PERIOD $PV = \dfrac{1-(1+r)^{-n}}{r}$

				Rate of Interest, %					
n	1.0	2.0	3.0	4.0	5.0	6	8	10	15
1	.99010	.98039	.97087	.96154	.95238	0.9434	0.9259	0.9091	0.8696
2	1.97040	1.94156	1.91347	1.88609	1.85941	1.8334	1.7833	1.7355	1.6257
3	2.94099	2.88388	2.82861	2.77509	2.72325	2.6730	2.5771	2.4869	2.2832
4	3.90197	3.80773	3.71710	3.62990	3.54595	3.4651	3.3121	3.1699	2.8550
5	4.85343	4.71346	4.57971	4.45182	4.32948	4.2124	3.9927	3.7908	3.3522
6	5.79548	5.60143	5.41719	4.24214	5.07569	4.9173	4.6229	4.3553	3.7845
7	6.72819	6.47199	6.23028	6.00205	5.78637	5.5824	5.2064	4.8684	4.1604
8	7.65168	7.32548	7.01969	6.73274	6.46321	6.2098	5.7466	5.3349	4.4873
9	8.56602	8.16224	7.78611	7.43533	7.10782	6.8017	6.2469	5.7590	4.7716
10	9.47130	8.98259	8.53020	8.11090	7.72173	7.3601	6.7101	6.1446	5.0188
11	10.36763	9.78685	9.25262	8.76048	8.30641	7.8869	7.1390	6.4951	5.2337
12	11.25508	10.57534	9.95400	9.38507	8.86325	8.3838	7.5361	6.8137	5.4206
13	12.13374	11.34837	10.63496	9.98565	9.39357	8.8527	7.9038	7.1034	5.5831
14	13.00370	12.10625	11.29607	10.56312	9.89864	9.2950	8.2442	7.3667	5.7245
15	13.86505	12.84926	11.93794	11.11839	10.37966	9.7122	8.5595	7.6061	5.8474
16	14.71787	13.57771	12.56110	11.65230	10.83777	10.1059	8.8514	7.8237	5.9542
17	15.56225	14.29187	13.16612	12.16567	11.27407	10.4773	9.1216	8.0216	6.0472
18	16.39827	14.99203	13.75351	12.65930	11.68959	10.8276	9.3719	8.2014	6.1280
19	17.22601	15.67846	14.32380	13.13394	12.08532	11.1581	9.6036	8.3649	6.1982
20	18.04555	16.35143	14.87747	13.59033	12.46221	11.4699	9.8181	8.5136	6.2593
21	18.85698	17.01121	15.41505	14.02916	12.82115	11.7641	10.0168	8.6487	6.3125
22	19.66038	17.65805	15.93692	14.45112	13.16300	12.0416	10.2007	8.7715	6.3587
23	20.45582	18.29220	16.44361	14.85684	13.48857	12.3034	10.3711	8.8832	6.3988
24	21.24339	18.91393	16.93554	15.24696	13.79864	12.5504	10.5288	8.9847	6.4338
25	22.02316	19.52346	17.41315	15.62208	14.09394	12.7834	10.6748	9.0770	6.4641
26	22.79520	20.12104	17.87694	15.98277	14.37519	13.0032	10.8100	9.1609	6.4906
27	23.55961	20.70690	18.32703	16.32959	14.64303	13.2105	10.9352	9.2372	6.5135
28	24.31644	21.28127	18.76411	16.66306	14.89813	13.4062	11.0511	9.3066	6.5335
29	25.06579	21.84438	19.18845	16.98371	15.14107	13.5907	11.1584	9.3696	6.5509
30	25.80771	22.39646	19.60044	17.29203	15.37245	13.7648	11.2578	9.4269	6.5660
31	26.54229	22.93770	20.00043	17.58849	15.59281	13.9291	11.3498	9.4790	6.5791
32	27.26959	23.46833	20.38877	17.87355	15.80268	14.0840	11.4350	9.5264	6.5905
33	27.98969	23.98856	20.76579	18.14765	16.00255	14.2302	11.5139	9.5694	6.6005
34	28.70267	24.49859	21.13184	18.41120	16.19290	14.3681	11.5869	9.6086	6.6091
35	29.40858	24.99862	21.48722	18.66461	16.37419	14.4982	11.6546	9.6442	6.6166
40	32.83469	27.35548	23.11477	19.79277	17.15909	15.0463	11.9246	9.7791	6.6418
45	36.09451	29.49016	24.51871	20.72004	17.77407	15.4558	12.1084	9.8628	6.6543
50	39.19612	31.42361	25.72976	21.48218	18.25593	15.7619	12.2335	9.9148	6.6605

A SUPPLEMENTARY DISCUSSION: THE TIME VALUE OF MONEY: COMPOUND INTEREST AND PRESENT VALUE

est compounded annually?" To find the answer, look at Table 10-4, row five ($n = 5$), in the 6 percent interest column, for the factor 4.2124. Multiplying this factor by $1,000 produces the answer to the problem, $4,212.40. This is the amount that would have to be deposited at the beginning of the first year to provide constant payments of $1,000 each at the end of the next five years. Notice that each factor in each column of Table 10-4 is a vertical accumulation of preceding factors from Table 10-3.

Key Terms

Deferred revenues
Liabilities
Contingent liabilities
Current liabilities
Voucher system
Liquidity
Working capital
Current ratio
Interest-bearing note
Noninterest-bearing note
Discounted note

Questions

1. List and describe three characteristics of all liabilities.
2. Identify the differences between current and long-term liabilities.
3. Define the term deferred revenue.
4. Under what major caption on the balance sheet should deferred revenue be disclosed?
5. Why are liabilities classified as current or long term?
6. How and why is working capital determined?
7. The current ratio is composed of which elements?
8. What is a tickler file and what function does it serve?
9. Describe the format of a voucher and explain its function.
10. How do accountants measure current liabilities?
11. Specify the objectives in accounting for current liabilities.
12. What are the advantages in reporting purchases net of discounts?
13. List some common payroll deductions.
14. Distinguish between payroll deductions and payroll taxes.
15. Why are payroll deductions a current liability?
16. When is a long-term liability reclassified as a current liability?
17. Distinguish between stated and effective interest rates.
18. What is a contingent liability and how is it reported in the financial statements?

1. Calculate the approximate effective annual rate of interest incurred by a firm that purchases $2,000 in merchandise and fails to take a discount of 3/15, n/30.

2. Calculate the amount of working capital and the current ratio for a firm with $400,000 in current assets and $260,000 in current liabilities.

3. How much interest is charged on a 6 percent, $15,000 interest-bearing note for 150 days?

4. Prepare the necessary entries to account for the issuance and payment of a discounted noninterest-bearing note of $1,000, discounted for 90 days at 9 percent interest.

5. Present journal entries to record the incurrence of a $500 trade account payable and the payment of that debt, assuming that a voucher system is used.

6. Prepare journal entries to account for the following events, assuming purchases are recorded at gross:
(a) Purchased merchandise on account for $5,000 at terms 2/10, n/30.
(b) Paid half of the liability within the discount period.
(c) Paid the remaining liability in 30 days.

7. Prepare journal entries to account for the transactions in Exercise 6, assume that the purchases are recorded net of discount.

8. What adjusting entry will accrue interest expense on a 90-day 8 percent, interest-bearing note of $2,000, if the year end date is 30 days before the maturity date of the note?

9. Record the issuance and payment of a $700, 60-day, noninterest-bearing note discounted at 6 percent.

10. Record employees' wages, given the following:

Gross Wages	$9,000.00
Less Federal Income Taxes	1,000.00
State Income Taxes	200.00
Union Dues	80.00
Employee FICA Taxes	526.50
Employer Taxes	
FUTA	45.00
State Unemployment	135.00
FICA Taxes	526.50

11. A partial list of assets and liabilities for the Jones Company on December 31 is shown below:

Current Assets		Liabilities	
Cash	$ 40,000	Accounts Payable	$ 60,000
Accounts Receivable	120,000	Accrued Liabilities	10,000
Inventory	180,000	Notes Payable (Due in 30 days)	100,000
		Long-Term Liabilities	200,000

Determine the following as of December 31:

(a) Working capital.

(b) Current ratio.

(c) Determine the current ratio, assuming that all of the cash was used to pay Accounts Payable.

12. On November 1, a firm received a check for $1,000 from a client for payment of six months' service in advance. How should receipt of this payment be recorded? What adjusting entry is needed on December 31?

13. During August, the G&S Department Store had total credit sales of $100,000. This amount includes $5,000 sales tax, which must be remitted by September 15. Will the Current Liability section of a balance sheet dated August 31 reflect an item related to these events?

14. On December 31, Watts Company issued a one-year noninterest-bearing note with a face value of $1,000 to acquire some production supplies. This was recorded as follows:

Purchases	$1,000	
Notes Payable		$1,000

If the cash value of supplies is $900, what adjusting entry should be made on December 31?

15. A payroll for the XYZ Company required $10,000 in salaries, of which $3,000 was withheld for income taxes. FICA taxes amounted to 13 percent of salaries, half of which is borne by the employer. FUTA taxes are fully borne by the employer: the state receives 2.7 percent and the federal government receives 0.4 percent. No payments on this payroll or on payroll taxes have been made by year-end. Present the current liability section of the balance sheet, at year-end.

16. Prepare the general journal entries to record the following transactions and any adjusting entries needed at year-end, April 30, 19X5:

(a) Issued a discounted $1,000, 90-day note to a bank on March 16, 19X5. Proceeds of the note were $985.

(b) Issued a 6 percent, 30-day, $200 note to a supplier on March 20, 19X5.

(c) Issued a 9 percent, 90-day, $1,000 note to another supplier on April 15, 19X5.

(d) Paid the 6 percent, 30-day, $200 note on time.

17. The following general ledger accounts are found in the RHD Corporation's general ledger after adjusting entries have been posted. Prepare the current liability section of the firm's balance sheet:

Accounts Payable	$ 32,000
Notes Payable (Due in 6 Months)	9,000
Discount on Notes Payable	600
Bonds Payable (Due in 18 Years)	150,000
Accrued Wages Payable	2,700
Accrued Interest Payable	12,000
Deferred Rental Income	400
Liability for Federal Income Taxes Withheld	1,800
Liability for State Income Taxes Withheld	300
FICA Taxes Payable	180
FUTA Taxes Payable	80

18. Present general journal entries to record the following transactions, assuming purchases are recorded net of discount.
(a) Purchased $600 in merchandise on account at terms 2/15, *n*/30.
(b) Purchased $1,500 in merchandise on account at terms 3/15, *n*/60.
(c) Paid purchase (a) within the discount period.
(d) Paid purchase (b) 57 days after the purchase date.

1. Marsha Donaldson is considering an investment in Bilge, Inc. Among other factors, she is evaluating the following data: **Problems**

Current Assets		
Cash		$ 35,000
Accounts Receivable	128,000	
Less Allowance for Bad Debts	13,000	115,000
Marketable Securities (Market Value and Cost)		10,000
Inventory		35,000
Prepaid Expenses		500
Current Liabilities		
Accounts Payable		108,000
Notes Payable		60,000
Interest Payable		8,000
Liabilities for Payroll Deductions		5.000

REQUIRED:
(a) Calculate the current ratio and working capital.
(b) Evaluate the impact of this firm's current liabilities and make a recommendation to Ms. Donaldson.
(c) Demonstrate the effect of accidentally classifying $20,000 in current liabilities as long term on the current ratio and working capital balance of Bilge, Inc. Assume the error has already been made in the preceding data.

2. The fiscal year for the Hemp Company ends on November 30. Hemp borrowed $500 from each of two banks and a stockholder on November 1, giving the following notes:

	Note 1	Note 2	Note 3
Face Amount	$500	$500	$500
Interest Rate	8%	—	—
Discount Rate	—	8%	—
Term of Loan	90 Days	180 Days	1 Year
Lender	Bank	Bank	Stockholder

REQUIRED:
(a) Record the borrowing of the money.
(b) Record the accrual of interest on November 30.
(c) Record the payment of the notes.

3. Baxter, Inc., has the following transactions involving accounts payable:
(a) Purchased merchandise, 2/10, n/30, for $1,500.
(b) Purchased merchandise, 3/15, n/30, for $1,800.
(c) Paid for first purchase within discount period.
(d) Paid for second purchase 30 days after the purchase.

REQUIRED:
(a) Record these transactions, assuming that purchases are recorded at the gross amount.
(b) Record these transactions, assuming that purchases are recorded net of discount.

4. The Weeks Company incurs $3,000 in wage expense this month. Assume this is the first month of the year and that the federal income tax withholding rate is in aggregate 15 percent and the state income tax withholding rate is 3 percent. FICA is 6 percent, and the employer's pension cost is 5 percent. The FUTA tax rate is 0.4 percent while state unemployment is 2.7 percent.

REQUIRED:
(a) Record the wage expense and payroll tax expense.
(b) Record the payment of payroll liabilities incurred.
(c) Determine the total cost to the Weeks Company of employing its workers for one month.

5. Reproduced below is a portion of the trial balance for Horn, Inc.:

	Debit	Credit
Accounts Payable		$66,000
Purchase Discounts Lost	$ 42	
FICA Taxes Payable		200
FUTA Taxes Payable		40
State Unemployment Taxes Payable		120
Notes Payable		8,000
Discounts on Notes Payable	180	

ADDITIONAL DATA:

(a) Wages of $3,000 are owed employees as of December 31, year end for Horn. No FUTA or state unemployment taxes are recognized because all employees have already earned above the $4,200 limit this year.

(b) The Notes Payable Account results from one 90-day note discounted at 9 percent by the bank on November 1.

(c) Estimated federal income taxes for Horn are $13,000. Estimated state income taxes for Horn are $3,000.

(d) FICA tax note is 12 percent, split between employee and employer.

REQUIRED:

(a) Make the necessary adjusting entries.

(b) Produce the current liability section of the balance sheet for Horn, Inc.

6. The following transactions involving current liabilities occurred during the current fiscal year of the North Company:

January 10	Purchased merchandise for $25,000 before a 2 percent discount from the supplier. Both purchases and accounts payable are recorded net of discounts.
January 19	Paid $15,300 on January 10 invoice. The invoice was billed at $15,612.
January 31	Paid balance of January 10 invoice after discount period.
April 1	Issued a one-year note to settle a March 27 invoice for $5,000. This invoice had been recorded net of the 2 percent discount, or $4,900. The note was recorded at a face value of $5,300 ($5,000 plus 6 percent interest).
December 31	Wages for December were $8,000 before the following withholdings:

Income taxes	$940
FICA, 5 percent	400
Union dues	175

The payroll taxes are recorded at the end of each month. December wages are subject to a 2.7 percent state unemployment tax and a 0.4 percent federal unemployment tax, all other withholdings and payroll taxes have been paid.

December 31   The company has sold service contracts on its products. Deferred Service Contract Revenue was credited on the receipt of customer payments and totals $37,000. Realized revenue from the service contracts for the current fiscal year is $5,300.

December 31   Interest expense on the April 1 note is recognized.

REQUIRED:

Prepare general journal entries.

Prepare the Current Liability section of the balance sheet, dated December 31.

7. The Boston Company's monthly payroll for November is as follows:

Officers' Salaries	$15,000
Sales Salaries	32,000
Clerical Salaries	12,000
Total Payroll	$59,000

Other data include the following:

Wages Subject to FICA Tax	$16,000
Wages Subject to FUTA Tax	3,000
Federal Income Taxes Withheld	8,700
State Income Taxes Withheld	3,000
Voluntary Deduction:	
Pension Contributions Withheld	600
Payroll Deductions for U.S. Savings Bonds	450
FICA Tax rate	6.13%
FUTA Tax Rate	2.50%
State Unemployment Rate	0.50%

REQUIRED:

Prepare the general journal entries to record the:
(a) Accrual of the November wages and related liabilities.
(b) Accrual of related employer's taxes.
(c) Payment of liabilities to employees and appropriate state, federal, and pension agencies.

8. The Art Mart frequently acquires supplies from Gordon Art Distributors, a wholesaler. The following transactions took place between these two firms:
(a) Mart purchased supplies costing $1,200 from Gordon on terms 2/15, n/30.
(b) Mart paid the amount due Gordon 13 days later. But financial problems were developing for Mart.
(c) Mart purchased $2,000 in supplies from Gordon on terms 2/15, n/30.
(d) Forty days later, Gordon agrees to accept a 90 day, 9 percent note in satisfaction of the $2,000 debt.
(e) Fifteen days later both Mart and Gordon's fiscal years end.
(f) Mart pays Gordon the full amount of the note and interest.

REQUIRED:

Prepare the general journal entries needed to account for these transactions, including any adjusting entries needed at year-end for *both* Mart and Gordon. Assume Mart records purchases net of discount.

9. Below is the trial balance before adjustments for the Iris Sales Company.

IRIS SALES COMPANY
Trial Balance
December 31, 19X4

	Debit	Credit
Cash	$ 2,000	$
Accounts Receivable	7,000	
Inventory	16,000	
Notes Receivable	3,000	
Supplies	900	
Furniture and Fixtures	18,000	
Accumulated Depreciation		6,000
Accounts Payable		1,200
Notes Payable		6,000
Discount on Notes Payable	90	
Liability for Federal Income Taxes Withheld		800
Liability for Pension Contributions Withheld		360
FICA Taxes Payable		180
Bonds Payable		10,000
Owner's Equity		9,750
Sales		89,000
Sales Discounts	1,200	
Purchases (Net of Discounts)	41,000	
Purchases Discounts Lost	250	
Wage and Salary Expense	22,000	
Payroll Tax Expense	2,500	
Utilities Expense	350	
Rental Expense	9,000	
	$123,290	$123,290

An analysis of the firm's financial records yields the following data:
(a) Bad debts of 1 percent of the current accounts receivable balance are anticipated.
(b) Ending inventory is $18,000.
(c) Supplies of $600 have been used this year.
(d) The assets being depreciated have a six-year useful life with no expected salvage value. Straight-line depreciation is used.
(e) The note payable is a discounted bank loan for 90 days dated December 1.
(f) The bookkeeper failed to record the employer's FICA taxes on the December payroll of $180.
(g) Bond interest expense of $900 is unpaid.

REQUIRED:
(a) Prepare adjusting general journal entries.
(b) Prepare a balance sheet for the Iris Sales Company.
(c) Calculate the current ratio for the firm as of December 31, 19X4.

□ 11
LONG-TERM LIABILITIES

☐ OBJECTIVES

AFTER STUDYING THIS CHAPTER, YOU SHOULD BE ABLE TO DO
THE FOLLOWING:

1. DESCRIBE THE MEASUREMENT AND REPORTING
   OBJECTIVES IN ACCOUNTING FOR LONG TERM
   LIABILITIES.

2. DISCUSS THE GENERALLY ACCEPTED ACCOUNTING
   TREATMENT FOR BONDS PAYABLE AND INTEREST EXPENSE.

3. IDENTIFY ACCOUNTING PROBLEMS AND THEIR
   RESOLUTION FOR LEASE AND PENSION LIABILITIES.

4. PRESENT FINANCIAL STATEMENT DISCLOSURES FOR
   DEFERRED TAXES.

Long-term liabilities are obligations of the firm that will not require satisfaction for a period of at least one year or one operating cycle, whichever is longer. They are sometimes referred to as *fixed liabilities*, because a particular liability may appear on the firm's balance sheet for several years. Long-term liabilities are usually incurred to meet the long-term financing needs of the firm, such as the acquisition of buildings, equipment, a new subsidiary, or new product lines from another firm. Frequently long-term liabilities are *secured*, which means that creditors are granted the right to seize specific assets in satisfaction of the debt if a debtor is unable to repay. Security is provided in a *mortgage contract*, which legally establishes the rights and duties of both parties to the lending transaction. It usually specifies which property may be seized if the debtor firm cannot meet its obligations. If a long-term liability is unsecured, the creditors of the firm do not have special rights or privileges in the event of default. Their rights are no greater than other creditors of the firm. Consequently, weaker firms may have difficulty borrowing on unsecured liabilities, or they must pay a higher rate of interest to compensate the lender for the additional risk.

Several types of long-term liabilities are commonly found on balance sheets. Long-term notes and bonds are the most common debt instruments used in long-term borrowing. In addition, a firm may incur long-term liabilities in connection with lease contracts, pension plans, or deferred income taxes. All of these obligations are reported on the balance sheet under the separate heading "Long-term Liabilities." Disclosure of long-term liabilities clearly distinguishes them from current liabilities, thus indicating the nature and amounts that must be satisfied in the more distant future as opposed to debts that must be satisfied in the near future.

Why Incur Long-term Debt?

There are several reasons why the majority of businesses choose to acquire some of their operating funds by incurring long-term liabilities instead of by selling additional shares of common stock or other ownership interests. The major advantages of long-term liabilities lie in the basic distinction between the rights and duties of creditors and owners and in the differing income tax treatment of interest and dividends. Creditors have preference over owners in the event of the dissolution of the business. Creditors must be completely repaid before owners can receive anything if business is discontinued. In addition, creditors must be paid the interest prescribed in the note or bond, while profit distributions received by owners depends in part on how profitable the firm has been. Consequently, new enterprises or weaker firms find it difficult to raise funds by selling stock: thus they raise funds by borrowing on notes or bonds because of the protection and privileges accorded creditors. At times, general economic conditions are so poor that even stronger firms have difficulty selling new issues of stock and must raise needed funds through long-term debt.

Even the strongest and most successful firms choose to raise funds by long-term borrowing, since creditors do not normally acquire the rights of owners. Current owners will not dilute their control of the firm if needed funds are borrowed. In addition, the cost of using borrowed funds is interest, a fixed amount (rate) determined by negotiation upon issuing the bond or note. The interest rate on a particular debt does not change over the life of the debt. If the firm has an extraordinarily profitable year, the amount paid creditors is no higher than in poor years, leaving the bulk of the profits to be divided among the current owners of the business. Using debt with fixed costs to fund business operations is referred to as *leverage*. However, the fixed costs of borrowing must be paid in less successful years as well as in profitable years. When a firm generates only small profits, the interest costs can consume the bulk of the earnings. In years with losses, interest payments may consume funds needed for operations. Leverage increases business risk, since inability to pay the interest may force the business into bankruptcy. Leverage generally increases the earnings available to the owners of the business in highly profitable years while reducing them in less successful years.

The benefits of leverage are heightened by the income tax treatment of interest. While distributions of profits, such as dividends to owners, create no income tax savings to the firm, the payment of interest is tax deductible. Consequently, the cost of borrowing is considerably less than it initially seems to be. For example, if the Wilson Corporation, in a 48% income tax bracket, borrows $100,000 at 8 percent interest, it will pay $8,000 interest per year. But the effective cost of using that $100,000 is actually less than $8,000, because Wilson saved $3,840 by deducting the interest as an expense for federal income tax purposes. As shown, the net cost of using these borrowed funds was only $4,160 per year, or 4.16 percent—not 8 percent.

Annual Interest Expense	$8,000
Less Taxes Saved by Interest Deduction (Interest Deduction × Tax Rate) ($8,000 × 0.48 = $3,840)	3,840
Net Cost of Using Borrowed Funds	$4,160
Effective After-Tax Rate of Interest ($4,160/$100,000)	4.16%

The benefits and risks of leverage are available to all business organizations, regardless of their form—proprietorship, partnership, or corporation. Because most large businesses are incorporated, however, the remainder of our discussion of long-term liabilities will be directed to corporations, although it would be equally applicable to other forms of business.

Measurement and Reporting Objectives

The measurement and reporting objectives of long-term liabilities are guided principally by the cost, matching, and adequate disclosure principles. When liabilities are incurred, they are measured and recorded in accordance with the cost principle. If a $1,000 bond is issued for $1,000, it is recorded as a $1,000 liability. Thereafter, long-term liabilities are measured and reported at the net present value of the liability. This amount is called the *net liability* or the *current cash equivalent* of the liability. If a liability is issued for exactly its principal amount,[1] the current cash equivalent of the liability exactly equals the amount of cash that must be repaid at maturity. Therefore no change is required in the reported amount of the liability over its life.

If the proceeds of a liability are greater than the principal amount of the liability, it is said to have been issued at a *premium*. On the other hand, a liability whose proceeds are less than the principal amount is said to have been issued at a *discount*. Where liabilities are issued at a premium or discount, the current cash equivalent of the liability differs from the ultimate amount that must be repaid. Consequently, each year the accountant recalculates the current cash equivalent and adjusts the liability account to its appropriate current cash valuation. This entry also reduces the amount of the premium or discount. As will be noted later, this process of reducing or *amortizing* the premium or discount also affects the interest expense of the firm and, as such, is governed by the matching principle. At maturity date, the liability's current cash equivalent will be equal to the amount required to be repaid, all premium or discount having been completely amortized.

Adequate disclosure requires enough information to be presented so that financial statement users can intelligently assess the effect of the liability on the firm. This information is presented either parenthetically in the body of the balance sheet or in footnotes to the financial statements. Generally, this information should include amounts authorized to be borrowed, due date or dates, interest rate, property mortgaged or pledged, and any other significant characteristics of the liability or indenture agreements that might be useful to the financial statement reader.

Bonds Payable

A *bond* is a written unconditional promise to pay the holder of the bond the *principal* or *face value* of the bond at *maturity date* and interest on the face

---

[1] The principal amount of a debt is the contractual amount that must be paid to satisfy the obligation at its maturity date. Normally, this is equal to the amount borrowed. The term "face amount" is a common synonym for principal.

value of the bond at a specified rate on specified dates. Most bonds carry a face value, sometimes called *par value*, of $1,000. Maturity dates vary greatly, some being as little as 5 years from the issuance date of the bonds, while other bonds mature as much as 100 years or more after issuance. Terms of 25 to 30 years are common for corporate bonds. The rate of interest paid on the bond is called *nominal* or *coupon rate* and is a fixed percentage of the face value of the bond. Interest is normally paid semiannually.

When a company issues bonds, it normally sells the entire bond issue to an *underwriter*. An underwriter is an investment firm (or, for large bond issues, a syndication of several investment firms) that sells the individual bonds to investors. Because there may be several thousand geographically dispersed individual bondholders for any one bond issue, the issuing company selects a *trustee*, who serves as representative for the individual bondholders. The rights of the bondholders are specified in a *bond indenture agreement*, and the trustee insures that the company lives up to the terms of the agreement. If the terms are violated, the trustee will take whatever action is necessary to protect the bondholders, including foreclosure.

Since a bond is a legal contract between a borrower and a lender, an almost infinite variety is possible. Normally, bond types are differentiated on the basis of their security, interest payment, or duration. The accounting procedures focus on the economic substance of the bond transaction. Consequently, two bond issues would be recorded in the same manner, even if one is secured by a mortgage against the buildings and the other is unsecured. Common characteristics of different types of bonds are described in the supplementary discussion at the end of this chapter.

Accounting for Bonds Payable

Several complex factors interact in determining the amount that investors will pay for newly issued bonds. Investors must assess the risk associated with investing in the bonds of a particular firm. If the investment is perceived as being fairly risky, a higher interest rate may be required to sell the bonds. In addition, the *market rate of interest* must be determined by the investor. This is the rate of interest at which willing borrowers and willing lenders would agree to borrow and lend at a given level of risk. The market rate of interest fluctuates daily as a function of the supply of and demand for loanable funds.

When a corporation issues bonds, it must obtain the approval of its stockholders to the major features of the bond issue in advance of its issuance. Weeks or even months before the bonds are sold, the indenture agreement must be drawn up and bond certificates must be printed. Consequently, the rate of interest that is paid on the bonds must be determined well in advance of the day on which they are first available for sale. As a result, the nominal rate of interest printed on the bond certificates may differ from the anticipated market rate of interest for an investment with that level of risk. Since the interest paid on the bonds is fixed and cannot be changed, the issuance price is adjusted to convert the nominal rate into the current market rate of interest.

Bonds Issued at Par

Bonds are issued at par when the contract rate printed on the bonds are perceived by investors as being approximately equal to the market rate of interest for the risk level involved. If the Smith Corporation sells $1,000,000 of 6 percent, 10-year bonds, paying interest semiannually, and receives $1,000,000 in proceeds from the sale, the entry to record the sale of these bonds at par would be:

```
Cash                        $1,000,000
    Bonds Payable                        $1,000,000
    Sold $1,000,000 6% 10-Year Bonds Payable at Par on 12/31/X5
```

If the Smith Corporation makes the semiannual interest payments on June 30 and December 31 of each year, one-half of annual bond interest will be paid on each date and recorded as follows:

```
Bond Interest Expense      $30,000
    Cash                                 $30,000
    Paid Semiannual Bond Interest Expense ($1,000,000 × 6% × ½) on 6/30/X6
```

```
Bond Interest Expense      $30,000
    Cash                                 $30,000
    Paid Semiannual Bond Interest Expense ($1,000,000 × 6% × ½) on 12/31/X6
```

When the Smith Corporation prepares financial statements at the end of its accounting period on December 31, 19X6, the financial statements would report the following with respect to this issue of bonds:

```
Income Statement:
    Bond Interest Expense                $60,000

Balance Sheet:
    Long-term Liabilities:
        Bonds Payable, 6%, due 12/31/Y5      $1,000,000
```

At the maturity date, the Smith Corporation would record the retirement of this bond issue as follows:

```
Bonds Payable    $1,000,000
    Cash                         $1,000,000
    Retired Bond Issue at Maturity
```

Bonds Issued at a Discount

If the market rate of interest on the day that bonds are issued is higher than the contract rate of interest provided by the bond, a reduction in the issue price of the bonds is required to sell the bonds. This reduction, or discount, should be sufficient to make the effective rate of interest earned by the bondholders equal to the current market rate of interest. For example, if the

Jay Corporation were selling $1,000,000, 6 percent, 10-year bonds, and the market rate of interest had risen above 6 percent on the date of issue, investors would expect to pay less than $1,000,000 for the bonds. If investors bid $975,000 for the bonds, the corporation's effective interest rate may be approximately calculated as follows:

Amount to Be Repaid:
Principle Amount of Bonds	$1,000,000
Interest—$60,000/Year for 10 Years	600,000
	$1,600,000
Less Proceeds of Sale of Bonds	−975,000
Cost of Borrowing for 10 Years	$ 625,000

Cost of Borrowing per Year $625,000/10 = $62,500
Effective Interest Rate $62,500/975,000 = 6.41%[2]

By selling the bonds at a discount, the Jay Corporation has increased the effective interest rate that it must pay (and investors will receive) to approximately 6.41 percent. The Jay Corporation would record the sale of these bonds on January 1, 19X6, by making this entry:

Cash	$975,000	
Discount on Bonds Payable	25,000	
Bonds Payable		$1,000,000

Sold $1,000,000, 6%, 10-year Bonds Payable at a Discount of 1/1/X6

Note that the face amount of the bonds payable is credited to the Bonds Payable account. The discount, which is the difference between the principal amount of the liability and the actual proceeds of the sale of the bonds, is recorded in a separate Discount on Bonds Payable account. This account is reported as a contra liability. A balance sheet produced on January 1, 19X6, would report bonds as follows:

Balance Sheet:
Long-term Liabilities:
Bonds Payable, 6%, due 12/31/X5	$1,000,000	
Less: Discount on Bonds Payable	25,000	$975,000

In this way the financial statement user is given all relevant information about the bonds, including the principal amount of the bonds that must be repaid at maturity. The objective of reporting the bonds at the current cash equivalent is accomplished by subtracting the unamortized discount from the principal amount of the bonds payable at maturity.

As noted earlier, the effect of a discount is to increase the effective rate of interest that the corporation must pay for the use of the borrowed funds.

---

[2]A precise calculation would utilize compound interest and present value concepts. This estimate is correct to the second decimal place.

BONDS ISSUED AT A
DISCOUNT

This additional interest expense is reflected in the income statement by the process of amortizing the discount in accordance with the matching principle. That is, the additional interest expense is recognized periodically over the life of the bond issue by matching the revenues earned through the use of borrowed funds with this additional cost of those funds.

There are two methods for calculating the amount of premium or discount to be amortized each interest payment period: the straight-line method of amortization and the effective-interest method of amortization. The straight-line method is a simple method that amortizes an equal amount of discount each period. It is, however, theoretically less acceptable than the more complex effective-interest method.[3] The effective-interest method accelerates amortization so that more discount is reclassified as expense earlier in the life of the bond issue than late in its life.

Straight-Line Amortization.   Under the straight-line method of amortizing bond discount, the total amount of discount is amortized equally over the life of the bond. In the case of the Jay Corporation, the amount amortized each interest payment period would be calculated as follows:

Amount of Discount to Be Amortized:	$25,000
Number of Interest Periods: (10-Year Bonds, Interest Paid Annually)	10
Amount to Be Amortized Each Interest Period	25,000/10 = $2,500

Effective-Interest Amortization. The effective-interest method provides discount amortization such that reported interest expense equals the effective-interest rate. The calculation is based on the carrying value of the bonds. Carrying value is the face amount adjusted for unamortized discount or premium. A partial amortization table for Jay Corporation is shown below:

JAY CORPORATION
Amortization Schedule—Interest Method

Year	Bond Carrying Value[a]	×	Effective Interest Rate	=	Annual Interest Expense	−	Cash Interest Payment	=	Discount Amortization
1	975,000		0.0641		62,498		60,000		2,498
2	977,498		0.0641		62,658		60,000		2,658
3	980,156		0.0641		62,828		60,000		2,828
4	982,984		0.0641		63,009		60,000		3,009
5	985,993		0.0641		63,202		60,000		3,202

[a]Bond carrying value equals the face amount of the bonds less unamortized discount. As discount is amortized each year, the bond carrying value increases.

The Jay Corporation would record the payment of the first year's interest as

[3]Methods other than the effective interest method may be used only if the results are not materially different from those that would result from using the effective interest method.

follows:

Bond Interest Expense	$62,498	
Discount on Bonds Payable		$ 2,498
Cash		60,000
Paid annual interest 12/31/X6		

Financial statements prepared on December 31, 19X6, would report:

Income Statement:
Bond Interest Expense $ 62,498

Balance Sheet:
Long-term Liabilities:

Bonds Payable, 6%, due 12/31/Y5	1,000,000	
Less Discount on Bonds Payable	22,502	$977,498

The amortization of bond discount properly reflects the additional cost of selling bonds at a discount by increasing the firm's interest expense. Also note that the amortization of discount reduces the balance in the Discount on Bonds Payable account, thereby increasing the net present value of the liability, as reported on the balance sheet, from $975,000 to $977,498. By the bond maturity date, the Discount on Bonds Payable account will have a zero balance (it will be fully amortized), and the liability's reported net present value will be $1,000,000—the exact amount due on that date.

If the market rate of interest on the bond issue date is lower than the nominal interest provided, the bonds will sell for an amount greater than par value. Like discounts, the premium that investors will pay equates the bond's effective interest rate to the current market rate of interest. For example, if investors bid $1,020,000 for the Jay Corporation's $1,000,000, 6 percent, 10-year bonds, the effective rate of interest paid can be approximately calculated as follows:

Bonds Issued at a Premium

Amount to Be Repaid:	
Principal Amount of Bonds	$1,000,000
Interest—$60,000/year for 10 years	600,000
	$1,600,000
Less Proceeds of Sale of Bonds	1,020,000
Cost of Borrowing for 10 years	$ 580,000
Cost of Borrowing per Year $580,000/10 = $58,000	
Effective Interest Rate 58,000/1,020,000 = 5.69%	

The Jay Corporation would record the issuance of $1,000,000, 6 percent, 10-year bonds at a $20,000 premium on January 1 in this entry:

Cash	$1,020,000	
Premium on Bonds Payable		$ 20,000
Bonds Payable		1,000,000

BONDS ISSUED AT A PREMIUM

A premium reduces the effective interest rate. To record the payment of annual interest, the bond premium is amortized, thus reducing bond interest expense. The amount of premium amortized each period is calculated under the straight-line method in the same fashion as was discount amortization:

Amount of Premium to Be Amortized: $20,000
Number of Interest Periods: (10-Year Bonds, Paying Interest Annually)   10
Amount to Be Amortized Each Interest Period: $20,000/10 = $2,000

The Jay Corporation would record the first year's interest payment as follows:

Bond Interest Expense	$58,000	
Premium on Bonds Payable	2,000	
Cash		$60,000

The Jay Corporations's financial statements prepared on December 31, 19X6, would report bonds and bond transactions as follows:

Income Statement:
    Bond Interest Expense $ 58,000

Balance Sheet:
    Long-term Liabilities:
        Bonds Payable, 6%, due 12/31/Y5   1,000,000
        Add Premium on Bonds Payable   18,000 $1,018,000

Bonds Issued After Date on Bond Certificate

Although bonds may be dated January 1, they are likely to be sold after January 1. This may be caused by actions of investors, underwriters, or issuers. Potential investors or underwriters may be reluctant to purchase bonds on the stated date. Alternately, the corporation may voluntarily withhold the bonds for a short while in hopes that the market rate of interest will fall, thus reducing its future interest expense. When bonds are issued after their initiation date, two problems result. The amortization of premium or discount must be adjusted to reflect the fact that the bonds will not be outstanding for their full term, and the measurement of bond interest expense for the first interest period must reflect the "shortness" of the first period.

The Amortization Problem. Bonds issued after the date printed on the certificates actually span a period shorter than the stated life. For example, bonds dated January 1, 19X6, maturing December 31, 19Y5, and actually sold on March 1, 19X6, are outstanding only for 118 months instead of the anticipated 120 months. In accordance with the matching principle, amortization of premium or discount should occur within the time period over which the bonds are actually outstanding. For example, on March 1, 19X6 the Northwestern Corporation issued $1,000,000, 6 percent, 10-year bonds dated January 1, 19X6, at a discount of $20,060. The discount amortization would be calculated as follows:

Amount of Discount to Be Amortized:	$20,060
Number of Months Outstanding:	118
Amount to Be Amortized Each Month:	$20,060 / 118 = $170

The Northwest Corporation would record semiannual June 30 and December 31 interest payments for 19X6 in these entries:

Bond Interest Expense	$30,680	
Discount on Bonds Payable		$ 680
Cash		30,000

Paid Semiannual Bond Interest and Amortized 4 Months Discount at $170/Month

Bond Interest Expense	$31,020	
Discount on Bonds Payable		$ 1,020
Cash		30,000

Paid Semiannual Bond Interest and Amortized 6 Months Discount at $170/Month

Interest for the short first period. When bonds are sold between interest payment dates, interest expense for that period should be less than if the bonds had been outstanding for the full period. Keeping records of the exact bond sales dates on large issues could be an extremely time-consuming task. Therefore investment bankers established an alternate mechanism: the buyer of a bond customarily pays the fair market value of the bond *plus accrued interest*. The bond issuer receives an amount equal to the interest the investor has not earned for that interest period. On the first interest payment date, that "prepaid" amount is returned to the investor in addition to the interest that has been earned.

For example, On March 1, 19X6, the Northwest Corporation issues $1,000,000, 6 percent, 10-year bonds, dated January 1, 19X6, at par. Investors will pay Northwest $1,000,000 plus the two months interest for the period between January 1 and March 1, or $10,000 ($1,000,000 × 6% × $\frac{2}{12}$). On the next interest payment date, Northwest will pay $30,000 interest to bondholders. Only $20,000 will be actual payments of interest; the other $10,000 will *simply be a return* of amounts paid by the bondholders. The sale of the Northwest Corporation's bonds and the payment of interest would be recorded in these entries:

Cash	$1,010,000	
Bonds Payable		$1,000,000
Bond Interest Expense		10,000

To Record the 3/1/X6 Sale of $1,000,000 6% Bonds Dated 1/1/X6, at Par Plus Accrued Interest

Bond Interest Expense	$30,000
Cash	$30,000

Paid Semiannual Bond Interest 6/30/X6

BONDS ISSUED AFTER DATE ON BOND CERTIFICATE

Recording the receipt of $10,000 as a credit to the Bond Interest Expense account greatly simplifies the accounting for the short interest period: the standard expense entry is quite sufficient to measure bond interest expense for the period correctly. Note the effect of these two entries on the Bond Interest Expense account:

BOND INTEREST EXPENSE

6/30/X6 $30,000	3/1/X6 $10,000
Balance $20,000	

Accrued Bond Interest Expense

When bond interest payment periods differ from the corporation's accounting period, an adjusting entry is required to measure bond interest expense for the year correctly. For example, if the Mesa Corporation, a calendar year corporation, issues $1,000,000, 6 percent, 10-year bonds on the face date, April 1, 19X6, at a $20,000 discount, the entry to record semiannual interest on September 30 would be:

Bond Interest Expense	$31,000	
Discount on Bonds Payable		$ 1,000
Cash		30,000
Payment of Semiannual Bond Interest and Amortization of Bond Discount, 9/30/X6		

On December 31 of this year and each year thereafter, the following adjusting entry must be made to measure bond interest expense for the year correctly:

Bond Interest Expense	$15,500	
Discount on Bonds Payable		$ 500
Bond Interest Payable		15,000
Accrual of 3 Months' Bond Interest Expense and Amortization of Discount, 12/31/X6		

When this interest is actually paid on March 31, 19X7, the entry will be:[4]

Bond Interest Expense	$15,500	
Bond Interest Payable	15,000	
Discount on Bonds Payable		$ 500
Cash		30,000
Payment of Current and Accrued Bond Interest and Amortization of Discount, 3/31/X7		

[4]Alternately, the December 31 entry would be reversed on January 1 as described in the Supplementary Discussion of Chapter 4. The reversal entry would accomplish the same end as is described in the March 31 entry shown here.

Instead of selling bonds to hundreds or thousands of bondholders, funds can often be borrowed from banks, insurance companies, or other financial institutions. These loans are usually evidenced by notes maturing in 2 to 10 years or more. Notes are especially common when firms need funds for a relatively short period of time (less than 5 years) or when bond interest rates are unfavorable. Borrowing on long-term notes allows the firm to avoid the costs of dealing with thousands of bondholders and trustees, and it avoids the necessity of registering bonds with the SEC.

Notes are accounted for in the same fashion as bonds. Much of the complexity of accounting for bond transactions is eliminated in the case of notes payable by the common practice of issuing notes at par and dating the notes on the date the funds are actually borrowed. The common entries for notes payable transactions are illustrated here for the Regency Corporation on the issuance of a $500,000, 6 percent, two-year note, paying interest annually:

Cash		$500,000
Notes Payable	$500,000	
Issued 2-Year 6% Note to First National Bank, 1/1/X6		

Interest Expense	$ 30,000	
Cash		$ 30,000
Paid 1 Year's Interest on First National Bank Note, 12/31/X6		

Interest Expense	$ 30,000	
Cash		$ 30,000
Paid 1 Year's Interest on First National Bank note, 12/31/X7		

Notes Payable	$500,000	
Cash		$500,000
Repaid First National Bank Note at Maturity, 12/31/X7		

Accrual entries are needed for notes with interest dates that do not coincide with the corporate year-end.

The popularity of leasing equipment and buildings has grown rapidly in the past decade, principally because of the substantial increase in the cost of purchasing these assets. In contrast, no large immediate outflow of cash is necessary if assets are leased. The growth of leasing has caused a heated controversy over the measurement of lease liabilities. Under what circumstances does a lease agreement give rise to a liability? When and how is this liability measured?

To answer these questions, accountants have divided leases into two classifications. *Operating leases* are generally cancelable and the lessor usually retains all or most of the incidents of ownership (such as paying property taxes, insuring the asset, and making repairs). *Financing leases* are characterized by long-term, noncancelable contracts that cover the approximate life of the asset and impose the rights and responsibilities of ownership on the lessee. Financing leases are considered, in substance, to be purchases in wich the lessee is allowed to pay for the asset in install-ments. Indeed, many financing leases provide that the lessee may purchase the asset at the end-of-lease period for only a nominal price.

If the lease is an operating lease, no long-term liability arises. This method of leasing is sometimes referred to as off-balance sheet-financing. Rental payments under the lease are recorded in this simple entry:

Rental Expense	$5,000	
Cash		$5,000

If the lease is considered a financing lease, most accountants believe that a long-term liability is incurred and that the lease transaction should be accounted for as if it were a purchase transaction. If the Southwest Cor-poration entered into a financing lease for a machine that could be purchased for $20,000 and agreed to pay $5,000 per year for five years (the estimated life of the equipment), the lease would be recorded in this entry:

Machinery	$20,000	
Deferred Lease Cost	5,000	
Financing Lease Liability		$25,000
Recorded 5-Year Financing Lease of Machinery		

The machinery is recorded at its current fair market value and difference between the total lease liability and the fair market value of the equipment would be recorded as a deferred financing lease cost. Each year part of the deferred cost would be amortized, thus increasing interest expense. The machine would also be depreciated. Depreciation, amortization, and the rental payment would be recorded as follows:

Financing Lease Liability	$5,000	
Cash		$5,000
Paid one Year's Rental of Machinery		
Depreciation Expense	$4,000	
Interest Expense	1,000	
Deferred Lease Cost		$1,000
Accumulated Depreciation		4,000
To Reclassify Expired Cost as Expenses		

The effect of this accounting treatment is to (1) record the lease as a purchase, (2) recognize that the difference between the fair market value of the leased assets and the total lease liability is interest, (3) recognize interest expense over the life of the lease by amortizing the financing lease discount[5] and (4) record the lease liability and report it on the balance sheet.

One of the most common fringe benefits provided employees is a pension or retirement plan. Pension plans provide payments to retired employees. Often the amount an employee will receive as a pension is determined by the length of employment, the size of his compensation while employed, or a combination of such factors. In these cases, the pension plan is called a *benefit plan.* If the amount to be received by a retired employee is not fixed or established by a formula, but varies as a function of contributions made by the employer and employee, the plan is called a *contribution plan.* Since most employees prefer to know how large a pension they will receive after retirement, the majority of organized pension plans in the United States are benefit plans.

A pension plan may be administered by the firm itself, or the firm may establish a pension trust or purchase employee annuities from an insurance company. If a trust administers a pension plan or if the firm purchases employee annuities, the obligation to make pension payments to retired employees is the obligation of the trust or insurance company. As a result, the trust or insurance company generally requires that the firm make annual contributions sufficient, along with earnings on those contributions, to meet future anticipated pension payments. Such a plan would be referred to as a *funded pension plan.* If the firm chooses to retain the obligation to make pension payments to retired employees, no payments are made to outside agencies, and a liability arises to make pension payments to retired personnel. The firm must undertake some provision to insure the proceeds from the plan for its employees.

Accounting for funded pension plans is relatively simple. Each year, employee pension expense is measured as the amount required to be paid to the trust or insurance company. For example, if the Boxcar Corporation is required to pay $18,000 each year to a trust administering its pension plan, the payment would be recorded in this entry:

Employee Pension Expense	$18,000	
Cash		$18,000
Paid Annual Pension Expense to Employee Pension Trust		

[5]Interest expense usually is calculated under the effective interest (annuity) method, which recognizes proportionately more interest in the early life of the asset. The straight-line method can be used for immaterial amounts, as in the example.

Measuring employee pension expense and the resultant long-term liability for a firm providing pension payments in company-funded pension plans is considerably more complex. To determine these amounts, professional actuaries must be consulted. After determining how long employees are expected to work with the firm, how long they are expected to live, and other factors, employee pension expense is measured as the present value of future pension costs incurred in the current year. The resulting long-term liability, recorded in the Employee Pension Liability account, is increased for each year's pension expense and reduced for actual payments made to employees under the pension plan, as illustrated in the following entries:

Employee Pension Expense	$126,200	
Employee Pension Liability		$126,200
Recorded Employee Pension Expense for the Year		

Employee Pension Liability	18,600	
Cash		18,600
Paid Employers $18,600 under Unfunded Pension Plan		

Deferred Income Taxes

Income tax laws and generally accepted accounting principles sometimes differ on the issue of *when* certain revenues or expenses are to be reported. This is not surprising, because the objectives of tax laws differ markedly from the objectives of generally accepted accounting principles. Tax objectives attempt to raise revenues and subsidize certain activities deemed to be socially desirable; accounting objectives are concerned with reporting fairly the financial position and results of operations of firms and providing timely and relevant information to investors and others. The timing differences arise when revenues or expenses are recognized in one period for accounting purposes and in another period for tax purposes. They cause accounting problems, because the matching principle requires that revenues and expenses be appropriately matched. For example, the income statement of the Regency Corporation for 19X6 may report an item of revenue of $1,000, while the Internal Revenue Code may require that this amount be reported in 19X7 for tax purposes. If the tax rate is 50 percent, the Regency Corporation would be mismatching revenues and related expenses if it reported the $1,000 item of revenue in 19X6 and waited until 19X7 to report the related $500 income tax expense.

To match revenues and expenses correctly, the Regency Corporation will recognize both the $1,000 revenue and the $500 income tax expense in 19X6, creating a *deferred tax liability* that must be paid in 19X7. For example, assume the following income statement data:

	19X6	19X7
Net Income per Income Statement (Including $1,000 Item in 19X6)	$80,000	$90,000
Revenue Reported on Income Statement in 19X6 but Taxable in 19X7	−1,000	+1,000
Taxable Income	$79,000	$91,000
Tax Rate	×0.50	×0.50
Income Tax Payable per Income Tax Return	$39,500	$45,500

To record this deferred tax liability in 19X6 and its satisfaction in 19X7, Regency Corporation would make the following entries:

```
Income Tax Expense                        $40,000
     Income Tax Payable                              $39,500
     Deferred Income Tax Liability                       500
     To Recognize Income Tax Liabilities for 19X6


Income Tax Expense                        $45,000
Deferred Income Tax Liability                 500
     Income Tax Payable                              $45,500
     To Recognize Income Tax Liabilities for 19X7
```

In each year, the amount entered as Income Tax Expense is 50 percent of the net income shown on the income statement (19X6 = $80,000 × 0.50 = $40,000 and 19X7 = $90,000 × 0.50 = $45,000). The current amount recorded as payable is the actual tax due for that year. The tax to be paid is computed by multiplying the tax rate by the amount of taxable income.

Recognition of a deferred liability matches revenue and expense. All of the income tax expense associated with revenues reported on the income statement in 19X6 are reported in 19X6, even though $500 of this amount is not due until 19X7. For 19X7, only that income tax expense associated with 19X7 income is reported on the 19X7 income statement; the additional $500 actually paid in 19X7 represents the reduction of the deferred income tax liability.

A great deal of controversy remains in the area of recognizing deferred income tax liabilities. Arguments against recognition of deferred income tax liabilities are: (1) no real liability to pay taxes exists until the Internal Revenue Code requires the filing of the income tax return, (2) future changes in tax laws or other uncertainties may reduce or expand future tax liabilities, and (3) future tax liabilities may be permanently deferred for stable or expanding firms, if the deferred income tax liability is viewed on an aggregate basis.

The example centered on timing differences that created a deferred income tax liability. These occur when accounting income is recognized before taxable income or tax deductions are recognized before accounting expenses. If taxable income is recognized before accounting income, or if accounting expenses are recognized before tax deductions, these timing differences require the recognition of a deferred cost or debit instead of a deferred income tax liability, or credit. This deferred cost may be viewed as a long-term prepaid asset and is treated in a manner parallel to the deferred income tax liability.

Reclassifying the Current Portion of Long-Term Debt

Generally, the significant determining question in classifying a liability as current or long term is "by when must the liability be satisfied." If satisfaction is required within one year or one operating cycle, whichever is longer, the liability is usually classified as current. A secondary criterion for the current classification is that the debt must be satisfied by expending current assets. Under these general rules, the character of a liability (or part of a liability) could change from one year to the next. For example, if the Research Corporation, a calendar year corporation, borrows money on an 18-month note on December 31, 19X6, the balance sheet for that date would report the note as a long-term liability. On the balance sheet prepared on December 31, 19X7, the note would be reclassified and reported as a current liability, because at that point in time satisfaction is due within less than one year. However, if the note is to be repaid out of funds deposited in a sinking fund or from other noncurrent resources, the note will not meet the requirements for reclassification as current liabilities in the year of maturity. Therefore the note should remain classified under long-term liabilities. Parenthetically or in a footnote, the accountant should indicate that the note is to mature within the upcoming year.

A related issue concerns refinancing short-term debt. In some cases, long series of short-term debt are used to finance an operation. Accordingly, it might not be appropriate to classify these obligations as current liabilities. Short-term debt may be excluded from current liabilities if two conditions are met: (1) there is *intent* to refinance the obligations; and (2) there is an *ability* to consummate the refinancing.

Summary

Chapter 11 considered the accounting problems associated with long-term liabilities. Long-term liabilities are defined as the obligations of the firm that do not require satisfaction for a period of one year or one operating cycle, whichever is longer. Because the rights and duties of creditors and owners differ, acquiring funds by incurring long-term liabilities can be easier and more advantageous for many firms than selling additional stock. Common long-term liabilities include bonds payable, notes payable, lease liabilities, pension liabilities, and deferred income taxes.

Bonds payable are accounted for at the exchange price at which they are issued. Thereafter they are reported at the net present value of the liability. Reporting them at their net present value may require amortization of premium or discount, which reduces or increases the interest expense of the firm. Issuance of the bonds after the date printed on the bond certificates requires that the rate of amortization be adjusted and that the expense of the firm for the short period be reduced.

Many of these problems in accounting for bonds are eliminated in accounting for notes payable. Notes are generally issued at par on the date of the note. Accounting for long-term lease liabilities, pension liabilities, and deferred taxes involves different problems than accounting for notes or bonds. Long-term liabilities are recognized in lease transactions only if the lease is a financing lease and not an operating lease. Long-term liabilities are recognized in pension transactions only if the pension plan is underfunded. The assistance of actuaries and other professionals is frequently required to establish the amount of a pension liability. Deferred tax liabilities arise whenever the time for recognizing income or expense differs for income tax and financial accounting purposes. While the recognition of deferred tax liability is currently required, much controversy continues to surround the propriety of recognizing these liabilities.

Although all the bonds in a single bond issue are similar bond issues have different characteristics. Bonds may differ on the basis of their underlying security, the method of paying interest, the method of repaying the principal of the bond, and early-retirement features.

| **A Supplementary Discussion: Common Bond Characteristics** |

SECURITY

All bonds are either secured or unsecured. A secured bond issue is accompanied by a mortgage contract or lien that specifies which property of the issuing company may be seized in satisfaction of the debt in the event of default. Secured bonds are often referred to by the type of security provided. Thus, an *equipment trust bond* is a bond secured by a mortgage on equipment such as railroad rolling stock. A *real estate mortgage bond* is secured by a mortgage on real property owned by the company. *Collateral trust bonds* are secured by the stocks, bonds, or other negotiable securities of other companies. These securities are commonly placed on deposit with the trustee to further protect the bondholders.

Unsecured bonds are called *debentures*. Bondholders must rely upon the general reputation and future earnings of the firm to provide for repayment of these bonds.

INTEREST PAYMENT

Bonds may pay interest in two ways. If the bond is *registered*, the name and address of each bondholder is retained as an up-to-date record by the firm and interest is paid only to the current registered owner of the bond. To avoid the record-keeping problem, *coupon bonds* have attached to the bond certificate a sheet of coupons —one for each interest payment. To receive interest on a coupon bond the bondholder must clip the appropriate coupon and mail it along with his name and address to the company or it may be deposited in a bank and cleared through the banking system. Registered bonds are considered somewhat safer, because proper ownership is a matter of record with the company.

REPAYMENT

The principal amount of a bond issue may be repaid in two ways. The entire bond issue may mature at the same time. Alternately, the bonds may be *serial* bonds. In a serial bond issue, a fixed proportion of the bonds within the issue mature each year, allowing the company to repay its bonded indebtedness over a period of years. For example, 10 percent of the bonds in a 10-year-life serial bond issue may mature at the end of each year.

RETIREMENT

Bond issues may also provide for early-retirement features. If a bond issue has no early-retirement feature, it is simply referred to as a *term bond*. Other bonds may be *callable bonds*, which give the company the right to buy them from the bondholder before maturity at a predetermined price that is usually slightly higher than face value, or *redeemable bonds,* which give the bondholders the right to sell them back to the company at some predetermined price prior to the maturity date. Other bonds may be *convertible bonds*, which give the bondholder the right to exchange the bond for some other security of the company, such as common stock, rather than holding the bond to maturity.

Key Terms

Long-term liabilities
Fixed laibilities
Leverage
Net liability
Premium
Discount
Amortizing
Bond
Principal
Maturity date
Par value
Operating leases
Financiing leases
Benefit plan
Contribution plan
Fixed pension plan
Deferred tax liability

1. Distinguish between an underwriter and a trustee. How does each relate to the issuance of bonds?

2. Define debenture.

3. List the relative advantages of raising money through issuing bonds rather than through issuing stock.

4. Define the word leverage and explain how leverage can be favorable for stockholders.

5. Under what circumstances are bonds sold at par, at a discount, or at a premium?

6. How should bonds payable be disclosed in the balance sheet?

7. Over what period is bond discount or bond premium amortized?

8. Describe the timing difference that causes a deferral of income taxes.

9. Why should taxes be allocated between accounting periods?

10. Cite the criticisms asserted against interperiod tax allocation.

11. Distinguish between an operating lease and a financial lease.

12. Distinguish between a funded pension plan and an unfunded plan.

13. Which concept, matching, conservatism, or materiality, is most closely associated with deferred taxes?

14. What is a nominal rate of interest associated with a bond?

15. What accounting problems are posed by bonds issued after the date printed on the bond certificate? How do accountants solve those problems?

16. When would a corporation recognize accrued bond interest expense associated with one of its own bonds?

17. When should long-term liabilities be reclassified as current liabilities?

1. ABC Company has outstanding $5 million, 5 percent bonds as of December 31 of the current year. These 10-year bonds are due in 5 years and 6 months. The unamortized premium on these bonds was $137,500 at July 1 of the current year. Prepare the journal entry to record the interest accrual and the amortization for the six months ended December 31.

2. Can Company issued $100,000, 5 percent, 20-year bonds at 98 on June 1, 19X6. The interest is payable on June 1 and December 1. Make the journal entries for the following:
(a) The issuance of the bonds on June 1, 19X6.
(b) Interest payments and amortization for 19X6.
(c) Adjusting entries for year-end, December 31, 19X6.

3. State whether the bond is sold at par, at a discount, or at a premium for each of the following cases.
(a) The effective rate of interest is 6 percent and the stated rate is $5\frac{3}{4}$ percent.
(b) The 6 percent, $1,000 maturity-value bond sold at 100.

(c) The coupon rate is 6 percent but the bond yields $5\frac{1}{2}$ percent.

(d) The nominal rate is 4 percent and the market rate is 6.7 percent.

(e) A 4 percent bond is sold at 101.

4. If bonds are issued initially at a discount and the straight-line method of amortization is used for the discount, interest expense in the earlier years will be

(a) Greater than if the effective interest method were used.

(b) The same as if the effective interest method were used.

(c) Less than if the effective interest method were used.

(d) Less than the amount of the interest payments.

Explain your answer. (AICPA adapted)

5. In 19X5, Bottle Corporation was considering each of the bond issuance plans listed below. The date of issuance is to be January 1, 19X6.

Plan A: $1,000,000 par value 8 percent, 20-year bonds, with interest payable annually, issued at 114.

Plan B: $1,000,000 par value 6 percent, 20-year bonds, with interest payable annually, issued at 86.

Determine the effective interest rate that results under both plans.

6. The Fox Corporation issued $20,000,000 par value 5 percent bonds at 105 on March 1, 19X6, plus accrued interest of $166,667 from January 1, 19X6. Maturity date of the bonds is June 30, 19X9. Interest is paid by the Fox Corporation on June 30 and December 31 annually. The premium is amortized at year-end, December 31. Prepare all entries for 19X6 related to the Fox Corporation bonds.

7. Marco Corporation issued $200,000 par value 7 percent bonds on April 1, 19X6, at $102\frac{1}{2}$. Interest is payable on March 31 and September 30 each year. These bonds mature in 10 years. Prepare journal entries for the following dates:

(a) April 1, 19X6, to record the bond sale.

(b) September 30, 19X6, to pay the interest and amortize the premium.

(c) December 31, 19X6, to accrue interest and amortize premium.

(d) At the date of maturity to pay interest, amortize premium, and retire bonds.

8. Dee Corporation sold Zee Corporation $100,000 par value 4 percent bonds. The bonds are due in 10 years and pay interest on March 1 and September 1. Zee Corporation purchased the bonds for $97,000 on September 1. Prepare the first complete year's journal entries for Dee and Zee Corporations. Assume straight-line amortization and closing of the books on December 31.

9. Determine the effective interest rate for the following bonds:

(a) A 10-year $1,000 par value bond; annual interest at 6 percent; purchased at 103.

(b) A 5-year $5,000 par value bond; annual interest at 5 percent; purchased at 98.

(c) A 15-year $10,000 par value bond; annual interest at 5 percent; purchased at $101\frac{1}{2}$.

10. A company issued $30,000 par value bonds on July 1, 19X5, to yield 6 percent. Interest is payable on July 1 and January 1. The bonds are due at par on July 1, 19X8. At what price were they issued, assuming the stated interest rate is 5 percent?

11. The accounting income (before taxes) and taxable income for the Grossman Co. for a three-year period were as follows:

	Accounting Income Before Taxes	Taxable Income
19X7	$20,000	$15,000
19X8	30,000	26,000
19X9	36,000	45,000

The differences between the taxable income and accounting income before taxes resulted from the inclusion of revenue for accounting purposes for 19X7 and 19X8 that was not recognized for tax purposes until 19X9. Assuming that the corporate tax rate is 50 percent, prepare the entries required for each year to allocate income taxes.

12. On January 1, 19X0, Strawser Co. signed a five-year, noncancellable lease with Leasing, Inc. for a piece of equipment. The lease contract required an annual rental of $2,000 payable at the beginning of each year starting with January 1, 19X0. It was estimated that the equipment would have a useful life of 10 years, and Strawser Co. was given the option to purchase the equipment at the end of the lease period for $1. Assume that the lease is considered a financing lease, that the equipment could be purchased for $8,500 cash on January 1, 19X0, and that the management of Strawser Co. estimates a zero salvage value and uses straight-line depreciation. Prepare for Strawser Co. those sections of the balance sheet dated December 31, 19X0, relating to the lease.

13. Tummins Company entered into a contract on July 1, 19X5, to lease a minicomputer. The computer originally cost the lessor $9,000 and has an estimated useful life of 12 years. Tummins Company has signed a two-year lease, agreeing to pay $2,750 per year. The lessor remains responsible for repairs and maintenance. Is this lease a financing lease or an operating lease? What entries should be made to report the lease payment of $2,750 on July 1, 19X5, and at year-end, December 31, 19X5, assuming that Tummins always uses straight-line depreciation?

14. Klaus and Company is having difficulty keeping employees and has decided to offer a pension plan. A pension consultant has studied their employees and pension options and concluded that the firm will incur an annual pension liability of $13,500 for the unfunded plan Klaus has selected. If Klaus adopts this plan on January 6, 19X4, what entry is needed to recognize this liability and to record the payment of $1,200 in pension benefits during the year to one retired employee?

15. What entry is required to report the annual payment of $16,000 to United American Insurance Company to fund an employee pension plan for Xenon Company employees?

Problems

1. On April 1, 19X6, Duggs Corporation issued $100,000 par value bonds for $97,291.40. The bonds have a nominal interest rate of 5 percent and mature

April 1, 19X9. Interest is payable on April 1 and October 1. The bonds were issued to yield 6 percent.

REQUIRED:

(a) Prepare an amortization table using the straight-line method.

(b) Show the balance sheet presentation of these bonds for Duggs Corporation on December 31, 19X6.

2. The Cook Company prepared the following interest and amortization schedule for its 10-year bond issue.

Date	Cash	Interest Expense	Amount Amortized	Bond Book Value
1/1/X6				$104,491
19X6	$ 2,500	$ 2,090	$ 410	104,081
19X7	2,500	2,082	418	103,663
19X8	2,500	2,073	427	103,236
19X9	2,500	2,065	435	102,801
19X0	2,500	2,056	444	102,357
19X1	2,500	2,047	453	101,904
19X2	2,500	2,038	462	101,442
19X3	2,500	2,029	471	100,971
19X4	2,500	2,019	481	100,490
19X5	2,500	2,010	490	100,000
	$25,000	$20,509	$4,491	

REQUIRED:

(a) Were the bonds issued at a discount or a premium?

(b) Was the straight-line method of amortization used?

(c) Prepare the journal entry to record the bond issuance on January 1, 19X6.

(d) Prepare the necessary journal entries for 19X1.

(e) Prepare the necessary journal entries for December 31, 19X5, recording the repayment of the bond.

3. The 19X6 balance sheet of Dean Company included the following accounts:

Six percent bonds payable, maturing on December 31, 19X9 $100,000
Discount on bonds payable   3,000

REQUIRED:

(a) Compute the annual interest expense assuming straight-line amortization is used.

(b) How would the accounts appear in the December 31, 19X8 balance sheet?

4. Company A issued $200,000 par value at 6 percent bonds on January 1, 19X6. These 10-year bonds pay interest semiannually on June 30 and December 31. The bonds were sold at 120. Company C issued $200,000 par value 4 percent, 10-year bonds on January 1, 19X6. Interest is payable semiannually on June 30 and December 31. The bonds were sold at 80.

REQUIRED:

(a) Prepare all the journal entries necessary for the two companies for 19X6.

(b) Show both balance sheet presentations of these bonds as of December 31, 19X6.

5. Ruth Perkins formed Perkins Soda Ash Corporation on January 1, 19X5. The corporation engaged in the following transactions:

(a) Sold on April 1 $2 million in 20-year bonds, dated April 1, 19X5, paying 9 percent interest, for $2,060,000, net.

(b) Entered into a lease for heavy equipment on June 1. The lease is for two years, requiring payments of $30,000 per year on June 1, 19X5, and 19X6. The lessor guaranteed to make all repairs required and to make all required insurance and property tax payments, when due. The life of the equipment was estimated to be 12 years.

(c) Entered into a lease for 10 heavy trucks on September 1. The lease was for the estimated useful life of the trucks—4 years—requiring payments on September 1, 19X5, and each September 1 for the term of the lease thereafter, of $50,000. Perkins assumed all ownership responsibilities for the trucks and the lease was noncancellable. Estimated current purchase price for the trucks is $190,000.

(d) Made the first semiannual interest payment on the bonds on October 1.

REQUIRED:

(a) Prepare the general journal entries necessary to record these transactions. Amortize bond premium or discount with each interest payment.

(b) Prepare the adjusting entries required to adjust these accounts on December 31, 19X5.

(c) Prepare the long-term Liability section of Perkins' balance sheet as of December 31, 19X5.

6. The Watson Corporation went into business on July 1, 19X1, and uses a July 1 to June 30 fiscal year. The corporation has considered several pension plans and has narrowed the possible alternatives down to these two:

(a) To acquire a pension annuity for its employees from an insurance company by paying an annual premium of $9,000.

(b) To operate its own pension plan. Actuarial estimates of its first-year pension costs are $12,200 but, since none of its employees will retire for a number of years, no payments will be made in the first year.

REQUIRED:

(a) Prepare the general journal entries to record pension costs and liabilities for *each* of these alternatives.

(b) Which pension alternative results in the recognition of a long-term liability?

7. Camelback Corporation had the following transactions dealing with long-term liabilities during 19X8:

(a) Issued $400,000 of 10-year, 7 percent bonds for $396,000 on January 1, 19X8. The bonds pay interest on June 30 and December 31.

(b) Paid $6,000 annual lease payment on heavy equipment. The lease contract is a one-year renewable lease, providing for the lessor to retain major incidents of ownership.

(c) Paid semiannual interest on bonds. Management elects to amortize premium or discount related to bonds semiannually along with bond interest payments.

(d) Paid $29,000 to pension trust fund.

(e) Renewed a 270-day, $10,000 note with a bank, paying $800 in interest.

(f) Paid semiannual interest on bonds and amortized premium or discount.

REQUIRED:

(a) Give the general journal entries to record these transactions.

(b) Prepare the long-term liability section of Camelback Corporation's balance sheet at December 31, 19X8.

8. The following data are extracted from Bluff Corporation's financial records for 19X1 and 19X2:

	19X1	19X2
Net Income before Extraordinary Items	$180,000	$205,000
Extraordinary Gains	20,000	0
Net Income per Income Statement	$200,000	$205,000

The relevant tax rate is 46 percent.

A review of the tax laws indicates that the $20,000 gain is not taxable in 19X1, but is to be taxed in 19X2, as summarized below:

	19X1	19X2
Taxable Income before considering the extraordinary gain	$180,000	$205,000
Taxable Extraordinary Gain	0	20,000
Taxable Income	$180,000	$225,000

REQUIRED:

(a) Give the general journal entry necessary to record any deferred income tax liability resulting from these timing differences.

(b) Show how these items would be reported on the financial statements in 19X1 and 19X2.

9. Below is the unadjusted trial balance for Pima Sales Company, Inc.

PIMA SALES COMPANY, INC.
Trial Balance
December 31, 19X8

	Debit	Credit
Cash	$ 60,000	$
Accounts Receivable	26,000	
Inventory	60,000	
Prepaid Expenses	4,000	
Deferred Lease Cost	4,000	
Equipment, Furniture, and Fixtures	306,000	
Accumulated Depreciation		125,000
Accounts Payable		15,000
Note Payable		5,000
Bonds Payable		102,000
Employee Pension Liability		30,000
Financing Lease Liability		20,000
Deferred Income Tax Liability		3,000
Owner's Equity		83,000
Sales		600,000
Cost of Goods Sold	380,000	
Salary Expense	80,000	
Rental Expense	36,000	
Interest Expense	19,000	
Utilities Expense	8,000	
	$983,000	$983,000

Data needed for liability adjustments are as follows:

(a) The note payable is a one-year, 6 percent note due on March 1, 19X9.

(b) Bonds payable are 10-year, 9 percent bonds issued June 30, 19X8, paying interest on December 31 and June 30. Interest payable on December 31 has been recorded, but the premium has not been amortized (straight-line).

(c) The firm has an unfunded pension plan for its employees. Pension consultants estimated the current year's additional pension liabilities to be $2,200.

(d) The financing lease is a six-year lease requiring $5,000 in lease payments each December 31. While these amounts were properly handled in the previous two years, this year, on the hectic last day of the year, a new bookkeeper recorded the lease payment as rental expense. The equipment would have cost $24,000 to purchase and depreciation was properly recorded.

(e) The deferred income tax liability relates to a gain in the previous year that was reported on the income statement last year but not taxed until this year.

(f) Assume income tax expense, exclusive of the deferred tax liability, to be $35,000.

REQUIRED:

(a) Give the adjusting general journal entries necessary to record the adjustments.

(b) Prepare an income statement and balance sheet for Pima Sales Company, Inc.

☐ 12
ACCOUNTING FOR OWNER'S EQUITY

PART I SOLE PROPRIETORSHIPS

PART II PARTNERSHIPS

LEGAL CHARACTERISTICS

VOLUNTARY CONTRACTUAL ASSOCIATION

DECISION: SHOULD WE ORGANIZE AS A PARTNERSHIP?

ALLOCATING PARTNERSHIP PROFIT AND LOSS

PARTNERSHIP DRAWINGS

PARTNERSHIP FINANCIAL STATEMENTS

PARTNERSHIP CHANGES AND LIQUIDATIONS

PART III CORPORATIONS

CHARACTERISTICS OF A CORPORATION

ADVANTAGES AND DISADVANTAGES OF THE CORPORATE FORM

ACCOUNTING FOR STOCKHOLDERS' EQUITY

TYPES OF STOCK

ISSUANCE OF STOCK

TREASURY STOCK TRANSACTIONS

OTHER SOURCES OF CONTRIBUTED CAPITAL

ACCOUNTING FOR RETAINED EARNINGS

ACCOUNTING FOR DIVIDENDS

ADEQUATE DISCLOSURE

SUMMARY

A SUPPLEMENTARY DISCUSSION: CORPORATIONS AND THE SEC

SECURITIES LEGISLATION

☐ OBJECTIVES

AFTER STUDYING THIS CHAPTER, YOU SHOULD BE ABLE TO DO THE FOLLOWING:

1. LIST CHARACTERISTICS OF BUSINESS THAT ARE RELATED TO THE FORM OF ORGANIZATION (PROPRIETORSHIP, PARTNERSHIP, AND CORPORATION).

2. PRESENT THE BALANCE SHEET EQUITY SECTIONS FOR PROPRIETORSHIPS AND PARTNERSHIPS.

3. CALCULATE THE DIVISION OF PROFITS IN A PARTNERSHIP.

4. PRESENT JOURNAL ENTRIES FOR STOCK ISSUES, TREASURY STOCK REPURCHASES, DIVIDENDS, AND CLOSING ENTRIES TO TRANSFER EARNINGS TO RETAINED EARNINGS.

5. PREPARE A BALANCE SHEET PRESENTATION FOR CORPORATE OWNERS' EQUITY.

6. PREPARE A STATEMENT OF CHANGES IN RETAINED EARNINGS.

The owners' equity in the firm is reported in the Owners' Equity section of the balance sheet. This section of the balance sheet will vary, both in form and content, depending on the form of organization selected by the business. If the business is a sole proprietorship, there is only one owner whose equity must be accounted for. In a partnership, there are multiple owners, each of whose equity must be accounted for separately. In the corporate form of business, the reporting of the stockholders' equity varies significantly from either sole proprietorships or partnerships. All the principal differences in the financial reports of sole proprietorships, partnerships, or corporations lie in the reporting of owners' equity. The remainder of the balance sheet and the income statements of sole proprietorships, partnerships, and corporations are otherwise identical in form. Consequently, a discussion of the differences in accounting for these various forms of business organization is basically a discussion of the owners' equity section of the balance sheet. In this chapter we consider the reporting of sole proprietorships, partnerships, and the more complex reporting problems of corporate stockholders' equity.

Part I Sole Proprietorships

Any business owned by only one person is a sole proprietorship. Accounting for and reporting the owner's equity in a sole proprietorship is relatively simple, because all changes in the residual equity of the firm affect only one owner. A sole proprietorship requires only two accounts: a capital account and a drawing account. The capital account is usually entitled using the name of the sole owner of the business. For example, John Smith's shoe repair business would use a capital account, entitled John Smith, Capital, or John Smith, Owner's Equity. The capital account is debited or credited for all transactions directly affecting owner's equity, except owner withdrawals from the firm. For example, the capital account is credited for investments that the owner makes. The capital account is also debited or credited for profits or losses in closing the accounts at the end of the accounting period.

The drawing account is also usually entitled using the owner's name, such as John Smith, Drawing, or John Smith, Withdrawals. The drawing account is debited for the _book value_ of assets that are withdrawn from the business by the owner. Neither common law nor tax recognize a sole proprietor as an employee of his own business, because he would be hiring himself. Therefore, the drawing account is used to record all payments made to the owner—even regular weekly or monthly checks—instead of a salary account. The drawing account is closed directly to the capital account of the proprietor at the end of the accounting period. The capital account at that point in time reflects the claim of the owner against the book value of the assets of the business—the net result of the investments and withdrawals plus or minus the results of business transactions, all measured on the basis of historical costs.

The following transactions and entries illustrate the accounting for owner's equity in sole proprietorships:

January 1, 19X1: John Smith invests $5000 in a shoe repair business:

Cash	$5,000	
John Smith, Capital		$5,000
Initial investment by owner		

January 31, 19X1: John draws his monthly $500 check to meet living expenses.

John Smith, Withdrawals	$500	
Cash		$500
Regular monthly withdrawal by owner		

November 15, 19X1: John withdraws typewriter from business for personal use.
Typewriter cost $300 and has $30 accumulated depreciation.

John Smith, Withdrawals	$270	
Accumulated Depreciation—Office Equipment	30	
Office equipment		$300
Withdrew typewriter		

December 31, 19X1: At the end of the year, after closing revenue and expense accounts, the following balances remain:

	Debit	Credit
Income Summary		$12,000
John Smith, Withdrawals	$6,270	
John Smith, Capital		5,000

To complete the closing process, the following entries would be made:

Income Summary	$12,000	
John Smith, Capital		$12,000
Closed Income Summary account		
John Smith, Capital	$ 6,270	
John Smith, Withdrawals		$ 6,270
Closed Withdrawals account.		

The owner's equity section of John Smith Shoe Repair Service's balance sheet, dated December 31, 19X1, would be reported as follows:

Owner's Equity	
John Smith, Capital, January 1, 19X1	$ 5,000
Add: Net Income for 19X1	12,000
Total	$17,000
Less John Smith, Withdrawals for 19X1	6,270
John Smith, Capital, December 31, 19X1	$10,730

In keeping with the adequate disclosure concept, the owner's equity section of the balance sheet details those changes in owner's equity resulting from business transactions reported on the income statement and *separately* reports other changes to owner's equity, such as withdrawals and additional investments.

Part II Partnerships

A *partnership* is defined by the Uniform Partnership Act as "an association of two or more persons who carry on as co-owners a business for profit." All of the elements in this definition are required before a partnership is recognized. If only one person is the owner of a business, it is not a partnership. The term "persons" should be viewed in a broad sense, however. Thus, corporations, estates, or trusts may be partners in a partnership. The relationship of the partners must be that of co-owners. Therefore, no partnership exists if the relationship between, for example, the two people who run a plumbing company is an employer-employee relationship or an agent-principal relationship. At the same time, there must be an intent to carry on a business and divide profits. Simple co-ownership of property does not create a partnership.

Partnership accounting is very similar to the accounting for sole proprietorships. Because there are multiple owners in a partnership, however, there must be a capital account and a withdrawals account for each partner. In addition, some means of dividing the profit or loss of the partnership among the partners must be determined, and the result of this division must be reflected in the capital accounts of the partners. Further complications in partnership accounting are caused by the withdrawal of a partner or by the complete liquidation of the partnership. Before illustrating the proper treatment of these accounting problems, it will be useful to examine the legal characteristics of a partnership. Business executives frequently ask accountants to help them decide whether to operate a business as a partnership or as a corporation. An understanding of the characteristics of a partnership is critical to that decision.

Legal Characteristics

The partnership form of organization has four significant legal characteristics: (1) voluntary contractual association; (2) limited life; (3) mutual agency; and (4) unlimited liability.

Voluntary Contractual Association. A partnership results from partners voluntarily entering into a contract to form and operate a partnership. A partner may not be forced into a partnership. Because of the mutual agency and unlimited liability of each partner, great care is required in selecting partners. Consequently, the law requires that each partner *voluntarily* contract with others to form the partnership. The contract may be written or oral. Because of the significance of the partnership relationship, legal advisors strongly urge that it be written and that it provide a set of operating rules covering all situations on which there may be future disagreement. For example, the contract should establish the formula for dividing profits and losses among the partners, rules for making major business decisions, and rules for dividing the assets at the liquidation of the partnership.

Limited Life. A partnership has a limited life. Many possible events can cause the partnership to be dissolved. The death, bankruptcy, insanity, or other legal incompetence of any partner automatically causes the partnership to dissolve. Any partner may at any time voluntarily withdraw from the partnership, which dissolves the partnership. Of course, this does not mean that the business operated by the partnership must cease to operate. Remaining partners can form a new partnership, but the old partnership exists no longer.

Mutual Agency. Each partner in a partnership is an agent for the partnership. In other words, each partner has the authority to bind the partnership to contracts that are within the scope of the business. This places enormous importance on the careful selection of partners, since each partner has the authority to singly make decisions, without consultating with other partners, that could be of immense importance to the business. For example, if one partner agrees that the partnership will buy assets, the resulting contract is binding on the partnership, even if the other partners knew nothing of the contract. Of course, the partnership can limit the authority of any partner, but such a limitation is not effective with respect to outsiders who have no knowledge of this limitation of authority. Outsiders unaware of this limited authority can successfully bind the partnership to contracts entered into by this partner.

Unlimited Liability. The liability of each partner in a partnership is *joint and several liability*. This means that if the assets of the partnership are not sufficient to meet the claims of creditors, each partner is personally liable for paying his prorata share of the remaining debt out of his personal assets. In addition, if one partner has insufficient personal assets to pay all of his share of the remaining debt, his fellow partners are liable for the part he is unable to pay. Of course, this partner with insufficient assets now owes his fellow partners for the amount of his debt they paid for him, but he may never be able to pay them.

The combination of the partnership characteristics of mutual agency and unlimited liability are strong disadvantages to the use of the partnership form of organization. Errors in judgment of partners can have disastrous consequences for each partner. These disadvantages can at least partly be

Decision: Should We Organize as a Partnership?

DECISION: SHOULD WE ORGANIZE AS A PARTNERSHIP?

overcome by the careful selection of responsible and capable partners. Strengths of the partnership form of organization can mitigate these disadvantages in some cases. Partnerships are generally easily formed and easily dissolved. The operations of partnerships are much simpler than those of corporations. Mutual agency provides the partnership with greater flexibility, allowing any partner to respond to a crisis rather than requiring that the appropriate corporate officer be located and act for the corporation. In addition, the partnership pays no federal income taxes. Instead, the individual partners report the results of partnership transactions on their personal income tax returns.

The decision as to the best form of organization is not an easy one. It can be made only by carefully examining the objectives of the owners and all the relevant circumstances in each case. It should also be noted that these circumstances may change over time. A business originally formed as a partnership or a corporation may, because of a change in business circumstances or owners' objectives, require reorganization in another form. The owners of the business should periodically review its operations to insure that the most advantageous form of organization is being employed.

Allocating Partnership Profit and Loss

Each partner in a partnership has a capital account and a withdrawals account. Both accounts are usually entitled using the name of the partner, that is, Joan Davis, Capital, or Joan Davis, Withdrawals. At the end of the accounting period, the net income or loss of the partnership is determined in the usual fashion. Once determined, this net income or loss is then allocated to the partners' capital accounts on some predetermined basis. If the partnership agreement is silent as to the manner in which partnership profits and losses are to be divided, the law provides that they be divided equally among the partners. In the partnership agreement the partners may agree to divide profits and losses in any way that they choose. The partners may also agree to divide profits on one basis and to divide losses differently.

There are several common methods of dividing profits and losses. Perhaps the most common method of division is the method that allocates a fixed percentage of profits or losses to each partner. Under this method, the partnership agreement establishes a profit-and-loss sharing ratio. For example, a two-person partnership might establish a 60 to 40 percent ratio for the sharing of profits and losses between partners Jim Smith and Joan Davis. If this partnership had a $10,000 profit (i.e., a $10,000 credit balance in the Income Summary account), the Income Summary account would be closed to the partners' capital accounts in this entry:

```
Income Summary              $10,000
     Jim Smith, Capital                  $6,000
     Joan Davis, Capital                  4,000
To allocate profits to partners' capital accounts.
```

Instead of allocating profits on the basis of a fixed sharing ratio, the partners could choose to reward specific partners for investments of time or property by making special allocations to these partners. One agreement might provide, for example, for Joan Davis to receive a special allocation of $5,000 for working full-time in the partnership, with the *remaining* profits and losses to be divided on a 60 to 40 percent basis between Jim Smith and Joan Davis. If this partnership had $10,000 in profits, the allocation would be determined as follows:

	Allocation to Jim Smith	Allocation to Joan Davis	Amount Remaining to be Allocated
1. Net Income			$10,000
2. Special Allocation to Joan Davis		$5,000	5,000
3. General Allocation 60%—Smith 40%—Davis	$3,000	2,000	
Total	$3,000	$7,000	

Although it appears that the partnership is allocating Joan Davis a salary, it is important to note that this amount is not a salary but a division of partnership profits. It should not be recorded in a salary account, but is reflected in the accounts of the partnership in this closing entry:

```
Income Summary              $10,000
     Jim Smith, Capital                  $3,000
     Joan Davis, Capital                  7,000
```

Another form of special allocation is to provide partners with allocations measured as a percentage of investment in the partnership. Investment could be measured as the amount of the partners' initial investment, or the balance of capital accounts at the beginning of the year, or in other ways. For example, the partnership agreement between Jim Smith and Joan Davis might provide for a special allocation of 8 percent of each partner's initial investment in the partnership, with the remaining profits or losses to be divided in a 60 to 40 percent ratio. If Jim Smith invested

$8,000 and Joan Davis invested $2,000 in the partnership, net income of $10,000 would be allocated as follows:

	Allocation to Jim Smith	Allocation to Joan Davis	Amount Remaining to be Allocated
1. Net Income			
2. Special Allocation to Partners (8% of 8,000 to Smith, 8% of 2,000 to Davis)	$ 640	$ 160	$10,000
			9,200
3. General Allocation 60%—Smith 40%—Davis	5,520	3,680	
Total	$6,160	$3,840	

Special allocations are usually made even if they result in allocating more income than has been earned by the partnership or even in the event that the partnership has a loss in the year. For example, assume the same facts as in the preceeding example, except the partnership had a net loss in the year of $3,000. The allocation would be made as follows:

	Allocation to Jim Smith	Allocation to Joan Davis	Amount Remaining to be Allocated
1. Net (Loss)			($3,000)
2. Special Allocation to Partners (8% of 8,000 to Smith, 8% of 2,000 to Davis)	$ 640	$ 160	(3,800)
3. General Allocation 60%—Smith 40%—Davis	(2,280)	(1,520)	
Total	($1,640)	($1,360)	

The entry to reflect this allocation of loss in the partnership accounts would be as follows:

Jim Smith, Capital	$1,640	
Joan Davis, Capital	1,360	
Income Summary		$3,000

A partnership agreement could provide for several special allocations. Since the partners may divide the profit and loss of the partnership in any fashion, an almost unlimited number of possibilities exist for profit or loss division. As a result, it is impossible to detail the various alternatives. The terms of the partnership agreement must be analyzed to determine the exact method or methods to be used. Tiered partnership distribution procedures are established to respond to varying involvements and commitments by the partners.

As partners receive cash or property from the partnership, each partner's withdrawal account is debited for the book value of the property or the amount of cash withdrawn, in the same manner as the withdrawals of sole proprietorship. At the end of the accounting period, the withdrawal account of each partner is closed to the partner's capital account. At this point in time, the partner's capital account reflects the equity of each partner in the book value of the partnership assets. The entry to close the withdrawal accounts of Jim Smith with $3,000 in withdrawals and Joan Davis with $4,000 in withdrawals would be as follows:

Partnership Drawings

Jim Smith, Capital	$3,000	
Joan Davis, Capital	4,000	
Jim Smith, Withdrawals		$3,000
Joan Davis, Withdrawals		4,000
To close withdrawal accounts to capital accounts.		

The financial statements of partnerships are very similar to the financial statements of sole proprietorships. The basic differences are found in the owners' equity section of the balance sheet. For example, the owner's equity section of the balance sheet for the Smith and Davis partnership would be shown as follows:

Partnership Financial Statements

SMITH AND DAVIS PLUMBING CO.
Balance Sheet
December 31, 19X1

Owners' Equity			
Jim Smith, Capital, January 1, 19X1		$8,000	
Add: Share of Net Income	$5,000		
Less: Withdrawals	3,000	2,000	
Jim Smith, Capital, December 31, 19X1			$10,000
Joan Davis, Capital, January 1, 19X1		$2,000	
Add: Share of Net Income	$5,000		
Less: Withdrawals	4,000	1,000	
Joan Davis, Capital, December 31, 19X1			3,000
Total Owners' Equity			$13,000

In keeping with the adequate disclosure principle, it is not uncommon to find the division of the partnership profits described at the bottom of the partnership income statement, in much the same fashion as earnings per share is shown on the bottom f the corporation's income statement. Where Smith and Davis share profits equally and have $10,000 in net income, their income statement might contain the following:

SMITH AND DAVIS PLUMBING CO.
Income Statement for the Year Ended
December 31, 19X1

Net Income	$10,000
Allocation of Net Income Among Partners:	
Jim Smith (50%)	$ 5,000
Joan Davis (50%)	5,000
Total Income Allocated to Partners	$10,000

The adequate disclosure principle also suggests that any other information helpful to the understanding of the financial statements should be included, either parenthetically or as footnotes to the financial statements.

Partnership Changes and Liquidations

The admission of a new partner, the sale of a partnership interest to an outsider, the retirement of a partner, and the liquidation of a partnership are all material changes that pose significant accounting problems for a partnership. A complete discussion of the accounting treatment of these events is complex and beyond the scope of this introductory text. In each of these events, however, the primary objective is to properly account for the equity of each partner. As noted earlier, the capital accounts of the partners in a partnership measure the claims of each partner to the *book value*—not necessarily the fair market value—of partnership assets. This is true because of the use of the historical cost principle in measuring and recording assets, liabilities, and owners' equity. A material change in the partnership, such as the retirement of a partner, may require that the assets and obligations of the firm be revalued so that the retiring partner may receive his fair share of the *fair market value* of partnership assets—not book value. The revaluation may take the form of a complete appraisal of all partnership assets made by professional appraisers or by estimates of the partners. Because appraisals by professional appraisers are relatively expensive, many partnerships estimate the changes in the value of assets themselves.

Summary

In Parts I and II we have examined the accounting problems of sole proprietorships and partnerships. A sole proprietorship is an unincorporated business with a single owner, while a partnership is an unincorporated business with more than one owner.

The decision as to the best form of organization for a business—sole proprietorship, partnership, or corporation—is a complex decision. It can be wisely made only after considering the objectives of the owners, the characteristics of each form of organization, and the pertinent advantages and disadvantages of each. Prudent business people will engage professional legal consultation before finalizing partnership agreements.

The basic differences in accounting for sole proprietorships and partnerships lie in the accounting and reporting of owners' equity. A sole proprietorship will have one capital account and one withdrawals account. All changes in owner's equity are ultimately reflected in the sole proprietor's capital account. In a partnership, each partner has a capital account and a withdrawals account. The profits and losses of the partnership are divided among the partners in accordance with the profit-and-loss division method agreed to by the partners, or equally, if there is no agreement. Additional accounting problems are posed by the admission of a new partner, the retirement of a partner, and the liquidation of the partnership. In each of these instances, care must be taken to properly account for the equity of each partner.

**Part III
Corporations**

The corporate form of organization is the third major form that may be selected by a business. Although some corporations are enormous in size, such as General Motors, the corporate form of business has advantages that lend its use to even small businesses like cafés or drug stores. There are more sole proprietorships or partnerships than corporations in the United States, but the corporation is clearly the dominant business form in this country, in terms of total assets and total revenues. Consequently, an understanding of the special accounting problems encountered in the corporate form is essential to the student of accounting. This part will discuss the characteristics of a corporation, the reporting of stockholders' equity on the corporation's balance sheet, the method of accounting for the issuance, repurchase, and reissuance of corporate stock, and the accounting and reporting problems of dividends and retained earnings.

Characteristics of a Corporation

A *corporation* is a separate, distinct legal entity. It has a separate legal existence, quite apart from that of its shareholders, who are the owners of the corporation. If a sole proprietorship or partnership is sued, it is the sole proprietor or partners who are liable for the damages that must be paid in the event the suit is lost. In the case of a suit against a corporation, however, only the corporation is liable for damages—not its stockholders. As a separate legal entity, a corporation may buy or sell property, sue or be sued, and enter into a wide variety of contracts with other parties. The existence of a corporation as a separate entity provides the corporate form of organization with most of the advantages that make its use appealing to businesses of all sizes.

Corporations acquire their legal existence by securing a *charter of incorporation* from a state or the federal government. This is accomplished by filing an *application for charter* with the appropriate government official. Since the federal government charters only a few kinds of corporations, such as banks and savings and loan associations, the appropriate official is usually the Secretary of State in the state of incorporation. The application for charter usually includes the names of the original stockholders, the name and address of the corporation, a statement of the purpose for which the corporation is formed, and a complete description of the kinds of stock the corporation is authorized to issue. After the legal requirements of the state of incorporation are met, the new corporation is granted a charter. At the first stockholders meeting the stockholders adopt a set of bylaws, which govern the operation of the corporation, and select a board of directors. The board of directors has the formal authority to oversee the operations of the corporation on behalf of the stockholders. The board of directors selects the officers of the corporation who have the day-to-day responsibility of managing the business of the corporation.

Because corporations are separate legal entities, they have the following characteristics.

Limited Liability. Shareholders of a corporation are not responsible for the actions or debts of their corporation. Creditors must look to the assets of the corporation alone to satisfy debts. In contrast, sole proprietorships and partnerships provide unlimited liability, holding sole proprietors and partners accountable for the actions and debts of their businesses.

Continuity of Life. The life of the corporation is determined by the laws in the state of incorporation or by its charter. In most states corporations are allowed to be incorporated into perpetuity, or to renew their charters after a maximum life, which effectively allows perpetual incorporation. The life of the business is unaffected by the death, insanity, or other legal incapacity of a shareholder. The sale of shares of stock has no effect on the life of the corporation. In contrast, sole proprietorships and partnerships are ended by any of these events and must be reorganized if the business is to continue.

Centralization of Management. The authority to bind the corporation to contracts is vested solely in the hands of the officers and board of directors of the corporation. Shareholders do not have this authority. As a result, shareholders are relieved of the burden of investigating the integrity of fellow shareholders and can rely on professional management to operate the business. The absence of the partnership's mutual agency may prove a substantial advantage where many capital providers are required to fund a business operation.

Ease of Transferability of Ownership Interests. The stock owned by shareholders, evidenced by stock certificates, represents the ownership rights of each stockholder. To transfer these ownership rights, all the stockholder must do is sell the stock. These transactions can be effected easily by simply endorsing the stock certificates over to the buyer. In contrast, the sale of a partnership interest is a much more complex process, requiring special legal documents to effect the sale and new partnership agreements if the new partner is acceptable to other partners.

The corporate form of organization provides its owners with many unique advantages that are unavailable to either sole proprietors or partners. Each of the major characteristics noted above provides strong incentive to select the corporate form. Limited liability protects the stockholder from the personal consequences of business operations. All the shareholder can lose is what he has invested in the stock of the corporation. Continuity of life helps to insure the stability of the business, regardless of what may happen to shareholders or officers. Centralization of management vests in professional management the right to bind the corporation to contracts, protecting shareholders from the misdeeds of other shareholders. Ease of transferability-of-ownership interests attracts small as well as large investors who wish to be able to change their investments as business conditions change.

Advantages and Disadvantages of the Corporate Form

The result of these advantages is the ability of corporations to raise the massive amounts of investment capital required by capital-intensive industries such as the automobile industry or the steel industry. The characteristics of the corporate form of organization allow thousands or even millions of individuals to pool their investment dollars and build the giant business that dominate American and world business.

There are some disadvantages of the corporate form that should be considered, too. The primary disadvantage of the corporate form lies in its federal and state income tax treatment. Corporations are taxable entities, paying federal income taxes at the rate of up to 48 percent of taxable income. In addition, dividends paid to shareholders are also taxable income to the shareholders. The resulting double taxation of corporate earnings can substantially increase the tax burden of a business if it selects the corporate form of organization. Most states also tax corporate income and dividends. Note that sole proprietorships and partnerships do not pay taxes at the business level. The owners are taxed on this income only once, as income on their individual income tax returns.

Another disadvantage of the corporate form of organization is its inflexibility. As a creature of the state, corporations are required to meet the requirements of state law. Periodic stockholders meetings are required, as well as meetings of the board of directors. Some states even require that the meetings be held in the state of incorporation. In addition, regular reports are usually required to be filed with the state government regarding the operation of the corporation. Many major business decisions require action by the board of directors and, in many instances, the stockholders. These and other requirements of state law not only contribute to inflexibility but also generate additional expenses that must be borne by the corporation. Because of this inflexibility, formality, and the income tax consequences of the corporate form, many businesses do not elect to incorporate.

Accounting for Stockholders' Equity

All of the principal differences found in reporting for corporations, sole proprietorships, or partnerships lie in the reporting of owners' equity. In sole proprietorships or partnerships, each owner of the business is provided with a capital account that measures at year-end the claim of each owner against the book value of the assets of the firm. This method of accounting for and reporting owners' equity is unwieldy and impractical for corporations for several reasons. Corporations may have thousands or even millions of shareholders. The exact makeup of the shareholder group changes constantly as shares of stock are bought and sold. In addition, the relative claims of stockholders against the assets of the corporation may differ if more than one class of stock is issued by the corporation. For example, the claims of common stockholders may differ substantially from the claims of preferred stockholders. Instead of accounting for stockholders' equity as a direct dollar measure of the claim of each shareholder, stockholders' equity is accounted for and reported by *source*. Exhibit 12-1 demonstrates the reporting of stockholders' equity by source.

Reporting stockholders' equity by source is not only a very practical solution to the problem of reporting the diverse equity interests of a large, everchanging group of stockholders, but it also clearly reports the *minimum legal capital* of the corporation. Minimum legal capital is the amount of original invested capital that the law does not allow to be impaired by the payment of dividends. Originally, the concept was designed to provide creditors with assurance that shareholders would not pay all of the assets out in dividends, leaving nothing to satisfy creditors' claims. A *par value* was established for stock and printed on the stock certificate. This establishes the amount of minimum *legal capital* per share of stock. For example, if 1,000 shares of stock with $10 par value are issued, the minimum legal capital of the corporation is $10,000. Thus, legal capital is a function of the number of shares of stock outstanding and the par value.

EXHIBIT 12-1
STOCKHOLDERS' EQUITY

Contributed Capital		
Common Stock, $100 par value, 100,000 shares authorized, 10,000 shares issued, 100 shares held as treasury stock		$1,000,000
Additional Contributed Capital from Common Stockholders		230,000
Preferred Stock, $100 par value, 6% cumulative and nonparticipating, 10,000 shares authorized, 1,000 shares issued and outstanding		100,000
Additional Contributed Capital from Preferred Stockholders		20,000
Contributed Capital from Plant-Site Donation		40,000
Contributed Capital from Treasury Stock Transactions		14,000
Total Contributed Capital		$1,404,000
Retained Earnings		
Appropriated Retained Earnings for Plant Expansion	$100,000	
Unappropriated Retained Earnings	606,000	
Total Retained Earnings		706,000
Total		$2,110,000
Less Cost of Treasury Stock		9,000
Total Stockholders' Equity		$2,101,000

The concept of a par value has proven very confusing to investors and has been largely unsuccessful in protecting creditors. Some naive investors may think that par value is a measure of fair market value, which it clearly is not. The corporation could dissipate its assets by unsuccessful operations or invest in equipment with resale values only a fraction of their original cost. In either instance, the concept of par value fails to provide creditors with assurance that funds are available to meet their demands. Many states now allow corporations to issue *no-par-value stock.* Where no-par-value stock is issued, the minimum legal capital is either a stated amount set by the corporation called stated value, or the full amount paid for the stock at issuance, depending on state laws.

All state laws now forbid the original issuance of stock at a *discount,* that is, below the amount of minimum legal capital per share. Stock may be issued at a *premium,* however, which is an amount above par or stated value. When it is issued at a premium, the amount above par or stated value is reported in a separate account. In Exhibit 12-1, the premium on common stock is reported as Additional Contributed Capital from Common Stockholders. In so doing, the amount of minimum legal capital is separately reported to provide information to creditors and investors.

Types of Stock   When an investor acquires stock of a corporation, he acquires a bundle of rights and privileges in exchange for his investment. One corporation may issue several different kinds of stock, each kind of stock granting to investors different rights. If only one class of stock is issued, it is called *common stock*. If more than one class of stock is issued, one class is common stock and the other class or classes are usually called *preferred stock*. Preferred stockholders usually receive certain dividend and liquidation preferences that common stockholders do not receive. Dividends are periodic earning distributions made by the company. By contrast, liquidation proceeds result from the partial or total dissolution of the company.

Common Stock.   The common stockholder is the residual equity holder of the corporation. Only after preferred stockholders are paid their dividends does the common stockholder receive dividends. Only after creditors and preferred stockholders have been satisfied does the common stockholder receive anything in the liquidation of the corporation. However, the common stockholders' dividends are not subject to fixed limits as is the usual case with preferred stock. Consequently, if the corporation is very successful, the common stockholders receive the greatest benefits, in higher dividends and appreciation in stock values. In addition, almost all common stock is voting stock. In effect, the common stockholders control the corporation by electing the members of the board of directors.

Preferred Stock.   Preferred stockholders receive rights and privileges that may differ from those of common stockholders in several ways. The most common preference given preferred stockholders is *current dividend preference*. Preferred stockholders must receive their stated current dividends before common stockholders may be paid a dividend. Dividend rates for preferred stock are stated as an annual dollar amount per share or a percentage of par value per share. For example, the preferred stock in Exhibit 12-1 is 6 percent, $100 par value preferred stock. This means that each share of preferred stock must be paid $6 in dividends during the year before common stockholders may be paid any dividends.

Notice that the payment of dividends—even preferred—is discretionary on the part of the board of directors. No liability to pay dividends exists unless the board of directors declares the dividend. If the stock has *cumulative dividend preferences*, dividends that are not declared in prior years must be paid in later years before common stockholders may receive dividends. If dividends are not declared on cumulative preferred stock, the unpaid dividends are called *dividends in arrears*. For example, if 6 percent, $100 par value cumulative preferred stock is two years in arrears in divi-

EXHIBIT 12-2
COMPARISON OF CUMULATIVE AND
NONCUMULATIVE DIVIDEND PREFERENCE

Assumptions: Preferred stock is 6 percent, $100 par value, two years in arrears,
1000 shares outstanding; common stock is $10 par, 1000 shares
outstanding

		Dividends Paid To:	
Case	*Total Dividends Declared*	*Noncumulative Preferred Stock*	*Common Stock*
A	$ 1,000	$1,000	0
B	7,000	6,000	1,000
C	13,000	6,000	7,000
D	19,000	6,000	13,000

		Dividends Paid To:	
Case	*Total Dividends Declared*	*Cumulative Preferred Stock*	*Common Stock*
A	$ 1,000	$ 1,000	0
B	7,000	7,000	0
C	13,000	13,000	0
D	19,000	18,000	$1,000

dend payments, the corporation must declare and pay all dividends in arrears plus the current dividend before common stockholders may be paid a dividend. In the absence of cumulative-dividend preference, preferred stockholders need to be paid only the current dividend before common stockholders can receive dividends, as illustrated in Exhibit 12-2.

One additional form of dividend preference that can be given preferred stock is *participating dividend preference*. Normally, the dividends paid to preferred stockholders are limited to their stated dividend rate. In rare instances, preferred stock may be given the opportunity to participate in additional dividends that are paid beyond their stated dividend rate. While participation features vary greatly, they usually require that the common stockholders receive the same percentage of par value in dividends as the preferred stockholders before preferred stockholders are allowed to share in any additional dividends. For example, if participating preferred stock is 6 percent, $100 par value, and the corporation's common stock is $10 par value, the corporation must declare sufficient dividends to pay the preferred-stock $6.00 dividend and a 60¢ dividend per share of common stock ($10 par value × 6% perferred-stock dividend rate) before the preferred stockholders participate in additional dividends. The rate of participation can be unlimited, that is, *fully participating*, or limited to a max-

EXHIBIT 12-3
DIVIDENDS PAID TO FULLY PARTICIPATING PREFERRED STOCKHOLDERS

Assumptions: Preferred Stock is 6 percent, $100 par value, fully participating, 10,000 shares outstanding. Common stock is $10 par value, 50,000 shares outstanding. Dividends declared total $135,000.

	Dividends to Preferred Stock	Dividends to Common Stock	Dividends Remaining to be Allocated
			$135,000
1. Current Dividends to Preferred Stock (6% × $100 × 10,000 shares)	$60,000		75,000
2. Pro Rata Dividend to Common Stock (6% × $10 × 50,000 shares)		$30,000	45,000
3. Participating Dividend*	30,000	15,000	0
Total	$90,000	$45,000	

*Calculated as follows:

Total Preferred Par Value = ($100 × 10,000 = $1,000,000)	$1,000,000
Total Common Par Value = ($10 × 50,000 = $500,000)	500,000
Total Par Values	$1,500,000

Part allocated to preferred stock:
$$\frac{\$1,000,000}{\$1,500,000} \times \$45,000 = \$30,000$$

Part allocated to common stock:
$$\frac{\$500,000}{\$1,500,000} \times \$45,000 = \$15,000$$

imum dividend, that is, *partially participating*. The exact manner in which common and preferred shareholders share in dividends is established in the corporate charter in the description of the various securities and varies from corporation to corporation. In the case of fully participating preferred stock, the two shareholder groups usually share in dividends by each receiving an equal percentage of par or stated value, as illustrated in Exhibit 12-3.

Following established priorities, the preferred stock is first allocated dividends up to the established 6 percent rate (step 1). Next, the common shareholders are allocated an equal rate of dividend on their investment (step 2). The remainder is allocated so that both common and preferred stockholders earn the same rate on the par value of their investment (step 3). When complete, each has earned 9 percent, calculated as follows:

	Number of Shares	×	Par Value	=	Legal Capital	÷	Dividend	=	Rate
Common	50,000		$10		$500,000		45,000		9%
Preferred	10,000		100		1,000,000		90,000		9%

Preferred stock may have other preferences in addition to dividend preferences. Almost all preferred stock is granted *liquidation preference*. In the event the corporation is liquidated, the preferred stockholders must receive a predetermined amount—usually at or slightly above par or stated value. Preferred stock may also carry a *conversion privilege*, which allows the investor to exchange the preferred stock for a predetermined amount of common stock in the same corporation. It should be noted, however, that preferred stock is rarely voting stock. Preferred stockholders rarely acquire a direct voice in the management of the corporation.

When a corporation issues stock in exchange for cash, the Cash account is debited for the proceeds of the sale, and the amount of minimum legal capital is credited to the Common Stock or Preferred Stock account, depending on the type of stock issued. If the stock has an assigned par value, this is the amount that is credited to the stock account. If the stock has a stated value determined by the corporation, this amount is credited to the stock account. In either instance, any excess proceeds above par or stated value are credited to an account entitled, for example, Additional Contributed Capital from Common (Preferred) Stockholders. If the stock is issued in a state in which all original proceeds from the sale of no-par-value stock are considered minimum legal capital, the entire proceeds are credited to the stock account.

Issuance of Stock

Issuing Par Value Stock

Cash	$180,000	
Common Stock		$100,000
Preferred Stock		25,000
Additional Contributed Capital from		
Common Stockholders		50,000
Additional Contributed Capital from		
Preferred Stockholders		5,000

Issued 100,000 shares of $1 par value common stock at $1.50 per share and 1,000 shares of $25 par value preferred stock at $30 per share.

Issuing No-Par-Value Stock with Stated Value Assigned

Cash	$180,000	
Common Stock		$100,000
Preferred Stock		25,000
Additional Contributed Capital from		
Common Stockholders		50,000
Additional Contributed Capital from		
Preferred Stockholders		5,000

Issued 100,000 shares of no-par-value common stock with $1 stated value at $1.50 per share, and 1,000 shares of no-par-value preferred stock with $25 stated value, at $30 per share.

Issuing No-Par-Value Stock without Assigned Stated Value

Cash	$180,000	
Common Stock		$150,000
Preferred Stock		30,000

Issued 100,000 shares no-par-value common stock at $1.50 per share and 1,000 shares no-par-value preferred stock at $30 per share.

Instead of issuing stock for cash, corporations may issue stock to individuals for performing services for the corporation or to suppliers in exchange for equipment or other assets. In these instances, the assets received should be recorded at the fair market value of the stock issued, which supports the cost principle. When the fair market value of the stock cannot be determined, the assets should be valued at their estimated fair market value. For example, if a corporation acquires machinery for the issuance of 1,000 shares of common stock with a fair market value of $15 and par value of $10, the entry would be as follows:

Machinery	$15,000	
Common Stock		$10,000
Additional Contributed Capital from Common Stockholders		5,000

Sometimes corporations sell stock on credit, taking installment payments for stock and issuing the stock after it is fully paid. Stock sold on credit terms is called *subscribed stock.* When the corporation and investor agree to the subscription, the corporation makes the following entry:

Cash	$1,000	
Subscriptions Receivable, Common Stock	9,000	
Common Stock Subscribed		$5,000
Additional Contributed Capital from Common Stockholders		5,000

Subscriptions to 1000 shares of $5 par value common stock taken at $10 per share, $1,000 paid and $9,000 receivable in six months.

Subscriptions Receivable is an asset, just as are other receivables, and the resulting Common Stock Subscribed and Additional Contributed Capital accounts are owners' equity items that reflect the increased claim of the stockholders against the assets of the corporation. When the stock is fully paid and the shares are issued, these entries are made:

Cash	$9,000	
Subscriptions Receivable, Common Stock		$9,000
Common Stock Subscribed	5,000	
Common Stock		5,000

Treasury Stock Transactions

When a corporation buys its own stock that previously has been issued the stock is called *treasury stock.* Corporations frequently reacquire their own shares to eliminate dissident minority shareholders, to acquire stock needed in employee stock bonus plans or executive stock options, to acquire shares to be used in acquiring other businesses, or to influence the market price of the stock. While treasury stock is technically still issued but no longer outstanding, treasury stock is not allowed to vote, nor are dividends paid on treasury stock. The purchase of treasury stock effectively reduces the stockholders' equity, as shown in Exhibit 12-1. Treasury stock is most frequently valued at the cost to reacquire the stock. For example, if a corporation purchases 100 shares of its own common stock for $3,000, it records the purchase as follows:

Treasury Stock	$3,000	
Cash		$3,000

Again note that the Treasury Stock account reduces stockholders' equity. It would be reported on the balance sheet in this manner:

STOCKHOLDERS' EQUITY

Contributed Capital:	
Common Stock, par value $10,	
100,000 shares authorized and issued,	
of which 100 are in the treasury	$1,000,000
Additional Contributed Capital from	
Common Stockholders	100,000
Retained Earnings:	
Unappropriated Retained Earnings	3,000,000
Total	$3,100,000
Less: Cost of Treasury Stock	3,000
Total Stockholders' Equity	$3,097,000

When treasury stock is later sold, it could be sold for its cost, or above or below its cost. If the stock is sold above its cost, the profit on the sale is treated as additional contributed capital—not as gain reported on the income statement. Sale of the treasury stock, acquired for $3,000, at the higher price of $4,000 is recorded as follows:

Cash	$4,000	
Treasury Stock		$3,000
Contributed Capital from Treasury Stock Transactions		1,000

If treasury stock is sold for less than its cost, the loss on the transaction is treated as a reduction in stockholders' equity. The Contributed Capital from Treasury Stock Transactions account is debited for as much of the loss as it is sufficient to absorb. Any remainder may be debited to Retained Earnings. If the balance of the Contributed Capital from Treasury Stock Transactions account is in excess of $1,000:

Cash	$2,000	
Contributed Capital from Treasury Stock Transactions	1,000	
Treasury Stock		$3,000

Sold treasury stock costing $3,000 for $2,000.

If the balance of the Contributed Capital from Treasury Stock Transactions account is $600:

Cash	$2,000	
Contributed Capital from Treasury Stock Transactions	600	
Retained Earnings	400	
Treasury Stock		$3,000

State laws normally prohibit purchases of treasury stock unless the corporation has a retained earnings balance at least equal to the cost of the treasury stock. Some states also require the appropriation of retained earnings, a subject described in more detail below. This continues to give some assurance to creditors that stockholders will not be able to remove the cushion provided by legal capital by having the company own itself.

Other Sources of Contributed Capital

Contributed capital may come from sources other than shareholders. For example, a city may donate land to a corporation in an effort to get the corporation to locate a plant in the city. These or other capital contributions made to a corporation by nonstockholders are reported on the balance sheet under a descriptive title that indicates the source of the capital contributed. The assets contributed are valued at their fair market value and entered in the books of the firm so that accounting control can be established over the assets, and the balance sheet can report the nature of this capital contribution. For example, if a city contributed land valued at $50,000 to a corporation, the entry to record the contribution would be:

Land	$50,000	
Contributed Capital from Plant Site Donation		$50,000

Accounting for Retained Earnings

The *Retained Earnings* account of the firm reflects the net result of its lifetime profits and losses, reduced by dividends declared during its life. Many studies have emphasized the importance of retained earnings as a source of capital to finance the growth and expansion of businesses. Retained earnings are normally the last major source of capital reported in the stockholders' equity section of the balance sheet. Just as with sole proprietorships and partnerships, the income of the business is summarized in the Income Summary account. For a corporation, this account is then closed to Retained Earnings in this entry:

```
Income Summary                          $500,000
     Retained Earnings                              $500,000
To close income summary account to retained earnings.
```

Retained earnings may be reported on the balance sheet as either unrestricted retained earnings or as retained earnings restricted for some special purpose. Retained earnings become restricted or appropriated by action of the board of directors. By appropriating retained earnings, the board of directors hopes to convey to shareholders information regarding the intended use of assets generated by these earnings and to explain why these assets were not paid out to shareholders in dividends. In addition, state laws may require the appropriation of retained earnings for the cost of treasury stock. If a corporation has issued bonds, the bond indenture agreement may require the corporation to appropriate retained earnings. Presumably, unappropriated retained earnings are not earmarked for specific projects. However, it must be remembered that retained earnings represents a claim against all assets in general and none in particular. An appropriation in no way assures that cash or other liquid resources are or will be available when needed.

To place a restriction on retained earnings merely requires the action of the board of directors to that effect. An appropriation of $300,000 in retained earnings for plant expansion would be recorded in this entry:

```
Retained Earnings                          $300,000
     Retained Earnings Appropriated for Plant Expansion     $300,000
```

Statement of Retained Earnings.   To fully disclose all relevant financial data, many corporations present a *Statement of Retained Earnings,* sometimes called a Statement of Changes in Retained Earnings. The function of the retained earnings statement is to summarize all changes in retained earnings during the year. A retained earnings statement is shown in Exhibit 12-4.

Prior Period Adjustments.   A large group of accountants has consistently sought to have all items that were nonrecurring or extraordinary in nature reported as changes in retained earnings. Thus, they would appear on the retained earnings statement rather than the income statement. However, the extraordinary items should be separated from the results of normal, recurring operations on the income statement (see Chapter 6). *Prior period adjustments* can be excluded from net income for only the following reasons:

1. Correction of an error in previous financial statements.
2. Adjustment for tax benefits realized on preacquisition, operating-loss carry-forwards of purchased subsidiaries.

EXHIBIT 12-4
THE KENYA CORPORATION
Statement of Retained Earnings
For the Year Ended December 31, 19X5

Retained Earnings Balance, January 1, 19X5	$114,000
Prior Period Adjustment:	
Decrease in 19X3 Federal Income Tax Liability	12,000
Adjusted Retained Earnings Balance, January 1, 19X5	$126,000
Add Net Income, 19X5	91,000
Balance	$217,000
Less Dividends Declared in 19X5	30,000
Retained Earnings Balance, December 31, 19X5	$187,000

The latter situation relates to a specific provision in the tax code and is not generalizable beyond this case. In the former situation an actual error must have been made—mathematical mistakes, incorrect application of accounting principles, or misuse of facts would qualify.

Prior period adjustments will be quite rare in practice. Nevertheless, users and preparers of financial statements should be aware of the potential to adjust the beginning balance of retained earnings.

Accounting for Dividends

Dividends are a distribution of the earnings of a corporation to its shareholders. The term dividend usually refers to a distribution of cash. The terms *property dividends* or *dividend in kind* refer to a distribution of assets other than cash. Before dividends may be paid to any shareholder, the board of directors must declare the dividend. It is important to note that no liability to pay dividends exists until they are declared by the board of directors. A typical declaration announcement would read as follows:

"The Board of Directors of Caddo Corporation today declared a quarterly dividend of $1 per share on the common stock, to be paid to shareholders of record on March 15, 19X5, payable on April 10, 19X5."

Three important dates are referred to in this announcement. The *date of declaration* is the day on which the board of directors declares the dividend and the corporation incurs the liability to make the dividend payment. This entry would be made:

Retained Earnings	$50,000	
Common Dividend Payable		$50,000

In this entry, the retained earnings account is directly reduced, and the liability to pay the dividend is recognized. The second date referred to in the announcement is the *date of record.* This is the date on which the shareholder records of the corporation are consulted to determine who will receive the dividends declared. A shareholder's name must appear in the corporation's records, that is, he must be a "shareholder of record" on this date before he is entitled to receive the dividend. On the *date of payment,* which may follow the date of record by a month or more in order to give the corporation an opportunity to prepare checks, the dividend is paid and this entry is made:

Common Dividend Payable	$50,000	
Cash		$50,000

Both assets and shareholders' equity have been reduced for the payment of the dividend.

In determining whether to declare and pay dividends to shareholders, the board of directors must consider many factors. Initially, they must decide if they are able to pay dividends. That is, do they have sufficient cash and retained earnings? Both are required before a dividend could legally and wisely be declared. More difficult considerations lie beyond these two essential ones. Does the corporation believe its business will prosper in the upcoming period, or does it need to retain its earnings? Does the business plan to expand or to invest in new equipment that will require extensive capital? Will the corporation suffer from some unforeseen event that will require large amounts of capital, such as a natural calamity like a flood or fire, or a lawsuit? Because of these and other considerations, corporations rarely pay all their earnings out in dividends to shareholders. Indeed, many corporations pay no dividends at all.

Stock Dividends. A *stock dividend* is a distribution of additional shares of stock in a corporation to the shareholders of the corporation. In effect, the corporation gives its shareholders additional evidence of their continuing interest in the corporation. A stock dividend accomplishes two things. First, it may relieve the corporation of shareholder pressure for the payment of cash dividends, which the board of directors may feel it is unwise to pay. Note that when cash dividends are paid, both assets and shareholders' equity are reduced. The distribution of a stock dividend does not reduce cash or total stockholders' equity. Second, the stock dividend causes a transfer of retained earnings to contributed capital. This permits the company to distribute additional shares of stock to existing stockholders. Each stockholder's proportionate interest in the firm remains the same. These are the entries to record a stock dividend of 500 shares of $5 par value common stock with a fair market value of $25:

EXHIBIT 12-5
EFFECT OF A COMMON STOCK DIVIDEND

Assumption: A 500-share, common stock dividend with total
fair market value of $25 per share is distributed
on $5 par value common stock.

Stockholders' Equity BEFORE STOCK DIVIDEND	
Contributed Capital:	
Common Stock (10,000 shares)	$ 50,000
Additional Contributed Capital	16,000
Retained Earnings	80,000
Total Stockholders' Equity	$146,000
Stockholders' Equity AFTER STOCK DIVIDEND	
Contributed Capital:	
Common Stock (10,500 shares)	$ 52,500
Additional Contributed Capital	26,000
Retained Earnings	67,500
Total Stockholders' Equity	$146,000

Retained Earnings	$12,500	
Common Stock Dividend Distributable		$ 2,500
Additional Contributed Capital from Common Stockholders		10,000
Declared a 500-share common stock dividend		
Common Stock Dividend Distributable	$ 2,500	
Common Stock		$ 2,500
Distributed common stock dividend		

Notice that the effect of the stock dividend is to reduce retained earnings by an amount equal to the fair market value of the stock dividend declared and to transfer these amounts to contributed capital. At the time of the declaration of the stock dividend, a contributed capital account entitled Common Stock Dividend Distributable is credited with the minimum legal capital for the stock to be distributed. While the title of the account suggests that it is a liability account, the account is a contributed capital account belonging in the stockholders' equity section of the balance sheet.

This process of transferring retained earnings to contributed capital is frequently referred to as *capitalizing* retained earnings. It is important to note that this process does not increase or reduce stockholders' equity; it merely rearranges the nature of that equity, as shown in Exhibit 12-5. This may eliminate some pressure on a company to distribute cash dividends.

The stock dividend in Exhibit 12-5 would be referred to as a 5 percent stock dividend, because the amount of the distribution totaled 5 percent of the outstanding stock (500 ÷ 10,000 = 5%). Each shareholder who owned 100 shares would receive 5 additional shares. But if assets and stockholders' equity remain unchanged as a result of the stock dividend, what has the shareholder really received? From the corporation he receives only additional evidence of his same interest in the corporation. If a stockholder owned 20 percent of the outstanding common stock of the corporation before the distribution, he would still own 20 percent of the outstanding common stock afterward.

Stock Splits. Corporations frequently have a range of prices within which they prefer their stock to trade. If the price per share grows too large, it discourages small investors from purchasing it. Corporations normally prefer that publicly held stock be widely distributed among as many shareholders as possible. This stabilizes the price of the stock, preventing wild fluctuations. To keep the price of the stock low and affordable to the average investor, a corporation may effect a stock split. A *stock split* occurs when the corporation calls all of its stock in and issues two or more shares for each share that was previously outstanding, reducing the par or stated value of the stock accordingly. For example, if stock selling at $125 per share has a par value of $20 per share and is split 2 for 1, the corporation calls all $20 par shares in and issues two $10 par shares for each $20 par share.

A stock split has no effect on total stockholders' equity or on the balances of contributed capital and retained earnings accounts. Since the only effect of a stock split is to reduce the par value of the shares and increase the number of shares outstanding, no accounting entries are required. However a memorandum, or parenthetical, entry would be made providing details of the split. Normally, the corporation would record the details of the stock split in the corporate records and adjust the description of the stock on the balance sheet.

Adequate Disclosure

The stockholders' equity section of the balance sheet can be long and very complex. To make it easy for shareholders, creditors, and potential investors to understand the items in the stockholders' equity section, it is important that all relevant information regarding the sources of equity capital be presented, either parenthetically or in footnotes to the statements. The various classes of stock issued by the corporation should be fully described, including the number of shares authorized, issued, outstanding, and in the treasury, as well as the par or stated value. The preferences granted to preferred stock should be clearly described, although lengthy descriptions are usually placed in footnotes rather than made parenthetically in the body of the balance sheet. Other items should be described in sufficient detail to allow a knowledgeable creditor or investor to understand the item and to judge its impact.

Summary

The corporate form of organization is the dominant business form in the United States and the world. A corporation is a separate legal entity with the characteristics of limited liability, continuity of life, centralization of management, and ease of transferability of ownership interests. These characteristics provide the corporation with significant advantages over other forms of business. These may, in part, be offset by the disadvantages of double taxation, organizational rigidity, and numerous legal requirements imposed by the state of incorporation.

Stockholders are the owners of the corporation. Many corporations issue more than one class of stock, providing owners with different rights and privileges. If only one class of stock is issued, it is called common stock. If more than one class of stock is issued, one class is common stock and the other are usually called preferred stock, providing preferred stockholders with one or more special rights or privileges.

Corporate accounting differs from the accounting for sole proprietorships or partnerships principally in accounting for owners' equity. Instead of accounting for the equity of each owner in the book value of the firm's assets, corporate owners' equity is accounted for by source—common stockholders, preferred stockholders, gains on treasury stock transactions, capital contributed by nonstockholders, retained earnings, and other sources. The financial statements prepared for corporations may also include a Retained Earnings Statement, summarizing the changes in retained earnings during the accounting period. Because of the complexity of corporate accounting, it is especially critical that accountants make extra effort to ensure that sufficient disclosure of corporate events is made in the body of the financial statements or in their footnotes to allow financial statement users to interpret the statements.

A Supplementary Discussion: Corporations and the SEC

The historical growth of the corporate form of business accelerated dramatically from the midnineteenth century into the twentieth century. With this dramatic increase in the number of corporations and corporate securities being issued came inevitable abuses in security sales—inflated claims by brokers, simultaneous buying and selling to give the appearance of volume trading, completely fraudulent issues of stock for nonexistent companies, and other illegal actions. From 1918 to 1928, over $50 billion in securities was issued in the United States. A committee of the House of Representatives reported in 1933 that fully half of the securities issued during this period—$25 billion—proved to be worthless. In this climate of abuses, accentuated by the stock market crash of 1929 and the advent of the Great Depression, Congress created the Securities and Exchange Commission (SEC) and gave it broad powers to enforce full and fair disclosure of information about securities offered for sale. The impact of the SEC on accounting, stemming from its charge to ensure full and fair disclosure, has been significant and appears to be increasing.

SECURITIES LEGISLATION

In the early 1930s Congress passed legislation to curtail the abuses in the securities industry. This legislation, the Securities Act of 1933 and the Securities Exchange Act of 1934, remains the primary statutory authority for securities regulation in the United States today. Its impact on corporations and accounting is far-reaching.

Securities Act of 1933.   The focus of this Act is the initial issuance of securities traded in interstate commerce. It has as its primary objectives providing investors with financial material or other information about securities to be issued and preventing misrepresentations and fradulent acts. These objectives are accomplished by requiring any firm issuing securities, except those specifically exempted, to file a registration statement with the SEC detailing a broad range of financial and other information about the firm. It also requires that the firm provide investors with almost this same information in a ***prospectus.*** The sale of securities covered by the Act is prohibited unless the SEC approves the registration statement and prospectus. Note that the act does not require nor allow the SEC to approve or disapprove an issue of securities. The SEC merely determines that appropriate disclosures of information are made to the investing public. The investing public must determine if the securities should be purchased.

The act provides severe criminal and civil penalties for fraud or misrepresentation in the registration statement and prospectus. Indeed, the act specifically provides that any investor who loses money due to false or misleading statements in the registration statement or prospectus may sue to recover losses and damages. It further provides that all parties to the registration statement, including the underwriters who market the issue, lawyers, and the accountants who express an opinion on the fairness of the financial statements, are responsible for the accuracy of the statements. Suits against the parties to the registration statement, including accountants, for alleged false or misleading statements in the registration statement are, unfortunately, not rare.

Securities Exchange Act of 1934.   Following the passage of the Securities Act of 1933, Congress set about providing legislation to regulate the operations of security exchanges and the trading of securities after issuance. Congress created a governmental body to manage and enforce securities regulation in this country. The Securities Exchange Act of 1934 created the Securities and Exchange Commission and gave it broad powers to enforce securities law, including the power to suspend trading of a security, to completely suspend trading of an exchange, to suspend or bar brokers from engaging in securities transactions, and to initiate investigations needed to enforce any of these provisions. It is further empowered to initiate court action to prevent or punish abuses in security transactions.

The Securities Exchange Act of 1934 attacked problems in the resale of securities by requiring that national exchanges and brokers register with the SEC. The exchanges are required to provide extensive data about their rules of operation and are required to aid in enforcing securities law. Brokers are required to submit periodic reports and must show that they are financially responsible.

In addition, the act specifically forbids a number of practices by corporate management, brokers, or stock exchanges designed to manipulate the price of securities. The act further gives the SEC the authority to regulate the solicitation of proxies from stockholders. A proxy is the right to vote the stock of a stockholder who will be absent from the stockholder's meeting. This regulation is designed to discourage deceptive attempts to get voting powers from stockholders.

One of the most significant provisions of the Securities Exchange Act of 1934 requires that corporations whose securities are traded on a national exchange or over-the-counter must file a registration statement of outstanding securities and update this information by filing periodic statements, perhaps monthly, with the SEC. The data required are extensive and are available to the public. Much of the data are financial data, and accountants are extensively involved in preparing these reports. Financial statements prepared for filing with the SEC must meet SEC accounting requirements.

THE SEC AND ACCOUNTING

Congress has given the SEC the authority to regulate the form, content, and methods to be followed in preparing financial statements for filing with the SEC. This authority is both broad and explicit. The SEC has formulated a set of rules that apply to all accounting filings and codified them in Commission Regulation S-X. Further pronouncements relating to accounting and financial disclosure are published in Accounting Series Releases (ASR). To date, over 250 ASRs have been published. Technically, the role of the SEC in prescribing accounting principles only extends to filings with the SEC and does not cover exempted firms, such as small or closely held corporations, or firms whose securities are not traded in interstate commerce. The impact of the SEC on accounting, however, extends far beyond its technical boundaries. Because of the significance of the corporations covered by the SEC rulings and the close interaction between the SEC and accounting profession, the SEC impact on the development of generally accepted accounting principles has been extensive.

Historically, the SEC has not exercised directly its authority to promulgate accounting principles. The first Chief Accountant of the SEC, Carmen Blough, fought pressure from several Commissioners of the SEC in the middle 1930s to prescribe accounting principles, choosing instead to rely on the public accounting profession for this development. The fear that the SEC would assume a more active role in developing accounting principles played a crucial role in the establishment of the Committee on Accounting Procedure (CAP), the supplanting of the CAP by the Accounting Principles Board (APB), and the replacement of the APB by the Financial Accounting Standards Board (FASB). The role of the SEC in the development of individual principles and accounting rules was also critical. In addition to a constant interplay of ideas and viewpoints, the SEC has frequently responded directly to CAP, APB, or FASB pronouncements. On more than one occasion, the SEC's views have caused the accounting profession to modify its position.

The role of the SEC in developing generally accepted accounting principles today is a more active and direct one than ever before. Where the SEC believes change to be desirable, the Office of the Chief Accountant has taken an active role in encouraging the accounting profession to examine the issues or, in some instances, has simply made the desired changes on filing requirements without waiting for the accounting profession to act. Some accountants fear that this increased involvement forebodes a reduction in the role of CPAs in the development of generally accepted accounting principles. In any event, the SEC clearly intends to be an active participant in the development of accounting in the future.

Key Terms

Book value
Partnership
Corporation
Par value
Legal capital
No-par-value stock
Discount
Premium
Common stock
Preferred stock
Subscribed stock
Treasury stock
Retained earnings
Statement of retained earnings
Prior period adjustments
Dividends
Date of declaration
Date of record
Date of payment
Capitalizing
Stock dividend
Stock split

Questions

1. Distinguish between a sole proprietorship and a partnership.

2. A partnership is distinguished by what characteristics?

3. What are the accounting differences between partnerships and sole proprietorships?

4. Describe the major characteristics of a corporation.

5. Accounting and reporting for partnerships and corporations differ in which respects?

6. Describe the attributes of common stock.

7. How does preferred stock differ from common stock?

8. What is minimum legal capital, and what function does it serve?

9. Is the minimum legal capital of a corporation disclosed on its balance sheet? How?

10. Define the term subscribed stock.

11. Identify the attributes of treasury stock.

12. How are gains or losses on treasury stock transactions reported?

13. What are the principal effects of declaring a stock dividend?

14. Distinguish between a stock split and a stock dividend.

15. When a sole proprietor receives a check from his or her business, is an asset, a liability, or an equity account debited?

16. When assets are withdrawn from a sole proprietorship, partnership, or corporation by the owners of the business, what determines the dollar *value* used to record the transaction?

17. Are losses of a partnership usually shared in the same ratio as the profits of the partnership?

18. What are the major advantages and disadvantages in operating a business as a corporation?

19. What dates are important to accountants in the process of declaring and paying dividends by a corporation?

20. What factors must a corporation's board of directors consider in the decision to pay dividends to shareholders?

Exercises

1. A sole proprietorship has a net profit of $6,000 for its first year of operation. The owner invested $15,000 to start the business and has withdrawn $7,000 for living expenses during the year. Calculate the balance of the sole proprietor's Owner's Equity account.

2. Record the investment, withdrawal, and the closing of the Withdrawal and Income Summary accounts in Exercise 1.

3. Frank and Cindy are partners, sharing profits equally after Frank is allocated a salary share of $5,000. How much is allocated to each partner if the partnership earned $26,600?

4. How much profit is allocated to John Jones and Jim Smith if their partnership earned $16,500 in profits and they divide their profits as follows:
(a) Salary shares: $3,000 to John Jones
$2,000 to Jim Smith
(b) Eight percent interest on original investments of $10,000 for Jones, and $6,000 for Smith.
(c) Remainder: 60% to Jones
40% to Smith

5. Record the closing of the income summary account if the total profit (Income

Summary balance) is $18,000, allocating $6,000 to partner A and $12,000 to partner B.

6. What entry is made to close the Income Summary Account of a corporation if its balance is $18,000?

7. Record the sale of 6,000 shares of $1 par value common stock and 1,000 shares of $100 par value preferred stock for $5 per share and $105 per share, respectively.

8. Calculate the total dividends paid common stockholders and the total dividends paid preferred stockholders if Homex Corporation, one year in arrears in the payment of dividends on its $100 par value 8 percent cumulative preferred stock, 10,000 shares outstanding, declares and pays $240,000 in dividends this year.

9. Calculate the total dividends paid to common and preferred stockholders, given these data:
(a) Preferred stock is 6 percent, $100 par value, fully participating, 10,000 shares outstanding.
(b) Common stock is $10 par value, 100,000 shares outstanding.
(c) No dividends are in arrears.
(d) $300,000 in dividends are declared.

10. Record a purchase of 1,000 shares of $10 par value common stock by the issuing corporation for $18 per share and a subsequent sale of this treasury stock for $21 per share.

11. Record the sale of 100 shares of $10 par value treasury stock for $60.00 per share. The stock was acquired for $90 per share. An account, Additional Contributed Capital from Treasury Stock Transactions, has a credit balance of $600.

12. How would a corporation report the issuance of 1,000 shares of common stock for $13 per share if:
(a) The stock has a $10 par value.
(b) The stock is no-par-value stock with a stated value of $3 per share.
(c) The stock is no-par-value stock without assigned stated value.

13. Record the subscription of 500 shares of $10 par value common stock, $1,000 received in advance and $6,000 to be received three months later in full payment.

14. What entries, if any, are needed to record the declaration and later payment of $3,000 in cash dividends to common stockholders, on these dates:
(a) Date of declaration.
(b) Date of record.
(c) Date of payment.

15. Record the declaration and distribution of a common stock dividend of 1,000 shares of stock with a fair market value of $6 per share and a par value of $1 per share.

16. What entries are required to record a 2 for 1 stock split if 100,000 shares of common stock are outstanding with a par value of $10 per share and a fair market value of $220 per share?

17. The Owners' Equity section of Hinton Corporation's balance sheet is shown below on December 31, 19X5:

Contributed Capital:	
Common Stock, $10 par value,	
100,000 shares authorized,	
issued, and outstanding	$1,000,000
Additional contributed capital	
from common stockholders	110,000
Retained Earnings	205,000
Total Stockholders' Equity	$1,315,000

Net income for calendar year 19X6 was $250,000. The Board of Directors appropriated $100,000 for contingencies during the year—a big lawsuit looms on the horizon—and declared and paid dividends totaling $40,000 during the year. Prepare the retained earnings statement for Hinton Corporation and the owners' equity section of the corporation's balance sheet for December 31, 19X6.

18. In reviewing the financial records, the following data are discovered, affecting retained earnings:

(a) The corporation acquired treasury stock costing $6,000. Local law requires an appropriation of retained earnings equal to the cost of treasury stock.

(b) The corporation has decided to appropriate $100,000 in retained earnings for plant expansion to reduce stockholder pressure for dividends.

(c) The corporation declared and paid $125,000 in cash dividends.

Prepare general journal entries to record these events. Prepare the related statement of changes in retained earnings, assuming net income for the year is $400,000 and the beginning retained earnings balance was $665,000.

19. Record the investment of $100,000 in a new business under the following cases:

(a) The firm is a sole proprietorship owned by Jim Smith.

(b) The firm is a partnership of Jim and Jane Smith, who contribute equally to the new business.

(c) The firm is a corporation that issued 10,000 shares of $5-par-value stock for $10 per share.

20. On January 1, 19X7, Wilson, Inc., declared a 5 percent stock dividend when the market value of the common stock was $15 per share. Stockholders' equity before the stock dividend was declared consisted of:

Common stock, $10 par value;	
authorized 200,000 shares;	
issued and outstanding 100,000 shares	$1,000,000
Additional paid-in capital on common stock	150,000
Retained earnings	700,000
Total stockholders' equity	$1,850,000

(a) Prepare the journal entry to record the stock dividend.

(b) Prepare the stockholders' equity section of a balance sheet immediately after the stock dividend is issued. (AICPA adapted)

1. Marston's Shoe Shop was formed this year by a capital contribution of $15,000. The business was successful and earned a profit of $22,000 in its first year. During the year, the owner(s) withdrew $16,000 for personal living expenses.

REQUIRED

(a) Give the entries to record the initial capital contribution; the withdrawals (assume the entire amount is withdrawn at once); and the closing of the Income Summary and withdrawal accounts, under the following assumptions. Also, prepare the Owner's Equity section of the balance sheet under each assumption as of the end of the first year of operation.

(1) The business is a sole proprietorship owned by Joe Marston.

(2) The business is a partnership of Joe and James Marston, making equal ($7,500) capital contributions, sharing profits equally, and each withdrawing $8,000 during the year.

(3) The business is a corporation with 1,000 shares of common stock having a par value of $1 per share, and the $16,000 is declared and paid to shareholders in dividends.

2. Fay Rice and Lise Stone are partners in a plumbing supply business. They made initial capital contributions of $18,000 and $26,000, respectively. Calculate the amount of profit or loss allocated to their respective capital accounts under the following assumptions:

	A	B	C
Profit and Loss Sharing Ratio (Rice/Stone)	6:4	3:2	1:1
Salary Allocated	None	$3,000 to Rice	$2,000 to Rice $1,000 to Stone
Interest on Initial Capital Contributions	6%	8%	10%
Profit (Loss) to be allocated	$8,000	$21,000	($3,000)

3. Bill and Roger Evans, cousins, are partners in a restaurant. The following transactions occurred during the first year of operation:

(a) Bill invested $25,000 and Roger invested $37,000 in the partnership on January 1.

(b) Bill contributed equipment to the partnership with a fair market value of $6,000 on May 1.

(c) Bill and Roger each withdrew $500 per month for living expenses.

(d) Roger contributed an automobile to the partnership with a fair market value of $4,000 on July 1.

(e) The partnership had a profit of $19,000 for the year, and closed all nominal accounts.

REQUIRED:

(a) Determine the division of profits between Bill and Roger, assuming they share profits equally after allocating 8 percent interest on the weighted average capital investment of each partner not including allocated profits for the year or withdrawals.

(*Note:* Weighted average capital investment can be determined by weighting each investment by the number of months it was invested in the business, and dividing the sum of weighted investments for each partner by 12.)

(b) Give the necessary entries to record these transactions.

(c) Prepare the Owners' Equity section of the balance sheet.

4. Hempstead Corporation was formed this year on March 1 to engage in the manufacture of preassembled roof joists. The charter of the corporation authorized the issuance of 10,000 shares of $5 par value common stock and 1,000 shares of 6 percent, $100 par value, cumulative preferred stock. Hempstead Corporation engaged in the following transactions during its first year of operation.

(a) Sold 3,000 shares of common stock for $9 per share.

(b) Sold 5,000 shares of common stock on subscription basis receiving $1 per share immediately, with $10 per share to be received in six months.

(c) Sold 1,000 shares preferred stock for $103 per share.

(d) Declared a dividend of $3 per share on preferred stock.

(e) Received $50,000 in full payment for subscribed common stock.

(f) Paid $3 per share preferred dividend.

(g) Declared a 2 percent stock dividend of common stock to common stockholders. Fair market value of common stock was $13 per share of this date.

(h) Issued the stock dividend declared in (g) above.

(i) Corporation had net income of $39,000 (close this account).

REQUIRED:

(a) Give the entries necessary to record these transactions.

(b) Prepare the Owners' Equity section of the balance sheet for Hempstead Corporation.

(c) Prepare a Retained Earnings Statement for Hempstead Corporation.

(d) Determine the amount of dividends that must be paid preferred stockholders next year before common stockholders may receive any dividends.

5. Mission Candle Corporation has been in business for three years. Although it has barely been profitable in its short history, its business has improved steadily. The

Owners' Equity section of its balance sheet as of December 31, 19X3, is reproduced below:

MISSION CANDLE CORPORATION
Balance Sheet
December 31, 19X3

Stockholders' Equity
Contributed Capital:
Common Stock, no-par-value,
10,000 shares authorized,
issued, and outstanding $300,000
Preferred Stock, $2 no-par-value,
noncumulative, 2,000 shares
authorized, issued, and outstanding   50,000
Retained Earnings:
Unappropriated Retained Earnings   29,000
Total Stockholders' Equity $379,000

Mission Candle Corporation has the following transactions affecting capital this year (19X4):

(a) Mission purchases 200 shares of its common stock for $16 per share.

(b) A local community gives the corporation 3 acres of land worth $18,000 for use as a warehouse site in the city's new industrial park.

(c) Mission sells 100 shares of treasury stock for $18 per share.

(d) The board of directors vote to split the corporations common stock, issuing two shares for each one outstanding, in order to further encourage broad ownership of the stock.

(e) The corporation has a profit of $53,000 for the year

(f) The corporation declares $2 in dividends to its preferred shareholders, to be paid early next year.

REQUIRED:

(a) Give the entries necessary to record these transactions.

(b) Prepare the Owners' Equity section of Mission Candle Corporation's balance sheet.

(c) Prepare a Retained Earnings Statement for Mission Candle Corporation.

6. Phyllis Glover owns and operates an antique shop that she purchased this year. Transactions affecting capital accounts during the year are as follows:

(a) Phyllis acquired the following assets in acquiring the business:

Asset	Cost to Phyllis
Land	$20,000
Building	44,000
Furniture and Fixtures	6,000
	$70,000

(Hint: In purchasing a sole proprietorship, the credit entry should record Phyllis' investment in the business.)

(b) Phyllis invested her substantial collection of antiques in the business, costing $110,000, as inventory.

(c) Phyllis withdrew $16,000 from the business to meet personal living expenses. The money was obtained from sales of antiques.

(d) Phyllis withdrew a special antique lamp that she wished to use for personal purposes rather than sell as inventory, costing $3,000 but with a fair market value of $9,000.

REQUIRED:

(a) Give the general journal entries needed to record these transactions.

(b) Assuming the firm made a profit of $14,000 this year, give the general journal entries necessary to record the closing entries for Phyllis' antique shop.

(c) Prepare the Owner's Equity section of the balance sheet for this business.

7. The partnership of Linn & Ward has the following transactions involving capital accounts this year:

(a) Because of the increased need for capital, both partners invested an additional $8,000 each in the partnership.

(b) Linn manages the business and took an annual salary of $12,000 for his efforts.

(c) Ward withdrew an automobile from the partnership, costing $6,000 with a fair market value of $3,000, and accumulated depreciation of $4,000.

An unadjusted trial balance for the firm at year-end on December 31, 19X5, prepared *after* properly recording these transactions, is shown below:

LINN WARD PARTNERSHIP
Trial Balance
December 31, 19X5

	Debit	Credit
Cash	$ 75,800	
Accounts Receivable	100,000	
Inventories	200,000	
Prepaid Expenses	36,500	
Equipment	260,000	
Accumulated Depreciation		83,000
Accounts Payable		34,400
Notes Payable		200,000
Linn, Capital		116,000
Linn, Withdrawals	12,000	
Ward, Capital		198,500
Ward, Withdrawals	2,000	
Sales		600,000
Cost of Goods Sold	354,300	
Selling Expenses	92,000	
Administrative Expense	81,300	
Interest Expense	18,000	
	$1,231,900	$1,231,900

(d) In addition to the salary paid Linn, the partnership agreement allows each partner an interest allocation equal to 6 percent of January 1, 19X5, capital account balances, and divided profit or loss thereafter equally.

REQUIRED:
(a) Record the transactions affecting capital.
(b) Prepare an income statement.
(c) Prepare a balance sheet for the partnership as of December 31, 19X5.

8. The ABC Corporation was formed this year on January 1, 19X3. Its charter authorizes the issuance of 10,000 shares of no par common stock and 10,000 shares of no par cumulative preferred stock. State law requires all proceeds received from the sale of no par stock to be treated as minimum legal capital. The corporation had the following transactions dealing with owners' equity in its first year ended December 31, 19X3:
(a) Issued 6,000 shares of common stock for $15 per share.
(b) Issued 1,000 shares preferred stock in exchange for land valued at $40,000.
(c) Entered into subscription agreements to issue 1,000 shares of common stock at $16 per share, $5 per share received at the signing of the agreement, the remainder to be received in six months.
(d) Declared the semiannual dividend of $3,000 on the preferred stock.
(e) Paid the preferred dividend.
(f) Received the remainder of the subscription payments described in (c) above.
(g) Declared a 5% common stock dividend at a time when the common stock had a fair market value of $20 per share.
(h) Distributed the stock dividend noted above in (g).
(i) Declared the semiannual preferred dividend of $3,000.
(j) Declared a 20¢ per share annual dividend on common stock.

REQUIRED:
(a) Give the general journal entries necessary to record these transactions.
(b) Prepare the Owners' Equity section of the balance sheet for this corporation at December 31, 19X3, assuming the corporation had net income of $15,000.

□ 13
STATEMENT OF CHANGES IN FINANCIAL POSITION

CONCEPT OF FUNDS

STATEMENT OF CHANGES IN FINANCIAL POSITION: WORKING CAPITAL DEFINITION OF FUNDS

PREPARING THE STATEMENT (WORKING CAPITAL)

ANALYSIS OF CHANGES IN WORKING CAPITAL

ANALYSIS OF FINANCIAL DATA

FUNDS FROM OPERATIONS

SALE OF NONCURRENT ASSET

ISSUANCE OF CAPITAL STOCK

DECLARATION OF DIVIDENDS

RETIREMENT OF LONG-TERM DEBT

EXCHANGE TRANSACTIONS

STATEMENT OF CHANGES IN FINANCIAL POSITION: CASH DEFINITION OF FUNDS

PREPARING THE STATEMENT

CASH USED OR PROVIDED BY OPERATIONS

CASH USED OR PROVIDED FROM OTHER SOURCES

USE OF CASH FLOW DATA

SUMMARY

A SUPPLEMENTARY DISCUSSION: WORKSHEET APPROACH TO PREPARING THE STATEMENT OF CHANGES IN FINANCIAL POSITION

☐ OBJECTIVES

AFTER STUDYING THIS CHAPTER, YOU SHOULD BE ABLE TO DO THE FOLLOWING:

1. LIST SOME QUESTIONS THAT CAN BE ANSWERED BY REFERENCE TO THE STATEMENT OF CHANGES IN FINANCIAL POSITION.

2. PREPARE A STATEMENT OF CHANGES IN FINANCIAL POSITION USING THE WORKING CAPITAL DEFINITION OF FUNDS.

3. PREPARE A STATEMENT OF CHANGES IN FINANCIAL POSITION USING A CASH DEFINITION OF FUNDS.

In previous chapters, we have focused primarily on two of the financial statements that must be provided to external financial statement users—the income statement and the balance sheet. The income statement summarizes the results of operations, and the balance sheet presented in comparative form indicates the amount of assets, liabilities, and owners' equity, as well as net changes in these amounts between two periods. However, certain information that would be very useful to a variety of financial statement users regarding the financing and investment activities of a firm can be obtained only partially from the income statement and balance sheet. For example, the fact that a corporation acquired machinery with a fair market value of $80,000 for 5,000 shares of its common stock might be deduced by an extremely observant balance sheet reader who notes that the common stock account and machinery account have both increased, but the reader could not be certain that his deduction was correct. A variety of other financing and investment activities are obscured by their presentation in the income statement and balance sheet. What were the sources of liquid assets used by the firm this period? To what use were the firms liquid assets placed? Were there transactions that did not involve liquid assets in the current period but that were, nonetheless, material financing and investment activities of the firm this period? Neither the income statement nor the balance sheet provide the necessary information to allow the investor or creditor to answer these questions. As a result, it may be difficult for the financial statement user to determine the likelihood that dividends will be paid in the future, to determine if the present level of financial resources is sufficient to continue operations at their present or increased levels, or to determine if expansion of the firm will require additional resources.

Because of the perceived value of this information to the financial statement user, the Accounting Principles Board issued Opinion 19, "Reporting Changes in Financial Position," in 1971. This opinion recognized the importance of adequately disclosing the financing and investment activities of a firm. It requires that a third financial statement, called a Statement of Changes in Financial Position, be prepared by accountants and presented to financial statement users along with the income statement and balance sheet. This third major financial statement will be discussed in this chapter.

Concept of Funds The *statement of changes in financial position* focuses on reporting the inflows and outflows of resources during the period. The basic objectives of the statement are: (1) to summarize the financing activities that result in inflows of resources and the investing activities that result in outflows of resources; and (2) to explain the changes in asset, liability, and owners' equity accounts during the period.

STATEMENT OF CHANGES IN FINANCIAL POSITION

The Accounting Principles Board was faced with a dilemma in its deliberations of APB Opinion 19. If the statement was to focus on inflows or sources of resources, and outflows or uses of resources, how was the term resources, often called *funds,* to be defined? Some assountants argued that funds should be defined to mean only *cash*. The statement would have as its primary objective in this event the explanation of changes in the cash account, perhaps also including near-cash accounts such as temporary investments. All transactions during the period that increase or decrease cash would be summarized and disclosed in the statement. Many accountants believed, however, that such a narrow definition of funds would seriously limit the usefulness of a statement of changes in financial position. It would fail to disclose many material transactions, such as the exchange of common stock for equipment, because they did not involve cash.

Another common definition of funds is *working capital*. As you recall, working capital is the difference between current assets and current liabilities. When funds are defined as working capital, the statement summarizes and explains the financing and investing activities that caused increases or decreases in working capital during the period. For example, the issuance of bonds for cash would be reported on the statement, because it results in an increase in working capital. Not only would transactions involving cash be reported but also the statement would report a broad range of transactions not involving cash. For example, using the working capital definition of funds, the acquisition of equipment for short-term notes would be reported on the statement, because it results in a decrease in working capital. Most accountants feel that the working capital definition of funds is more meaningful to financial statement users, because it encompasses changes in the net amount of all current liquid resources available to the firm—not just changes in cash.

In explaining changes in financial positions, the use of either the working capital or the cash definition of funds sometimes excludes certain transactions involving significant financing or investing activities, because they do not directly affect cash or working capital during the period. Transactions that represent major financing and investing activities and do not involve changes in working capital or cash include the issuance of bonds or capital stock to acquire long-term assets and the conversion of preferred stock into common stock. The Accounting Principles Board concluded that such transactions should be reported in the statement of changes in financial position, even though they do not result in changes in cash or working capital balances. This approach is referred to as the *all-financial-resources concept* of the statement of changes in financial position. It is applied by defining funds as either cash or working capital—whichever the accountant feels is most appropriate under the circumstances—followed by the disclosure of other significant financial activities excluded by the definition of funds used. In this fashion, the statement of changes in financial position emphasizes changes in the liquid resources of the firm but also reports the effect of other financing activities.

Because of the extensive use of the working capital definition of funds, we will first examine the statement prepared using the all-financial-resources concept in conjunction with the working capital definition of funds. The last section of this chapter discusses the principles involved in preparing the statement using the cash definition of funds. A supplementary discussion will review a work sheet approach for preparing the statement.

Statement of Changes in Financial Position: Working Capital Definition of Funds

A statement of changes in financial position prepared using the working capital definition of funds is presented in Exhibit 13-1. The statement is divided into two parts. The first part details the sources and uses of funds, including both changes in net working capital items and material financing as well as investment activities not involving working capital accounts. The second part is a summary of changes in specific working capital accounts.

There are several important things to note about the nature and form of the statement. APB Opinion No. 19 recognized the need for flexibility in the form, content, and terminology of the statement of changes in financial position. The Opinion indicated that, provided certain guidelines are met, "...the Statement may take whatever form gives the most useful portrayal of the financing and investing activities and the changes in financial position of the reporting entity." Consequently, the specific form of presentation has varied considerably in practice.

Note also that the emphasis of the statement of changes in financial position is on the net movement of resources to and from working capital. Events affecting *only* working capital are generally neither sources nor uses of working capital. For example, the collection of $1,000 in accounts receivable involves increasing one working capital account and decreasing another—increasing cash and decreasing accounts receivable—resulting in no net change in working capital. The statement is not designed to highlight such changes, although their net result will be shown in the latter part of the statement.

Preparing the Statement (Working Capital)

The data for Courtney Corporation in Exhibits 13-2 and 13-3 will be used to illustrate the preparation of the statement using a working capital definition of funds. Comparative balance sheets provide most of the essential data needed to prepare a statement of changes in financial position. However,

EXHIBIT 13-1
COURTNEY CORPORATION
Statement of Changes in Financial Postion
(Working Capital)
For The Year Ended December 31, 19X2

Sources of Funds:			
Operations:			
Net Income			$ 25,000
Add Expenses Not Affecting Working Capital:			
Depreciation Expense			10,000
Working Capital Provided by Operations			$ 35,000
Issuance of Capital Stock			15,000
Sale of Land			15,000
Financial Transactions Not Affecting Working Capital:			
Bonds Payable Issued in Exchange for Equipment			50,000
Total Sources of Funds			$115,000
Uses of Funds:			
Retirement of Bonds Payable			$ 35,000
Declaration of Cash Dividends			5,000
Financial Transactions not Affecting Working Capital:			
Acquisition of Equipment by Issuance of Bonds Payable			50,000
Total Uses of Funds			90,000
Increase in Working Capital			$ 25,000

Summary of Changes in Working Capital			
Working Capital Items	12/31/X2	12/31/X1	
			Increase (Decrease) In Working Capital
Current Assets:			
Cash	$38,000	$30,000	$ 8,000
Accounts Receivable (Net)	35,000	40,000	(5,000)
Inventory	99,000	88,000	11,000
Prepaid Expenses	3,000	2,000	1,000
Current Liabilities:			
Accounts Payable	84,000	95,000	11,000
Accrued Liabilities	6,000	5,000	(1,000)
Increase in Working Capital			$ 25,000

some other information is also required, such as income statement, and details about various financing and investing transactions.

Working capital is equal to the difference between current assets and current liabilities. The change in working capital from the beginning to the end of the year for Courtney Corporation can be determined by examining the

Analysis of Changes in Working Capital

ANALYSIS OF CHANGES IN WORKING CAPITAL

EXHIBIT 13-2
COURTNEY CORPORATION
Comparative Balance Sheet
As of December 31, 19X1 and 19X2

	December 31, 19X2	December 31, 19X1
Assets		
Current Assets:		
Cash	$ 38,000	$ 30,000
Accounts Receivable (Net)	35,000	40,000
Inventory	99,000	88,000
Prepaid Expenses	3,000	2,000
Total Current Assets	$175,000	$160,000
Buildings and Equipment	350,000	300,000
Less: Accumulated Depreciation	(70,000)	(60,000)
Land	105,000	120,000
Total Assets	$560,000	$520,000
Liabilities and Stockholders' Equity		
Current Liabilities:		
Accounts Payable	$ 84,000	$ 95,000
Accrued Liabilities	6,000	5,000
Total Current Liabilities	$ 90,000	$100,000
Bonds Payable	145,000	130,000
Capital Stock ($1 par Value)	55,000	50,000
Additional Paid-in Capital	210,000	200,000
Retained Earnings	60,000	40,000
Total Liabilities and Stockholders' Equity	$560,000	$520,000

current asset and current liability sections of the balance sheet (Exhibit 13-2):

	12/31/X2	*12/31/X1*	*Change*
Current Assets	$175,000	$160,000	$15,000
Current Liabilities	90,000	100,000	10,000
Working Capital	$ 85,000	$ 60,000	$25,000

The net increase or decrease in working capital is shown as one amount at the bottom of both parts of the statement of changes in financial position, and it is considered as the amount to be explained by the body of the statement. The $25,000 increase in working capital for Courtney Corporation is a result of the $15,000 net increase in the components of current assets and a $10,000 decrease in the components of current liabilities.

EXHIBIT 13-3
COURTNEY CORPORATION
Income Statement
For The Year Ended December 31, 19X2

Sales		$200,000
Cost of Goods Sold		105,000
Gross Margin		95,000
Expenses:		
Operating Expenses (excluding depreciation)	$50,000	
Depreciation Expense	10,000	60,000
Income Before Taxes		35,000
Income Tax Expense		10,000
Net Income		$ 25,000

Supplementary Information:
1. Cash dividends declared and paid amounted to $5,000.
2. Acquired equipment with a market value of $50,000 by issuing bonds payable with a maturity value of $50,000.
3. Bonds Payable of $35,000 were retired at an amount equal to maturity value.
4. Land was sold for $15,000. Since it originally cost $15,000, no gain or loss was recorded on the sale.

The relationship between working capital accounts and nonworking capital accounts provides the basis for preparing the statement of changes in financial position. Any transaction that results in an increase in working capital is a source of working capital, and any transaction that results in a decrease in working capital is a use of working capital. Thus, a necessary step in preparing the statement is separation of the transactions that result in a change in working capital from those that have no effect on working capital. In this process, all transactions may be divided into three groups:

1. *Transactions that affect only current asset and/or current liability accounts.* These transactions affect the components of working capital, but they do not change the net amount of working capital. For example, receipt of payment for a receivable will increase cash and decrease accounts receivable. However, net current assets will remain the same. Such transactions are not considered in preparing the statement. APB Opinion 19 requires, however, that the net changes in each element of working capital be disclosed in a supplementary schedule or be included in the body of the statement, as shown in Exhibit 13-1.

2. *Transactions that affect only nonworking capital accounts.* These transactions result in no change in working capital. As discussed previously, however, these transactions must be analyzed to determine if they represent significant financial activities. For example, the declaration of a stock dividend would not appear on the statement, because it does not rep-

resent a significant financial activity. No substantive economic transaction regarding funds of the firm has occurred as yet. However, the declaration could have significance to investors, creditors or others. On the other hand, the issuance of long-term bonds to acquire a long-term asset is a significant financial transaction. Note how such a transaction is reported on the statement of changes in financial position in Exhibit 13-1. The issuance of the bonds is treated as a source of funds, and the acquisition of the equipment is treated as a use of funds. Both are under descriptive headings that make it clear that working capital was not directly affected.

3. *Transactions that affect both a working capital account and a nonworking capital account.* These transactions result in either an increase in working capital (by increasing a current asset or decreasing a current liability) or a decrease in working capital (by decreasing a current asset or increasing a current liability). These transactions are reported on the statement as either a source or a use of funds. The sale of a building for cash will increase working capital and is reported as a source of funds. Likewise, converting short-term bank notes (current liability) into long-term debt will also increase working capital and will be reported as a source of funds.

Thus, the basic information necessary for preparing the statement is obtained by dividing the elements of the condensed balance sheet into two categories: (1) working capital accounts, and (2) all other (nonworking capital) accounts. The statement is prepared by analyzing the changes in nonworking capital accounts to determine the effects of these changes on working capital and to determine the existence of any significant activities that did not affect working capital.

In general, with the exception of significant financial activities that do not affect working capital, the transactions that are summarized on the statement are those that affect both a working capital account and a nonworking capital account. Those events that result in a source or a use of funds can be divided into the following categories:

Sources of funds:

1. Revenues from operations.
2. Sale of noncurrent assets.
3. Borrowing by issuing long-term debt.
4. Issuance of capital stock.

Uses of funds:

1. Expenses related to a decrease in current assets or an increase in current liabilities.
2. Declaration of cash dividends.
3. Acquisition of noncurrent assets.
4. Retirement of long-term debt.
5. Purchase of treasury stock.

Normally, the source of funds from revenues and the use of funds from expenses are netted and reported as either a source or a use of funds from operations, as shown in Exhibit 13-1.

Analysis of Financial Data. As indicated above, the statement of changes in financial position normally includes two sections. The first section reports sources and uses of working capital (including significant financial activities not affecting working capital) and the net change in working capital for the period. The second section summarizes the changes in the individual working capital accounts during the period.

The $25,000 increase in working capital from the beginning to the end of the period is determined by examining the current assets and current liabilities in the comparative balance sheet shown in Exhibit 13-2. The causes of the net increase in working capital are explained by analyzing the changes that occurred in the remaining accounts (other than working capital accounts) in the comparative balance sheet. The sources and uses of funds for Courtney Corporation are analyzed in the following paragraphs.

Funds from Operations. Normally, the reported amount of net income is not the same as the source of funds from operations, because the income statement usually includes expenses that did not cause a decrease in working capital during the period. Expenses such as depreciation and amortization result in decreases in noncurrent assets and reduce net income, but they do not reduce working capital. For example, the entry to record depreciation is a debit to depreciation expense and a credit to accumulated depreciation. Although net income is reduced by this entry, working capital is unaffected. As a result, adjustments are required in the reported net income or loss to determine the amount of funds provided from operations.

The amount of working capital from operations can be determined by subtracting from revenues only those expenses that resulted in an outflow of working capital during the period. Since the "nonfund" expenses reduce net income without reducing working capital, an alternative approach for computing funds from operations is to add to net income those expenses that did not reduce working capital. This approach is simpler and is the one normally followed. Thus, the working capital provided by operations for Courtney Corporation is determined as follows:

Net Income	$25,000
Add Expenses Not Requiring Use of Working Capital	
Depreciation Expense	10,000
Working Capital Provided by Operations	$35,000

Although expenses not using working capital are shown as an addition in this approach, it is important to understand that they do not really represent a source of funds. Instead, they are added because the net income figure, which includes expenses not reducing working capital, is less than the amount of actual working capital provided by operations.

Sale of Noncurrent Asset. An examination of the comparative balance sheet and a consideration of additional information relating to these accounts are necessary to determine whether funds have been generated through the sale of noncurrent assets. The comparative balance sheet for Courtney Corporation shows that the noncurrent asset, land, decreased by $15,000 during the year. Since no gain or loss on the sale is reported in the income statement, the proceeds on the sale must be equal to the book value of the land sold. Therefore, a sale of land for $15,000 is reported as a source of funds in the statement. If a gain or loss had been present, an adjustment to the income account would be made.

Issuance of Capital Stock. To determine if funds have been provided by the issuance of capital stock, we must examine the comparative balance sheet to see if any capital stock accounts have increased. The balance sheet of Courtney Corporation reveals that capital stock increased by $5,000 and additional contributed capital increased by $10,000. Since there is no indication in the additional information provided that the increase was a result of a stock dividend or other nonfund transaction, the increase must be the result of the issuance of capital stock for cash. The entry to record the issuance of the stock was:

Cash	$15,000	
Capital Stock		$ 5,000
Additional Contributed Capital		10,000

Accordingly, a source of funds of $15,000 is reported in the statement, because the transaction resulted in a $15,000 increase in working capital.

Declaration of Dividends. The $20,000 increase in the retained earnings account may be explained as follows:

Retained Earnings (January 1, 19X2)	$40,000
Add: Net Income	25,000
Deduct: Cash Dividends	(5,000)
Retained Earnings (December 31, 19X2)	$60,000

The effect of net income in determining working capital from operations has already been discussed and is shown on the statement. However, Courtney Corporation apparently declared and paid cash dividends during 19X2, since no dividend payable liability appears on the balance sheet. The cash dividend of $5,000 reduces working capital and is reported on the statement as a use of funds. If the declaration of a dividend occurs during one period and the payment occurs during a subsequent period, the reduction in working capital is reported in the period of the declaration. This occurs because a current liability, dividends payable, is recorded at the declaration date, increasing current liabilities and reducing working capital. The entry of payment, a debt to dividends payable and a credit to cash, has no effect on working capital.

Retirement of Long-Term Debt. An examination of the comparative balance sheet for bonds payable indicates that the balance in this account decreased by $15,000 during the year. The additional data provided indicates that bonds payable of $35,000 were retired at an amount equal to maturity value and that $50,000 of bonds payable were issued in exchange for equipment.

The information that the bonds were retired at maturity value and the absence of bond premium or discount accounts is consistent with the fact that there was no gain or loss on retirement reported in the income statement. Thus, the retirement is reflected as a use of funds of $35,000 on the statement. The issuance of bonds payable in exchange for equipment, which does not affect working capital, is discussed in the following section on exchange transactions.

Exchange Transactions. Under the all-financial-resources concept discussed previously in the chapter, the statement of changes in financial position should reflect all significant financing and investing activities during the period. Consequently, exchange transactions affecting only non-working capital accounts that have significant financing and investing aspects are reported as both a source and use of working capital.

During 19X2, Courtney Corporation issued long-term bonds payable with a maturity value of $50,000 in exchange for equipment with a fair market value of $50,000. The entry to record this exchange was:

Equipment	$50,000	
Bonds Payable		$50,000

Although this exchange transaction did not affect any current asset or current liability account, under the all-financial-resources concept, the issuance of the bonds is reported as a source of funds, and the purchase of equipment is considered to be a use of funds. Of course, since the transaction has no direct effect on working capital, the source and the use are equal in amount and offset each other in the statement. This transaction would be shown in the statement as follows:

Source of Funds	
Financial Transactions Not Affecting Working Capital	
Bonds Payable Issued in Exchange for Equipment	50,000
Uses of Funds	
Financial Transactions not Affecting Working Capital	
Acquisition of Equipment by Issuance of Bonds Payable	50,000

Some transactions not affecting working capital are not considered to be significant financial transactions, and they are not reported in the statement. For example, a stock dividend is not considered to be a significant exchange transaction.

The resulting statement of changes in financial position for Courtney Corporation, prepared by using the working capital definition of funds, is shown in Exhibit 13-1. The increase in working capital reported in the first section of the statement ($25,000) agrees with the net change in working capital in the second section, which is determined from the analysis of the changes in the individual current asset and current liability accounts.

Statement of Changes in Financial Position: Cash Definition of Funds

As we indicate earlier in the chapter, the term "funds" may be defined in different ways in developing a statement of changes in financial position. Although a majority of companies define funds in terms of working capital, APB Opinion No. 19 states that each firm should adopt the presentation that is most informative in presenting its financing and investing activities and changes in financial position. Consequently, some firms find it more meaningful to interpret funds as cash (or cash and its equivalents, such as temporary investments). The resulting statement is a summary of sources and uses of cash. As in the working capital approach, the statement based on the cash definition should also reflect the financing and investing aspects of significant transactions that do not affect cash. A statement of changes in financial position for Courtney Corporation prepared by using the cash definition of funds is shown in Exhibit 13-4.

The form of the statement in Exhibit 13-4 differs somewhat from one prepared using the working capital definition of funds. Because funds are defined in terms of the balance of only one account that uses a cash definition, it is not necessary to detail the makeup of the specific account changes as it was when funds were defined in terms of a group of accounts. Consequently, there is no need to prepare the second portion of the statement summarizing specific account changes. In addition, the determination of the amount of cash provided by operations is somewhat more involved than the determination of the amount of working capital provided by operations. As a result, a substantial portion of the typical statement of changes in financial position prepared by using the cash definition of funds is devoted to showing the adjustments necessary to calculate cash used or provided by operations.

In other respects, the statement prepared on the basis of a cash definition of funds is very similar to the statement prepared using the working capital definition of funds. The statement discloses material financing and investment activities that do not involve cash in the same way that they

EXHIBIT 13-4
COURTNEY CORPORATION
Statement of Changes in Financial Position (Cash)
For the Year Ended December 31, 19X2

Sources of Funds
Operations

Net Income		$25,000	
Add (Deduct) Items Not Requiring or Providing Cash in the Current Year			
Depreciation Expense	$10,000		
Accounts Receivable Decrease	5,000		
Inventory Increase	(11,000)		
Accounts Payable Decrease	(11,000)		
Prepaid Expenses Increase	(1,000)		
Accrued Liabilities Increase	1,000	(7,000)	
Cash Provided by Operations			$18,000
Issuance of Capital Stock			15,000
Sale of Land			15,000
Financial Transactions Not Affecting Cash:			
Bonds Payable Issued in Exchange for Equipment			50,000
Total Source of Funds			$98,000
Uses of Funds			
Retirement of Bonds Payable			$35,000
Payment of Cash Dividends			5,000
Financial Transactions Not Affecting Cash:			
Acquisition of Equipment by Issuance of Bonds Payable			50,000
Total Uses of Funds			$90,000
Increase in Cash			$ 8,000

would if funds had been defined as working capital. It is important to emphasize, however, that by narrowing the definition of funds to only one account, Cash, the search for material financing and investing transactions not included in the definition of funds must be broadened to encompass a greater number of accounts and potential transactions. For example, if machinery is acquired in exchange for short-term notes, this should be disclosed on the statement. If we defined funds to be working capital, no special analysis would be required to note and report this transaction. Our analysis of working capital changes would have noted that a current liability had increased, reducing working capital. By defining funds as cash, however, an analysis of changes in cash would fail to pick up this transaction, since cash was not involved in the transaction. In practice, the decision as to which definition of funds is most appropriate may depend, in large measure, on the presence or absence of these kinds of transactions. If there are several material transactions affecting working capital but not affecting cash, the accountant may decide that the working capital definition of funds is more meaningful than the cash definition. In any event, if funds are defined to be cash, such transactions should be disclosed on the statement under a descriptive title indicating that cash was not directly affected.

**Preparing
the Statement
(Cash Definition)**

Here we use the financial data for Courtney Corporation that are shown in Exhibits 13-2 and 13-3 to illustrate the preparation of a statement of changes in financial position using the cash definition of funds. By referring to Exhibit 13-2, note that cash has increased $8,000 between December 31, 19X1, and December 31, 19X2. The objectives of the statement are to explain the causes of the $8,000 increase in cash and to disclose other material financing and investing transactions. The change in cash may be explained by analyzing the changes that occurred in the remaining accounts (other than cash) in the comparative balance sheet. The causes of the change in the cash balance are determined in the same fashion as is described for the working capital approach, with the addition of certain adjustments to determine cash from operations.

Cash Used or Provided by Operations. Using the working capital approach, the funds provided by operations were determined on the accrual basis of accounting. For example, revenues were considered a source of funds regardless of whether the sales were for cash or on account. To determine cash used or provided by operations requires conversion from the accrual basis to the cash basis of accounting. One way to calculate cash used or provided by operations is to adjust the components of the entire income statement from the accrual basis to a cash basis. For example, Courtney Corporation had sales of $200,000 during 19X0, and the accounts receivable balance decreased from $40,000 at the beginning of the year to $35,000 at the end of the year. In this case, the cash inflow is $205,000, the amount of sales plus the decrease in accounts receivable. Similarly, the cost of goods sold of $105,000 on an accrual basis is converted to a cash basis by adding two items: the $11,000 increase in inventory, since purchases (an outflow of funds) exceeded the related accrual charge to cost of goods sold, and the $11,000 decrease in accounts payable (an outflow of funds), since cash disbursements for purchases exceeded purchases during the year. Cash disbursements during the year for purchases were, therefore, $127,000 [cost of goods sold (105,000) + increase in inventory (11,000) + decrease in accounts payable (11,000)]. The adjustments that are normally required to convert an accrual basis income statement to a cash basis income statement are as follows:

Accrual Basis Item	± Adjustments	=	Cash Basis Item
Sales	− Increase in Accounts Receivable + Decrease in Accounts Receivable		Cash Collected from Customers
Cost of Goods Sold	+ Increase in Inventory − Decrease in Inventory − Increase in Accounts Payable + Decrease in Accounts Payable		Cash Payments for Purchases
Prepaid Expenses	+ Increase in Corresponding Prepaid Asset − Decrease in Corresponding Prepaid Asset		Cash Payments for Prepaid Expenses
Accrued Expenses	− Increase in Corresponding Accrued Liability + Decrease in Corresponding Accrued Liability		Cash Payments for Accrued Liabilities

Once the income statement to a cash-basis income statement has been changed, all that must be done to determine cash used or provided by operations is to reduce expenses by the amount of noncash depreciation or amortization. Then cash expenses are simply subtracted from cash revenues. The computation of cash provided by operations for Courtney Corporation during 19X2 is shown in Exhibit 13-5.

Instead of separately converting each item on the income statement to the cash basis, a second approach to computing the cash provided by operations is to adjust the amount of net income for the effect of changes during the period in working capital items other than cash. This is the format normally used on the statement of changes in financial position, as shown in Exhibit 13-4, to calculate cash provided or used by operations. The calculation is made by adding to net income those adjustments that result in an increase in cash collected from customers or a decrease in cash payments for operations, and subtracting those adjustments that result in a decrease in cash collected from customers or an increase in cash payments for operations. The format for this adjustment procedure is somewhat different than that used to convert the full income statement to a cash basis and is illustrated below:

Net Income (Loss)

Add (Deduct) Items Not Requiring or Providing Cash in Current Year:

− Increase in Accounts Receivable

EXHIBIT 13-5
Cash Provided by Operations For
Courtney Corporation During 19X2
Calculated by Adjusting the Entire Income Statement

Revenues:			
Sales		$200,000	
+ Decrease in Accounts Receivable		5,000	
Cash Collections from Customers			$205,000
Expenses:			
Cost of Goods Sold		$105,000	
+ Increase in Inventory		11,000	
+ Decrease in Accounts Payable		11,000	
Cash Payments for Purchases			127,000
Operating Expenses and Income Taxes		$ 70,000	
− Depreciation	$(10,000)		
− Increase in Accrued Liabilities	(1,000)	(11,000)	
Balance		$ 59,000	
+ Increase in Prepaid Expenses		1,000	
Cash Payments for Operating Expenses and Income Taxes			60,000
Total Cash Payments for Operations			187,000
Cash Provided by Operations			$ 18,000

+ Decrease in Accounts Receivable

− Increase in Inventory

+ Decrease in Inventory

+ Increase in Accounts Payable

− Decrease in Accounts Payable

− Increase in Prepaid Asset Accounts

+ Decrease in Prepaid Asset Accounts

+ Increase in Accrued Liability Accounts

− Decrease in Accrued Liability Accounts

+ Depreciation, Amortization

Cash provided by operations for Courtney Corporation for 19X2 using this calculation format is shown in Exhibit 13-6. It is the same as that used in the statement of changes in financial pposition shown in Exhibit 13-4.

The amount of cash provided by operations calculated by adjusting the full income statement is, of course, the same as that calculated by adjusting net income, but note that the signs of the adjustments affecting expenses are reversed. For example, an increase in inventory has the effect of increasing cash payments for purchases and, hence, it is shown as a posi-

EXHIBIT 13-6
Cash Provided By Operations
For Courtney Corporation During 19X2
Calculated by Adjusting Net Income

Net Income		$25,000
Add (Deduct) Items Not Requiring		
or Providing Cash in Current Year		
Depreciation Expense	$10,000	
Decrease in Accounts Receivable	5,000	
Increase in Inventory	(11,000)	
Decrease in Accounts Payable	(11,000)	
Increase in Prepaid Expenses	(1,000)	
Increase in Accrued Liabilities	1,000	(7,000)
Cash Provided by Operations		$18,000

tive (+) adjustment in adjusting cost of goods sold. However, when the adjustment is made directly to net income, from which cost of goods sold had already been subtracted, the adjustment for an increase in inventory is negative (−), because it results in a decrease in cash provided by operations. With a little practice, adjustments to determine cash provided or used by operations will become easy to handle.

Cash Used or Provided from Other Sources. In this example, all changes in current assets and current liabilities were related to operations. In some instances, for example, the payment of dividends that have been declared, a current liability account and a current asset account are reduced in a transaction not related to operations. Care should be exercised to insure that such transactions are not reported as resulting from operations. Transactions of this kind should be reported separately.

Other sources and uses of funds should be reported in the same fashion under the cash definition of funds as under the working capital definition of funds. Transactions that are material financing or investing transactions but that do not involve cash should be reported both as a source and a use of funds under descriptive titles which clearly indicate that cash was not directly affected by the transaction (see Exhibit 13-4).

The statement of changes in financial position with funds defined as cash provides a summary of the effect of all transactions on a firm's cash (or cash and equivalents) position during a period. Cash flow data, however, are subject to misinterpretation by financial statement users. The APB, in Opinion 19, is very concerned that the presentation of cash flow data, especially figures such as cash flow per share, might confuse and mislead fi-

Use of Cash Flow Data

nancial statement users, causing them to believe that this figure is an improvement on or a substitute for properly determined net income—which it clearly is not. The Board recommends that:

"...isolated statistics of working capital or cash provided by operations, especially per share amounts, not be presented in annual reports to shareholders."

If per share or other cash flow data is to be provided, the Board gives specific recommendations as to the manner in which it should be presented to minimize the chance of misleading or confusing financial statement users.

Summary

The statement of changes in financial position provides the financial statement user with important information about the financing and investing activities of the firm that is not available on the income statement or balance sheet. APB Opinion 19 requires that the statement of changes in financial position be presented in all instances where an income statement and balance sheet are presented. The statement summarizes and explains the changes in the funds of the firm during the year, plus discloses other material financing and investing transactions of the firm. The APB concludes that funds may be defined as cash, cash and cash equivalents, working capital, or other fund concepts that in the opinion of the accountant presents the financing and investing activities of the firm most meaningfully to financial statement users. The working capital definition of funds is used most often, since it highlights the changes in all liquid resources of the firm during the year. The cash definition of funds is also found in practice. The form of the statement will vary greatly, depending on the definition of funds chosen and the presentation that the accountant believes most meaningfully details the source and use of funds during the year. APB Opinion 19 directs that the statement be prepared and presented on the basis of an "all-financial-resources concept," explaining not only the sources and uses of funds, as defined, but also material financing and investing transactions not directly affecting funds.

Supplementary Discussion: Worksheet Approach to Preparing the Statement of Changes in Financial Position

In the illustration presented in this chapter, the statement of changes in financial position was prepared directly from the changes in the comparative balance sheet accounts. In more complex situations, various methods are used to aid in the preparation of the statement. One of the most common is the use of a work sheet to categorize and summarize the information to be presented in the statement of changes in financial position. A worksheet for Courtney Corporation is shown in Exhibit 13-7. In this example, it is assumed that funds are defined as working capital.

The worksheet described in this section is composed of four columns and an upper and a lower section. Comparative balance sheet data are entered in the upper

EXHIBIT 13-7
COURTNEY CORPORATION
Worksheet for Statement of Changes in Financial Position
(Working Capital)
For the Year Ended December 31, 19X2

	Balances December 31, 19X1	Analysis of Entries for 19X2 (Source) Debit	(Use) Credit	Balances December 31, 19X2
Working Capital	$ 60,000	$ 25,000(1)		$ 85,000
Building and Equipment	300,000	50,000(9)		350,000
Land	120,000		$ 15,000(5)	105,000
Total	480,000			540,000
Accumulated Depreciation	60,000		10,000(3)	70,000
Bonds Payable	130,000	35,000(7)	50,000(6)	145,000
Capital Stock	50,000		5,000(4)	55,000
Additional Contributed Capital	200,000		10,000(4)	210,000
Retained Earnings	40,000	5,000(8)	25,000(2)	60,000
Total	480,000			540,000
Sources of Funds:				
From Operations:				
Net Income		25,000(2)		
Add:			Total from	
Depreciation Expense		10,000(3)	operations	
Issuance of Capital Stock		15,000(4)		
Sale of Land		15,000(5)		
Issuance of Bonds Payable in Exchange for Equipment		50,000(6)		
Uses of Funds:				
Retirement of Bonds Payable			35,000(7)	
Declaration of Dividends			5,000(8)	
Acquisition of Equipment in exchange for Bonds Payable			50,000(9)	
Increase in Working Capital			25,000(1)	
		230,000	230,000	

section, and the statement of changes in financial position is developed in the lower section. The steps involved in preparing a worksheet are as follows:

1. The net amount of working capital and the balances of the noncurrent items appearing on the balance sheet at the beginning of the period (or end of the previous period) are listed in the first column of the upper section of the worksheet. The corresponding balances at the end of the period are entered into the fourth column.

2. The transactions that explain the changes in the balances of the noncurrent accounts from the beginning to the end of the period are entered in the upper section of the middle pair of columns, and the effect of each transaction is listed as a source or use of working capital in the lower section. A source of working capital appears in the debit column, and a use of working capital is shown in the credit column in the lower portion of the worksheet. The change in net working capital is entered in the upper section as a debit or credit, and this amount is entered in the lower section as the increase (credit) or decrease (debit) in working capital for the period.

Explanations for the individual entries that appear in the middle pair of columns on the worksheet are given below. The number preceding each explanation corresponds with the numbers appearing in parentheses with the entries on the worksheet.

1. The net working capital increased from $60,000 at the beginning of the year to $85,000 at the end of the year. The increase in working capital, $25,000, is entered as a debit to working capital in the upper section to reconcile the change, and as a credit in the lower section to indicate an increase in working capital.

2. The net income for the period of $25,000 is included in the ending retained earnings balance. This amount is credited to retained earnings to explain a portion of the change in that account, and is credited to "sources of funds: from operations" in the lower section. The $25,000 net income does not represent all entries affecting funds from operations, since adjustments may be necessary for expenses that do not require an outlay of working capital.

3. The accumulated depreciation account increased by $10,000 during the year as a result of the entry to record depreciation expense. Since depreciation expense does not involve an outflow of working capital, this amount is credited to accumulated depreciation in the upper section, and is debited to "source of funds: from operations" in the lower section. In this illustration, this is the only adjustment to net income required in determining working capital provided by operations. The net income and the adjustment are bracketed on the worksheet to indicate the amount of working capital from operations.

4. The sale of capital stock for $15,000 is recorded as a source of working capital. The par value of the stock sold is credited to the capital stock account, the amount of proceeds in excess of par value is credited to additional contributed capital, and a source of working capital is debited in the lower section of the worksheet.

5. The sale of land for $15,000 is recorded on the worksheet as a credit to land in the upper section of the worksheet, and as a source of working capital (debit) in the lower section.

6. and 9. Equipment valued at $50,000 acquired in exchange for long-term bonds of $50,000 par value. Since this is a significant financial activity not affecting working capital, it is recorded as both a source and a use of funds. The bonds payable account is credited for $50,000, and a source of funds is recorded on the lower section of the worksheet. Similarly, the equipment account is debited for $50,000, and a use of funds is credited.

7. During the year, $35,000 of bonds payable were retired at an amount equal to

maturity value. This is recorded in the lower section of the worksheet as a use of working capital (credit), with the corresponding debit in the upper section explaining the net change in the bonds payable account.

8. The cash dividend of $5,000, which caused retained earnings to decrease, is reported as a use of funds by debiting retained earnings in the upper section and crediting use of funds from dividends in the lower section of the worksheet.

When all of the changes in the noncurrent accounts are explained, the statement may be prepared from the worksheet. Note, again, that the debits in the analysis (that is, the middle two) columns in the lower section of the worksheet are the sources of funds, and that the credits are the uses of funds. With all the necessary items to be included on the statement summarized on the worksheet, the preparation of the statement should follow easily. The statement of changes in financial position that was prepared from the completed worksheet is shown in Exhibit 13-1.

Statement of changes in financial position	**Key Terms**
Funds	
Cash	
Working capital	
All-financial-resources concept	

1. Describe the all-resources concept of a statement of changes in financial position. **Questions**

2. Identify factors that explain the difference between net income and increases in working capital.

3. Identify at least one accounting event that would not be reflected on a statement of changes in financial position, even though it would be reflected on other financial statements.

4. Losses on operations (negative income) must be reflected in the financial statements. Describe how these losses would be disclosed on a statement of changes in financial position. How would these losses be disclosed on a statement of sources and applications of working capital?

5. Will a conventional statement of sources and applications of funds disclose the disposition of fully depreciated machinery that is scrapped? Explain.

6. List transactions that would appear as applications of funds on a conventional all-resources funds statement, but that would not appear on a traditional working-capital funds statement.

7. Can treasury stock ever be an element of working capital? Explain.

8. Can noncash assets ever be included under the classification of cash?

9. Explain the nature of increases and decreases in working capital.

10. Why must the conventionally determined net income number be modified before it is reflected in the cash-basis statement of changes in financial position?

1. Determine the change in working capital that results from the following events.
(a) $1,000,000 par value bonds are reacquired by issuer at 98 and retired. The amount of unamortized premium on the bonds is $25,000.
(b) A 15 percent stock dividend is declared on $200,000 par value common stock outstanding.
(c) Equipment was purchased for $600,000 by paying $150,000 in cash and signing a note for $450,000, payable $150,000 every year for the next three years.
(d) Inventory is written down $20,000 below cost (in a lower of cost or market adjustment).

2. What is the working capital increase or decrease from operations, if the ABC Company shows a net loss of $8,000 on its income statement and if the following items were included?

Amortization of Patents	$ 5,000
Amortization of Discounts on Bonds Payable	3,000
Depreciation Expense	22,000

3. The balance sheet of the Crow Company is as follows:

	December 31	
	19X1	19X2
Cash	$ 24,000	$ 16,000
Accounts Receivable (Net)	2,000	7,000
Inventory	6,000	5,000
Permanent Investments	1,000	
Fixed Assets	70,000	83,000
Treasury Stock		10,000
	$103,000	$121,000
Accumulated Depreciation	$ 38,000	$ 30,000
Accounts Payable	9,000	2,000
Bonds Payable	5,000	20,000
Common Stock	40,000	51,000
Retained Earnings	11,000	18,000
	$103,000	$121,000

REQUIRED:
Determine the change in working capital that occurred during the year.

4. The balance sheet for the Cooper Company is as follows:

	December 31	
	19X3	*19X4*
Cash	$ 3,000	$ 4,000
Accounts Receivable (Net)	4,000	8,000
Inventory	9,000	11,000
Permanent Investments	2,000	
Fixed Assets	15,000	45,000
	$33,000	$68,000
Accumulated Depreciation on Fixed Assets	$ 4,000	$ 6,000
Accounts Payable	2,000	4,000
Notes Payable Short Term (Nontrade)	3,000	2,000
Long-Term Notes Payable	5,000	17,500
Common Stock	15,000	28,000
Retained Earnings	4,000	10,500
	$33,000	$68,000

Additional data reflecting changes in the noncurrent accounts:

A. Net income for the year 19X4, $13,000.
B. Depreciation on fixed assets for the year, $2,000.
C. Permanent investments were sold at cost.
D. Dividends of $6,500 were paid.
E. Fixed assets purchased for $10,000 cash.
F. Fixed assets purchased giving a $20,000 long-term note payable.
G. $7,500 long-term note payable paid by issuing common stock.
H. Unissued common stock sold for $5,500.

REQUIRED:
Determine the net change in working capital (working-capital basis).

5. The balance sheet of the Saco Company is as follows:

	December 31	
Debits	*19X5*	*19X6*
Cash	$ 8,000	$ 10,000
Accounts Receivable (Net)	18,000	22,000
Inventory	50,000	48,000
Prepaid Expenses	2,000	4,000
Permanent Investments	8,000	
Buildings	88,000	118,000
Machinery	38,000	60,000
Patents	5,000	3,000
	$217,000	$265,000

Credits		
Accounts Payable	$ 10,000	$ 6,000
Notes Payable Short-Term (Nontrade)	8,000	12,000
Accrued Wages	2,000	1,000
Accumulated Depreciation	38,000	37,000
Notes Payable, Long-Term	28,000	34,000
Common Stock	120,000	150,000
Retained Earnings	11,000	25,000
	$217,000	$265,000

Additional data affecting the noncurrent accounts are:

A. Net income for the year was $20,000.

B. Depreciation of $6,000 was recorded on fixed assets.

C. Patents were amortized, $2,000.

D. Machinery was purchased for $12,000 paying one-half in cash and a seven year interest-bearing note for the balance.

E. Machinery was purchased for $20,000 by issuing common stock.

F. Machinery was sold for $3,000. It originally cost $10,000 ($7,000 depreciated).

G. Added on to building; paid $30,000 cash.

H. Sold $10,000 common stock.

I. Sold permanent investments for $8,000.

J. Cash dividends of $6,000 were paid.

K. Sales on Account were $100,000.

L. Accounts receivable collected were $96,000.

REQUIRED:

(a) Develop a cash basis statement of changes in financial position.

(b) Prepare a statement of changes in financial position on a cash basis.

6. Data from the Haki Company's latest financial statements are as follows:

	Beginning of Year	End of Year
Cash	$ 25,000	$ 30,000
Marketable Securities	65,000	50,000
Accounts Receivable	40,000	60,000
Inventories	70,000	80,000
Short-Term Prepayments	13,000	15,000
Noncurrent Assets (Net)	219,000	252,500
Accounts Payable	40,000	70,000
Notes Payable (Short-term)	60,000	35,000
Accrued Liabilities	12,000	12,500
Long-term Debt and Stockholders' Equity	320,000	370,000

Determine the change in working capital during the year.

7. The following items are descriptions of business transactions and adjustments.

State whether each increases, decreases, or does not effect working capital. Explain your answer.

(a) Sold common stock for cash.

(b) Sold a fixed asset, receiving cash, a short-term note receivable, and a mortgage receivable.

(c) Borrowed from the bank, giving a short-term and a long-term note payable.

(d) Purchased a fixed asset, giving cash, a short-term note payable, and a mortgage payable.

(e) Declared a cash dividend.

(f) Paid a cash dividend.

(g) Paid debts, debiting both accounts payable and long-term notes payable.

(h) Purchased treasury stock for cash.

(i) Retired bonds by issuing common stock.

(j) Depreciation.

8. Given the following comparative financial statements at December 31 for the Tree Corporation, prepare a statement of changes in financial position using the working-capital concept. Income for 19X6 equalled $26,000.

	19X5	19X6
Cash	$ 60,000	$ 75,000
Accounts Receivable (Net)	105,000	91,000
Inventory	87,000	63,000
Machinery	131,000	121,000
Land	73,000	58,000
Accumulated Depreciation	(46,000)	(60,000)
Total Assets	$410,000	$348,000
Accounts Payable	$ 67,000	$ 60,000
Accrued Wages	10,000	
Common Stock	225,000	200,000
Retained Earnings	108,000	88,000
Total Liabilities and Owners' Equity	$410,000	$348,000

Additional data:

(a) Machinery was purchased for $10,000 by issuing common stock.

(b) Depreciation expense was $20,000.

(c) Common stock was retired by giving land worth $15,000.

(d) Dividends of $46,000 were paid.

(e) Machinery was sold for $14,000 that had originally cost $20,000 (accumulated depreciation for the machinery was $6,000).

(f) Common stock of $20,000 was purchased for cash and retired.

9. Given that the accrual-basis net income was $63,000, determine the net income on a cash basis. Dividends during 19X6 amounted to $134,000.

	19X5	19X6
Currents Assets:		
Cash	$ 35,000	$ 50,000
Accounts Receivable	21,000	37,000
Inventory	54,000	20,000
Prepaid Expenses	17,000	19,000
Noncurrent Assets:		
Patents	14,000	10,000
Machinery	330,000	330,000
Accumulated Depreciation	(54,000)	(64,000)
Land	163,000	
Total	$580,000	$402,000
Current Liabilities:		
Accounts Payable	$ 89,000	$ 96,000
Accrued Wages	54,000	40,000
Noncurrent Liabilities:		
Mortgage Payable	300,000	200,000
Owners' Equity	137,000	66,000
Total	$580,000	$402,000

10. Using the information given in Exercise 9, prepare a statement of changes in financial position using the cash concept.

11. Calculate the increase in working capital from current operations by analyzing the income statement below:

HENDERSON CORPORATION
Income Statement
For the Year Ended December 31, 19X3

Sales		$360,000
Cost of Goods Sold		209,000
Gross Margin on Sales		$151,000
Operating Expenses:		
Selling Expenses	$38,000	
Administrative Expenses	19,400	
Salaries and Wages	62,000	
Amortization of Goodwill	6,000	
Depreciation Expense	21,000	146,400
Net Income Before Income Taxes		4,600
Income Tax Expense		2,000
Net Income		$ 2,600

12. Which of the following transactions would not be listed as (or directly affect an item listed as) a source or use of funds on a statement of changes in financial position that defines funds as cash:
(a) Cash sales of $16,000.
(b) Collections of accounts receivable, $9,000.
(c) Credit sales uncollected in the current year.
(d) Declaration of a dividend.
(e) Payment of a dividend.
(f) Sale of stock for cash.
(g) Exchange of preferred stock for bonds outstanding.
(h) Acquisition of equipment for cash.
(i) Acquisition of equipment for short-term notes.
(j) Acquisition of equipment for bonds.
(k) Acquisition of equipment for stock.

13. Which of the items in Exercise 12 would affect the balance of an item listed as a source or use of funds, where funds are defined as working capital? Which items, if any, would be ommitted from a statement of changes in financial position prepared on an all-financial-resources basis?

14. Kirt, Incorporated, had net income for 19X7 of $3,000,000. Additional information about this company is as follows:

Amortization of Goodwill	$ 80,000
Depreciation of Fixed Assets	3,200,000
Long-term debt	
Bond Discount Amortization	130,000
Interest Expense	2,600,000
Provision for Doubtful Accounts	
Current Receivables	700,000
Long-term Receivables	210,000

The company uses the working capital definition of funds. Using this information, prepare a schedule showing the working capital provided from operations in the statement of changes in financial position for the year ended December 31, 19X7 (AICPA adapted).

1. Use the following statements of the Leathers Company to answer questions (a) to (e).

LEATHERS COMPANY
Balance Sheet
January 1, 19X0

Assets

Current Assets	$35,000
Buildings and Equipment	48,000
Accumulated Depreciation (Buildings and Equipment)	(15,000)
Patents	5,000
	$73,000

Equities

Current Liabilities	$ 9,000
Capital Stock	27,000
Retained Earnings	37,000
	$73,000

LEATHERS COMPANY
Statement of Source and Application of Funds
(All-Financial-Resources)
for 19X0

Working Capital, January 1, 19X0		$26,000
Funds Provided:		
Operations:		
Net Income	$20,000	
Depreciation (Buildings and Equipment)	10,000	
Amortization (Patents)	1,000	31,000
Issue of Capital Stock		13,000
Sale of Buildings		7,000
		$77,000
Funds Applied:		
Dividends	12,000	
Purchase of Land	14,000	
Purchase of Buildings and Equipment	30,000	56,000
Working Capital, December 31, 19X0		$21,000

Total assets on the Balance Sheet at December 31, 19X0, are $105,000. Accumulated Depreciation on the building sold was $6,000.

(a) What was the amount of the credit made to the Buildings and Equipment account when the building was sold?

(b) What was the book value of the buildings and equipment at December 31, 19X0?

(c) What were the Current Liabilities at December 31, 19X0?
(d) What was the balance in the Retained Earnings account at December 31, 19X0?
(e) What was Capital Stock (plus capital in excess of par or stated value) at December 31, 19X0 (AICPA adapted)?

2.

RETAIL ESTABLISHMENT, INC.
Balance Sheets

	December 31	
	19X1	19X0
Assets		
Current assets:		
Cash	$ 150,000	$100,000
Marketable securities	40,000	
Accounts receivable (net)	420,000	290,000
Merchandise inventory	330,000	210,000
Prepaid expenses	50,000	25,000
Land, buildings and fixtures	565,000	300,000
Less accumulated depreciation	55,000	25,000
	$1,500,000	$900,000
Equities		
Current liabilities:		
Accounts payable	$ 265,000	$220,000
Accrued expenses	70,000	65,000
Dividends payable	35,000	
Note payable (due 19X4)	250,000	
Common stock	600,000	485,000
Retained earnings	280,000	130,000
	$1,500,000	$900,000

RETAIL ESTABLISHMENT, INC.
Income Statements

	Year Ended December 31	
	19X1	19X0
Net sales, Including Service Charges	$3,200,000	$2,000,000
Cost of Goods Sold	2,500,000	1,600,000
Gross Profit	700,000	400,000
Expenses (Including Income Taxes)	500,000	260,000
Net Income	$ 200,000	$ 140,000

Although Retail Establishment, Inc., will report all changes in financial position, management has adopted a format emphasizing the flow of cash.

All accounts receivable and accounts payable relate to trade merchandise. Cash discounts are not allowed to customers, but a service charge is added to an account for late payment. Accounts Payable are recorded net and always are paid to take all of the discount allowed. The allowance for doubtful accounts at the end of 19X1 was the same as at the end of 19X0; no receivables were charged against the allowance during 19X1.

The proceeds from the note payable were used to finance a new store building. Capital stock was sold to provide additional working capital.

(a) How much cash was collected from customers during 19X1?

(b) How much cash was paid on Accounts Payable to suppliers during 19X1?

(c) What was the amount of 19X1 cash dividend payments?

(d) What were the 19X1 cash receipts not provided by operations?

(e) What were the 19X1 cash payments for assets that were not reflected in operations (AICPA adapted)?

3. The comparative balance sheets at December 31 of the Glass Corporation are as follows:

	19X5	19X6
Cash	$ 60,000	$ 65,000
Receivables	78,000	70,000
Inventory	122,000	120,000
Prepaid Expenses	18,000	19,000
Fixed Assets	227,000	322,000
Accumulated Depreciation	(73,000)	(96,000)
Patents	51,000	45,000
	$483,000	$545,000
Accounts Payable	$ 93,000	$ 80,000
Taxes Payable	75,000	75,000
Mortgage Payable	110,000	
Preferred Stock		160,000
Additional Paid-in Capital-Preferred		14,000
Common Stock	160,000	160,000
Retained Earnings	45,000	56,000
	$483,000	$545,000

(1) Accumulated Depreciation was credited for the period's depreciation expense only.

(2) The retained earnings account entries are for cash dividends of $5,000 and net income.

(3) The 19X6 income statement is as follows:

Sales	$235,000
Cost of Sales	100,000
Gross Profit	$135,000
Operating Expenses	$119,000
Net Income	$ 16,000

REQUIRED:

(a) Prepare a statement of changes in financial position using the working-capital concept.

(b) Prepare a statement of changes in financial position using the cash concept.

4. The Food Company had the following changes in the account balances during 19X6, its first year of operations.

	Debit	Credit
Current Assets	$ 70,000	
Plant and Equipment	120,000	
Accumulated Depreciation		$35,000
Current Liabilities		10,000
Capital Stock		90,000
Additional Paid-in Capital		30,000
Retained Earnings		25,000

Plant and equipment were purchased for $120,000 of stock. No plant and equipment retirements were made. Dividends of $30,000 were paid.

REQUIRED:

Prepare a statement of changes in financial position using the working-capital basis.

5. The following statements are those prepared for the Wood Company.

WOOD COMPANY
Balance Sheet
January 1, 19X6

Current Assets	$ 45,000
Fixed Assets	123,000
Accumulated Depreciation	(32,000)
Patents	15,000
Total Assets	$151,000
Current Liabilities	$ 36,000
Common Stock	101,000
Retained Earnings	14,000
Total Liabilities and Owners' Equity	$151,000

WOOD COMPANY
Statement of Changes in Financial Position
(For the Year Ended December 31, 19X6)

Working Capital, Beginning Balance		$ 9,000
Working Capital Generated:		
From Operations:		
Net Income	$42,000	
Add:		
Depreciation Expense	11,000	
Amortization of Patent	3,000	56,000
Common Stock Issued		25,000
Fixed Assets Sold		41,000
Total Working Capital Generated		$131,000
Working Capital Applied:		
Dividends Paid	$ 8,000	
Machinery Purchased	53,000	81,000
Working Capital, Ending Balance		$ 50,000

The ending balance of total assets was $190,000. When the fixed assets were sold, the accumulated depreciation debit was for $10,000.

REQUIRED:

Prepare the December 31, 19X6 balance sheet for the Wood Company.

6. The Greta Corporation's comparative balance sheet accounts for 19X3 and 19X4 are shown below:

	December 31, 19X4		December 31, 19X3	
	Debit	Credit	Debit	Credit
Cash	$ 8,400	$	$ 9,500	$
Accounts Receivable	26,600		27,300	
Allowance for Bad Debts		600		800
Inventory	68,700		64,200	
Prepaid Expenses	1,100		800	
Equipment	45,000		44,000	
Accumulated Depreciation		10,600		7,600
Accounts Payable		15,000		14,700
Common Stock, No Par		105,000		100,000
Retained Earnings		18,600		22,700
	$149,800	$149,800	$145,800	$145,800

The firm's financial records indicate the following:
(a) Net income for the year totaled $900.
(b) Depreciation expense for the year totaled $3,000.
(c) Acquired $1,000 in equipment this year.
(d) Cash dividends of $5,000 were declared and paid during the year.
(e) Sold stock for $5,000 to new investor.

REQUIRED:

Prepare a statement of changes in financial position using a working capital definition of funds.

7. Comparative balance sheets for the Mar Corporation are presented below:

THE MAR CORPORATION
Comparative Balance Sheets
December 31, 19X1 and 19X2

	December 31, 19X2	December 31, 19X1
Assets		
Current Assets:		
Cash	$ 25,400	$ 23,600
Accounts Receivable (Net)	69,800	66,800
Inventory	171,800	173,400
Supplies	4,000	3,600
Total Current Assets	$271,000	$267,400
Fixed Assets:		
Equipment	10,800	12,200
Accumulated Depreciation	(5,000)	(4,800)
Building	80,000	80,000
Accumulated Depreciation	(35,000)	(31,000)
Land	20,000	20,000
Total Fixed Assets	$ 70,800	$ 76,400
Total Assets	$341,800	$343,800
Equities		
Current Liabilities:		
Accounts Payable	$ 39,000	$ 41,000
Notes Payable	6,000	7,000
Income Taxes Payable	6,000	6,200
Total Current Liabilities	$ 51,000	$ 54,200
Long-term Liabilities:		
Long-term Notes Payable	10,000	0
Total Liabilities	$ 61,000	$ 54,200
Owner's Equity:		
Common Stock ($10 Par)	$190,000	$180,000
Additional Contributed Capital, Common Stock	15,000	15,000
Retained Earnings	75,800	94,600
Total Owners' Equity	$280,800	$289,600
Total Equities	$341,800	$343,800

An analysis of the financial records shows the following:

(1) Net income for the year totaled $6,200.

(2) Equipment costing $1,400 was sold for $200 during the year. Related Accumulated Depreciation of $1,200 was removed from the account.

(3) Depreciation Expense for equipment totaled $1,400 and Depreciation Expense for building totaled $4,000.

(4) A two-year $10,000 note payable was taken out on December 30.

(5) A 1,000 share stock dividend was declared and distributed when the stock was selling for $10 per share.

(6) Cash dividends totaling $15,000 were declared and distributed to stockholders during the year.

REQUIRED:

Prepare the statement of changes in financial position.

8. The Concordia Corporation has the following net changes in its account balances for 19X4:

	Debit	Credit
Working Capital	$20,000	$
Plant and Equipment	60,000	
Accumulated Depreciation		15,000
Bonds Payable		40,000
Common Stock		20,000
Retained Earnings		5,000

Plant and Equipment were acquired for the issuance of bonds. Another issue of bonds totaling $20,000 was retired during the year. A stock dividend requiring the capitalization of $20,000 in retained earnings was declared and distributed. Cash dividends of $15,000 were declared and paid during the year. No plant or equipment disposals occurred.

REQUIRED:

(a) Calculate net income of Concordia Corporation for 19X4.

(b) Prepare a statement of changes in financial position, sources and uses of funds section, from these data.

9. The Habersham Company's financial records disclose the following:

Sales	$290,000
Beginning Accounts Receivable	88,000
Ending Accounts Receivable	80,000
Cost of Goods Sold	160,000
Beginning Inventory	40,000
Ending Inventory	45,000
Beginning Accounts Payable	19,000
Ending Accounts Payable	20,000
Depreciation Expense	16,000
Beginning Prepaid Expenses	2,000
Ending Prepaid Expenses	1,000
Beginning Accrued Liabilities	3,000
Ending Accrued Liabilities	3,000
Operating Expenses and Income Taxes	70,000

The records also show the following transactions:
(1) Issued stock for equipment costing $30,000.
(2) Retired $50,000 in bonds for cash.
(3) Purchased land for $75,000.

REQUIRED:
(a) Calculate "Cash Provided by Operations" from these data.
(b) Prepare a statement of changes in financial position using the cash definition of funds for Habersham Company for the year ended March 31, 19X7.

□ 14
FINANCIAL STATEMENT ANALYSIS

THE ANALYTIC PROCESS

PLAN OF ANALYSIS

ANALYTIC TECHNIQUES AND INTERPRETATION

COMPARATIVE ANALYSIS

COMMON-SIZE ANALYSIS

RATIO ANALYSIS

PROFITABILITY RATIOS

PROFIT MARGIN ON SALES

RATE OF RETURN ON ASSETS

RATE OF RETURN ON COMMON STOCK EQUITY

EARNINGS PER SHARE

LIQUIDITY RATIOS

CURRENT RATIO

ACID TEST RATIO

RECEIVABLES TURNOVER

INVENTORY TURNOVER

SOLVENCY RATIOS

DEBT TO TOTAL EQUITY

TIMES INTEREST EARNED

MARKETABILITY RATIOS

PRICE EARNINGS RATIO

PAYOUT RATIO

SUMMARY OF RATIOS

LIMITATIONS OF RATIO ANALYSIS

SUMMARY

A SUPPLEMENTARY DISCUSSION: THE FINANCIAL ANALYST

Liquidity
Solvency
Profitability
Marketability
Absolute data
Historic base
Like-kind base
Horizontal analysis
Vertical analysis

1. Why must financial statements be analyzed?

2. Effective analysis requires that financial data be compared with standards, historical data, or industry data. Why is comparison critical?

3. What measurement bases can be used by a financial statement analyst?

4. Define the term, liquidity, and explain its relevance to financial statement analysis.

5. Contrast the concepts of liquidity and solvency.

6. How long a period is required for historical analysis? How do conventional financial statements attempt to accommodate this form of analysis?

7. What are common-size financial statements?

8. Identify ratios that address the issue of profitability.

9. For what purpose is the ratio, rate of return on assets, calculated? How does the interpretation of this ratio differ from that of the ratio, rate of return on common stock equity?

10. Waltham Corporation reports earnings per share of $0.20, and Ridgeland Company reports earnings per share of $2. Is Ridgeland more profitable than Waltham? Explain.

11. Is a high inventory turnover preferable to a low turnover? Does this also hold true for a receivables turnover? Explain.

12. Wilson Company offers trade terms of 2/10, n/30, and it reports an accounts receivable turnover of 5.2. How do you interpret these facts?

13. Sampson Company reports a current ratio of 1.3. What conclusion can you draw?

14. List the two comparative analysis techniques described in the chapter, and explain the differences between them.

15. List the categories under which ratios are typically classified.

16. What do liquidity ratios attempt to measure?

17. What must the analyst know to be able to use ratio analysis properly?

18. List the primary user groups of financial statements, and state what goals each group has in examining the statements.

19. In general, what are the interests shared by all groups who examine financial statements?

20. Why are historical comparisons useful to financial statement analysts?

Exercises

1. Data for Wyatt Corporation are shown below:

	19X2	19X1
Sales	$60,000	$52,000
Cost of Goods Sold	41,000	37,000
Gross Profits	$19,000	$15,000
Expenses	13,000	11,000
Net Income Before Income Taxes	$ 6,000	$ 4,000
Income Tax Expense	1,200	800
Net Income	$ 4,800	$ 3,200

Perform a horizontal analysis of these income statements.

2. Perform (a) vertical analysis of Wyatt Corporation's income statement for 19X2, using the data in Exercise 1. (b) Calculate gross margin percentage for Wyatt Corp. in 19X2.

3. (a) Combine vertical *and* horizontal analysis for Wyatt Corporation by using the data provided in Exercise 1.

(b) What question does this form of analysis allow you to answer with the use of comparative industry data?

4. Prepare a vertical analysis of North Corporation's balance sheet from these accounts:

	Debits	Credits
Cash	$ 16,000	
Accounts Receivable	39,000	
Notes Receivable	5,000	
Inventory	120,000	
Prepaid Expenses	2,000	
Long-Term Investment	60,000	
Building	80,000	
Equipment	35,000	
Land	10,000	
Accounts Payable		$ 29,000
Notes Payable		40,000
Mortgage Payable		40,000
Bonds Payable		100,000
Common Stock		100,000
Retained Earnings		58,000
	367,000	367,000

5. Below are accounts abstracted from Benson Corporation's balance sheet:

	Debits	Credits
Cash	18,000	
Marketable Securities	40,000	
Accounts Receivable	37,000	
Inventory	88,000	
Plant and Equipment	155,000	
Land	40,000	
Accounts Payable		33,000
Notes Payable		21,000
Wages Payable		9,000
Property Taxes Payable		8,000
Long-term Bonds Payable		100,000

Calculate: (a) working capital, (b) current ratio, and (c) acid test ratio.

6. Calculate the following ratios and give a preliminary interpretation of the results for Jones Corporation:

Ratio	Industry Average	Jones
(a) Profit Margin on Sales	5.8%	
(b) Rate of Return on Assets	5.2%	
(c) Rate of Return on Common Stock Equity	7.8%	
Financial Data for Jones Corporation		
Sales		$1,500,000
Net Income		96,000
Total Assets, Current Year-End		$1,800,000
Total Assets, Last Year-End		1,500,000
Common Stockholders' Equity, Current Year-End		1,000,000
Common Stockholders' Equity, Last Year-End		920,000

7. The following data are abstracted from the financial statements of ABC, Inc. All sales in the industry in which this firm operates are made on trade terms N/30.

Net Sales	$18,000,000
Current Year-End Net Accounts Receivable	1,480,000
Previous Year-End Net Accounts Receivable	1,260,000

(a) Calculate receivable turnover and the average collection period.

(b) What conclusions can be drawn abut the liquidity of these receivables and the firm's credit and collection policies if the industry average collection period is 28 days?

8. Smith Company reports the following data with respect to inventory:

Sales	$290,000
Cost of Sales	160,000
Year End Inventory Balance	60,000
Previous Year-End Inventory Balance	48,000

(a) Calculate inventory turnover and average inventory turnover in days.
(b) How would you interpret these data?

9. From the data given below, (a) calculate two leverage ratios, and (b) determine the margin of safety for creditors and the ability of the firm to withstand adverse business conditions:

Total Liabilities	$6,300,000
Total Stockholders' Equity	4,600,000
Net Income	400,000
Interest Expense	380,000
Income Tax Expense	140,000

10. Below are given some financial data for Apex Company:

Total Assets	$1,500,000
Income Taxes	60,000
Sales	1,800,000
Interest Expense	15,000
Common Stockholders' Equity	600,000
Preferred Dividends	30,000
Net Income Before Income Taxes	150,000

(a) Calculate rate of return on Total Assets.
(b) Calculate rate of return on Common Stock Equity.
(c) Calculate rate of return on sales.
(d) What generalizations can be drawn from your rate of return calculations, if any?

11. Consider the following income statement data from Chairs, Inc.:

	Last Year	This Year
Sales	$880,000	$1,560,000
Cost of Goods Sold	660,000	770,000
Selling Expenses	79,200	83,600
General Expenses	33,000	35,200
Income Taxes	52,800	79,200

(a) Prepare Common-size income statements for each year.
(b) Prepare a comparative income statement.
(c) Evaluate these statements.

12. Prepare a horizontal analysis of both absolute and relative changes from the comparative income statements shown below:

AAA CORPORATION
Comparative Income Statements
For the Years Ended December 31, 19X3 and 19X4

| | Year Ended December 31 | |
	19X4	19X3
Sales	$226,000	$219,000
Sales Returns and Allowances	9,000	6,000
Net Sales	$217,000	$213,000
Cost of Goods Sold	119,000	106,000
Gross Profit	$ 98,000	$107,000
Operating Expenses		
Selling Expenses	$ 37,000	$ 33,000
General Administrative Expenses	46,000	42,000
Interest Expense	9,000	1,000
Total Expenses	$ 92,000	$ 76,000
Net Income Before Income Taxes	6,000	31,000
Income Taxes	3,000	15,000
Net Income	$ 3,000	$ 16,000

13. Prepare a common-size analysis of the comparative income statements shown in Exercise 12. What insights are provided by this analysis into the firm's problems?

14. Calculate the following ratios from the financial data given below for Webster Corporation:
(a) Current ratio.
(b) Acid test ratio.
(c) Inventory turnover.
(d) Debt to equity ratio.
(e) Times interest earned.

WEBSTER CORPORATION
Income Statement
For the Year Ended December 31, 19X5

Sales		$290,000
Cost of Goods Sold		
Inventory, January 1, 19X5	$ 30,000	
Purchases	188,000	
Goods Available for Sale	218,000	
Inventory, December 31, 19X5	21,000	
Cost of Goods Sold		197,000
Gross Margin on Sales		93,000
Operating Expenses	57,000	
Interest Expense	3,000	
Total Expenses		60,000
Net Income Before Income Taxes		33,000
Income Tax Expense		16,000
Net Income		$ 17,000

WEBSTER CORPORATION
Balance Sheet
December 31, 19X5

Assets	
Cash	$ 4,700
Accounts Receivable (Net)	20,000
Inventory	21,000
Prepaid Expenses	1,000
Property, Plant, Equipment	160,000
Accumulated Depreciation	(40,000)
Total Assets	$166,700
Equities	
Accounts Payable	$ 18,000
Notes Payable (Due in 10 Years)	40,000
Common Stock (No Par)	60,000
Retained Earnings	48,700
Total Equities	$166,700

15. On January 1, 19X6, the River Company's beginning inventory was $400,000. During 19X6, River purchased $1,900,000 of additional inventory. On December 31, 19X6, River's ending inventory was $500,000. What is the inventory turnover for 19X6 (AICPA adapted)?

1. Given the financial data below, reconstruct the balance sheet and income statement for AAA, Inc., by using ratio formulas to solve for unknowns:

AAA, INC.
Balance Sheet
December 31, 19X0

Assets	
Current Assets:	
Cash	$ 12,000
Accounts Receivable (Net)	?
Marketable Securities	28,000
Inventories	?
Total Current Assets	$?
Long-Lived Assets:	
Plant and Equipment (Net)	$?
Total Assets	$?
Equities	
Current Liabilities	$?
Long-term Liabilities	
Bonds Payable at 10%	$?
Stockholders' Equity:	
Common Stock	$240,000
Retained Earnings	$460,000
Total Stockholders' Equity	$700,000
Total Equities	$?

AAA, INC.
Income Statement
For the Year Ended December 31, 19X0

Sales (Net)	$?
Cost of Goods Sold	?
Gross Margin	$560,000
Operating Expenses	?
Operating Income	$?
Other Expenses:	
Interest Expense	?
Net Income Before Taxes	?
Income Taxes (50%)	$ 112,000
Net Income	$?

Other financial data for the year 19X0 include the following:

(1) Total Debt to Common Equity was 50 percent.

(2) Average number of days to collect accounts receivable was 45 (based on a 360-day year). Beginning accounts receivable balance was $200,000.

(3) Inventory turnover was four times during the year. Beginning inventory balance was $120,000.

(4) Gross Margin was 35 percent of net sales.

(5) Times interest earned was 15.

(6) Acid test ratio was 1.60.

(7) Operating expenses were 20 percent of sales.

2. The following are the financial statements of the E-Z Company:

E-Z COMPANY
Comparative Balance Sheets
December 31, 19X1 and 19X0

Assets	19X1	19X0
Current Assets:		
Cash	$ 8,000	$ 11,920
Marketable Securities	120,000	56,000
Accounts Receivable	80,000	64,000
Inventory	160,000	120,000
Total Current Assets	$368,000	$251,920
Long-Term Assets:		
Plant and Equipment	$320,000	$320,000
Accumulated Depreciation	240,000	224,000
Net Total Long-term Assets	$ 80,000	$ 96,000
Total Assets	$448,000	$347,920
Equities		
Current Liabilities:		
Accounts Payable	$120,000	$ 64,000
Taxes Payable	40,000	24,000
Total Current liabilities	$160,000	$ 88,000
Long-term liabilities:		
Bonds Payable, 6% interest	$ 80,000	$ 80,000
Stockholders' Equity:		
Preferred Stock, 5% dividend rate	$ 40,000	$ 40,000
Common Stock (10,000 Shares)	80,000	80,000
Capital in Excess of Par	16,000	16,000
Retained Earnings	72,000	43,920
Total Stockholders' Equity	$208,000	$179,920
Total Equities	$448,000	$347,920

E-Z COMPANY
Income Statement
For the Year Ended December 31, 19X1

Sales	$648,000
Cost of Goods Sold	420,000
Gross Margin	$228,000
Operating Expenses	146,400
Net Operating Income	$ 81,600
Other Expenses:	
Interest Expense	4,800
Net Income Before Income Taxes	$ 76,800
Income Taxes	30,720
Net Income	$ 46,080

REQUIRED:
  (a) Calculate the following ratios for the year 19X1:
    (1) Current ratio.
    (2) Acid test ratio.
    (3) Accounts receivable turnover.
    (4) Average collection period (assume a 360-day year).
    (5) Inventory turnover.
    (6) Number of times interest earned.
    (7) Earnings per share (common stock).
    (8) Rate of return on common stockholders' equity.
    (9) Rate of return on total assets.
    (10) Total debt to stockholders' equity.
  (b) From the information supplied in (a) above, write out your comments about the condition of the company for the year 19X1.
3. The 19X0 income statement data for two electronics companies, Transistor, Inc., and Computer Company, shown below:

Income Statement
For the Year 19X0

	Transistor, Inc.	Computer Co.
Sales and Other Income	$294,474	$393,482
Cost of Sales	273,260	380,870
Pension Contributions	2,245	2,956
Depreciation	4,546	2,558
Interest Expense	154	469
Miscellaneous Taxes	1,195	1,605
Income Taxes	6,192	2,214
Miscellaneous Expenses	192	—
Total Expenses	$287,784	$390,672
Net Income	$ 6,690	$ 2,810

REQUIRED:

Prepare common-size income statements for the two companies and comment on the results. If Transistor, Inc., used LIFO in valuing inventories and Computer Company used FIFO, what effect, if any, could this have on the reported net income of the two companies.

4. Information selected from the Center Supply Company's financial statements for the current year and the preceding year is presented below:

	Current Year	Last Year
Sales (Net)	600,000	375,000
Cost of Goods Sold	360,000	277,500
Bond Interest Expense	11,250	11,250
Federal Income Taxes	13,500	9,000
Net Income After Taxes	30,000	22,500
Accounts Receivable, Dec. 31	67,500	56,250
Merchandise Inventory	150,000	90,000
Common Stockholders' Equity	240,000	225,000
Total Assets	450,000	337,500

REQUIRED:

Calculate the following ratios for the current year:

(a) Inventory Turnover.

(b) Number of times interest earned.

(c) Average Collection Period.

(d) Return on Sales.

(e) Return on Assets.

(f) Return on Common Stockholders' Equity.

5. XYZ Company had $300,000 of current assets, a 2 to 1 current ratio, and a 1.5:1 acid test ratio. The following transactions then took place:

(1) $2,000 accounts receivable collected.

(2) Sold marketable securities for $34,000 that cost the company $30,000.

(3) Allowance for bad debts increased $1,000.

(4) $0.15 per share cash dividend was declared on 90,000 shares of outstanding common stock valued at $10 par.

(5) The cash dividend was paid.

(6) $15,000 was borrowed from a bank for 90 days at 9.5 percent interest.

(7) A stock dividend was declared that required 4,500 additional shares to be distributed. Market value of the stock was $14 per share on the declaration date.

(8) Merchandise was purchased for $15,000 on credit, and the company uses a perpetual inventory system.

REQUIRED:

Prepare a schedule that shows the XYZ Company's current ratio and acid test ratio after all of the above transactions.

6. Comparative income statements for Boot Company are shown below:

	19X4	19X3
Sales	$945,000	$827,000
Cost of Goods Sold	650,000	557,000
Gross Profit	295,000	270,000
Operating Expenses:		
General Administrative	48,000	43,000
Selling Expenses	82,000	77,000
Depreciation	80,000	84,000
Net Income from Operations	85,000	66,000
Other Income	400	250
Net Income Before Income Tax	85,400	66,250
Income Tax Expense	42,700	33,125
Net Income	$ 42,700	$ 33,125

REQUIRED:

(a) Perform horizontal analysis on these income statements. What general conclusions could you gather from a horizontal analysis if you were provided with industry data?

(b) Perform vertical analysis on the data provided. What conclusions could you draw from a vertical analysis, given that you had industry data?

7. The BBB Company's comparative income statements for 19X7 and 19X8 are shown below:

BBB COMPANY
Comparative Income Statements
For the Years Ended December 31, 19X7 and 19X8

	Year Ended December 31	
	19X8	19X7
Sales, Net	$8,950	$6,410
Cost of Goods Sold	4,150	2,500
Gross Margin on Sales	4,800	3,910
Operating Expenses		
Selling Expenses	950	840
Administrative Expenses	2,900	2,600
Total Operating Expenses	3,850	3,440
Net Income	$ 950	$ 470

Industry data gathered by a trade association indicate that cost of goods sold averaged 40 percent of sales, selling expenses averaged 18 percent of sales, and administrative expenses averaged 25 percent of sales during this period.

REQUIRED:
(a) Perform a comparative vertical analysis on these data, similar to that shown in Exhibit 14-3.
(b) Using the industry data shown, what observations would you make about the operations of this firm?

8. Comparative income statements for the Evans Company are shown below:

THE EVANS COMPANY
Comparative Income Statements
For the Years Ended December 31, 19X7, and 19X8

	Year Ended December 31	
	19X8	19X7
Sales	$600,000	$500,000
Sales Discounts	11,000	8,500
Net Sales	$589,000	$491,500
Cost of Goods Sold	395,000	268,000
Gross Margin on Sales	$194,000	$223,500
Operating Expenses		
Selling Expenses	$ 62,000	$ 55,000
Administrative Expenses	88,000	81,000
Total Operating Expenses	$150,000	$136,000
Net Income	$ 44,000	$ 87,500

REQUIRED:
(a) Prepare a comparative analysis of both absolute and relative changes in the income statements for the Evans Company.
(b) What conclusions would you draw from this technique if you independently discovered that the costs of merchandise in this industry have risen, on average, 8 percent during this period? What other trends do you note?

9. The Jenson Marine Company sells boats and accessories. Comparative financial statements for the firm for 19X8 and 19X9 are as follows:

THE JENSON MARINE COMPANY, INC.
Comparative Income Statements
For the Years Ended December 31, 19X8, and 19X9

	Year Ended December 31	
	19X9	19X8
Sales	$1,130,000	$887,000
Cost of Goods Sold	640,000	501,000
Gross Margin on Sales	$ 490,000	$386,000
Operating Expenses		
Selling Expenses	180,000	141,000
Administrative Expenses	140,000	138,000
Interest Expense	21,000	4,000
Total Expenses	$ 341,000	$283,000
Net Income Before Income Taxes	149,000	103,000
Income Taxe Expense	74,500	51,500
Net Income	$ 74,500	$ 51,500
Earnings Per Share (1,000 shares common stock outstanding)	$ 7.45	$ 5.15

THE JENSON MARINE COMPANY, INC.
Comparative Balance Sheets
December 31, 19X8 and 19X9

	19X9	19X8
Assets		
Cash	$ 22,000	$ 18,000
Accounts Receivable, Net	131,000	89,000
Notes Receivable	28,000	3,000
Inventory	239,000	115,000
Prepaid Expenses	9,000	10,000
Equipment	62,000	37,000
Accumulated Depreciation	(16,000)	(12,000)
Total Assets	$475,000	$260,000
Equities		
Liabilities:		
Accounts Payable	$ 39,000	$ 14,000
Notes Payable, Short-term	215,000	65,000
Miscellaneous Accrued Expenses	3,000	2,500
Bonds Payable (due in 10 years)	100,000	100,000
Total Liabilities	$357,000	$181,500
Owners' Equity:		
Common Stock (1,000 shares, $10 par)	$ 10,000	$ 10,000
Additional Contributed Capital,		
Common Stockholders	8,000	8,000
Preferred Stock (500 shares, $10 par)	5,000	5,000
Retained Earnings	95,000	55,500
Total Owners' Equity	$118,000	$ 78,500
Total Equities	$475,000	$260,000

REQUIRED:
    (a) Calculate the following ratios for 19X9:
        (1) Profit margin on sales.
        (2) Rate of return on assets.
        (3) Rate of return on common stock equity (a $.60 preferred cash dividend was paid this year).
        (4) Current ratio.
        (5) Acid-test ratio.
        (6) Accounts receivable turnover.
        (7) Inventory turnover.
        (8) Debt to total equity.
        (9) Times interest earned.

(b) Compare your results with the following industry data for these ratios:

Profit margin on sales	7.1%
Rate of return on assets	19.7%
Rate of return on common stock equity	29.0%
Current ratio	3.1
Acid-test ratio	1.1
Accounts receivable turnover	12.0 times
Inventory turnover	4.8 times
Debt to total equity	48.0%
Times interest earned	14.3 times

(c) If a client were considering an investment in this firm, how would you evaluate the potential risks and rewards associated with this firm?

□ 15
LONG-TERM INVESTMENTS AND CONSOLIDATIONS

LONG-TERM STOCK INVESTMENTS

COST AND EQUITY COMPARED

OWNERSHIP AND CONTROL

CREATING A PARENT-SUBSIDIARY RELATIONSHIP

TRANSFER OF ASSETS

STOCK-FOR-STOCK EXCHANGE

PURCHASE TRANSACTIONS

EXCESS COST OVER NET BOOK VALUE

CONSOLIDATION OF A PURCHASED SUBSIDIARY

CONSOLIDATED WORKSHEETS

CONSOLIDATED INCOME STATEMENT

REPORTING PARENT-SUBSIDIARY RELATIONSHIPS

SUMMARY

A SUPPLEMENTARY DISCUSSION: MINORITY INTERESTS

☐ OBJECTIVES

AFTER STUDYING THIS CHAPTER, YOU SHOULD BE ABLE TO DO THE FOLLOWING:

1. RECOGNIZE INCOME FROM LONG-TERM INVESTMENTS UNDER THE COST AND EQUITY METHODS.

2. DESCRIBE PARENT-SUBSIDIARY RELATIONSHIPS.

3. PREPARE A WORKSHEET TO HELP CONSOLIDATE FINANCIAL STATEMENTS FOR PARENT AND SUBSIDIARY CORPORATIONS.

4. CONSTRUCT CONSOLIDATED FINANCIAL STATEMENTS.

In Chapter 9 we introduced accounting for long-term investments in the capital stock of another company. The nature and extent of the financial relationship between two organizations can vary depending on the amount of stock that is owned. Alternatives are available so that the accountant can provide the most relevant information about an investment, consistent with economic reality.

This chapter discusses the cost and equity methods of accounting for long-term investments, principles of business combination and consolidated financial statements.

Long-term Stock Investments

All long-term investments are recorded and valued at their cost on the date of acquisition. Acquisition cost includes all necessary costs to purchase the stock, including brokerage fees and transfer taxes. After acquisition, long-term investments in stock may be accounted for either under the cost method or the equity method.

The *cost method* treats both the investor and investee as separate, distinct entities. The investing company records its acquisition at cost and leaves the account substantially unchanged until all or part of the investment is sold. Profits or losses by the investee firm are not reflected in the investor's accounts.

Operations can lead to dividend payments by the investee. In these cases, the owner will recognize dividend income by increasing cash and an appropriate revenue account. For example, if a dividend of $1,000 was received, the investor would make the following entry:

Cash	$1,000	
Dividend Revenue		$1,000

At the time of sale, any gain or loss from the original cost would be recognized.

The *equity method* assumes a significant economic relationship between the investor and investee. This relationship justifies adjustments to the investment account reflecting net changes in the investee's assets. While initially recorded at cost, the equity method permits the investor to record its proportionate share of changes in the net assets (assets less liabilities) of the investee. Net assets of the investee increase as it earns income, and decrease as it incurs losses or pays dividends. Thus, the investor's account, Investment in Common Stock of X Company, will be adjusted upwards and downwards to reflect events associated with the investee.

Cost and Equity Compared. The mechanics and differences involved in each method can best be illustrated by a comparative example. Assume that Able Company purchased 1,000 of the 4,000 outstanding shares of

Baker Company stock for $15,000. The acquisition and subsequent events are shown in Exhibit 15-1. All entries are as they would be made in the books of Able Company.

The acquisition of Baker Company stock is recorded in the same manner under both the cost and the equity methods. Historical cost is used to record the acquisition.

The report of an operating loss by Baker will lead to no entry if the cost method is used. However, the equity method takes account of the loss. The investment account is reduced and a loss is recognized for the extent of Able's ownership of Baker (1,000/4,000 × $2,000). If financial statements were prepared at this time, the investment would be valued at $15,000 under the cost method and $14,500 under the equity method.

Profits or gains are also not recognized under the cost method. The equity method does provide for a proportionate share to be recorded by Able Company (1,000/4,000 × $6,000). At this point in time, a balance sheet would disclose an investment in Baker valued at $15,000 under the cost method and $16,000 under the equity method. An income statement for this period would include $1,500 of investment income if the equity method was used.

The payment of a dividend is recognized by increasing cash under each method. The cost method leads to the realization of an equal amount of revenue. Under the equity method, income equal to the earnings of the firm was already recognized. Receipt of a dividend indicates a distribution of some of these earnings by Baker. Therefore, the investment account is reduced.

The entry to record the sale of the investment in Baker Company depends on the investment carrying value. Under the cost method, the cash received exceeds the carrying value, leading to the recognition of a gain. The investment carrying value under the equity method responded to income and dividends. Since the investment was valued at more than the cash received, a loss is recognized.

Over the total life of this investment, both the cost and equity methods provide for recording the same basic facts. Differences in the timing of recognition account for the major contrast between them. A firm is free to select either method depending on the level of economic influence exerted by the investor. If an investor acquires more than 50 percent of the outstanding stock of a firm, the relationship changes and the investor must consider consolidated financial statements.

When more than 50 percent of the outstanding capital stock of a company is acquired by one stockholder, a controlling interest is created: the controlling stockholder can elect a majority of the acquired company's directors.

Ownership and Consolidation

EXHIBIT 15-1
COMPARISON OF COST AND EQUITY METHODS

Event	Cost Method		Equity Method	
Able buys 1,000 shares of Baker for $15,000.	Investment in Baker $15,000 Cash	$15,000	Investment in Baker $15,000 Cash	$15,000
Baker reports loss of $2,000 for the period.	No entry		Loss from Investment $ 500 Investment in Baker	$ 500
Baker reports gain of $6,000 for the period.	No entry		Investment in Baker $ 1,500 Investment Income	$ 1,500
Baker pays dividend of $1,600; Able receives $400 as its share.	Cash $ 400 Dividend Revenue	$ 400	Cash $ 400 Investment in Baker	$ 400
Able sells its investment in Baker for $15,500.	Cash $15,500 Investment in Baker Gain on Sale	$15,000 500	Cash $15,500 Loss on Sale 100 Investment in Baker	$15,600

When the controlling interest is held by another corporation, the investing company is called a _parent_ and the acquired company is known as a _subsidiary_. Since the stockholders of the parent own the parent, which in turn owns the subsidiary, the stockholders of the parent have an indirect ownership interest in the subsidiary. That is, the parent and the subsidiary can be viewed by the parent's stockholders as a single entity. _Consolidated financial statements_ report on the financial position and results of operations of a parent and subsidiary. Consolidation involves the combination of like data obtained from the separate financial statements for the parent and subsidiary. For example, combining the cash balances for the parent and subsidiary produces the consolidated cash balance. Consolidated reporting provides readers with a concise summary of the activities and balances for a group of related, but separate, legal entities.

The following sections describe the construction of consolidated financial statements and focus on the related problems of measurement and interpretation. Three events related to consolidation will be considered: creation of a parent-subsidiary relationship, recognition of earnings of the subsidiary, and reporting to the public. The supplementary discussion at the end of the chapter will discuss _minority interests_ that are created in the consolidation of partially owned subsidiaries.

A parent-subsidiary relationship may be created whenever one corporation either (1) acquires more than 50 percent of the outstanding voting stock of an existing corporation, or (2) transfers some assets to a newly organized subsidiary in exchange for a controlling interest in the subsidiary. Both approaches for creating a parent-subsidiary relationship are extremely common. Accounting for parent-subsidiary relationships is relatively complex, since the underlying business transactions themselves are very complex. To simplify the issues, we discuss only 100 percent owned subsidiaries in this section and deal with partially held controlling interests in the supplementary discussion at the end of this chapter. Three cases of 100 percent owned subsidiaries are given in order of complexity. In the first case, the parent gains control by transferring some of its assets to a wholly owned subsidiary. In the second case, the parent acquires all of the subsidiary's stock in exchange for its own common stock and records the investment at the book value of the subsidiary's net assets. In the third case, the parent purchases the subsidiary's stock or assets and values the investment at the market value of consideration given in the exchange.

Creating a Parent-Subsidiary Relationship

Transfer of Assets. A parent corporation may create a subsidiary by transferring some of its assets to a newly organized legal entity controlled by the parent. For example, the Major Corporation wishes to create a new sub-

EXHIBIT 15-2
Major Corporation, Before and After Reorganization

	Major Corp. Before Reorganization	Major Corp. After Reorganization	Minor Corp.
Cash	$ 80,000	$ 60,000	$20,000
Accounts Receivable	200,000	150,000	50,000
Plant and Equipment	700,000	700,000	0
Investment in Subsidiary	0	45,000	0
Total Assets	$980,000	$955,000	$70,000
Current Liabilities	$100,000	$ 75,000	$25,000
Long-term Liabilities	500,000	500,000	0
Common Stock ($10 par)	55,000	55,000	45,000
Additional Paid in Capital	130,000	130,000	0
Retained Earnings	195,000	195,000	0
Total Liabilities and Capital	$980,000	$955,000	$70,000

sidiary that will be called the Minor Corporation. Legal counsel for Major obtains a corporate charter for Minor from the secretary of the state of incorporation. The charter specifies that Minor is authorized to issue up to 1,000,000 shares of $10 par common stock. Major then exchanges one-quarter of its cash, accounts receivable, and current liabilities for common stock in Minor. The balance sheets for Major and Minor corporations, both before and after the reorganization, are reflected in Exhibit 15-2.

Major Corporation transfers net assets valued at $45,000 to Minor Corporation for 4,500 shares of $10 par (Minor) common stock. This transaction is reflected in Major's journal by the following entry:

Investment in Subsidiary	$45,000	
Current Liabilities	25,000	
Cash		$20,000
Accounts Receivable		50,000

The Investment account has a value equal to the net asset value of accounts transferred to Minor Corporation. The 4,500 shares of Minor Corporation common stock provide evidence to support the existence of the Investment account. Except for the four accounts affected by the journal entry listed above, the remaining accounts in Major's ledger are totally unaffected by the transaction. For example, the Retained Earnings account, after reorganization, reflects the same $195,000 balance recognized before the reorganization.

Minor Corporation would record the organization transaction in its journal as follows:

Cash	$20,000	
Accounts Receivable	50,000	
Current Liabilities		$25,000
Capital Stock		45,000

The Capital Stock account is credited at par: in this case, 4,500 shares of the $10 par stock is valued at $45,000. Exhibit 15-2 presents a balance sheet for the Minor Corporation that reflects this journal entry.

For any number of valid business reasons, management may issue common stock at some dollar value above par. For example, management might attribute a value of $15 per share for Minor common stock used in the reorganization. At this "price," only 3,000 shares are needed to equal the $45,000 net asset value. A journal entry to record the reorganization transaction on Minor Corporation's books at $15 per share is as follows:

Cash	$20,000	
Accounts Receivable	50,000	
Current Liabilities		$25,000
Common Stock (par)		30,000
Additional Paid in Capital		15,000

Common stock is recorded at par, while Additional Paid in Capital reflects the remainder (in this case, $5 per share for 3,000 shares). See Chapter 12 for further discussion of accounting for the issuance of common stock.

The example described in Exhibit 15-2 is ideal for comparing consolidated and unconsolidated balance sheets. Stockholders of Major Corporation are interested in the economic reality of the total business entity, without regard to internal organizational (and legal) structure; therefore, they would prefer the "before reorganization" balance sheet. A consolidated balance sheet would appear exactly as shown in the "before adjustment" column. To produce a consolidated balance sheet, the accountant would start with balance sheets prepared for the parent and all subsidiaries. Those balances that reflect unique information would then be added together. Thus, the consolidated Cash of $80,000 would be determined by adding together the Cash of Major and Minor corporations ($60,000 + $20,000). *Reciprocal accounts* would be ignored in consolidation, since one account reflects a debit balance for the same amount as the other account reflects a credit balance. For example, the Investment in Subsidiary account (debit) and the Common Stock of Minor (credit) both refer to 4,500 shares of Minor common stock, par value $10. Neither of these $45,000 balances would be reflected in the consolidated balance sheet.

EXHIBIT 15-3
BEFORE AND AFTER POOLING OF INTERESTS: BALANCE SHEETS
FOR PATER, INC., AND SUNCO
(Assuming Merged Operations)

	Part A *Before Pooling*		*Part B* *After Pooling*
	Pater, Inc.	*Sunco*	*Pater, Inc.*
Assets	$700,000	$200,000	$900,000
Liabilities	$400,000	$ 50,000	$450,000
Capital Stock ($10 par)	100,000	25,000	125,000
Additional Paid In Capital	35,000	110,000	145,000
Retained Earnings	165,000	15,000	180,000
Total Liabilities and Equities	$700,000	$200,000	$900,000

In contrast, an unconsolidated balance sheet is reflected in the middle column of Exhibit 15-2, "Major Corp. After Reorganization." The balance associated with the account, "Investment in Subsidiary," clearly indicates that the accounts of the subsidiary have not been combined with those of the parent. An unconsolidated balance sheet would interest the creditors of Major Corporation: those creditors associated with the $75,000 current liabilities only have recourse against the assets of Major Corporation and have no claim against the assets of Minor Corporation. (Remember, the corporate form of organization is recognized by the courts as having limited legal liability.) All of the asset and liability accounts of the subsidiary are summarized in the Investment account in unconsolidated parent-company balance sheets.

Stock-for-stock Exchange. Some parent-subsidiary relationships are created when a parent acquires all of the capital stock of a subsidiary in exchange for its own capital stock. This form of business combination is commonly known as a *pooling of interests.* A business combination resulting from a pooling of interests is viewed by the accounting profession as a modification in existing reporting entities rather than as an accounting transaction requiring revaluation of assets and liabilities. Financial statements after a pooling of interests will maintain the same book values for assets and liabilities for the entities as existed before the business combination.

A pooling of interests may best be described with reference to an example. Part A of Exhibit 15-3 presents summarized balance sheets for two companies, Pater, Inc., and Sunco. Although the common stock of both companies has a $10 par value, no single stockholder owns stock in both companies. Managers for both companies agree on a pooling of interests in which Sunco stockholders will receive one newly issued Pater share for each Sunco share they hold. The stockholders of both companies agree to the plan, and the stock-for-stock exchange occurs.

Assuming that Sunco operations will be merged into those of Pater, Inc., and that Sunco will cease operating as a separate legal entity, the following entry will be recorded in Pater's journal to reflect the pooling of interests.

Assets	$200,000	
Liabilities		$ 50,000
Capital Stock (par)		25,000
Additional Paid in Capital		110,000
Retained Earnings		15,000

The first two lines of the journal entry carry over to Pater's books the balances that had been recorded in Sunco's individual asset and liability accounts. Obviously, if Sunco had hundreds of such accounts, the journal entry would be quite extensive. The last line of the journal entry carries forward to Pater (the surviving entity) all of the accumulated Sunco Retained Earnings: in effect, this is a retroactive recognition of Sunco's prior earnings history. The Capital Stock credit reflects the par value of new Pater stock issued to the old Sunco stockholders. Since this pooling of interests involved a one-for-one exchange of shares with identical par values, the equity accounts after the pooling represent the sum of the prepooling balances for both Pater and Sunco. Thus, the equity accounts were summed because of the nature of the exchange and the equality of par values. Part B of Exhibit 15-3 presents a postpooling balance sheet for Pater, Inc. In contrast to the previous example, if it is assumed that Sunco would continue to operate as a separate legal entity after the pooling of interest, the Pater journal entry, to record the pooling, appears as follows:

Investment in Subsidiary	$150,000	
Capital Stock (par)		$ 25,000
Additional Paid in Capital		110,000
Retained Earnings		15,000

The Investment in Subsidiary account receives a balance equal to the net assets carried on Sunco's books. After the exchange of stock, all of the outstanding Sunco shares would be held by Pater and would serve as evidence to support the Investment account. No journal entry would be required by Sunco, since the exchange of stock occurred between the shareholders of Sunco and Pater, Inc. Postpooling balance sheets for Pater, Inc., and Sunco are displayed in Part A of Exhibit 15-4. Part B of Exhibit 15-4 presents a consolidated statement, which would be most meaningful to stockholders, since all stockholders hold Pater, Inc., stock. Notice that the consolidated balances reflect the sum of all accounts for both compa-

| | Part A Unconsolidated | | Part B Consolidated |
	Pater, Inc.	Sunco	Pater, Inc.
Investment	$150,000	0	0
Assets	700,000	$200,000	$900,000
Total Assets	$850,000	$200,000	$900,000
Liabilities	$400,000	$50,000	$450,000
Capital Stock ($10 par)	125,000	25,000	125,000
Additional Paid in Capital	145,000	110,000	145,000
Retained Earnings	180,000	15,000	180,000
	$850,000	$200,000	$900,000

nies, except the reciprocal $150,000 Investment in Subsidiary account of Pater and the three equity accounts of Sunco, which total $150,000. (Also note that Part B of Exhibits 15-3 and 15-4 contain identical balances: the former balance sheet reflects the actual combination of Pater and Sunco, while the latter reflects the consolidation of the two.)

Whenever the par value of stock given by the parent differs from the par value of stock received from stockholders of the subsidiary, the equity accounts after a pooling of interests will not be identical to the sum of the separate equity accounts of the parent and subsidiary. Full discussion of this point is well beyond the scope of this book. Interested readers are directed to any standard advanced accounting textbook. We can state, however, that the consolidated Common Stock balance equals the par value of outstanding parent common stock. The consolidated Retained Earnings balance will never be larger than the combined parent and subsidiary Retained Earnings balances, although it is often smaller than the combined sum.

Purchase Transactions. A parent-subsidiary relationship can be created whenever a parent purchases the stock or assets of a subsidiary. Stock would be acquired from the subsidiary's stockholders, while assets would be acquired directly from the subsidiary.

As compensation for its acquired investment, the parent may distribute cash, marketable debt securities (bonds), or newly issued common stock. In any event, the market value of compensation given in the purchase of a subsidiary determines the value of the investment. Obviously, the Investment account is most easily valued when a parent makes a cash purchase. It is less easily valued when the parent acquires the subsidiary for its own common stock, since stock values tend to change on a day-to-day basis. Most often, the managers of the parent and subsidiary agree on a method for valuing the stock, such as a six-month average of the daily closing prices. Once the method is agreed on, the valuation itself is relatively easy.

For example, the Gramp Company acquires all of the assets of the Junior Company for $4,675,000 in cash. The purchase would be recorded in Gramp's journal by the following entry:

Investment in Subsidiary	$4,675,000	
Cash		$4,675,000

If Gramp issued new common stock having a market value $4,675,000 to acquire Junior's assets, the specific journal entry used would depend on the market price per share, par value per share, and the number of shares issued. If the market price per share was $50, par value was $20, and 93,500 shares were issued, Gramp's journal would reflect the following entry:

Investment in Subsidiary	$4,675,000	
Common Stock (par)		$1,870,000
Additional Paid in Capital		2,805,000

Several comments should be made about these journal entries used to record the purchase of Junior by Gramp. First, the Investment in Subsidiary account is always valued at the market value of consideration that is given to consummate the purchase. Second, the Common Stock account always reflects the par value of securities issued, and the additional Paid in Capital account reflects the difference between par value and market value: the Retained Earnings account is never credited as part of a purchase transaction. Third, the acquisition journal entry is not affected by the means in which the parent gains control over the subsidiary; an acquisition of assets or of subsidiary common stock would be recorded with journal entries. Finally, it is highly unlikely that the value attributed to the Investment in Subsidiary account is equal to the values of the underlying subsidiary net assets. Further elaboration of this final point appears in the following section.

A parent can acquire a subsidiary in exchange for newly issued parent company common stock. The market price of parent company stock is determined by many factors, including the parent's earnings, dividends, and financial leverage (associated with liquidity and solvency risks). In addition, interest rates, inflation, economy growth, and other environmental factors also affect the price of common stock. In other words, much of the day-to-day change in the price of the parent's stock are associated with elements beyond the control of the parent.

CREATING A
PARENT-SUBSIDIARY
RELATIONSHIP

At the same time, the individual assets and liabilities of the subsidiary reflect historical costs altered by accounting adjustments. For example, inventories are reflected at LIFO, FIFO, and/or Lower of Cost or Market adjustments. Net Plant and Equipment valuations reflect estimated project lives and alternative depreciation methods. Few of the assets or liabilities reflect changed market conditions, such as inflation or supply/demand factors associated with current replacement costs or disposal values. The accounting convention of "conservatism" generally tends to understate asset market values.

Additionally, accountants face the problem of valuing the total package consisting of the subsidiary's separate assets and liabilities. For many elements of the package, the total value is not equal to the sum of the values of the separate parts. For example, the value of a fleet of cars is not the same as the sum of the value of the individual cars; the value of the individual parts of an automobile are not equal to the value of the automobile. Even if the accountant could determine the value of the subsidiary's individual assets, the sum of these probably would not equal the total value of the subsidiary.

Excess Cost over Net Book Value. Whenever the acquisition price for a subsidiary is larger than the book value of the subsidiary's net assets, goodwill may be recognized when the transaction is recorded as a purchase. Accountants presume that a difference between the price and book value indicates that the individual acquired assets are undervalued or that some positive goodwill is associated with the subsidiary. Goodwill is an intangible asset that is recognized under the account name *Goodwill* or *Excess Cost Over Book Value of Acquired Subsidiary.* For example, if Parent Company acquires a 100% interest in Sub Corp. for $100,000 when the net assets of Sub are appraised to only $80,000, the transaction may be journalized as follows:

Goodwill	$20,000	
Investment in Subsidiary	80,000	
Cash		$100,00

This excess cost over net book value may reflect the fact that the parent has acquired two elements in one package, the net assets of the subsidiary and an additional intangible asset that had not been previously recognized on the subsidiary's book. Generally accepted accounting procedures require that the excess cost over net book value must first be assigned to specific undervalued assets of the acquire subsidiary (to revalue them at their current purchase value). That is, the excess cost is used to correct any undervaluation that may appear on the subsidiary's book. The remaining excess will be labeled Goodwill. Goodwill is not to be written off as a lump sum immediately after the purchase; instead, it should be amortized by systematic charges against income for a period not to exceed forty years. Revaluation of acquired assets and recognition of Goodwill occur as part of the consolidation process, a subject discussed in the following section. That is, these two types of accounting events may not be reflected in the subsidiary's records.

Consolidation of a Purchased Subsidiary. Consolidation of a purchased subsidiary is best described with reference to a specific case. For example, the Parent Company acquires (from Subsidiary's stockholders) all of the outstanding common stock of Subsidiary, Inc., for $200,000. Immediately preceding the acquisition, the financial position of each company appeared as follows:

	Parent	*Subsidiary*
Current Assets	$230,000	$ 15,000
Plant and Equipment	200,000	95,000
Total	$430,000	$110,000
Current Liabilities	$ 5,000	$ 10,000
Common Stock	130,000	20,000
Additional Paid In Capital	120,000	5,000
Retained Earnings	175,000	75,000
Total	$430,000	$110,000

Parent's journal would reflect the following entry to record the acquisition transaction:

Investment in Subsidiary	$200,000	
Cash		$200,000

This $200,000 acquisition price is $100,000 larger than the net assets recognized on Subsidiary's books. For the sake of this illustration, assume that the excess $100,000 is attributable to a $65,000 undervaluation of Plant and Equipment and the remaining $35,000 is associated with Goodwill. In other words, the account, Investment in Subsidiary, reflects a whole host of factors. A detailed journal entry to merge the Subsidiary account balances directly into the Parent account balances would have appeared as follows:

Current Assets	$ 15,000	
Plant and Equipment	160,000	
Goodwill	35,000	
Liabilities		$ 10,000
Cash		200,000

Consolidation will allow the Parent Company to prepare a balance sheet as if the detailed journal entry had been used, even though the summarized

EXHIBIT 15-5
CONSOLIDATION OF A PURCHASED SUBSIDIARY:
BALANCE SHEETS, IMMEDIATELY AFTER THE ACQUISITION

	Parent Company	Subsidiary, Inc.	Consolidated Entity
Current Assets	$ 30,000	$ 15,000	$ 45,000
Plant and Equipment	200,000	95,000	360,000
Goodwill	0	0	35,000
Investment in Subsidiary	200,000	0	0
Total	$430,000	$110,000	$440,000
Liabilities	$ 5,000	$ 10,000	$ 15,000
Common Stock	130,000	20,000	130,000
Additional Paid In Capital	120,000	5,000	120,000
Retained Earnings	175,000	75,000	175,000
Total	$430,000	$110,000	$440,000

journal entry is actually used. Thus, consolidation allows the combination of accounts for two seqparate entities: each entity can maintain its own set of accounting records, but the financial reports will reflect the combined financial position of the total economic entity. Balance sheets for the Parent Company, Subsidiary, Inc., and the Consolidated Entity are illustrated in Exhibit 15-5.

The consolidated balances of Current Assets and Liabilities are determined by adding the separate Parent and Subsidiary balances. Half of the Investment in Subsidiary balance, $100,000, relates to (and offsets) the three Subsidiary equity accounts. The remaining $100,000 in the Investment in Subsidiary account is allocated to Plant and Equipment, and Goodwill. Thus, consolidated Plant and Equipment represents the sum of $200,000, $95,000, and $65,000. The consolidated equity accounts are identical to Parent's equity accounts, since the owners of the parent are the direct and indirect owners of the consolidated entity.

The underlying events in this case were relatively simple; yet the consolidated balances are not intuitively obvious. Accountants often prepare worksheets to aid in the preparation of consolidated financial statements. The following section describes consolidation work sheets.

Consolidation Worksheets

The accountant who prepares consolidated financial statements usually develops a worksheet to help determine the correct consolidated balances. First the year-end parent and subsidiary financial statements are entered in

EXHIBIT 15-6
CONSOLIDATION WORKSHEET
December 31, 19X1

	Separate Balance Sheets		Adjustments		Consolidated Balance Sheet
	P	S	Debit	Credit	
Debits					
Cash	$ 2,200	$ 1,500			$ 3,700
Accounts Receivable	9,800	7,600			17,400
Notes Receivable	15,000	10,000		$ 6,000 (a)	19,000
Dividends Receivable	8,000	0		8,000 (b)	0
Investment in Bonds of P	0	9,800		9,800 (c)	0
Investment in Stock of S	110,000	0		110,000 (d)	0
Inventory	50,000	25,000			75,000
Other Assets	252,000	77,100			329,100
Total	$447,000	$131,000			$444,200
Credits					
Accounts Payable	$ 23,000	$ 7,000			$ 30,000
Notes Payable to P	0	6,000	6,000 (a)		0
Dividends Payable	0	8,000	8,000 (b)		0
Bonds Payable	98,000	0	9,800 (c)		88,200
Capital Stock	105,000	30,000	30,000 (d)		105,000
Additional Paid-In Capital	50,000	10,000	10,000 (d)		50,000
Retained Earnings	171,000	70,000	70,000 (d)		171,000
Total	$447,000	$131,000			$444,200

parallel columns, as shown in Exhibit 15-6, columns P and S. The accountant then compiles information about the extent of intercompany activity and the methods used by the separate entities to record this activity. This additional information is used to prepare adjustment entries that eliminate intercompany balances, as shown in the middle set of columns in Exhibit 15-6. These adjustment entries suppress balances associated with interfirm activities that do not involve transactions with independent parties outside of the consolidated group. The numbers across each row of the worksheet are then combined (giving proper recognition to debit and credit balances) to derive consolidated balances. The last column of Exhibit 15-6 lists consolidated balances that will appear in the consolidated balance sheet.

The worksheet in Exhibit 15-6 is keyed to the following explanations.

(a) Scan the list of accounts from top to bottom. The first account, which contains reciprocal balances, is Notes Receivable. S owes P $6,000. This balance is reflected in the S Notes Payable as well as in the P receivables but affects no party outside the consolidated entity; the consolidated entity owes itself the $6,000. Since the final consolidated balance in both accounts is produced by the process of cross-footing, the worksheet adjustment needed is as follows:

Notes Payable	$6,000	
Notes Receivable		$6,000

This entity eliminates the redundant reciprocal balances.

(b) The Dividend Receivable account of P is directly related to the Dividend Payable account of S: the directors of S have declared, but have not yet paid, an $8,000 dividend. P owns all of the stock of S: it will be the sole recipient of the dividend. Since the asset account, Dividends Receivable, has a debit balance, the suppressing adjustment must credit this account, as follows:

Dividends Payable	$8,000	
Dividends Receivable		$8,000

(c) The Investment in Bonds of P account on the S books relates directly to the Bonds Payable account on the P books. An adjustment would remove all of the investment and 10 percent of the payable as follows:

Bonds Payable	$9,800	
Investment in Bonds		$9,800

If S had acquired its Investment in Bonds of P from third parties, the cost of the investment might well differ from the original issuance price. However, discussion of this additional complexity is beyond the scope of this text.

(d) An adjustment to the Investment in Stock of the S account offsets $110,000 against the equity accounts of S: Capital Stock, Additional Paid In Capital, and Retained Earnings. That is, all four accounts are linked to the outstanding shares issued by S and wholly owned by P.

Worksheets are not absolutely necessary; in simple cases where little intercompany activity has occurred, the accountant may prepare consolidated reports directly from the original separate company reports. However, there are several advantages in preparing worksheets for all consolidations. By preparing worksheets, accountants are forced to formalize their thinking and to explicitly state any necessary adjustments. Worksheets allow for a division of labor, so that more than one person may be engaged on the project. They also facilitate review of the consolidating work by others. Finally, having a worksheet will help in next year's preparation, since it represents a model to be followed.

Consolidated Income Statement

Consolidated income statements are prepared by combining balances for like accounts from the parent and all subsidiaries. The Revenue account balances for all units would be accumulated to determine Consolidated

Revenue. Similarly, the expense account balances would be accumulated to produce Consolidated Expense. However, consolidated balances would have to be adjusted to eliminate the double-counting effects of reciprocal transactions. Two types of reciprocal transactions are commonly found when preparing consolidated income statements: recognition by the Parent of subsidiary earnings and intercompany sales of goods or services.

Consolidation adjustments for reciprocal income statement transactions are best described with reference to an example. The S Company is a wholly owned subsidiary of the P Corporation. Income statements for both companies are presented in Part A of Exhibit 15-7. The account, Income from Subsidiary—$20,000 (disclosed on the P income statement)—clearly indicates that P recognizes income from the subsidiary under the equity method. This $20,000 balance should not be disclosed in the consolidated income statement, since all of the separate revenue and expense items underlying the $20,000 will be reflected in the statement. That is, including this $20,000 would constitute double counting.

Additional information about the relationship between P and S might indicate that one unit sold goods or provided services to the other unit at a profit. For example, assume that S Company provided maintenance services to P Corporation. Actual costs to S Company of labor and supplies for these services amounted to $5,000, but S charged P $9,000 for these services. That is, the S Revenue account reflects $9,000 while its Expense account reflects $5,000. Since P acquired these services from S, the P Expense account also reflects $9,000. From a consolidated entity point of view, total expense for maintenance should be $5,000 rather than $14,000 ($5,000 + $9,000). Furthermore, Revenue will be overstated by $9,000 if no adjustment is made for the intercompany service.

Part B of Exhibit 15-7 illustrates a consolidation income statement worksheet. The accounts have been reordered so that all credit balance accounts appear together. The total of the debit balance accounts is set equal to the total credit balance by including a line item for Net Income. Two adjustments are reflected on the worksheet: adjustment (a) suppresses the double counting of $9,000 expenses and the intercompany Revenue item. Adjustment (b) removes the redundant $20,000 Income from Subsidiary. Neither of these adjustments change the $48,000 Net Income that accrues to the benefit of the P stockholders. After the adjustments, however, the consolidated Revenue and Expense accounts only reflect transactions that involved third parties: no intraconsolidated-group transactions are reflected in the income statement.

Additional adjustments are required whenever intercompany sales of goods occur. These adjustments become quite complicated whenever some of these goods remain within the consolidated group at the end of the accounting period, that is, when they have not been sold to third parties. Ad-

EXHIBIT 15-7
SEPARATE COMPANY INCOME STATEMENTS AND CONSOLIDATION WORKSHEET

Part A
SEPARATE COMPANY STATEMENTS
Period Ended December 31, 19X1

Income Statement	P Corporation	S Company
Sales Revenue	$1,000,000	$500,000
Cost of Sales	850,000	325,000
Gross Profit	$ 150,000	$175,000
Expenses	(122,000)	(155,000)
Income from Subsidiary	20,000	
Net Profit	$ 48,000	$ 20,000

Part B
CONSOLIDATION WORKSHEET

	Separate Income Statements		Adjustments		Consolidated Income Statement
	P	S	Debit	Credit	
Revenue	$1,000,000	$500,000			$1,491,000
Income from Subsidiary	20,000		$ 9,000 (a)		
			20,000 (b)		
	$1,020,000	$500,000			
Cost of Sales	$ 850,000	$325,000			(1,175,000)
Expenses	122,000	155,000		$ 9,000 (a)	(268,000)
Net Income	48,000	20,000		20,000 (b)	
Total	$1,020,000	$500,000			$ 48,000

ditional complexities arise whenever a subsidiary involved in these intragroup transactions is not completely controlled by the parent, that is, when the parent owns less than 100 percent of the outstanding common stock of the subsidiary. Other than noting the existence of these adjustment problems, further discussion is well beyond the scope of this book. Interested readers are referred to any standard advanced accounting textbook.

Parent-subsidiary relationships can be reported to the public in a number of ways. First, consolidated financial statements may be prepared and issued. Second, financial statements might be prepared for each separate legal entity. Third, the parent might issue its own unconsolidated financial statement. Each of these alternatives has been persuasively defended (and also attacked) in the financial literature.

Reporting Parent-Subsidiary Relationships

Consolidated reporting is the predominant mode in the United States. The American financial community presumes that consolidated financial statements are more meaningful than separate legal entity or unconsolidated parent company statements. Institutions such as the Securities and Exchange Commission and the American Institute of Certified Public Accountants believe that consolidation is necessary for fair presentation of operating results and the financial position for groups of entities organized in parent-subsidiary networks. The widespread acceptance of consolidated reporting amply demonstrates the usefulness of this form of financial reporting. Primary beneficiaries of consolidated reporting are the stockholders of the parent company.

Unconsolidated parent company statements are the common mode of reporting in several foreign countries. This form predominates in Germany, for example, where ownership interests are not widely held and where central bankers play an important part in the long-term financing of business operations. Complete reporting for each legal entity isn't especially popular, given the large number of units used by most large organizations. Some large American corporations have several hundred separate legal entities within the consolidated group.

Not all corporations within the parent-subsidiary relationship should be consolidated. To be considered for consolidation, the parent must currently control and plan to have continued control over the subsidiary management. The subsidiary and parent operations must be homogeneous (e.g., a bank cannot be consolidated with a manufacturing organization). The fiscal years of parent and subsidiary should close within a short period of each other, and the consolidated financial statements must afford a valid reflection of the financial position and results of operations of the constituent units. Consolidation may not be appropriate if these criteria are violated.

Summary

A controlling interest is acquired whenever more than 50 percent of the common stock of a corporation is acquired by one stockholder. Where the one stockholder is a corporation, a parent-subsidiary relationship is created. From the viewpoint of the parent's stockholders, both the parent and the subsidiary can be viewed as a single economic entity. Consolidated financial reports do present the financial position and results of operations for parent-subsidiary relationships as if they represented a single economic entity.

Parent-subsidiary relationships can be created by having the parent transfer assets to a newly created subsidiary or by acquiring the controlling interest directly from the subsidiary's stockholders. Alternately, the parent might acquire a controlling interest by obtaining the assets of a subsidiary in exchange for cash, debt securities, or its own common stock. Acquired subsidiaries may result from the pooling of interests or a purchase transaction. In a pooling, assets of the subsidiary are valued at existing book value and retained earnings of the subsidiary are carried forward to the surviving entity. Under the purchase method, the acquired assets are recorded at market value, while any additional excess of cost over book value is recognized as an intangible asset, Goodwill. Goodwill must be amortized periodically to income over the period not to exceed forty years.

Consolidation is the process of aggregating parent and subsidiary account balances into a single set of asset, liability, owners' equity, revenue, and expense accounts. While combining accounts, care is taken to exclude reciprocal balances that only relate to activities or relationships within the parent-subsidiary group. Worksheets can be prepared to facilitate the consolidation process. Consolidated financial reporting is appropriate in most instances and is the most commonly used method of reporting parent-subsidiary relationships in the United States.

Supplementary Discussion: Minority Interests

Whenever a parent acquires less than 100 percent ownership af a subsidiary, consolidated financial statements will reflect a subordinated ownership claim commonly labeled Minority Interest. *Minority Interest* represents ownership rights in the subsidiary held by parties other than the parent. The dollar balance in Minority Interest is determined by multiplying the subsidiary's net assets by the percentage of stock held by minority stockholders.

For example, consider a case in which the parent acquires 90 percent of the outstanding stock of Subco for $90,000. Subco had net assets of $100,000 on the day of the acquisition, so no Goodwill is associated with the acquisition. The parent would journalize the transaction in summary form as follows:

Investment in Subsidiary	$90,000	
Cash		$90,000

Immediately after recording the acquisition entry, balance sheets for the parent and

EXHIBIT 15-8
CONSOLIDATION WORKSHEET DISCLOSURE OF MINORITY INTEREST

	Parent	Subco	Debit	Credit	Consolidated Entity
Current Assets	$ 50,000	$ 15,000			$ 65,000
Plant and Equipment	200,000	95,000			295,000
Investment in Subsidiary	90,000	0		$90,000	0
Total	$340,000	$110,000			$360,000
Liabilities	$ 35,000	$ 10,000			$ 45,000
Common Stock	40,000	20,000	$20,000		40,000
Additional Paid-In Capital	120,000	55,000	55,000		120,000
Retained Earnings	145,000	25,000	25,000		145,000
Minority Interest	0	0		10,000	10,000
Total	$340,000	$110,000			$360,000

Subco would appear as in the first two columns of the consolidation work sheet illustrated in Exhibit 15-8.

The consolidation adjustment offsets the Investment in Subsidiary balance of $90,000 against the equity accounts of Subco, Common Stock, Additional Paid In Capital, and Retained Earnings, for a total of $100,000. Obviously, an additional credit of $10,000 is required to maintain the equality between debits and credits. The $10,000 credit is attributed to the account, Minority Interest. In retrospect, it can be seen that the original $100,000 net asset value of the subsidiary was claimed as $90,000 by the parent and $10,000 by the minority stockholders.

The account, Minority Interest, usually is disclosed on consolidated balance sheets in one of three places: within the liability section, between the liability and owners' equity sections, or within the owners' equity section. In theory, Minority Interest is not a liability, since there is no legal obligation for the parent to ever pay the minority shareholders any amount at any known future date, for any services rendered. In reality, Minority Interest reflects an ownership interest claim against some of the assets reflected on the balance sheet: in this sense, Minority Interest is a subordinated ownership claim, since the parent stockholders have ownership claims against all of the assets. Nevertheless, Minority Interest is most often found on consolidated balance sheets within the liability section.

Cost method
Equity method
Subsidiary
Consolidated financial statements
Reciprocal accounts
Pooling of interests
Goodwill

Key Terms

1. Why are the stockholders of a parent company considered indirect owners of subsidiary companies, in contrast to being considered direct owners?

2. By what two methods are parent-subsidiary relationships created?

3. Identify the most frequent types of intercompany transactions encountered in preparing consolidated financial statements.

4. What does a controlling interest refer to? Describe the relationship between a corporation that exercises a controlling interest and the controlled corporation.

5. Why might the price paid to acquire a controlling interest in a subsidiary be different from the book value of the equity acquired?

6. What determines the value of an investment of a subsidiary acquired by a pooling of interests, as reflected on the books of the parent?

7. Wood Sales, Inc., has an 80 percent ownership interest in Oak Corp., a 100 percent interest in Maple Co., and a 50 percent interest in Lumber Ltd. Which entities may Wood consolidate for financial reporting purposes?

8. List and describe two criteria that must be satisfied before a subsidiary may be consolidated in the financial statements.

9. How is the value of a minority interest determined when preparing consolidated financial statements?

10. Should an account identified as Excess Cost Over Book Value of Acquired Subsidiary be classified as an asset, a liability, or an equity account? What is another common name for this account?

11. Should an account identified as Minority Interest be classified as an asset, a liability, or an equity account?

12. Company A owns a 100 percent interest in Corporation B, acquired in a purchase transaction. Which account on A's balance sheet will indicate that B has not been consolidated, assuming that it has not been consolidated? If B is included within the consolidated financial statements, the presence of which account may reflect the fact of consolidation?

13. Company B acquired a 100 percent interest in Corporation C through a purchase transaction at a cost in excess of book value. What is the accounting disposition of the account, Cost in Excess of Book Value, as reflected in the current and future consolidated financial statements?

1. Lee Company paid $480,000 cash for all of the capital stock of Mob Corp. At the date of acquisition, Lee's total stockholders' equity consisted of $1,700,000 Capital Stock and $1,100,000 Retained Earnings, while Mob reflected $460,000 Capital Stock and $20,000 Retained Earnings. Prepare the stockholders' equity section for a consolidated balance sheet immediately after the acquisition.

2. Kar Corporation purchased all the outstanding shares of Lab Co. for cash of $2,800,000. At that time, Lab's accounts reflected total assets of $3,400,000 and total liabilities of $1,400,000. In consolidation, Lab's assets will be reflected at what dollar amount?

3. Total assets of S Company reflect a book value of $200,000, even though their fair market value is $280,000. S also has liabilities of $10,000. P Corporation purchases all the outstanding shares of S for cash of $270,000. Prepare a journal entry to record the acquisition of S by P, assuming you are P's bookkeeper.

4. Prepare the stockholders' equity section for a consolidated balance sheet, assuming that a 100 percent equity in the subsidiary was acquired in a pooling of interests transaction.

	Unconsolidated Account Balances	
	Parent	Subsidiary
Investment in Subsidiary	$600,000	$ 0
Capital Stock, $10 par	800,000	480,000
Additional Paid-in Capital	150,000	70,000
Retained Earnings	160,000	50,000

5. Okay Company entered into an agreement with ABC Company whereby Okay acquired all 3,000 shares of ABC's $50 par value stock. In return Okay transferred 1,200 shares of its $100 par value stock (currently selling for $200/share). Before the agreement the two firms had the following balance sheets:

	Okay	ABC
Net Assets	$600,000	$180,000
Common Stock	$480,000	$150,000
Retained Earnings	120,000	30,000
	$600,000	$180,000

(a) Prepare a consolidated balance sheet immediately after the transaction, assuming that the acquisition will be treated as a purchase.
(b) Prepare a consolidated balance sheet immediately after the transaction, assuming that the acquisition will be treated as a pooling of interests.

6. (a) Circle Corp. acquired 90 percent of the outstanding stock of Fan Company for $270,000. The net assets of Fan Company on the day of acquisition were $200,000. What is the dollar balance in Minority Interest? Where is this balance recorded on the balance sheet?
(b) Thunder Company owns all of the voting shares of Wall Company. During the year Thunder earned $80,000 (including its share of Wall's earnings) while Wall earned $50,000. Determine the amount of consolidated net earnings for the year.

7. The Pears Company acquired the Sunny Company for $80,000. Immediately after acquisition, an appraisal of the fixed assets for Sunny established their fair market value at $90,000. Nonconsolidated balance sheets for the two companies are as follows:

Balance Sheets
Immediately After Acquisition

	Pears Company	Sunny Company
Cash	$ 15,000	$ 13,000
Note Receivable from Pears Co.		5,000
Investment in Sunny		
Co. (100%), at cost	80,000	
Fixed Assets	105,000	85,000
Total	$200,000	$103,000
Liabilities	$ 25,000	33,000
Note Payable to Sunny Co.	5,000	
Common stock, $1 par	130,000	50,000
Retained Earnings	40,000	20,000
Total	$200,000	$103,000

Prepare a consolidated balance sheet, assuming that the transaction was treated as a purchase.

8. On January 1, Carr Corp. purchased 100 percent of the common stock of Motor Company. At the end of the year, Carr's general ledger reflected Revenue of $150,000; Cost of goods sold of $100,000; Expenses of $40,000; Income from investments (in Motor Company) of $10,000. Motor's general ledger reflected Revenue of $80,000; cost of goods sold of $40,000; Expenses of $30,000. Motor Company had performed services for Carr Corp., billing $14,000 for services that cost Motor only $8,000 to perform. Prepare a consolidation worksheet similar to those described in the text. Complete the worksheet. Explain the adjustments.

9. On January 1, Stemm Company purchased 60 percent of the outstanding common stock of Dodd Company for $160,000 cash. The fair-market value of the assets equalled their book values. Immediately after the acquisition the balance sheets reflected the following:

Balance Sheets
Immediately After Acquisition

	Stemm Company	Dodd Company
Cash	$ 80,000	$ 30,000
Accounts Receivable	200,000	80,000
Investment in Dodd Co.	160,000	
Fixed Assets	300,000	150,000
Total	$740,000	$260,000
Liabilities	$ 65,000	$ 20,000
Common Stock, $5 par	100,000	25,000
Additional Paid-in Capital	300,000	125,000
Retained Earnings	275,000	90,000
Total	$740,000	$260,000

Prepare calculations to determine the amount of goodwill purchased.

10. On January 1, the Martin Corp. acquired 100 percent of the outstanding shares of stock of Dixie, Inc., in a transaction treated as a pooling of interests. After the acquisition, Dixie, Inc., will cease operations and be merged into the Martin Corp. Immediately before the transaction, a balance sheet of Dixie, Inc., showed the following:

Cash	$15,000	
Accounts Receivable	95,000	
Service Trucks	100,000	(fair market value, $120,000)
Current Liabilities	85,000	
Common Stock, $5 par	55,000	
Retained Earnings	70,000	

Journalize the acquisition transaction for Martin Corp., assuming that Martin exchanges one share of $5 par stock for each share of Dixie's common stock.

11. The following information relates to P Company and its subsidiary, S Company, one year after consolidation:

	P	S	Consolidated
Assets			
Cash	$ 60,000	$ 25,000	$ 85,000
Accounts Receivable	90,000	75,000	80,000
Inventory	280,000	170,000	450,000
Investment in S	500,000		
Long-term Assets	750,000	350,000	1,100,000
Excess of Cost over Book			20,000
Value of Investment in S	$1,680,000	$620,000	$1,735,000
Liabilities and Stockholders' Equity			
Accounts Payab;e	75,000	30,000	20,000
Long-term Payables	420,000	110,000	530,000
Capital Stock	800,000	300,000	800,000
Additional Paid-in Capital	210,000	60,000	210,000
Retained Earnings	175,000	120,000	175,000
	$1,680,000	$620,000	$1,735,000

For some accounts, the sum of the balances for P and S equals the balance reflected in the consolidated statement. Cash, is determined as follows: $60,000 + $25,000 = $85,000. This relation does not exist for other accounts. Please explain the nature of each adjustment required to reconcile the sum of balances for P and S to the Consolidated balance.

12. River Company and Current Company have entered into a contract to pool their firms into a single company. Using the following data answer the questions below.

	River	Current
Total Assets	$1,600,000	$1,300,000
Total Liabilities	500,000	600,000
Capital Stock (par value $10 for each)	700,000	500,000
Additional Paid-in Capital	100,000	100,000
Retained Earnings	300,000	100,000

(a) Prepare a journal entry for River Company that will account for a pooling of interests, assuming that 50,000 shares of River are exchanges for all of the stock of Current.

(b) Prepare a consolidated balance sheet that reflects the transaction recorded in requirement (a).

13. The Penn Corporation owns all of the outstanding common stock of the Sawyer Corporation. During 19X0 Sawyer declared a $10,000 cash dividend payable in 19X1. In addition, in 19X0 Penn borrowed $5,000 from Sawyer. The loan and $300 interest was repaid at the end of 19X0. Record the adjusting entries to eliminate these intercompany balances for 19X0.

14. During the course of the year 19X4, Glen Corporation, a 100 percent subsidiary of Ross Corporation, engaged in the following transactions with its parent:
(a) Sold assets costing $600,000 to Ross Corporation at a $100,000 loss.
(b) Loaned Ross Corporation $250,000, earning $12,500 in interest income.
(c) Leased from Ross Corporation equipment (on an operating lease contract) for $50,000.
Record these transactions by Glen Corporation, then give the entries necessary to adjust these intercompany balances.

15. On November 30, 19X7, File, Incorporated, purchased all 300,000 shares of the outstanding common stock of Mooney Company for cash of $25 per share. Mooney's balance sheet at November 30, 19X7, reflected net assets of $6,000,000. Additionally, the fair value of Mooney's property, plant and equipment on November 30, 19X7, was $800,000 in excess of its book value. What amount, if any, will be shown in the balance sheet caption "Goodwill" in the November 30, 19X7, consolidated balance sheet of File, Incorporated, and its wholly-owned subsidiary, Mooney Company (AICPA adapted)?

16. On January 1, 19X6, Brevity Corporation acquired as a long-term investment for $130,000 a 40 percent common stock interest in Astute Company. On that date, Astute had net assets of $300,000. During 19X6 Astute reported net income of $60,000 and declared and paid cash dividends of $15,000. (a) What is the maximum amount of income that Brevity can report from this investment for the calander year 19X6? (b) Determine the balance in Brevity's Investment account at the end of 19X6. (AICPA adapted)

17. On January 2, 19X6, Malt Corporation sold equipment costing $100,000 with accumulated depreciation of $25,000 to its wholly-owned subsidiary, Pacer, Inc. The selling price was $90,000. Malt was depreciating the equipment on the straight-line method over twenty years with no salvage value. Pacer continued this deprecia-

tion. At what amounts are the equipment and accumulated depreciation reflected in the December 31, 19X6, consolidated balance sheet (AICPA adapted)?

1. Ham Company owns 100 percent of the stock of Son Company. Below are the two income statements for the year after consolidation. **Problems**

	Ham	Son
Sales	$900,000	$450,000
Cost of Goods Sold	600,000	300,000
Gross Margin	$300,000	$150,000
Operating Expenses	(94,000)	(45,000)
Interest Expense	(6,000)	(11,000)
Interest Income	12,000	
Tax Expense	(90,000)	(38,000)
	$122,000	$ 56,000

Son sold merchandise to Ham for $40,000, which cost $32,000. None of this merchandise is included in Ham's ending inventory. Son paid $11,000 interest charges to Ham during the year. Ham's income statement does not include its equity interest in the subsidiarys' income.

Prepare a consolidated income statement for the year just ended.

2. On January 1, the Cosgrove Company exchanged one-third of its cash, one-fourth of its inventory, one-fourth of its current liabilities for all of the outstanding common stock of Nills Corporation, a new entity created by Cosgrove on this date. The number of shares received by Cosgrove is determined by the book value of assets transferred to Nills. Nills Corporation is authorized to issue up to 1,000,000 shares of $10 par value stock. Management attributes a value to Nills Common Stock of $20 per share. The balance sheet for Cosgrove Co., immediately before the exchange, is as follows:

COSGROVE COMPANY
Balance Sheet
Immediately Before the Exchange

Cash	$ 90,000
Accounts Receivable	260,000
Inventory	160,000
Plant and Equipment	550,000
Total Assets	$1,060,000
Current Liabilities	$ 120,000
Long-term Liabilities	400,000
Common Stock, $10 par	150,000
Additional Paid-in Capital	255,000
Retained Earnings	135,000
Total Liabilities and Capital	$1,060,000

(a) Is the transaction a pooling of interests, a purchase, or neither? Explain.

(b) Prepare an entry made by Cosgrove Company to record the exchange.

(c) Prepare an entry made by Mills Corp. to record the exchange.

(d) Prepare unconsolidated balance sheets for Cosgrove Co. and for Nills Corp. after the above exchange. Prepare a consolidated balance sheet.

3. The unconsolidated balance sheets of the Ladd Corp. and King Company, immediately after the Ladd Corp. acquired King, are given below:

Balance Sheets
Immediately After Acquisition

	Ladd Corp.	King Company
Cash	$ 80,000	$ 40,000
Accounts Receivable	40,000	15,000
Inventory	170,000	80,000
Investment in King Co., cost	240,000	
Plant and Equipment	160,000	130,000
Total Assets	$690,000	$265,000
Current Liabilities	$ 25,000	$ 45,000
Bond Payable, 7%	100,000	20,000
Common Stock, $10 par	450,000	150,000
Retained Earnings	115,000	50,000
Total Liabilities and Capital	$690,000	$265,000

After Ladd Corp. acquired King Company, it was determined that King Company's inventory was overstated by $6,000 and Plant and Equipment was understated by $31,000.

(a) Was this a pooling of interests or a purchase? Explain.

(b) Determine the amount of goodwill that would be reflected on the consolidated balance sheet, after considering all adjustments.

(c) At what amount will the assets of King Company be included in the consolidated balance sheet? Explain.

4. The Rass Company acquired a 100 percent interest in Tass Company from Tass's stockholders for $850,000. The fair market value of Tass' long-term assets are $900,000, even though their book value is $700,000. Balance sheets for the two companies immediately before the acquisition are presented below.

	Rass	Tass
Assets		
Current Assets	$1,800,000	$ 400,000
Long-term Assets	2,100,000	700,000
Total Assets	$3,900,000	$1,100,000
Liabilities and Stockholders' Equity		
Current Liabilities	$ 300,000	$ 250,000
Long-term Liabilities	850,000	350,000
Capital Stock	1,100,000	380,000
Retained Earnings	1,650,000	120,000
Total	$3,900,000	$1,100,000

Prepare a consolidated balance sheet.

5. On January 1 the Vast Company acquires 100 percent of the assets of the Mite Company from Mite's stockholders for $900,000 cash. The balance sheets of both companies *before* the acquisition are as follows:

Balance Sheets
Immediately Before the Exchange

	Vast Company	Mite Company
Cash	$1,100,000	$100,000
Accounts Receivable	600,000	200,000
Plant and Equipment	900,000	600,000
Total Assets	$2,600,000	$900,000
Current Liabilities	$ 400,000	$150,000
Long Term Liabilities	1,300,000	400,000
Common Stock, $1 par	100,000	50,000
Additional Paid-in Capital	500,000	250,000
Retained Earnings	300,000	50,000
Total Liabilities and Equity	$2,600,000	$900,000

On the date of acquisition, an appraisal determined the fair market value of Mite's Plant & Equipment to be $720,000.

REQUIRED:
(a) Should the transaction be recorded as a pooling of interests or a purchase? Explain.
(b) Prepare the entry required by Vast Company to record the acquisition.
(c) Analyze the acquisition to determine the amount of goodwill associated with the purchase.
(d) Prepare a consolidated balance sheet.

6. Assume the same facts as in Problem 5, except that Vast Company acquired 100 percent of the assets of Mite Company in exchange for 45,000 shares of newly issued stock. The Market price of Vast's common stock on the date of the acquisition was $20 per share.

REQUIRED:
(a) Is the acquisition a purchase or pooling of interests?
(b) Record the acquisition.
(c) Prepare a consolidated balance sheet as of the date of acquisition.

7. Condensed unconsolidated balance sheets at December 31, 19X2, for Boyd and Wynn Corporations prior to Boyd's acquisition of 100 percent of the stock of Wynn Corporation, are shown below:

	Boyd Corporation	Wynn Corporation
Assets		
Current Assets	$2,800,000	$ 600,000
Long-term Assets	3,100,000	1,000,000
Total Assets	$5,900,000	$1,600,000
Equities		
Current Liabilities	$ 500,000	$ 300,000
Long-term Liabilities	900,000	500,000
Capital Stock	1,000,000	500,000
Retained Earnings	3,500,000	300,000
Total Equities	$5,900,000	$1,600,000

On December 31, 19X2, Boyd acquired 100 percent of the stock of Wynn Corporation for $1,200,000, paid out of current assets. Wynn Corporation's long-term assets had a fair market value on the date of purchase of $1,400,000.

REQUIRED:
(a) Record the acquisition of the stock by Boyd Corporation.
(b) Prepare a consolidated balance sheet for these corporations immediately after the acquisition.

8. On July 14, 19X8, Pitt and Brown Corporations entered into a pooling type combination in which Pitt acquired all of Brown's 50,000 shares of $10 par value common stock by issuing 10,000 shares of its own $10 par value common stock. The fair market value of Pitt's common stock on the day of the transfer was $80 per share. Balance sheets for these two corporations on the day of the transaction, before pooling, are shown below:

	PITT CORPORATION Balance Sheet July 14, 19X8	BROWN CORPORATION Balance Sheet July 14, 19X8
Assets		
Current Assets	$ 200,000	$300,000
Long-term Assets	1,000,000	400,000
Total Assets	$1,200,000	$700,000
Equities		
Current Liabilities	$ 100,000	$ 50,000
Long-term Liabilities	500,000	100,000
Total Liabilities	$ 600,000	$150,000
Common Stock	$ 400,000	$500,000
Retained Earnings	200,000	50,000
Total Stockholders' Equity	$ 600,000	$550,000
Total Equities	$1,200,000	$700,000

REQUIRED:

(a) Record the acquisition of Brown's stock by Pitt Corporation.

(b) Prepare a consolidated balance sheet for these corporations immediately after the acquisition.

☐ 16
ANALYSIS OF OTHER DISCLOSURES AND A REVIEW OF POTENTIAL CHANGES IN FINANCIAL REPORTING

PART I: ANALYSIS OF OTHER DISCLOSURES

SIGNIFICANT ACCOUNTING POLICIES

FOOTNOTE DISCLOSURE

THE AUDITOR'S REPORT AS AN INFORMATION DISCLOSURE

SCOPE OF THE AUDIT

INTERIM REPORTING

REPORTING FOR SEGMENTS OF A BUSINESS

PROBLEMS IN PROVIDING SEGMENT DATA

TECHNICAL PROBLEMS

SEC REPORTING REQUIREMENTS

ANNUAL REPORT TO THE SEC

OTHER REPORTS TO THE SEC

REQUIRED REPLACEMENT COST DISCLOSURES

PART II: CONCEPTUAL FRAMEWORK OF FINANCIAL ACCOUNTING

IMPLICATIONS OF THE CONCEPTUAL FRAMEWORK PROJECT

MEASUREMENT OF THE ELEMENTS OF FINANCIAL STATEMENTS

SUMMARY—CONCEPTUAL FRAMEWORK PROJECT

A SUPPLEMENTARY DISCUSSION: ACCOUNTING FOR INTERNATIONAL OPERATIONS

FOREIGN ACCOUNTING PRINCIPLES

ACCOUNTING FOR MULTINATIONAL TRANSACTIONS

TRANSLATION OF FOREIGN BALANCES

SUMMARY

□ OBJECTIVES

AFTER STUDYING THIS CHAPTER, YOU SHOULD BE ABLE TO DO THE FOLLOWING:

1. LIST OTHER INFORMATION INCLUDED WITH THE FINANCIAL STATEMENTS.

2. DESCRIBE THE CONTENT AND INTERPRETATION OF THE AUDITOR'S OPINION.

3. EXPLAIN REQUIREMENTS FOR INTERIM REPORTING, BUSINESS SEGMENT REPORTING, REPLACEMENT COST DISCLOSURES, AND OTHER DISCLOSURES REQUIRED BY THE SECURITIES EXCHANGE COMMISSION.

4. DISCUSS THE EXTENSIONS TO CURRENT ACCOUNTING PRACTICES PROPOSED IN THE "CONCEPTUAL FRAME-WORK OF ACCOUNTING".

The first part of this chapter examines several disclosures included as a part of comprehensive financial reports in addition to the basic financial statements discussed in previous chapters. We will review six additional subjects:

1. Accounting policy disclosures.
2. Footnote and other information disclosures.
3. Auditor's report.
4. Interim reports.
5. Reporting for segments of a business.
6. Securities and Exchange Commission requirements.

The second part of this chapter focuses on potential changes in the direction of accounting and financial reporting in the future.

**Part I—
Analysis of Other
Disclosures**

**Significant
Accounting
Policies**

Management of each organization has considerable flexibility in selecting from alternative generally accepted accounting methods. The accounting methods selected by a firm can significantly affect the determination of financial position, changes in financial position, and results of operations. A hypothetical example of the effects of alternative accounting methods is provided in Exhibit 16-1. In this example, earnings per share could range from $1.00 to $1.95, depending on accounting methods, given one set of underlying economic circumstances. Therefore, the usefulness of the financial data will be enhanced if disclosure includes information regarding the methods used by the firm. When financial statements are supplemented by such information, the financial data of different firms can be adjusted for differing accounting alternatives to make them comparable.

Those accounting principles and methods of applying the principles selected by management are referred to as the *accounting policies* of the entity. Accounting Principles Board Opinion 22, "Disclosures of Accounting Policies" requires that "a description of all significant accounting policies of the reporting entity should be included as an integral part of the financial statement." Such disclosure should describe the accounting principles followed by the reporting entity and the method of applying those principles that materially affect the determination of financial position, changes in financial position, or results of operations. In general, the disclosure should identify principles and describe methods peculiar to the industry or other unusual or innovative applications of accounting principles. Accounting policy disclosure would include such items as the basis of consolidation, depreciation methods, amortization of intangibles, inventory cost-flow assumptions, income realization on long-term contracts, and recogni-

EXHIBIT 16-1
EFFECTS OF ALTERNATIVE GENERALLY ACCEPTED
ACCOUNTING PRINCIPLES
(WITH IDENTICAL ECONOMIC EVENTS)

	A Company	B Company
Sales Revenues (Net)	$10,000,000	$10,000,000
Expenses:		
Cost of Goods Sold[1]	$ 6,000,000	$ 5,600,000
Depreciation[2]	400,000	300,000
Pension Costs[3]	200,000	50,000
Salaries and Bonuses[4]	400,000	200,000
Miscellaneous Expense	2,000,000	2,000,000
Total Expenses	$ 9,000,000	$ 8,150,000
Income Before Taxes	$ 1,000,000	$ 1,850,000
Income Tax Expense	500,000	875,000
Net Income	$ 500,000	$ 975,000
Earnings Per Share (500,000 shares outstanding)	$ 1.00	$ 1.95

[1] A Company uses the last-in, first-out method for pricing inventories and B Company uses the first-in, first-out method.
[2] A Company uses accelerated depreciation for book and tax purposes, and B Company uses the straight-line method for financial accounting and accelerated depreciation for tax purposes.
[3] A Company expenses the normal cost plus amortization of past service costs (i.e., the maximum). and B Company expenses only the normal cost plus an amount equivalent to interest on unfunded prior service cost (i.e., the minimum).
[4] A Company pays incentive bonuses to officers in cash, and B Company grants stock options to officers.

Source: Adapted from Leonard Spacek, "Business Success Requires an Understanding of Unsolved Problems of Accounting and Financial Reporting," in James Lorie and Richard Brecky (eds.), *Modern Developments in Investments in Investment Management* (New York: Praeger Publishers, 1972), pp. 643–44.

tion of revenue from franchising or leasing operations. The Opinion did not require a specific format for accounting policy disclosures, but it did recommend that the disclosures could appear in a separate "Summary of Significant Policies" preceding the notes to the financial statements or as the initial note. In recent years, most large business enterprises have included in their annual reports a separate summary of their significant accounting policies.

**Footnote
Disclosure**

The information used in financial analysis is basically derived from the financial statements. Normally, however, the statements alone cannot provide all the information needed to understand the subtleties impounded in the financial position and results of operations. Consequently, *footnotes* are an important means of disclosing additional quantitative and qualitative information required for a proper interpretation of the statements. These footnotes are considered an integral part of the financial statements. Although footnote disclosures tend to be detailed and lengthy, they generally represent a vital input to the analysis process. Some of the more important topics covered by footnotes are the following:

1. Accounting methods used.
2. Changes in accounting principles and retroactive adjustments.
3. Contingent assets and liabilities.
4. Description of liabilities outstanding and credit agreements.
5. Information regarding stockholders' equity.
6. Long-term commitments.
7. Subsequent events.
8. Other useful disclosures.

These subjects are discussed and illustrated in the following paragraphs.

Accounting Methods Used. APB Opinion No. 22 requires that the accounting principles followed and methods of applying those principles must be described within the financial statements, preferably as the initial footnote or as a separate summary preceding the norms to the financial statements. Frequent disclosures concern the consolidation basis, depreciation methods, interperiod tax allocation, inventory cost flow assumptions, translation of foreign currencies, and revenue recognition.

Changes in Accounting Principle. APB Opinion No. 20—"Accounting Changes"—concluded that a change in accounting may significantly affect the financial statements, and therefore disclosures should be made to facilitate financial analysis. For most changes in principle, footnotes to the financial statements generally disclose the nature of and justification for the change as well as the effect of the change on net income and the related earnings per share. Footnotes are also frequently used to disclose the effect on income of a change in estimate. The excerpts from actual annual reports, shown in Exhibit 16-2, illustrate both types of footnotes.

Contingent Assets and Liabilities. A contingency involves circumstances shrouded in a considerable degree of uncertainty that *may* result in gains or losses through potential effects on asset or liability balances. Contingent liabilities arise from current or prospective litigation against the company, guarantees of indebtedness, and tax reassessments. Contingent assets may arise from loss carryforwards, claims for tax refunds, and patent in-

**ANALYSIS OF OTHER
DISCLOSURES AND A
REVIEW OF POTENTIAL
CHANGES IN FINANCIAL
REPORTING**

EXHIBIT 16-2
FOOTNOTE DISCLOSURE

Change in Accounting Principle:

MONSANTO COMPANY
Notes to Financial Statements
($ millions, except per share)
Depreciation, Obsolescence,
Depletion

	1972	1971
Charges against income:		
Depreciation and amortization	$168.4	$167.4
Obsolescence	21.7	14.7
Depletion	3.8	4.8
	$193.9	$186.9

Effective January 1, 1972, the Company changed from the sum of the years digits method to the straight line method of computing depreciation for financial statement purposes on domestic assets placed in service on or after that date. The reason for the change in policy was the desire to conform with prevailing industry practice. The change resulted in reduced depreciation charges of $5.0 and an increase in net income of $2.0 or 8 cents a share for the year.

It is estimated that the cumulative effect of the change in method will have a greater impact upon earnings in subsequent years.

The Company continued the use of the sum of the years digits method of computing depreciation on most domestic assets placed in service prior to 1972. The excess of depreciation provided by this method over straight line depreciation on such assets was $13.0 in 1972 and $18.3 in 1971.

Change in Accounting Estimate:

EMPIRE GAS CORPORATION
Notes to Consolidated Financial State-ments
Note 1 (in part): Summary of Significant Accounting Policies: Depreciation—Depreciation is provided for financial statement purposes by the straight-line method over the following estimated useful lives:

Buildings and improvements	20–40 years
Storage facilities	33 years
Customer service facilities	25 years
Transportation equipment	4–10 years
Office and other equipment	10 years

As a result of a survey conducted during the year, the Company extended the lives on bulk storage facilities from 20 to 30 years and on customer service facilities from 20 to 25 years. As a result of extending these lives, the net earnings of the Company for the current year were increased $185,000 or $.09 per common share on a fully diluted basis.

For income tax purposes, depreciation is computed by accelerated methods.

fringement suits against other parties. The usual means of disclosing contingencies is in the footnotes to the financial statements. An example of a footnote disclosure of a contingent liability is shown in Exhibit 16-3.

Description of Liabilities Outstanding and Credit Agreements. Typically, footnotes are used to disclose supplementary information regarding the na-

EXHIBIT 16-3
CONTINGENT LIABILITIES

WEIGHT WATCHERS INTERNATIONAL, INC.

Notes to Consolidated Financial Statements

Note 4: Commitments and Contingent Liabilities—The aggregate annual rentals under long-term leases expiring at varying dates to 1981 amount to approximately $175,000. Certain leases require payment of real estate taxes in excess of base period taxes.

A lawsuit seeking among other things, specific damages totalling $2,740,000 has been instituted by two commonly owned corporations which are franchisees of the Company. The most significant claim asserted is that the Company unlawfully limited the amount of the fees which the Plaintiffs could impose upon persons registering for and attending the weight reduction classes they operate. It is the opinion of special antitrust counsel that the issue presents a factual question requiring ultimate resolution by trial. However, it is the opinion of such counsel that the amount, if any, that the Plaintiffs are likely to recover, would be substantially less than the amount claimed.

The Company has also been named as defendant in various other actions but in the opinion of counsel, the outcome of these matters will have no material effect on the financial condition of the Company.

ture of current liabilities, long-term debt, and loan commitments for future loans or extensions of existing loans. In addition, footnote disclosure is often used to describe imputed interest on long-term payables not bearing interest or bearing an interest rate lower than the prevailing rate.

Information Regarding Stockholder's Equity. Companies present some information in the body of the balance sheet regarding the nature of equity securities. However, additional disclosure is usually presented in footnote form. The need for disclosure in connection with the capital structure of a corporation is stated APB Opinion No. 15—"Earnings per Share" as follows:

"...financial statements should include a description in summary form, sufficient to explain the pertinent rights and privileges of the various securities outstanding. Examples of information which should be disclosed are dividend and liquidation preferences, participation rights, call prices and dates, conversion or exercise prices or rates and pertinent dates, sinking fund requirements, unusual voting rights, etc."

This disclosure should also include a description of stock options or purchase plans outstanding. In addition, it is important to disclose the nature of any restrictions such as the amount of retained earnings available for cash dividends.

ANALYSIS OF OTHER DISCLOSURES AND A REVIEW OF POTENTIAL CHANGES IN FINANCIAL REPORTING

Long-term Commitments. Many businesses make various types of commitments for future performance. Such commitments include long-term

EXHIBIT 16-4
SUBSEQUENT EVENTS

CARNATION COMPANY

Notes to Consolidated Financial Statements

Note 9: Subsequent Events—To provide working capital for current and future expansion of its foreign operations, the Company issued on January 25, 1973 outside the United States, $25,000,000 of 4% Convertible Subordinated Debentures due in 1988. The debentures are convertible on and after August 1, 1973 and prior to maturity unless previously redeemed at the rate of 9.153 shares of common stock for each $1,000 principal amount (equivalent to a conversion price of $109¼ per share), subject to adjustment under certain circumstances. Initially, 228,825 shares of common stock have been reserved for conversion of the debentures.

lease agreements and pension and retirement plans. Some of these events are typically not reflected in their entirety in the accounts, but they are sufficiently important so that disclosures should be made in the notes to financial statements. Certain disclosures are required for pension plans (APB Opinion No. 8) and for long-term leases (APB Opinions No. 5 and No. 31).

Subsequent events. Events or transactions that occur subsequent to the end of the accounting period but prior to the issuance of financial statements and which have a material effect on the financial statements should be disclosed in the statements. Examples of subsequent events that may require disclosure are business combinations pending or affected, litigation settlements, issues of sale of bonds or capital stock, and catastrophic loss of plant or inventories. A footnote disclosing a subsequent event is presented in Exhibit 16-4.

Other Useful Disclosures. Footnote disclosure is often used to provide any other information relevant to the understanding and interpretation of the financial statement data. Examples of such information relate to foreign operations, product lines, sales backlogs, and inventory profits.

The Auditor's Report as an Information Disclosure

Financial statements are representations of the management of an entity to interested parties. Although management has a responsibility to disclose sufficient information to ensure that financial statements are not misleading, an independent auditor may evaluate these statements to express an opinion to third parties about the fairness of presentation of the statements. This independent audit provides confidence to readers of the financial statements about the quality of information provided to them. Consequently, the report prepared by the auditor may serve as an important input to the financial reporting process. However, readers must understand the meaning of the auditor's opinion and the implications of the opinion for financial statement analysis.

The *auditor's report* is written after the auditor has undertaken an extensive and objective study of the accounting process and the financial statements prepared by management. Auditors indicate in a report to the stockholders the scope of their examination and then express an opinion regarding the fairness of the financial statements. The standard format of a report that indicates no qualifications as to the fairness of the financial statements is as follows:

TO THE STOCKHOLDERS OF X COMPANY:

We have examined the balance sheet of X Company as of December 31, 19XX, and the related statements of income and retained earnings and changes in financial position for the year then ended. Our examination was made in accordance with generally accepted auditing standards, and accordingly included such tests of the accounting records and such other auditing procedures as we considered necessary in the circumstances.

In our opinion, the aforementioned financial statements present fairly the financial position of X Company at December 31, 19XX, and the results of its operations and the changes in its financial position for the year then ended in conformity with generally accepted accounting principles applied on a basis consistent with that of the preceding year.

This report is referred to as an *unqualified (clean) opinion* because the auditor has not qualified his opinion in any way.

Scope of the Audit. In the scope paragraph, the statement "Our examination was made in accordance with generally accepted auditing standards" relates to both general standards and standards of field work. Conformance to general standards implies that the examination was performed by adequately trained, proficient auditors who maintained an independent mental attitude and who exercised due professional care. Conformance to field standards implies that the work was properly planned, that assistants were adequately supervised, and that a sufficient study and evaluation of the internal control (of the business) was made.

Another important phrase in the scope paragraph states that the examination "accordingly included such tests of the accounting records and such other auditing procedures as we considered necessary in the circumstances." This statement relates principally to the standards of field work. The auditor's use of tests must be based on a proper study and evaluation of the client's system of internal control, and sufficient competent evidential matter must be obtained to justify an opinion on the financial statements.

ANALYSIS OF OTHER DISCLOSURES AND A REVIEW OF POTENTIAL CHANGES IN FINANCIAL REPORTING

The Opinion. The opinion paragraph of the auditor's report requires the auditor to express an opinion on the financial statements; or, if he cannot express an opinion, to clearly indicate so and state all the reasons. The four reporting standards are listed below:

1. The report shall state whether the financial statements are presented in accordance with generally accepted principles of accounting.
2. The report shall state whether such principles have been consistently observed in the current period in relation to the preceding period.
3. Informative disclosures in the financial statements are to be regarded as reasonably adequate unless otherwise stated in the report.
4. The report shall either contain an expression of opinion regarding the financial statements, taken as a whole, or an assertion to the effect that an opinion cannot be expressed. When an overall opinion cannot be expressed, the reasons therefore should be stated. In all cases where an auditor's name is associated with financial statements the report should contain a clear-cut indication of the character of the auditor's examination, if any, and the degree of responsibility he is taking.

Thus, if an auditor's examination is made in accordance with generally accepted auditing standards, and if the financial statements are fairly presented in conformity with generally accepted accounting principles, applied on a consistent basis, and include all necessary disclosures, the auditor will issue a "clean" (unqualified) opinion. In all other circumstances, the auditor must give either a qualified opinion, an adverse opinion, or disclaim an opinion.

In a *qualified opinion,* the auditor expresses certain reservations in his report concerning the scope of his examination and/or the financial statements. When the auditor's reservations are more serious, an adverse opinion or a disclaimer of opinion is given. In an adverse opinion, the auditor indicates that the financial statements do not present fairly the financial position and results of operations of the company. A disclaimer of opinion indicates that the auditor is unable to express an opinion. The inability to express an opinion usually occurs because of limitations in the scope of the audit.

The four major types of conditions that require the auditors to express an opinion other than unqualified opinion are as follows:

1. The scope of the auditor's examination is limited by:
   (a) Conditions that prevent the application of auditing procedures considered necessary in the circumstances.
   (b) Restrictions imposed by the client.
2. The financial statements do not present fairly the financial position or results of operations because of:
   (a) Lack of conformity with generally accepted Accounting Principles or Standards.

THE AUDITOR'S REPORT
AS AN INFORMATION
DISCLOSURE

(b) Inadequate disclosure.

3. Accounting principles are not consistently applied in the financial statements.

4. Uncertainties exist concerning the future resolution of material matters whose effects cannot be reasonably estimated.

The auditor's report for Bausch & Lomb Incorporated shown in Exhibit 16-5 illustrates a qualified opinion based on unusual uncertainties.

It should be apparent that information very relevant to the process of financial analysis may be revealed in the auditor's report. Consequently, the user of financial statements should carefully examine the auditor's opinion in relation to the other financial data in the annual report.

Interim Reporting

Interim financial reports, usually issued on a quarterly basis, are designed to provide more timely information than annual reports. Interim financial information may include data on financial position, results of operations, and changes in financial position, and it may take the form of either complete financial statements or summarized financial data. The publication of interim reports is required by companies listed on both the New York Stock Exchange and the American Stock Exchange. The Securities and Exchange Commission also requires all listed companies to file quarterly reports on Form 10-Q.

Because the ultimate results of operations cannot be known with certainty until the business is finally liquidated, many problems are incurred when allocating costs and revenues to relatively short time periods. Consequently, interim reports are subject to even more significant limitations than annual reports.

Given the problems inherent in determining interim financial results, it is important that the user fully understand the limitations of such data. However, the pronouncements of the APB and the FASB should serve to enhance the comparability of interim reports. When analyzed with the proper caution, it appears that the information contained in interim reports can be used to improve the user decision-making process.

Reporting for Segments of a Business

Diversified companies are required to disclose financial information concerning the activities of individual segments of the business. The term *segment* generally is used to describe a component of an entity whose activities relate to a separate major class of customer or product. Individual segments of a diversified company may be uniquely affected by economic conditions and have different rates of profitability, degrees of risk, and opportunities for growth. Therefore, segment financial data can help financial analysts and other users of financial statements learn about and make in-

ANALYSIS OF OTHER
DISCLOSURES AND A
REVIEW OF POTENTIAL
CHANGES IN FINANCIAL
REPORTING

EXHIBIT 16-5
QUALIFIED OPINION

To The Shareholders and Board of Directors of
BAUSCH & LOMB INCORPORATED

We have examined the consolidated financial statements appearing on pages 13 through 21 of this annual report of Bausch & Lomb Incorporated and its consolidated subsidiaries at December 31, 1972 and December 26, 1971. Our examinations were made in accordance with generally accepted auditing standards and accordingly included such tests of the accounting records and such other auditing procedures as we considered necessary in the circumstances.

As described in the note on litigation in the accompanying consolidated financial statements, the company was named as defendant in several legal actions. The current status of all the actions is at an early stage and the ultimate liability, if any, cannot now be determined.

In our opinion, except for the effect, if any, of the litigation referred to in the preceding paragraph, the accompanying financial statements present fairly the consolidated financial position of Bausch & Lomb Incorporated and its consolidated subsidiaries at December 31, 1972 and December 26, 1971 and the results of their operations and changes in financial position for the periods then ended, in conformity with generally accepted accounting principles consistently applied.—Reported of Independent Accountants.

Notes to Financial Statements

Litigation—Actions were commenced during the year against the company, its Chairman of the Board, certain Wall Street brokerage firms and others. These actions allege, among other things, violations of disclosure requirements under federal securities laws. The allegations include an alleged failure to make timely disclosure of adverse information and the alleged disclosure on a selected basis of certain information, including projected earnings for the company's first quarter and the use of this information by others to effect sales prior to its dissemination to the public. The plaintiffs seek recovery of alleged damages of indeterminate amount to themselves and other persons who purchased shares of the company's common stock during specified periods. The company's answers deny any improper action.

Also during the year, National Patent Development Corporation served a complaint on the company commencing an action seeking a declaratory judgment as to the method to be used under the company's sublicense for hydrophilic soft contact lenses in the Western Hemisphere to determine the amount payable to National Patent Development Corporation. The complaint alleges that the company has overstated expenses by including therein items not properly includable, and has understated sales by excluding therefrom items not properly excludable. The amount alleged to be presently due is claimed to be at least $3,000,000. The company believes that it has paid National Patent Development Corporation all amounts due it to date under the sublicense.

formed decisions regarding such companies. Some of the more important sepecific uses of segmented data include the following:

1. To provide information regarding the nature of the businesses a company is involved in and the relative size of the various segments.
2. To use the sales and contributions toward profit as an input to the evaluation and projection of corporate earnings.
3. To appraise the ability of management in making acquisitions.
4. To make credit decisions by using information concerning the sources and use of funds by the various segments.

Problems in Providing Segment Data. There are several potential problems in providing financial data for diversified companies on a segment basis. We classify these problems technical problems that arise in preparing such reports and disadvantages to the reporting company of disclosing segment data.

Technical Problems. The three main technical problems that occur in developing financial data on a segment basis are (1) allocation of common costs to two or more segments, (2) pricing transactions between segments, and (3) determining segments to be used for reporting purposes. Each technical problem must be addressed if meaningful information is to be reported.

Disadvantages of the Reporting Company. Concern has been expressed by corporate management that disclosure of segment financial information may cause difficulties harmful to the reporting company. The disadvantages cited often include confidential information that would be revealed to competitions, technical problems inherent in the preparation of the data that might result in misleading information users, and, the cost of providing the data that could be significant.

Usefulness of Segment Data. Diversified companies present special problems in financial analysis and decision making. Since these companies may have varying degrees of profitability, uses, and growth potential for individual components, the analyst needs financial information regarding the components to make meaningful decisions. Despite the potential usefulness of segment information, however, the analyst must use extreme caution in assessments and evaluations of the data.

SEC Reporting Requirements

Other sources of financial information regarding a business entity are required filings with the Securities and Exchange Commission (SEC). The SEC is an agency of the United States government that administers the Securities Act of 1933 and the Securities Exchange Act of 1934.

After the crash of 1929, there was a campaign for better and more infor-

ANALYSIS OF OTHER DISCLOSURES AND A REVIEW OF POTENTIAL CHANGES IN FINANCIAL REPORTING

mative corporation reports. Congress responded by enacting legislation intended to provide investors with information about the issuer of a security so that informed decisions can be made on the merits of that security. The emphasis of these laws is to promote full disclosure by requiring all companies having securities traded publicly (with certain exceptions) to register and file periodic reports with the SEC.

Annual Report to the SEC

Regulation S-X prescribes the form and content of all financial statements and related schedules filed with the SEC. In general, the balance sheet, statement of operations, and statement of changes in financial position prepared under Regulation S-X are basically the same as financial statements presented in an annual report to shareholders.

An annual report to the SEC is filed by each registered company within 90 days after the end of its fiscal period. Industrial and commercial firms file this report on a *Form 10-K*. Form 10-K information is divided into the following two parts:

Part I
1. Description of the business.
2. Summary of operations.
3. Properties.
4. Parents and subsidiaries.
5. Legal proceedings.
6. Increases and decreases in outstanding securities.
7. Approximate number of equity security holders.
8. Executive officers of the registrant.
9. Identification of directors and officers.
10. Financial statements and exhibits filed.

Part II
11. Principal security holders and security holders of management.
12. Directors of the registrant.
13. Remuneration of directors and officers.
14. Options granted to management to purchase securities.
15. Interest of management and others in certain transactions.

Usually, the firm's annual report to shareholders is included in the filing.

Other Reports to the SEC

Registered companies are also required to file quarterly reports on a *Form 10-Q* after each of the first three fiscal quarters. The information required in the 10-Q includes the following:

1. Financial Statement (which may be condensed):
   (a) Comparative income statements for the quarter and year-to-date.

(b) Balance sheets as of the end of the quarter for the current and preceding years.

(c) Statement of changes in financial position for the year-to-date for the current and proceeding years.

2. Management's narrative analysis of the results of operations.

In addition to the requirements imposed by Form 10-K and 10-Q, Form 8-K is used to report certain important specified events concerning the reporting company. The report must be filed within 10 days after the close of the month in which the specified event occurs. Such events include defaults on senior securities, changes in the registrants' auditor, and other materially important events.

Required Replacement Cost Disclosures

Companies whose total inventories, gross property, and plant equipment exceed $100 million dollars and are ten percent or more of total assets are required to disclose certain replacement cost data on Form 10-K. Replacement cost is defined for this purpose as the lowest amount that would have to be paid in the normal course of business to obtain an asset of equivalent operating or productive capacity. The disclosures required include:

1. The current replacement cost of inventories.
2. The estimated current cost of replacing productive capacity (depreciable and amortizable property, plant, and equipment) together with the depreciated cost of such productive capacity.
3. The approximate cost of sales based on the replacement cost of goods and services at the time sales were made.
4. The approximate amount of straight-line depreciation, depletion and amortization based on average current replacement cost of productive capacity.

The methods used in determining the replacement cost data and any other information management believes necessary to prevent the information from being misleading must also be disclosed. Although the detailed disclosures are required only in SEC findings the annual shareholders report should include at least a general description of the nature of the replacement cost data.

Part II— Conceptual Framework of Financial Accounting

ANALYSIS OF OTHER DISCLOSURES AND A REVIEW OF POTENTIAL CHANGES IN FINANCIAL REPORTING

In recent years, members of the financial community have suggested changes in the principles of financial accounting and reporting to make financial data more useful to decision makers. Since accounting is a product of a complex and dynamic environment, accounting principles continually evolve in a responsive manner. However, it is often argued that the development of a general theory or conceptual framework for financial accounting and reporting would provide the basis for resolving many of the current (and future) issues facing the accounting profession.

Some have contended that the lack of a well-defined framework has resulted in an erosion of the credibility of corporate financial reporting. Among the often mentioned criticisms of financial accounting are:

1. Acceptability of two or more methods of accounting for the same facts.
2. Unwarranted assertion of immateriality to justify nondisclosure or unfavorable information or departures from standards.
3. Off-balance-sheet financing.
4. Unjustified optimism in estimates of recoverability.
5. Use of reserves to artificially smooth income.
6. Elevation of form over substance.

Although such criticisms may not in fact be valid, the attention given to those arguments has caused skepticism about financial accounting.

The most recent attempt to establish a basic theory of accounting comes from the Financial Accounting Standards Board in its project *Conceptual Framework for Accounting and Reporting*. This project is considered a major, continuing effort and current and future components include a consideration of the objectives of financial statements, the definitions and measurement procedures for the elements of financial statements, and the form and content of financial statements, allocation, and revenue recognition.

In describing the need for an importance of this project, the FASB has indicated:

"A conceptual frame work is a constitution, a coherent system of interrelated objectives and fundamentals that can lead to consistent standards and that prescribes the nature, function, and limits of financial accounting and financial statements."[1]

In essence, the conceptual framework should provide both support and guidance for individual financial accounting standards. Furthermore, the framework should lead to increased public confidence in corporate financial reporting.

At the present time there are certain fundamental concepts recognized in practice. The so-called "historical cost principle" permeates the entire accounting process. The cost principle states that the historical, or input, cost is the appropriate basis of accounting for assets and services acquired, ex-

Implications of the Conceptual Framework Project

[1]*Scope and Implications of the Conceptual Framework Project,* Financial Accounting Standards Board (December, 1976) p. 2.

penses, liabilities, and owners' equity. Basically, this principle means that the exchange price derived from completed transactions represents the amount to be recognized in the accounting process.

The cost principle has a very significant affect on the nature of corporate financial statements. However, historical cost is only one of several bases that could be used to measure the elements of accounting. For example, a wide range of values may exist for a single asset—historical cost, current replacement cost, current selling price, or present value of expected cash flows. The determination of the value to be recorded is clearly critical to the accounting process. Consequently, one important aspect of the conceptual framework project is to consider the attributes (i.e., historical cost, replacement cost, etc.) that should be measured to provide the most useful information in financial statements.

Measurements of the Elements of Financial Statements

In the accounting literature, various measurement bases have been proposed as representing the most relevant bases for financial accounting measurement. Some possible measurement methods are discussed below.

Historical cost is the amount paid to acquire an asset or the amount received when a liability was incurred. Historical cost uses actual transaction prices and to that extent is recognized as being objective and verifiable. Continued adherence to historical cost during the period the asset is held results in postponing recognition of changes in value (other than depreciation and amortization) until the changes are realized by sale or other disposition. Consequently, some assets may be substantially undervalued in the balance sheet.

Existing generally accepted accounting principles are essentially a modified historical cost approach because some assets and liabilities are carried at amounts other than historical cost. For example, accounts receivable are valued at historical cost less allowance for uncollectable accounts and marketable equity securities are valued at the lower of historical cost or market.

Current cost is the amount that would be required currently to obtain the *same* asset or the amount that would be required if the same obligation were incurred currently. The *same* asset may refer to either an identical asset or an asset with equivalent productive capacity.

Opponents of current cost contend that imprecise price data available for certain assets and liabilities would seriously reduce the reliability of the financial statements. Another problem in the application of this approach is how to reflect the impact of technological change in determining current cost.

Proponents of current cost argue that the balance sheet value would be more relevant and holding gains and losses would be separately reported in the income statement. The distinction between operating profit and holding gains and losses may be clarified with the following example. A firm acquired an item of inventory for $1 on January 1, 19X7, and sold that unit on December 31, 19X9, for $3. During the two-year period, there was no inflation, but due to a shift in supply and demand for the item, the cost to replace the same item on December 31, 19X8, was $2. During 19X9, the replacement cost of the item remained constant.

Using historical cost, the change in the price of the item during the two-year holding period is ignored. The asset, inventory, would be reported in the December 31, 19X8, balance sheet at $1—the historical cost. The expenses deducted from the sales revenue for the period ending December 31, 19X9, include only the $1 originally invested in the item. The income associated with the item would be computed as follows:

	19X8	19X9
Revenue	0	3
Expense	0	1
Income	0	2

In the current cost approach, however, the $1 increase in the current cost of the item during 19X8 is separately accounted for as a holding gain, and the asset, inventory, is reflected at the $2 current cost in the December 31, 19X8, balance sheet. Accordingly, the income reported in the year of sale (19X9) reflects only the difference between the revenue from the sale and the current cost of the item. The income associated with the item would be reported as follows:

	19X8	19X9
Revenue	0	3
Expense	0	2
Operating Income	0	1
Holding Gain	1	0
Income	1	1

Note that the difference between historical cost and current cost incomes is the timing and nature (i.e., holding gains) of the income but the total amount of income over the two years is unchanged.

Current exit value in orderly liquidation is the amount of cash that could be obtained currently by selling an asset (that is, current market value, if a market exists), or the amount required currently to eliminate an obligation.

Ideally, this amount is measured by quoted market prices for assets of a similar kind or condition. Current exit values are used by mutual funds and some insurance companies to account for marketable securities.

Some proponents consider current exit values as a relevant attribute of all assets and a means of assessing the firm's ability to adapt to changing conditions by redeploying its resources. Conversely, opponents of this measurement basis contend that asset liquidation values in financial statements are not relevant when there is no intention to liquidate the company.

Present value of expected cash flows is the discounted amount of net cash inflows pertaining to an asset or the discounted amount of net cash outflows required to eliminate a liability. Measurement of the present value of an asset requires information about three factors: (1) the amounts of future cash inflows and cash outflows expected to result from the use and/or disposition of the asset, (2) the timing of those expected cash flows, and (3) the appropriate rate of discount to relate future flows to the present. Measures of the present value of long-term receivables and long-term obligations are widely used in present financial statement.

To many, present value is considered the ideal valuation method. A business enterprise engages in a continuous process of acquiring goods and services (cash outflows) and converting them to cash (cash inflows). Therefore, it is argued that the essence of value of an asset is the present value of the future net cash receipts into which the asset will be converted.

To illustrate the process, assume an asset has expected net cash inflows of $1,000 per year for the next three years. The present value of the cash inflows assuming a 9 percent discount rate would be computed as follows:

Year	Gross Amount	9% Discount Factor	Present Value
1	$1000	.917	917
2	1000	.842	842
3	1000	.772	772
	$3000		$2531

Each year's payment is multiplied by the present value factor corresponding to the selected discount rate and these discount factors may be obtained from a present value table. The selection of the discount rate may have a significant effect on the present value calculation. In measuring present value, several possible rates of discount exist. A discussion of the process of selecting a discount rate is beyond our scope here.

The conceptual framework project represents an attempt to provide an underlying structure for accounting. Ultimately, it is intended to provide both support and guidance to the body responsible for establishing accounting standards. The project has multiple objectives that include stating the objectives of financial accounting and reporting, selecting an approach for developing accounting theory and practice, providing definitions of the elements of financial statements, and resolving how to measure financial statement items.

One key issue confronted in the conceptual framework project is: What attribute or attributes of financial statement items should be measured in financial accounting and reporting. Within the conceptual framework project, several measurement bases have been considered. However, the ultimate selection depends to great extent on the objectives of financial statements.

**Summary—
Conceptual
Framework Project**

Accounting policies
Footnotes
Auditor's report
Unqualified opinion
Qualified opinion
Interim financial reports
Segment
Form 10-K
Form 10-Q
Historical cost
Current cost
Current exit value in orderly liquidation
Present value of expected cash flows

Key Terms

The accounting system for multinational business organizations is designed to record business transactions that subsequently will be reflected on the balance sheet, the income statement, and the statement of changes in financial position. Accounting for multinational organizations introduces three complexities above and beyond those encountered by domestic businesses. This dicusssion highlights three major areas of international accounting complexities: differences in generally accepted accounting principles, international transaction gains and losses, and international translation of foreign balances.

**Supplementary
Discussion:
Accounting for
International
Operations**

**SUPPLEMENTARY
DISCUSSION:
ACCOUNTING FOR
INTERNATIONAL
OPERATIONS**

FOREIGN ACCOUNTING PRINCIPLES

Accounting principles differ from nation to nation, and reflect each nation's economic system, business environment, and its social and legal traditions. Some nations require that accounting systems in their countries must formerly recognize the impact of inflation, and that this impact must be reflected in publicly distributed financial statements. Businesses in other nations are allowed to artificially smooth year-to-year net income by creating discretionary "reserves" that can be expanded or contracted at will. Thus, income in these nations takes on a different meaning than income reported in the United States. Companies that are organized into several subsidiaries are not required to prepare consolidated financial statements in some countries, while comparable operations by U.S. concerns are required to do so. Depreciation policy in some countries permits immediate writeoff of the cost of fixed assets, or requires depreciation in excess of amounts that would be recognized by domestic United States concerns. In addition, inventory methods, goodwill amortization, treatment of stock dividends, and the accounting for pension plans or leases differs dramatically from country to country.

These differences between domestic and foreign generally accepted accounting principles produce financial statements that are not directly comparable from country to country. Differences in principles affect the assets, liabilities, owners' equity, revenues, and expenses reflected in balance sheets and income statements. Before a domestic United States business consolidates accounts of foreign subsidiaries or evaluates their financial statements, adjustments must be made to the financial statements to correct for differences in accounting principles.

ACCOUNTING FOR MULTINATIONAL TRANSACTIONS

Whenever a domestic United States firm engages in international transactions, accounting problems are liable to occur. In particular, importing involves the purchase of goods or services from foreign suppliers while exporting involves the sales to foreign customers. Importing or exporting transactions may require that the monetary measurement be denominated in a currency other than the U.S. dollar. An American corporation may purchase goods from a foreign supplier and promise to pay for the purchase with the foreign currency. Between the time of purchase and the time of payment, the relationship between the value of the foreign currency and the value of the dollar may change, thus creating an opportunity for gains or losses on foreign transactions. For example, assume that the ABC Corporation purchases some merchandise from a foreign supplier on May 1 for 10,000 Deutschmarks (DM). Each DM can be exchanged for $.60 on May 1. The following journal entry could be used to record the purchase:

```
Purchases                 $6,000
     Accounts Payable              $6,000
(To record a purchase for 10,000 DM when the exchange rate is $.60)
```

Suppose that the exchange rate on August 1, the date of payment, is DM = $.62. At that exchange rate, the 10,000 DM debt will require ABC Corporation to pay $6,200 in satisfaction of the debt. The journal entry to record payment at the rate of 62¢ is as follows:

Accounts Payable	$6,000	
Foreign Exchange Transaction Loss	200	
Cash		$6,200

(To record payment of 10,000 DM debt when exchange rate is $.62)

That is, a change in the exchange rate exposes an international trader to a foreign exchange loss that goes above and beyond the normal risks of business carried on by domestic corporations. At the same time, changes in exchange rates may enable domestic concerns to recognize gains on international transactions. For example, assume that the exchange rate on August 1 is DM = $.58. Then, ABC Corporation will save 2¢ on each Deutschmark that is spent to satisfy the foreign debt. The entry to record payment at a rate of 58¢ is as follows:

Accounts Payable	$6,000	
Cash		$5,800
Foreign Exchange Transaction Gain		200

(To record payment of 10,000 DM debt when the exchange rate is $.58)

Similar types of foreign exchange gains and losses can be recognized in a foreign sale that is denominated in terms of the foreign currency. Foreign exchange losses will be recognized whenever a sale is made at one exchange rate, and the payment occurs after the exchange rate has fallen. For example, if a sale had been made on July 1 for 10,000 DM when the exchange rate was 65¢, and the collection occurs on August 1 when the exchange rate is 60¢, then a $500 foreign exchange loss would be recognized as part of the collection transaction. Alternately, foreign exchange gains may be recognized on a sale transaction, whenever the sale is denominated in the foreign currency and the exchange rate rises. For example, a sale for 10,000 DM when exchange rates are DM = 65¢ will generate an accounts receivable balance of $6,500. If the exchange rate increases to DM = 70¢ at the time of settlement, cash receipts will be $7,000, and a foreign exchange gain of $500 will be recognized.

TRANSLATION OF FOREIGN BALANCES

Multinational corporations commonly organize foreign subsidiaries to facilitate an international transaction. Domestic American corporations will reflect these foreign subsidiaries on the domestic financial statements either as long-term investments, or as a consolidated element in the consolidated financial statements. To accomplish either of these practices, however, the account balances of the foreign subsidiaries must be translated in terms of dollars. A problem results whenever exchange rates fluctuate over time, so that the foreign account balances were incurred at different exchange rates. Current practice requires that monetary assets such as cash, receivables, and investments, as well as monetary liabilities must be translated at current exchange rates, while nonmonetary assets and liabilities must be translated at historic exchange rates. Under these translation rules, a balance sheet that is in balance when denominated in terms of the foreign currency may be out of balance when translated into dollars by use of these exchange rate translation rules. Under current accounting practice, the amount required to equate the translated assets and the sum of the translated liabilities and equities must be reflected in the U.S. financial statements as a translation gain or loss. Since exchange rates fluctuate greatly, translation gains and losses are commonly reflected on the income statements of multinational corporations. The relative size of translation gains and losses depends in part on the magnitude of the exchange fluctuation, as well as the net monetary position of the foreign subsidiary. Net monetary position represents the difference between the monetary assets and the monetary liabilities.

SUMMARY

Accounting for multinational operations introduces three additional complexities not found in the accounting for domestic operations: differences in generally accepted accounting principles, gains and losses on foreign exchange transactions, and foreign exchange translation gains and losses. Accountants who deal with multinational organizations must be thoroughly familiar with the accounting implications of each of these events. Multinational operations require a degree of sophistication and expertise of accounting that is not easily gained without extensive study and research.

Questions

1. What disclosures and reports, besides financial statements, are large businesses (such as large publicly held corporations) required to prepare or publish?

2. Describe the accounting policies section of footnotes found in financial statements.

3. Why are accounting policies required to be disclosed?

4. What kind of information should be included in the footnotes to the financial statements?

5. List some topics commonly covered in the footnotes to the financial statements.

6. Describe a typical auditor's report.

7. Is the management of a firm responsible for preparing the auditor's report on that firm's financial statements?

8. Identify the major parts of the auditor's report.

9. What kinds of opinions may an auditor express in an auditor's report regarding the fairness of a firm's financial statements?

10. Of what use is the auditor's report to the financial statement user?

11. How does an interim financial report differ from the annual financial report?

12. Why do the major stock exchanges require corporations listed on those exchanges to publish interim financial statements?

13. What limitations exist to the preparation and use of interim financial statements?

ANALYSIS OF OTHER DISCLOSURES AND A REVIEW OF POTENTIAL CHANGES IN FINANCIAL REPORTING

14. Define the term business segment.

15. Of what benefit is it to a financial statement user to be provided with financial reports that separately report business segment activities for diversified businesses?

16. Providing financial data for segments of a business is more complex than providing data for the whole business. List some additional accounting problems associated with segment reporting.

17. Describe the relationship between the SEC and other accounting institutions.

18. Which corporations must file reports with the SEC?

19. Describe the reports that some corporations must file with the SEC.

20. How are the objectives of the SEC implemented through its formal reporting requirements?

21. Only a portion of the companies filing reports with the SEC must make replacement cost disclosures. Which companies must do so?

22. How are replacement costs measured? Are these measures available through the conventional financial accounting systems currently used by most businesses?

23. What is the primary objective of the Financial Accounting Standard Board's project *Conceptual Framework for Accounting and Reporting?*

24. One aspect of the FASB's *Conceptual Framework* project is an examination of measurement bases for accounting purposes. List and describe some alternative measurement bases being considered by the FASB.

25. What should the student of accounting conclude about the basic nature of accounting from the FASB's *Conceptual Framework* project?

INDEX

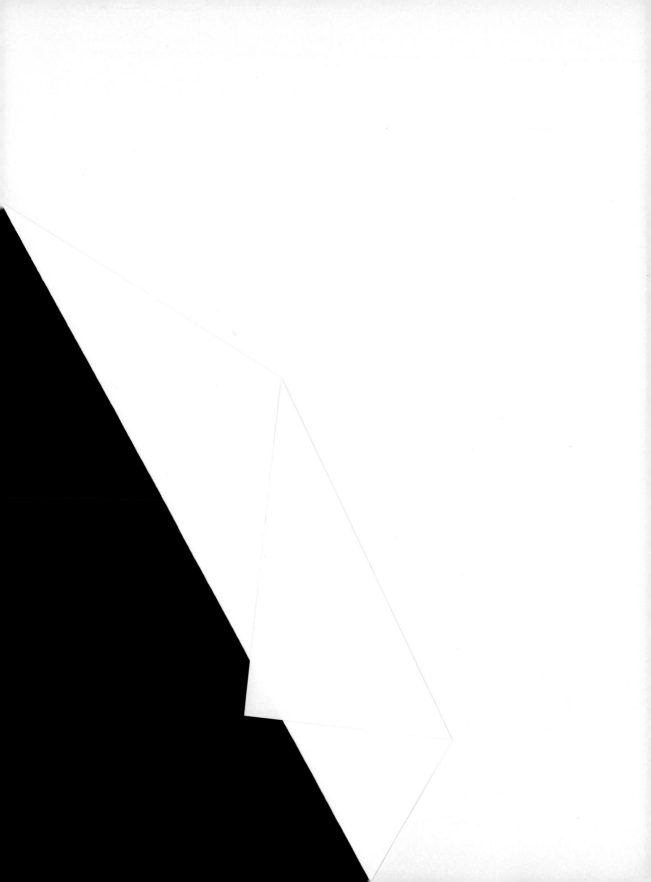

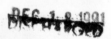